PROPERTY LAW: CURRENT ISSUES AND DEBATES

Property Law: Current Issues and Debates

Edited by

PAUL JACKSON
Professor of Law and Director of The Centre for Property Law
The University of Reading

DAVID C. WILDE
Lecturer in Law
The University of Reading

Ashgate

DARTMOUTH

Aldershot • Brookfield USA • Singapore • Sydney

Published by
Dartmouth Publishing Company Limited
Ashgate Publishing Ltd
Gower House
Croft Road
Aldershot
Hants GU11 3HR
England

Ashgate Publishing Company
Old Post Road
Brookfield
Vermont 05036
USA

Ashgate website: http://www.ashgate.com

British Library Cataloguing in Publication Data
Property law : current issues and debates
    1. Property - Congresses
    I. Jackson, Paul, LL. B. II. Wilde, David C.
    346'.04

Library of Congress Cataloging-in-Publication Data
Property law : current issues and debates / edited by Paul Jackson and David C. Wilde.
    p. cm.
  ISBN 0-7546-2040-9
    1. Property 2. Real property. I. Jackson, Paul, LL. B. II. Wilde, David C.

K720.P758 2000
346.04--dc21   99-049169

ISBN 0 7546 2040 9

Printed and bound by Athenaeum Press, Ltd.,
Gateshead, Tyne & Wear.

Contents

List of Contributors		*vii*
Foreword		*ix*
Preface		*xi*

PART I: COUNTRYSIDE, CONSERVATION, AND CHARITIES

1   Working Together for Access
J Rowan-Robinson   3

2   The "Right to Roam" - An Empty Dream?
Christine Willmore   14

3   Reforming Property Rights for Nature Conservation
Christopher P Rodgers   48

4   Reforming the Law on Charity Trading
Peter Luxton   69

PART II: COMMONHOLD

5   Is Apartment Ownership Genuine Ownership?
C G van der Merwe   87

6   Aspects of Condominium Law in The Bahamas
Gilbert Kodilinye   101

7   *Caveat* Commonholds
Peter Smith   117

8   The Proposed Commonhold Association - A Company Law
Perspective
Letitia Crabb   147

PART III: COMPARATIVE AND INTERNATIONAL PROPERTY LAW

9   Are Property Rights So Simple In Europe?
    Geoffrey Samuel   161

10 Limitations on Constitutional Property Rights
    Tom Allen   187

11 The Constitutional Property Clause and Police Power Regulation
    of Intangible Commercial Property - A Comparative Analysis of
    Case Law
    AJ van der Walt   208

12 The Reform of South African Land Law in its Roman-Dutch
    Context - New Wine?
    DL Carey Miller   281

13 Extending Security of Tenure in South Africa: Labour Tenants
    and Farm Workers
    Juanita Pienaar   307

14 Finland's New Electronic Title and Mortgage Register
    Matti Ilmari Niemi   333

vi

List of Contributors

Tom Allen   *Senior Lecturer in Law, The University of Durham*

DL Carey Miller   *Professor of Property Law, The University of Aberdeen*

BS Letitia Crabb   *Lecturer in Law, The University of Reading*

Gilbert Kodilinye   *Professor of Property Law, The University of the West Indies*

Peter Luxton   *Senior Lecturer in Law, The University of Sheffield*

Matti I Niemi   *Professor in Civil Law, The University of Lapland*

Juanita M Pienaar   *Professor of Law, The University of Stellenbosch, SA*

Christopher P Rodgers   *Professor of Law, and Director of the Centre for Law in Rural Areas, The University of Wales, Aberystwyth*

RJ Rowan-Robinson   *Professor of Law, The University of Aberdeen*

Geoffrey Samuel   *Professor of Law, The University of Kent at Canterbury*

Peter F Smith   *Reader in Property Law, The University of Reading*

Cornie G van der Merwe *Professor of Private and Roman Law, The University of Stellenbosch, SA*

AJ van der Walt *Professor of Private Law, The University of South Africa, Pretoria*

Christine Willmore *Lecturer in Law, The University of Bristol*

Foreword

On behalf of the Centre for Property Law

While this is not the place for a general valediction to mark Paul Jackson's retirement from Reading, I hope Paul will not mind that I have, with the connivance of the publishers, added to the proofs of the book this brief foreword on his standing down as Director of the Centre for Property Law. Invited to speak on behalf of the Centre, I should like to thank him for, and pay tribute to, his contribution to it.

Paul was behind the initiative to establish the Centre, and has served as its Director since it was set up in 1995. He is in large part responsible for its success. Many outside Reading will be familiar with the public work he has done for the Centre. To those within the Centre, perhaps his greatest contribution (among many) has been in setting standards of scholarship for others to aspire to.

We shall greatly miss his wisdom - and wit - as chair of the Centre. He has, of course, the very best wishes of all associated with the Centre for his retirement.

DAVID WILDE

Preface

By the Director of the Centre for Property Law

This is the second of two books based on papers given at the conference organised by the Centre for Property Law at Reading in March 1998 under the title, "Contemporary Issues in Property Law". Speakers represented jurisdictions from around the world. Their subjects ranged from the theoretical and jurisprudential to the severely practical. No one who attended the conference - or subsequently reads the papers in this and the preceding book, *Contemporary Property Law* - can believe in the picture of property law as archetypical, dry as dust, black letter, law. Questions of human rights, changes in social structures, technological developments are all shown to have their impact on property law, calling for careful analysis of the present law and practical proposals for reforms to reflect new developments.

The papers printed here must and can speak for themselves. The success of the conference which gave birth to those papers depended, however, on many whose contributions do not appear between these covers. The Centre is very glad to be able to record its thanks to them. Mr Justice Neuberger and David Wood QC, opened the proceedings in inimitable fashion. Lord Justice Millett, as he then was, kindly presided at the Conference Dinner. Judge Paul Baker QC, Professor Kenneth GC Reid, Professor Kevin Gray and Susan Bright undertook the duties of chairing various working sessions.

Mrs Sandi Murdoch again devoted her organisational skills to ensuring the efficient planning and running of the conference. Nicholas King gave up his summer vacation following graduation to assisting in the initial stages of the editorial work involved in reducing a disparate mass of texts and discs to something like a manuscript. More recently David Wilde has again brought his valuable eye for detail to the last, but onerous stage of producing a final version suitable for publication. Mrs Hennessey has again demonstrated her willingness to work far beyond the call of duty. To all of these the Centre is indeed deeply indebted.

PAUL JACKSON

PART I

COUNTRYSIDE, CONSERVATION, AND CHARITIES

1 Working Together for Access

J ROWAN-ROBINSON

Introduction

In February 1998 the government issued a consultation paper on the freedom to roam in England and Wales.[1] The paper does not immediately opt for a redistribution of rights in favour of those seeking access. Rather it places the onus on those with the right - the owners and managers of the land - to demonstrate that the expectations of public access can be realised without legislative intervention.

The *Concordat on Access to Scotland's Hills and Mountains,* launched by the Access Forum in 1996, offers a possible model. The Forum is a voluntary body established on the initiative of Scottish Natural Heritage. It comprises representatives of all the main organisations involved in recreation on the hills. Included are those who own and manage land, recreational bodies such as the Ramblers Association (Scotland) and public bodies involved in facilitating access.

The Concordat does not alter the distribution of property rights in the Scottish countryside. As Mackay[2] observes, it is about responsibilities rather than rights. It sets out four key principles relating to access:

   (i)   an acknowledgement of a common interest in the natural beauty and special qualities of Scotland's hills and the need to work together for their protection and enhancement;

   (ii)   acceptance by land managers of the public's expectation of having access to the hills;

   (iii)   agreement that there should be freedom of access exercised with responsibility and subject to reasonable constraints for management and conservation purposes;

   (iv)   recognition by visitors of the needs of land management and understanding of how this sustains the livelihood, culture and community interests of those who live and work on the hills.

The Concordat aims to create a better climate of opinion with regard to access and to move the debate forward in a positive way.[3]

The purpose of this chapter is *not* to measure the success of the Concordat. I simply do not know whether it is altering attitudes. What I want to do is to highlight some of the problems with the law relating to access which provide the context for the Concordat. I also want to speculate about why the parties have arrived at a Concordat rather than polarising over the prospect of legislation. I will look at the position, first of all, from the point of view of the owners and managers of land and, secondly, from the perspective of those seeking access.

The Owners and Managers of Land

Some landowners are genuinely interested in promoting public access to the countryside and will have little hesitation in subscribing to the objectives of the Concordat. The "not for profit owners",[4] such as the National Trust for Scotland, are an example. For others, the prospect of avoiding a compulsory redistribution of property rights through legislation is likely to have been an important motivating factor. In terms of property rights, the Concordat preserves the *status quo,* although it aims to introduce into land ownership something akin to a limited form of stewardship ethic. For others still, there will have been recognition that, by permitting freedom of access, landowners would be able to portray themselves as conceding something which, in practice, it is already very difficult to resist. This is because of shortcomings with the remedies available against trespass. These shortcomings are now examined.

It is sometimes suggested that there is no law of trespass in Scotland. This is probably because, unlike the position in England and Wales, trespass is not a wrong for which damages may be sought (in the absence of proof of damage). However, like England and Wales, the ownership of land in Scotland carries with it the right to exclusive use.[5] If a person enters land without right or permission, the owner may act to exclude that person. In other words, the landowner has control of the position in law. The problem is exercising that control in practice.

Control over trespassers may be exercised in practice through an application to the court for interdict or through self-help. These are considered in turn.

Interdict

Interdict is the Scottish equivalent of an injunction and, as in England and Wales, the award is discretionary. For example, in *Steuart v Stephen*[6] the Second Division declined to grant an application for interdict in respect of an alleged trespass. The defender appeared to be taking a short cut across the owner's land from time to time with the knowledge of, but without objection from, the tenant. To secure an interdict a petitioner will have to demonstrate reasonable anxiety that the trespass will be repeated. As Lord Gifford observed in *Hay's Trs v Young*,[7] "there must be reasonable grounds for fearing that the respondent in a petition such as this will do the act which he is to be interdicted from doing". Interdict is, therefore, essentially, a remedy against future acts of trespass and is suited to the case of persistent and known trespassers.

There is a further problem with what Reid refers to as "public trespass".[8] "There are", he says, "often formidable difficulties in identifying the persons concerned in order that they may be interdicted, and in any event an interdict against persons who trespassed on one occasion is no protection against different persons trespassing on another". He goes on to add that interdict will not be granted where the threatened trespass is considered too trivial to warrant the full weight of the law. Since, by definition, trespass is always temporary, an application for interdict may often be vulnerable to arguments of triviality. In other words, unless the petitioner can show that the trespasser is, in effect, asserting some right against ownership, the prospect of securing an interdict is not good. Interdict, therefore, has quite serious practical limitations as a remedy.

Self-help

Some seventy years ago, Gloag[9] commented that when people ask their legal adviser how far they may go with self-help, "the answer they get is qualified and cautious". That comment is as true today as it was then. The caution arises because by taking the law into their own hands, landowners may expose themselves to the risk of a civil action for damages by a trespasser for personal injury and/or a criminal prosecution for assault or worse.

There is no doubt that a landowner may take defensive measures to prevent or discourage trespass from happening. These could include putting up walls, fences and railings, installing lights and alarms, posting warning notices and operating security patrols. Defensive measures of this sort should be apparent so that if a person, nonetheless, trespasses and is injured by, for example, being caught on barbed wire, the owner should be able to establish the defence of *volenti non fit injuria* to a civil action for damages.

However, some of these measures might still expose the owner to potential criminal liability for recklessly causing injury to another, for recklessly endangering a subject or for causing real injury. Although no such prosecutions have been brought in Scotland in the context of trespass, these crimes are so broadly based that it is, in theory, possible that an owner might be criminally liable if a trespasser is injured by, for example, broken glass cemented into a wall.

More active defensive measures, such as the construction of electrically charged fences or the placing of mantraps or spring guns intended to injure trespassers, would be likely to expose the landowner in the event of injury to an intruder to both civil[10] and criminal[11] liability.

The more difficult question with regard to self-help is how far a landowner may use force to evict a trespasser once it happens. The position at criminal law would seem to be that reasonable force may be employed to remove a trespasser provided there is no intention to assault that person and there is no culpable recklessness. In *HMA v Harris*[12] a bouncer at a night-club seized and pushed a young woman so that she fell down a flight of stairs and into a road where she was struck and injured by a car. The bouncer was charged with assault or, alternatively, with reckless injury. In the course of his judgment, Lord Morrison said:

> Persons such as policemen, bus conductors or ambulancemen and others [*eg*, gamekeepers and wardens] have from time to time to seize and push people, without any criminal intent, in the course of their employment. I do not think that a bouncer is in a different position. He may have to eject people from the premises for which he is responsible by manhandling them with reasonable force. No criminal intent can be imputed to that. Of course, even lawful handling of another may spill over readily into assault. However, if reasonable force is not exceeded, ejection may nonetheless be culpably reckless, I consider, if insisted upon in the face of danger to the person being ejected or to that person's actual severe injury.[13]

The position seems to be much the same with regard to civil liability[14] and is well summarised in the *Stair Memorial Encyclopaedia of the Laws of Scotland*:[15]

A peaceful trespasser should first be invited to leave of his own accord and force should only be used as a last resort. In all cases where force is justifiable, the degree of force used must be properly matched to the circumstances of the trespass. Only the minimum force required by the circumstances may be employed and excessive force is actionable in delict.

The problem in practice is knowing what is reasonable in the circumstances. Even if that can be established, reasonable force can so easily escalate during the heat of a confrontation to the point at which a landowner may be exposed to criminal or civil liability.

There are, therefore, quite severe practical difficulties facing a landowner attempting to rely on a confrontational approach against trespassers. Interdict as a remedy has severe limitations and self-help is hedged around with uncertainties. There is also the further consideration that, with the large highland estates, effective control through interdict or self-help could only be exercised by employing an army of wardens to police the boundaries, an unrealistically expensive course of action. It may have been considerations such as these which have contributed to the decision by those representing the owners and managers of land to reject the "thou shalt not" approach in favour of the "let's work together" approach implicit in the Concordat.

Those Seeking Access

The motivation of those representing members of the public seeking access to the countryside to favour a "let's work together" approach is also fairly clear. To avoid being a trespasser, a person must show that they are on land either by right or by permission. There are difficulties in Scotland with both categories.

Access By Right

There are a number of circumstances in which a person may have a right in Scotland to be on land owned by another. For example, he or she may be a tenant in possession; a neighbour may have a servitude right to enter for specified purposes; a heritable creditor may enter land in exercise of powers under the security; or a group of people may negotiate a contractual right to enter land. The British Horse Society, for example, has been successful in negotiating a right of access to certain land for its members.

The public, generally, may have a right to be on someone else's land. This right may arise by virtue of a statutory agreement such as an access agreement or a public path creation agreement entered into under the Countryside (Scotland) Act 1967, as amended. Research suggests that only limited use has been made of these provisions, mainly in connection with long distance footpaths and country parks.[16] The former Countryside Commission for Scotland expressed disappointment at the low level of use of these powers.[17] It seems that neither landowners, nor planning authorities, welcome the commitment resulting from a formal agreement or order. There is also a feeling amongst some planning officers that agreements operate to restrict and regulate rather than extend access for the public and they see no reason why authorities should pay for something which hitherto has been enjoyed by tradition.[18]

Access may also be obtained by the public as of right because of the existence of a public right of way. Such a route is generally created by continuous use by the public, as of right, of a more or less defined line, running from one public place to another, for the period of 20 years prescribed by section 3(3) of the Prescription and Limitation (Scotland) Act 1973. The evidence must be sufficient to exclude the idea of tolerance.

Uncertainty about the status of linear routes in Scotland has resulted in a steady erosion of the heritage of public rights of way. The uncertainty stems from the lack of any definitive map, from the difficulty in satisfying the criteria for establishing a public right of way (for example, a "public place" is a place where the public have a right to be - most people have no right to be on top of a munro), and from the fact that prescription operates to extinguish as well as create routes.[19] In Scotland, it is manifestly not correct to say "once a highway, always a highway". The result is that owners, developers and those undertaking public works have no easy way of establishing what routes stand in the way of their plans and little incentive to enquire too closely. The public and planning authorities, for their part, do not have the resources, or cannot collect evidence, to safeguard routes. It is thought that a substantial part of the heritage of public rights of way has been lost to the public because of afforestation, hydro-electric schemes, agricultural improvements, changing estate management practices, major road schemes and the electrification of railways.[20]

Although a right of access along a defined line can be created by prescription, a right of access to an area cannot. The custom of straying over open, uncultivated land for the prescriptive period will confer no right on the public. In other words, it is not possible to acquire a prescriptive right to roam. In *Dyce v Hay,*[21] for example, the Second Division rejected a claim that a servitude right existed on behalf of the public from time immemorial of walking and recreation on land by the River Don in Old Aberdeen. This was not a servitude recognised by the law of Scotland and such a right could not be acquired by use. Lord Justice-Clerk Hope observed that "there is no case whatever in which a right to wander over, to rest or to lounge upon the ground of a private proprietor - under the name of recreation - has ever been established".[22]

Access By Permission

As already stated, a person who enters land with the permission of the landowner is not a trespasser. Such permission may be express or implied.[23] No difficulty arises with regard to express permission. The terms of access are governed by the permission. This sort of permission is sometimes secured by user groups.

The concept of implied permission for access gives rise to considerable difficulty. Walker states that "a person prima facie a trespasser may be deemed a licensee if trespass in such circumstances has been so repeatedly tolerated as to imply acquiescence by the occupier in his presence".[24]

As authority for that statement he cites *Dumbreck v Addie*[25] and *Breslin v The London and North Eastern Railway Co.*[26] The *Dumbreck* and *Breslin* cases are part of a long line of cases[27] involving damages claims by someone entering the land of another in the absence of a right or express permission. In *Dumbreck* an important question in determining the nature and extent of liability was whether the person injured was a trespasser, an invitee or a licensee. The landowner's duty of care was held to vary according to the status of the injured person.

These cases need to be treated with considerable caution when considering their relevance to the freedom to roam. This is because, although they were concerned with the law relating to access to land, their specific focus was on liability for personal injury and particularly injury to children - and the law relating to such liability has changed. An analysis of the cases shows the judges were prepared to go to considerable lengths to avoid the harsh application of the law resulting from the very limited duty of care owed, at that time, by occupiers of land to trespassers. Initially, the courts came close to suggesting that nothing short of a direct invitation was required to take a person out of the category of trespasser. Subsequently, the courts appeared to relax the position and accepted that habitual resort to land with the knowledge of the landowner could amount to implied consent. The Occupier's Liability (Scotland) Act 1960 later enlarged the duty of care owed by occupiers of land to trespassers. With this enlargement of the duty of care, it is no longer necessary for the courts to try to force a claimant into the category of a licensee for liability for injury to arise.

Nonetheless, the cases are significant because they recognise the concept of implied permission and serve to throw some light - and it can be put no stronger than that - on the circumstances in which implied permission may be said to exist. Implied permission will not, however, be lightly inferred. As Lord Justice-Clerk Inglis observed in *Buccleuch v Edinburgh Magistrates*[28] (a case involving encroachment), the doctrine of acquiescence "must be carefully guarded, especially when it affects heritable property. The facts from which acquiescence is to be inferred must be such as to leave no reasonable doubt as to what was the intention of the parties"; and in *Breslin* Lord Justice-Clerk Aitchison referred to the "clearly implied consent of the owner" being a necessary prerequisite for a licence.[29] It must be doubtful whether the concept of implied permission goes very far in underpinning the freedom to roam.[30]

The evident shortcomings in the legal arrangements for linear and area access provide an obvious motivation for those representing recreational interests to sign up to the Concordat. The Ramblers Association of Scotland and the Scottish Mountaineering Council are both signatories. The Concordat provides a basis for continued dialogue with representatives of landowning interests about access issues, a commitment to work collectively to improve matters, and a recognition of the need for more management of recreation in the hills.[31]

Conclusions

The Concordat does not, however, of itself, give the public the freedom to roam. It is a statement of intent. It aims to create a climate in which landowners will acknowledge the freedom of the public to roam in the countryside subject to reasonable constraints. In other words, it is likely to work through permission rather than rights.

This appears to stop short of what the late John Smith (a keen "munro-basher") had in mind when he committed the Labour Party to giving the public a *right* to roam. The introduction of such a right would require legislation and the consultation paper issued by the Land Reform Policy Group[32] set up by the Secretary of State for Scotland in February 1998 simply notes that this will be a matter for consideration by the Scottish Parliament. In the meantime, Scottish Natural Heritage has been asked to consider what changes in the law are required. A consultation paper on this is expected later this year.

Legislating for a right to roam would not be easy. It will qualify the landowner's entitlement to the exclusive use and enjoyment of land. In doing so, it will be necessary to tackle issues such as what land is to be covered by the right, what recreational activity is to be encompassed by the right, how such a right will interact with land management practices, how the privacy of those who live and work the land is to be safeguarded, and what will happen to public rights of way. However, I do not want to overstate the difficulties. Indeed, there is already a possible model for such legislation in the Countryside (Scotland) Act 1967.[33] This provides that people taking access to land under the terms of an access agreement are not to be treated as trespassers.

There is a further difficulty that may need to be addressed in legislating for a right to roam. That is the question of the exposure of owners and occupiers to liability for injury or damage sustained by members of the public enjoying such a right. The position would be governed very largely by the Occupier's Liability (Scotland) Act 1960.[34] This provides that the occupier must show towards a person entering the land such care as in the circumstances of the case is reasonable to see that the person will not suffer injury or damage by reason of any dangers due to the state of the land or anything done or omitted to be done. The case of *Johnstone v Sweeney*[35] shows that an occupier of land in Scotland owes a duty of care under the Act to someone exercising a *right* of access to the land (in that case, a public right of way). The position in England and Wales under the 1957 Act (as extended) appears to be different.[36]

It may be that any legislation on the right to roam would need also to look at the recreational user provisions in the Occupiers' Liability Act 1995 for Eire. This, in turn, seems to have drawn on the experience of recreational user provisions in a number of states in the USA. Broadly, these provisions reduce the occupier's potential for liability for injury to recreational users.   Liability in Eire is limited to that resulting from reckless disregard of their persons or property.[37]

These difficulties suggest that the prospect of moving forward by agreement should not lightly be cast aside. The Concordat provides a basis from which to work towards such agreement in Scotland, a basis which does not yet seem to exist south of the border. It may be that the threat of legislation will encourage landowners to demonstrate that the "let's work together" approach can achieve public policy goals on access to the Scottish countryside.

Postscript

Since this chapter was written, an enlarged Access Forum has recommended to Scottish Natural Heritage that the public should have a general *right* of access to land and water for informal recreation and passage, subject to responsible exercise of that right and subject to certain restraints in the interests of privacy, land management and conservation. Scottish Natural Heritage endorsed the proposal in its advice to government in January 1999, advice which the government have now accepted. Legislation is promised. Like the Concordat, this is a move forward by consensus. Unlike the Concordat, this proposal extends beyond the hills and mountains to include lowland areas and the urban fringe.

Notes

1   *Access to the Open Countryside in England and Wales*, DETR, February 1998.
2   Mackay J, "A Concordat on Access to Scotland's Hills and Mountains", (1996) 55 Scottish Planning and Environmental Law 45.
3   *Ibid*.
4   A term used by Wightman A in *Who Owns Scotland* (Canongate), 1996, Table 18.
5   Gordon WM, *Scottish Land Law* (The Scottish Universities Law Institute), 1989, para 13-06.
6   (1877) 4 R 873. See, too, *Hay's Trs v Young* (1877) 4 R 398.
7   (1877) 4 R 398 at 402.
8   Reid K, *The Law of Property in Scotland* (Butterworths), 1996, para 183.
9   Gloag WM, "The Limits of the Right of Self-Redress", (1917) 29 Juridical Review 124, 127; and see Rowan-Robinson J and McKenzie-Skene D, "Self Help and Access to the Countryside", Juridical Review, forthcoming.

10   *Bird v Holbrook* (1928) 4 Bing 911.

11   *Craw* 1827, Syme, at 188, 210.

12   1993 SCR 559.

13   *Ibid* at 566.

14   *Bell v Shand* (1870) 7 SLR 267; *Wood v North British Railway* (1899) 2 F 1.

15   *Property*, Vol 18, para 184.

16   Rowan-Robinson J, *Review of Rights of Way Procedures*, SNH Review No 9, 1994, paras 3.2.1 and 3.2.2.

17   *Ibid*, para 3.2.4.

18   *Ibid*, para 3.2.5.

19   *Ibid*, Section 4. See, too, the Scottish Rights of Way Society Ltd, *Rights of Way: A Guide to the Law in Scotland*, 1986; also the Scottish Rights of Way Society Ltd, *Proposals for the Reform of the Law relating to Public Rights of Way in Scotland*, 1990.

20   *Ibid*.

21   (1849) 11 D 1266; (1852) 1 Macq 305 (HL). See, too, *Harvey v Lindsay* (1853) 15 D 768.

22   *Ibid*, 1275.

23   *Duke of Buccleuch v Edinburgh Magistrates* (1865) 3 M 528.

24   Walker DM, *Principles of Scottish Private Law* (The Scottish Universities Law Institute), 1989, 4th edn, p 207.

25   1929 SC HL 51.

26   1936 SC 816.

27   See *Devlin v Jeffray's Trs* (1902) 5 F 130; *Cummings v Darngavil Coal Co* (1902) 5 F 513; *Cooke v Midland Great Western Railway of Ireland* [1909] AC 229 (HL); *Mackenzie v The Fairfield Shipbuilding and Engineering Co Ltd* 1913 SC 213; *Boyd v The Glasgow Iron and Steel Company Ltd* 1923 SC 758.

28   (1866) 3 M 528 at 531.

29   1936 SC 816 at 824.

30   See generally on this Rowan-Robinson J and Ross A, "The Freedom to Roam and Implied Permission", Edinburgh Law Review, 1998, vol 2 (2), pp 225-233.

31   Mackay, *supra* n 2.

32   *Identifying the Problems*, The Scottish Office, 1998.

33   S 11(1).

34   On this see, generally, *Liability and Access to the Countryside*, SNH Review No 74, 1996.

35   1985 SLT (Sh Ct) 2.

36   See *Greenhalgh v British Railways Board* [1969] 2 QB 286.

37   S 4.

2 The "Right to Roam" - An Empty Dream?

CHRISTINE WILLMORE

Introduction

Unbounded freedom ruled the wandering scene
Nor fence or ownership crept in between.[1]

The "right to roam" is often portrayed as a moral crusade.[2] Its proponents appeal to a romantic view of history, exemplified in the above quotation from John Clare, in which ancient public rights to roam were suppressed during enclosure. They see themselves as inheriting the mantle of the campaigners against the removal of ancient agricultural rights who tore down fences and continued to exercise ancient rights to take wood and other material in the face of trespass actions.[3] In much of the debate the term "right" is used in a loose sense, deliberately making a moral and political appeal to listeners. However, if these emotional and moral arguments are to be converted into changes in the law to provide increased lawful recreational access to the countryside, the rhetorical use of the language of rights needs to be backed by a more precise legal analysis of what this "right" entails. This paper explores the difficulties of defining a "right to roam" in English property law,[4] and concludes that the language of rights presents obstacles to the attainment of the goal of increased lawful public access - exemplified by the approach taken in the 1998 Green Paper on *Access to the Open Countryside*.[5]

The Emergence of the "Right to Roam"

A number of factors came together to produce a rapidly developing social movement for access to the countryside in the mid-nineteenth century. Concern at the loss of the agricultural rights of the poor became conflated with emerging urban aspirations through a complex range of factors:

growing population densities, recognition of the relationship between clean air, exercise and public health, pressure for open space associated with industrial communities and demands from a growing landless middle class for access. The critical point, however, in developing this romantic notion of "lost" rights, may well be the allegiance between those with essentially practical concerns for the poor, such as Octavia Hill,[6] the aesthetic concerns for natural beauty of the kind exemplified by Wordsworth,[7] and a more widespread social movement harking back to a mythical golden age.[8] The founding of the Commons, Open Spaces and Footpaths Preservation Society in 1865 is an example of the developing national status of the issues.[9]

Whilst some placed the "right to roam" in the context of wider philosophical statements about the nature of land ownership and taxation,[10] the movement for access was drawn from a wider social cross-section of interests than could be sustained behind any general movement for land ownership reform. There is not space in this paper to explore the complex pressures sustaining a movement and ethos containing such diverse strands, but it is essential to recognise the potential consequences of such a diverse base for the manner in which the claim to a right to roam has been advanced. This broad coalition of interests made an enduring political movement, but legal changes need to be precisely expressed. The movements were fighting on a broad front: preservation of public rights of way; an end to enclosure of commons and village greens; rights of access to remaining commons; a creation of local authority powers to provide parks and open spaces for recreation. The content of such rights was only defined from time to time in the context of particular campaigns, litigation or legislation. At different times both the land to be subject to this "right" and the nature of the right itself have varied. To say that it lacked certainty is not a criticism, more a statement of the inevitable result of the diversity of objective, and essential pragmatism of the access agenda. Excessive precision in the nature of the rights sought would have lead to fragmentation of the movement.

For the most part, attention has focused upon piecemeal gains, arguing for localised reallocations, within an accepted framework of property law.[11] The common feature has been a claim for increased public access to land, as of right, not on a permissive basis, leaving open for debate the area to be covered, the relationship between conflicting uses and the importance of accessibility as opposed to access.[12] With such a long agenda, it has seldom proven necessary for the access movement to look beyond immediate battles to identify an ultimate destination.

Lost Ancient Rights

Emotive approaches, based on claims of lost ancient rights are not confined to the last century.[13] They can be seen, to greater or lesser extent, deployed in the arguments for access today. The most recent manifestation of this view is the government's Green Paper on *Access to the Open Countryside*, which starts:

> The demand for access legislation followed the enclosure movement which reached its peak in the eighteenth and nineteenth centuries and greatly reduced the areas of open, uncultivated land available for public use.... This process became highly unpopular, and from the mid-nineteenth century Parliament progressively limited the scope for further enclosures. From that time onwards there was pressure to do more and to ensure people could again roam over some of the land which had been "lost".[14]

That language has shown a remarkable consistency, reflecting a widespread belief that a right to roam should exist, even if it does not already do so.[15]

At best this romanticism perpetuates a limited analysis of the nature of the access sought and the way in which this can be accommodated within English property law. At worst it is based upon misinterpretations of legal history. There is no doubt that large numbers of people were deprived of rights to use the countryside for subsistence purposes through processes such as emparkment and enclosure.[16] Suppression of commoners' rights, the judicial assault upon easements in gross[17] and customs in gross,[18] and the severe restrictions placed upon *profits à prendre* all combined to restrict those agricultural rights which were not incidents of land ownership. The loss of these rights from the sixteenth century onwards was important and contentious,[19] but was not about public access as such. Loss of the right to exploit did remove the rationale for being on the land, but these were accesses incidental to use of the right to exploit the land, not rights for the public at large.

To say that local peasants lost customary or manorial rights to use their environment, is not the same as saying a general right to roam existed. On land which was not being intensively farmed and had not been emparked, local residents enjoyed *de facto* access for recreation prior to enclosure. The fencing and hedging associated with enclosure hindered this.[20] However, it is a sizeable leap from that to an assertion of a *de jure* right of access for recreation for the public at large. The only role that rights available to the public at large play in enclosure is in relation to public rights of way.[21]

The right to roam now asserted is a right for the public at large, not a relational right dependent upon local residence or property tenure. Efforts to use the common law to defend such a right have been repeatedly rebuffed.[22] As far as the common law is concerned there seems to be no such right. Efforts to override public exclusion whether by the breaking of enclosures in the nineteenth century, or their modern equivalents such as the mass trespass on Kinder Scout in 1932, have drawn public and philanthropic attention to the issue, but not directly produced legal confirmation of prior public rights. After early largely unsuccessful attempts,[23] there has been no effective modern attempt to reassert those alleged rights through the courts.

Creating New Rights to Roam

Instead the focus has been upon the creation of new access rights through legislation to secure new public rights of access to countryside. This approach has achieved little in the past 150 years, despite much effort.[24] What has been secured? Access to Metropolitan Commons,[25] post-1876 enclosures,[26] urban commons,[27] and a smattering of individual local Acts provide for access.[28] These measures have a common feature, which may help to explain their success: it is not just that they take advantage of particular social contexts in which commons' conservators or schemes of management exist to provide tools for managing the conflict between acknowledged rights, which can be adapted to include access as just another issue in the layers of intermingled rights. They also relate to a relatively easily defined area of land - common land had already been defined in property law for other purposes and could, at least in theory, be identified exhaustively by way of maps. Identification of the land and a means of managing conflict between uses are critical hurdles in the path of a wider right of access. Even given these advantages, progress has been patchy, with many commons, particularly those away from urban areas, not carrying any public rights of access.[29]

Bills to secure access to wider areas of "open countryside" have had less success. This is not for want of effort, as Access to Mountains

Bills were put before Parliament in 1908, 1926, 1927, 1928, 1931, 1937, culminating in the Access to Mountains Act 1939.[30] These measures provided for blanket access to substantial areas of land. After the war, the importance of maximising agricultural production gave the rural landowner a strong negotiating position[31] resulting in a move away from such Bills into individual access orders and agreements within the 1949 legislation.[32]

Options for Further Access

Current options for extending access can learn from that historical experience. Four possible options for extending access appear to exist: legislation to secure new "rights", voluntarism, fiscal/financial incentives and public or quasi-public ownership. The post-war emphasis has been upon a combination of voluntarism and public ownership backed by fiscal and financial incentives. The post-war success of these must be considered before turning to the latest set of proposals.

Access agreements, agri- and tax incentive schemes illustrate the strengths and limitations of voluntarism. These operate within classic notions of property law, to confer contractual rights of access, as opposed to the permanent legal rights sought by the access movement. The 1949 National Parks and Access to the Countryside Act created a legal framework within which local access agreements and orders could be made, extended by the 1981 Wildlife and Countryside Act to the wider concept of management agreements, covering many aspects of land management, of which access may form a part. As with commons management schemes, access agreements offer a tailored site-specific approach to the relationship between public use and the interests of the site owner. Such approaches, based upon securing agreement on a site by site basis, can be costly to establish. In many cases a fiscal or financial incentive will be needed to secure the agreement, essentially transferring the cost of provision from the landowner to the state.[33]

As recently as 1990 a book sponsored by the Countryside Commission was able to claim that the access agreement concept had failed due to a lack of resources and landowner pressures.[34] The same book reflected that the access agreement "will be used less and less in the future".[35] Since then, however voluntary agreements appear to have made progress.[36] The 1998 Green Paper estimates that statutory schemes, including the Agri-Environment Regulation Schemes,[37] amount to a total area of 119 hectares - slightly more than the total of common land in England and Wales, but of that the largest single element is the 58,000 hectares recorded under the capital tax conditional exemption scheme.[38] This is not the large scale mass access to uplands envisaged by the promoters of the 1949 Act, mostly being small scale and individuated. Nonetheless, cumulatively it has provided as much access as the rights-based approach to common land to date.

Perhaps the largest contributions to public access have been secured through schemes of ownership of land by statutory bodies whose objectives include access: local authorities;[39] the National Trust;[40] the Woodland Trust;[41] agencies and utilities such as the Environment Agency.[42] The National Trust is particularly important in the context of access to open countryside.[43] Founded at the turn of the century, as one thread of the access and heritage movement, by using the traditional notions of property law, the Trust has secured ownership of, and thereby control over access to, vast acres of the country.[44] Although possessing statutory powers beyond those normally associated with land ownership, the Trust, in essence, is a landowner, allowing the public permissive access to its land. The wider public interest is protected through the parent statute which sets out the terms on which the Trust must hold the land.   The privatised utilities have specific remits to have regard to the need for public access as an incident of the transfer of land to them,[45] insofar as this is consistent with their other obligations.   Given current emphasis upon cost-benefit analyses by such bodies, there may be increasing pressure to reduce inconvenient access to or charge for access or at least for the incidents of access such as parking.   In that context the government assertion in its 1998 Green Paper that such bodies "have opened up their land wherever possible"[46] seems a trifle optimistic.[47]

To make land accessible, as opposed to providing a legal entitlement to access, requires easily available and relatively consistent public information about the existence and terms of such rights.[48] Whilst access agreement and agri-incentive/tax schemes have been productive in terms of acres of access, problems of public awareness of opportunities for access have arisen.[49] Being in essence permissive contractual arrangements as opposed to permanent legal rights, they are not recorded on ordnance survey maps or similar official records which are key sources of information for countryside users.   Access agreements and voluntary schemes are sometimes included in local recreation guides - indeed they may have been negotiated specifically for the purpose of establishing a circular route or access to a view point for such tourist activities. However, the variability of detail and duration make any consistent recording of these schemes difficult. Those resulting from tax agreements are even harder to locate, being private agreements protected by tax legislation.[50]   This lack of publicity is critical to the delivery of accessibility.[51]

Even were enhanced information to be made available, voluntarist schemes seldom deliver the "right to roam" sought by campaigners: usually being temporary and permissive as opposed to property rights. They may also be used as a justification for not extending legal rights. The Green Paper, for example, uses the *de facto* access provided by the Forestry Commission in many places as a basis for arguing that the extension of access to woodlands more generally is not an immediate priority, side-stepping the geographically skewed distribution of Forestry Commission woodlands,[52] and apparently ignoring Countryside Commission concerns about declining woodland access.[53] Such comments serve to reinforce suspicions about *de facto* access.

Human Rights Act 1998

The pressure for greater certainty and durability leads inevitably to requests for the creation of a statutory property right: indefeasible, permanent and binding *in rem*.   This at once presents problems for traditional property law concepts in the UK.   "Ownership" of land in England can be seen as the ownership of a bundle of twigs, in which each one represents a particular incident of ownership.[54] The bundle contains the totality of rights which the landowner currently exercises, and all those foreseeable and unforeseeable incidents of use associated with the property.   The notion is residual.   That is, the owner's bundle contains all those rights and incidents associated with the land which have not already been expressly allocated to someone else.

Thus, in English Law, the claim to a public right of access does not involve the creation of a new right; rather, it involves taking one stick from the bundle of rights currently held by the landowner, and giving it to someone else.   Within this commonly used model, the claim of a right of access therefore inherently involves not merely the creation of a new right vested in the public at large, but also the loss of control of public use by the landowner, in whom all rights are currently vested.   It is therefore not surprising that landowners perceive claims to a legal right to roam as a loss of part of their property. It is. The loser is bound to campaign against this loss of his exclusive rights, unless sufficiently compensated.[55] And this is a loss, irrespective of whether other concerns exist, such as the compatibility of public access with the landowner's chosen use of his land, in the exercise of his existing and remaining rights. Of course, one can argue that the bundle of rights analysis is neither useful, nor accurate. But for as long as it has a currency, use of the rights debate to seek to secure access faces a problem.

Jurisdictions which have different concepts of property ownership experience fewer problems in the introduction of a right of access to open countryside. Thus, in some jurisdictions (*eg* Finland) the landowner does not own all the foreseeable incidents associated with the land. He owns a specified list of rights. To create a right of access for someone else does not inherently involve taking away from his bundle of rights. Whilst issues of compatibility of the exercise of the rights may still exist, there is not the same problem with inherent loss of rights. That is not to say it is impossible to construct a public right of access to open countryside in England, but rather that it is harder than in some jurisdictions.

Any new statutory right of access is likely to be challenged in the domestic courts under the Human Rights Act 1998, and ultimately in the European Court of Human Rights.[56] As currently constructed the European Convention on Human Rights has proven a potent tool in the protection of current property rights from state intervention. Two elements of the Convention Rights in particular have been used to challenge efforts to create new rights which conflict with or restrict existing property rights: Article 1 of the First Protocol, and the procedural provisions in Article 6.

There is no right to acquire property. Article 1 of the First Protocol[57] protects existing property owners from unwarranted state intervention in the peaceful enjoyment of their property rather than conferring the opportunity to acquire new property rights.[58] Accordingly, Convention provisions relating to the protection of property are available to some, not others, depending upon whether their argument can be articulated in terms of the protection of existing property rights. This imbalance lies at the core of the problem rights arguments face in the context of the "right to roam". At the point at which new legislation is introduced to confer any new public right to roam, existing landowners would be in a position to seek to invoke their Convention Rights[59] to protect their current property rights. Whether, and when, users of a "right to roam" became entitled to use the same provisions would depend upon whether the legislation was seen as creating a property right vested in potential users.[60]

The Convention does not, even inadvertently, suggest there is a "correct" definition of property.[61] Instead the Convention seems to accept the diversity of definitions of property existing in signatory states at the time of signature and seeks to regulate efforts to change existing property rights.[62] As a result, this provision is not an inherent barrier to a right to roam: the Swedish "*allemansratt*" passes the Article 1 test. But that is in the context of a concept of property law which does not see the *allemansratt* as taking anything away from the property of the landowner, and which predated Sweden's signature of the Convention. This means an effort to change definitions of property in State A towards those of State B might be in breach of Article 1, even if the existing law in State B is not in breach.

Under Article 1 the state can expropriate property in the public interest or control[63] property in the general interest, but only in accordance with prevailing law. This limit upon state action only applies to statutory restrictions upon the holding or use of existing property rights, so it only affects efforts to secure a "right to roam" and does not in any way affect voluntarist or fiscal approaches to increasing access.

The crux of the Convention test lies in the requirement that any restrictions on existing property rights must be "in the public interest".[64] In determining this, the Court of Human Rights looks at whether a fair balance has been struck between the public interest to be served and the resulting burden on a particular individual, bearing in mind the opportunities for compensation.[65] As any attempt to take rights out of the English landowner's bundle, to create a right to roam, involves a loss of property right, this proportionality test must be applied. A new public right can only be safely granted where the loss of property rights and ancillary difficulties in the use of remaining incidents of ownership, are proportionate to the public benefit gained. At the same time as providing this sensitivity to differing landowner needs, the legislation must be accessible and certain.[66] Whilst the European Court of Human Rights has been prepared to give a wide margin of appreciation to signatory states in determining what is in the public interest,[67] this does impose some restrictions upon the ability of a state to alter the "English bundle" of property rights - particularly if a state wishes to remain well within the margin of appreciation.[68]

Avoidance of successful legal challenge will require careful use of language. The blunt language of the early twentieth century Access Bills will not work. Rhetoric about the loss of ancient rights must be avoided from the outset: even loose wording in a government Green Paper could taint later cautiously worded proposals. From the outset the proposal must speak of action limited to the minimum necessary in the public interest and must seek to ensure that in any particular case the restriction on the holding or use of existing private property rights is restricted only to the extent justifiable under the Convention. It must demonstrate that the government has addressed the Convention issues and consider whether compensation is necessary to minimise the opportunity for successful legal challenge. This immediately presents a difficulty for English draftsmen. Balance of convenience tests are inherently uncertain legal tools. They require a different form of purposive drafting to that historically used in property law, where certainty of outcome has tended to take priority over purposive statements. They run counter to the experience of right to roam discussions over the past century, where successful legislation has been precise.

Perhaps a more significant obstacle to a right to roam is the extent to which the Convention jurisprudence links compensation to the ability to create a robust right to roam. One of the obstacles to increased provision of voluntary access has been the lack of money to provide suitable financial incentives. There is no evidence of money being more forthcoming for right to roam compensation. The availability of compensation may be critical to the success of any measure and may permit things which would otherwise lie outside the scope of the state's power under Article 1 of the First Protocol. The Human Rights Act 1998 does not confer a right to damages if a failure to deliver Convention Rights results from the legislation *per se* as opposed to its implementation, but this omission may mean little in this context because of the importance placed upon the distribution of the economic costs and benefits of change[69] by the jurisprudence of the European Convention.[70] The cost of the new benefit must be distributed across the community and not borne excessively by any one property owner. Compensation for loss of rights is not required within the Convention, but compensation is a critical tool in spreading the costs of the change across the wider community and will generally be required where otherwise there would be private loss.[71] Only minimal schemes for enhanced mandatory public access could be pursued without compensation, if they are to restrict the landowner's rights.

Quite apart from questions of whether such a "right to roam" would be a high priority for public sector spending, the principle of paying compensation poses a problem for those who subscribe to the "lost rights" approach. Thus, Alan Mattingly argued[72]

> Those who support proposed access to open country legislation believe that it will restore to the general public a freedom of which they should never have been deprived in the first place. They therefore do not see a case for compensating owners of open country in the event of a right of access being created. They further believe that there would be strong public opposition to the payment of such compensation.

If the assertion of lost rights is correct in law, then the Convention would not require the payment of compensation, but unless that is the case, compensation must at least be considered. Opposition to compensation must therefore depend on proof of the loss of ancient rights in law, as opposed to romantic or folklore notions of lost right. As we have seen, that has not been successful to date.[73]

Compensation would not need to be the same in all cases,[74] and the state has considerable discretion in valuing the loss,[75] but it will require a process through which this can be adjudicated. That procedure will be subject to the requirements of Article 6.

Any "right to roam" legislation will need to make provision for the determination of disputes concerning the effect upon landowners, to comply with Article 6.[76] This will require a procedure for determining individual disputes which has a degree of independence. Experience of the interminable and costly processes under the Definitive Map provisions,[77] raises concern about the likely cost and juridification of a "right to roam" inquiry procedure, even if limited to questions of quantum. Yet these are brushed aside in the Green Paper.[78]

In the wake of the Convention, any right to roam must now be phrased carefully, in terms of proportionality of the public gain to the private loss. This is no longer required purely to avoid electoral unpopularity with landowners, or to secure a majority in the House of Lords, it is required as a matter of law. With it comes a further complication. Proportionality is a useful word to encapsulate the wide range of social and economic policy factors which can be used in deciding *ex post facto* whether a particular change is or is not proportional. Seeking to draft general legislation which offers the precision necessary in English property law, whilst it at the same time reflects the wide range of issues related to a proportionality test, is a somewhat taxing brief. Yet, that is what, in effect, legislation associated with the right to roam has been seeking to do for more than a century. Even if the proportionality test *per se* is a relative newcomer to the debate, it is not essentially different from the wide range of interests which needed to be accommodated to secure the passage of earlier attempted measures.

The 1998 Consultation

The 1998 government consultation on *Access to the Open Countryside* illustrates the difficulties reform faces. It sets the context that " ... we wish to work as far as possible with the assent of those owning and managing land and to keep compulsion to the absolute minimum necessary to achieve our objectives".[79] The emphasis is entirely on voluntarism, although the paper explores what a right may contain in the very limited context in which the government envisages a role for compulsion. The Green Paper shows just how limited the "right to roam" debate becomes, when placed in that context. It is easy to suggest that the government consultation is simply trying to be all things to all people, but this essay seeks to argue that the limitations of the proposal are inherent in the concept of the "right to roam".

The issue of access to open countryside was raised in parliament immediately after the general election by a backbencher,[80] but Labour general election manifesto promises on this have become caught up in the wider countryside debate.[81] The focus of both the back bench initiative and government proposal is not upon an unrestricted "right to roam" but upon a cautious extension of voluntary access to open country.[82] Although badged as part of the "Third Way" initiatives, the 1998 Green Paper fits snugly into the traditions of the access debate. The Green Paper reaffirms a commitment to "securing greater access to open countryside",[83] but stresses that this is to be achieved by voluntary agreement. Compulsion will only be used to the minimum level necessary to achieve the aim of increased access. As the level of increase in access sought is not quantified,[84] it is difficult to judge the extent to which reliance upon new statutory rights will be required.

This very much reflects the agenda of the last 70 years. It is a proposal which could have been published at any time in the last 70 years. Indeed some of it was: the Green Paper lists some exceptions to the potential list of access land, including, *inter alia,* "tramways and aerodromes".[85]   Aerodrome may be a term of art, but it is curious that the consultation so closely mirrors the wording of section 60 of the 1949 National Parks and Access to the Countryside Act.   The scanner and word processor look to have been at work.   But it is not just the language which harks back two generations.   The keystone of the Green Paper is the idea of public use where that use is compatible with the owner's chosen use.   It emphasises voluntarism, as in the 1949 legislation, with the possibility of a right of access held out as a residual option.   This may be a lack of radicalism, an assertion of the "Third Way", or a pragmatic response to the limitations of the Convention.   Voluntarism, backed up by economic instruments, is also more in line with the broad thrust of European approaches to behaviour modification in the wider environmental field.[86]

The Green Paper sees the "rights based" and "fiscal" approaches as mutually exclusive.   It seeks to promote voluntarism through the fiscal approach with the potential of further statutory intervention only to supplement this.[87]   As we have seen, systems for providing permissive public access, in exchange for financial or fiscal advantages have been in place for 50 years.   Whilst one can argue about the success of such schemes, recent experience in the context of non-linear access, and in terms of public rights of way, has shown a lack of political will at all levels to provide the necessary funding to support such a non-rights-based approach.[88]   In consequence there is every likelihood that any measure which made increased access contingent upon payment of compensation, would lie on the shelves little used.   The Green Paper does not address this crucial gap between theory and implementation.[89]   Nor does it explain why so much of the work carried out by the Common Land Forum, the Royal Commission on Commons and the work leading to the Dartmoor Commons Act 1985 has been ignored in favour of a return to uniform and simplistic global solutions.

For Treasury reasons it is necessary for the Green Paper to assert that the proposals have no major financial implications.[90]   As we have seen, the European Convention sees compensation as having a potentially significant role in distributing the costs of achieving public benefits.   The Green Paper sees the costs falling upon owners, local authorities, statutory agencies and the courts.   It rejects the idea of a general right to compensation,[91] but instead refers to the availability of grants or payments under existing voluntary schemes,[92] and the scope for landowners to secure indirect income, such as from the provision of parking facilities.[93]

Any proposal must:

(a)   define the land to be covered;

(b)   reconcile recreational and ownership uses reflecting Convention obligations;

(c)   provide sufficient permanence or universality for the sites to be publicised and made accessible;

(d)   provide an adjudication process; and

(e)   consider the need for compensation.

Defining the Land

The Green Paper, by seeking to address the question of "open countryside" is faced from the outset with a definitional problem. Defining the land to be covered by any enhanced right of access has always been problematic. The phrase "access to open countryside" is fine as a campaign slogan, or as part of the writings of the access movement over the last century, but if it is to be included in legislation must be subject to precise definition. Just as the nature of the "right" sought by users has never been defined precisely,[94] so too the land to which the access is sought has never been defined accurately. We all know what we think is "open countryside" - but our ideas might not coincide and are unlikely to be amenable to precise definition: indeed this is an argument for saying the statutory right should be dealt with by way of map not generic classification. A glance at any upland fringe will demonstrate how ephemeral such concepts as enclosure are: the tumble down stone walls, where once moorland cottages and enclosures stood are sufficient testimony.

Earlier attempts at "right to roam" legislation, have dealt with the problem of geographical definition in a different way. The most precise definition is found in the Law of Property Act 1925, which provided for access to commons which still had commoners' rights on 1st January, 1926 and fell within an Urban District.[95] At least this relied upon recognised legal concepts of commoners and Urban Districts. Even so, evidential problems have arisen in establishing whether commoners' rights did exist at that time. The Access to Mountains Act 1939 took a different route, providing a precise mechanism under which landowners, local authorities, and anyone legitimately speaking for users could seek an order from the Minister applying the provisions of the Act to a piece of land.[96]

Other measures,[97] such as the 1949 National Parks and Access to the Countryside Act sought to provide a complete map of all the land to which the Act applied.[98] The 1949 Act required local planning authorities to map "open country" in their area and report to government on the steps being taken to secure public access to it.[99] Such a reporting system, even if widely executed would not have given rise to the sort of pressure for detailed interpretation which is likely to flow from attaching a right of access to any land falling within the definition.

The 1998 Green Paper, in contrast, expressly rejects a statutory map approach.[100] Mapping, in the form of a Countryside Commission register, is to have unspecified evidential value in the case of dispute. Beyond that the government relies rather vaguely upon statutory countryside agencies to build upon existing sources of information to ensure public accessibility.[101] As an initial stage in the process the Countryside Commission is carrying out terrestrial surveys and the government has announced a satellite survey of the UK which will provide a map and database on a field by field basis.[102]

Whichever definition is chosen, the difficulties of identifying the land covered and disseminating information are multiplied if land can move in and out of the access category.[103] By rejecting a statutory map, increased pressure is placed upon finding a legally robust definition of the land covered. The 1998 Green Paper aims to tackle this by defining "open countryside" as "mountain, moor, heath, down and common".

Only the word "common" has any recognised and tested legal definition. One can say with a degree of certainty whether something is, or is not, a common, as sites not registered under the 1965 Commons Registration Act are no longer legally classified as commons. But the other definitions are fraught with problems. Mountains could be defined in relation to altitude; but the ordinary meaning of the word mountain is not wholly altitude linked: Denver, Colorado is not a mountain, but at an altitude of a mile is rather higher that any English peak. Even in the solely English context an altitude test may cause problems for communities in high altitude valleys. Nonetheless, there is a chance of defining "mountain": at least, like the elephant, we would all probably recognise it when we see it. The Green Paper opts for the simplistic solution of an ordinance datum test of 600 metres. It is silent as to the problem of high altitude communities.

The categories "moor, heath and down" are rather more problematic. We would not all necessarily recognise them when we see them. Whilst there are some areas we would all probably agree are one of those, around the margins of each would lie a peripheral area of disagreement. As to the differences between them, we would struggle.

The 1998 Green Paper uses a biodiversity view, where these are defined by their species mix.[104] "Heath", for example is defined as having dwarf shrubs such as heather and gorse and may occur on uplands or lowlands. This is an inherently weak basis for defining property law rights: unless supplemented by a legally binding map and adjudication process,[105] it relies upon people out for a roam having sufficient habitat skills to know whether the species mix on a particular piece of land falls within the botanical definition and provides problems of winter identification. Whilst the Green Paper proposes a statutory duty upon the Countryside Commission to provide guidance to enable the identification of the countryside affected, it is difficult to see how this can overcome the inherent uncertainties of the definition. Some of these identification problems could be reduced if courts accept it is only necessary to show a particular site is a "moor, heath and down", rather than needing to show whether it is a moor, or heath or down. Nonetheless, problems will remain in relation to marginal land and the vulnerability of species mix to changing management practices.

As conservationists and those working to protect SSSIs report, landowners are susceptible to "improving" such sites. If such changes will also remove public access a further temptation for site destruction is added. The government is sanguine about the extent to which the Green Paper proposals will result in further habitat loss, because they see the resulting use as low pressure, but the habitat risk here is not from the possible use, but from the choice of legal definition of the locations of the possible use. By defining the areas covered in relation to habitats, you make habitat change a critical tool in excluding unwanted access. A different definition would at least remove that risk.

Proportionality Tests: Reconciling Uses

Having considered the difficulties of defining the land over which access will be permitted, it is necessary to consider the relationship between the access sought and the landowner's chosen use of the land. The proportionality of the public benefit to be gained from increased access set against the loss of private property freedom is central to the European Convention on Human Rights, quite apart from the need for sufficient consensus to secure the passage of legislation. Any legislation to increase public access therefore needs to tackle these questions. One can be critical of the particular route chosen in the Green Paper,[106] but any proposal will struggle with trying to translate the proportionality required by the Convention into sufficiently precise language to give effect to changed property rights. The proposal merits attention as an illustration of the difficulties any proposal of this kind faces.

The first task is to define the nature of the public use to be granted. The Green Paper does this in terms of a "freedom of access", rather than a "right to roam". The access is to be "on foot for the purposes of open-air recreation".[107] This use by walkers[108] is likely to exclude dogs[109] and may be further restricted by local by-laws. Even with such a limited scope, the "right" proposed is only the negative one of immunity from action as a trespasser,[110] modelled on the 1949 Act[111] rather than the Dartmoor Commons Act model. The owner will have no greater liability to the users than to a trespasser. A user exceeding the limited scope for use, within the by-laws, would be excluded for the day / duration of their breach.[112] This may be an effort to resist claims that the proposals will remove part of a landowner's "property right". If so, it fails. The "right" to bring an action for trespass is part of the hypothetical bundle of rights of ownership in English law. Whilst this is a smaller loss than the positive right to roam would confer, it is nonetheless a loss of "rights" triggering the application of the Convention. The only way to avoid Convention issues is to opt for voluntarist solutions which do not affect property rights.

The Convention does not prohibit a "right to roam", however broadly or narrowly defined: it requires the change to be justified under a proportionality test. Whether from a concern to win support from landowners or from fears of the operation of the Convention, the Green Paper goes on to propose than even its limited interference with property rights will not apply where the landowner's chosen use of the land would be affected.

Given the vast range of uses to which "mountain, moor, heath, down and common" can be put, and the differing pressures for use, it is difficult for legislation to specify the degree of intervention in property use which is to be authorised. Beyond the very simple levels of exclusion considered above ("*Defining the Land*") lies a category of land over which access at some times in some circumstances may be appropriate. Here legislation needs to identify the circumstances and period for which access becomes inappropriate, or at least a mechanism by which such matters are to be determined.[113] We would all object to a public right of access to our back garden. Beyond that, upon which criteria should exclusion be based?

Risk analysis could offer a basis for exploring the emotional, environmental, economic, agricultural and cultural issues which affect perceptions of where the benefit of increased access is disproportionate to the interference with individual property interests. It would not remove all uncertainties, but might provide a more consistent approach. For example, the Green Paper seems to assume that it is intensity of husbandry, as opposed to its nature, which is the source of incompatibilities between farmer and recreationist: this is not necessarily the case - two sheep are as easily scared as a whole flock. Lower intensity use by the farmer may affect the chances of a harmful encounter, but does not necessarily reduce the harm should the encounter occur. If the risk of harm were at the core of the government's concern, then intensity of anticipated recreational use is as significant as the intensity of the landowner's use to the likelihood of harm.

The Green Paper considers that access should not extend to "developed or agricultural" land,[114] unless only extensively grazed. This seeks to reflect the proportionality idea at a high level of generality. In doing so it makes essentially urban and growth-based assumptions that land which is not under active cultivation or development is somehow "underused" and assumes extensive grazing is more compatible with public access than other uses. It fails to recognise the sustainability questions associated with appropriate levels of use of land and the extent to which apparently "unused" land may nonetheless be playing a significant role in biodiversity systems or estate management.[115]

Whilst not seeking to define agriculture, or extensive grazing, further, the Green Paper recognises a need to define "developed" land. It contemplates doing so by reference to a list: buildings and their curtilage, parks, gardens, pleasure gardens, land used for surface working of minerals, land used by statutory undertakers, golf courses, racecourses, railways, tramways and aerodromes.[116] The clue to the origin of this list lies in the rather archaic language used for the last two: they come from section 60 of the 1949 National Parks and Access to the Countryside Act. What would be the rationale for making explicit reference to these uses, but leaving others to be excluded by the general words "developed land"? Why, for example is a racecourse on the draft list, whereas a rugby pitch or bowling green is not? Perhaps the list approach avoids difficulties in identifying criteria, but it should at least be consistent. Repetition of previous legislation does not seem to offer sufficient justification for this.

The vague definition of agriculture as excluding land "extensively grazed" means that small changes in estate management or animal husbandry will take land in or out of "access land". The public right of access will depend upon the ephemera of the landowner's choice of agricultural practice. This conjures up visions of "rentaflock", being moved around uplands in advance of visits by inspectors to assess whether the land is extensively grazed. Practices also legitimately change from year to year in reflection of normal husbandry or agricultural rotation, or in response to market or subsidy pressures. Will the right of access ebb and flow with such changes? If only long term changes are to affect access, at what stage will a modest change in practice amount to a longer term change in the character of the land?[117]

The Dartmoor Commons Act 1985 illustrates the complexity of the relationship between access and agriculture/husbandry, which the Green Paper seeks to roll into this one tight phrase. The Green Paper says little about the effect of seasonal changes in the compatibility of access with agricultural use,[118] or temporary exclusion as a pre-condition to securing maximum landowner compliance. Whilst there has been much debate about what is a "legitimate" reason for such closures, apart from the normal list of exclusions for health, military and heritage grounds[119] the Green Paper speaks in very vague terms of a right for the landowner to suspend access for short periods "if the owner or occupier so wish".[120] This proposal is headed "Protecting people's way of life" and gives equal weight to the idea that owners may have "personal or social reasons" for excluding the public as to management or financial ones. Reliance by the Green Paper upon the notion of landowners being given a Code of Practice by the Countryside Commission offering guidance on how to use this provision does little to remove concerns of it being a licence to exclude at will.

One sees in the Green Paper the dilemma posed by efforts to increase access: a proposal which substantially increases public access and is used by the public will increase pressure upon landowners to use whatever exceptions are available. Intensification of grazing or cropping, short of a change in habitat such as to stop the land being "moor, heath or down", may nonetheless create an additional opportunity through which landowners can seek to exclude land from access,[121] possibly at the expense of the environment. Proposals for drainage or habitat change which were previously marginal economically may be promoted by this provision. The government seems remarkably optimistic that landowners will not take advantage of these loopholes:

There may be some risk that farmers will be reluctant to re-establish these [biodiversity action plan] habitats because of the access implications, making the achievement of Biodiversity Action Plan targets more difficult. However we expect that a realistic appraisal of the likely impact of our proposals should prevent this.[122]

Whilst the particular wording of the Green Paper may create unnecessary loopholes, any wording of a proportionality test will reflect in some form the landowner's chosen use of the land. That will make it prey to change of land use, and thence of habitat. If, as the government says, the likely impact of the proposals is modest, then what is the purpose of the entire process of trying to define a statutory right to roam at all?

Uncertainty and Universalism

There are very few universalist access measures in force, but this is not for want of effort on the part of campaigners and the proposers of Bills.[123] Almost all the rights acquired in the past 150 years have been through the sub-universalism of commons legislation, local Acts or the fiscal and voluntarist routes: measures which have set up a framework within which location-specific solutions can be reached.[124]

The Common Land Forum, looking at the way to extend the experience of access to commons to cover all common land, suggested the concept of a management scheme, where all involved negotiated site-specific terms against the background of a model set of terms which would apply in default of local agreement. This model of schemes tailored to particular local needs is one which seems to have been forgotten in the current Green Paper, but has much to commend it in terms of providing local solutions rather than uniformity. It would provide a potent tool for reaching local agreement about precisely which fields to include within the right. The drawing of the boundaries provides an opportunity to negotiate quality as well as quantity of access. There seem no obvious reasons why its approach could not be extended to open countryside which is not part of a common: with the owners, occupiers and local authority negotiating the terms of a scheme for each relevant site within the local authority area. The disadvantage of course is the lack of uniformity, making it difficult for the public to know their entitlements. Instead the Green Paper opts for universalism.

Whatever definition is chosen, however precise, there will be practical disputes about whether a piece of land has the right species mix, altitude or common land status to be subject to this freedom from trespass. Disputes will then arise as to whether the current use of the land is within one of the defined exceptions or for *ex post facto* dispute adjudication. The Green Paper offers little by way of explanation for how this will happen; indeed, it seems to assume recourse to the courts. The Green Paper proposes a duty upon the Countryside Commission to issue guidance helping to identify the land affected which would be taken into account by courts, coupled with a Code of Practice for users, analogous to the current Countryside Access Charter. As far as disputes are concerned the Green Paper contemplates that local authorities and statutory agencies may need to use existing or new by-law powers, possibly including some model by-laws.[125] The concept of management is not spelt out, although it seems local authorities will be expected to undertake a new role and may be given new powers to do so.[126] If this is the management model finally adopted it moves away from management by consensus of the kind proposed by the Common Land Forum, where all interested parties were to be represented on management bodies.

Lack of management mechanisms does not just affect procedural questions.   It also affects the Green Paper's conceptualisation of complexity. This can be seen in the way the Green Paper addresses the relationship between public use and habitat damage. The government concludes that, "We do not expect increased access to have major environmental implications",[127] the argument being that where access might threaten its "wildlife or archaeological interest" closure orders could be made. This suggests that access is an all or nothing concept. Many habitats[128] benefit from some public access - for example to provide path breaks in grass by use. However the precise extent of the use which is not harmful or even beneficial will depend on the particular site. In such cases management, rather than exclusion, is needed: are local authorities the appropriate bodies to do this?

It is unclear how such a low status "right" will be protected.[129] Will these rights be reflected in the property register? How will changes in land use which take land in and out of the access category be recorded and publicised?   Nor is there any suggestion of public consultation or notification prior to changes in land use which may affect public access. Yet the availability of an effective adjudication mechanism is essential under Article 6 of the European Convention on Human Rights. Without such procedures, the only way to test the application of the provision will be by reference to the courts by way of judicial review, or actions for trespass.[130]

This paper has highlighted some of the unnecessary uncertainties in the Green Paper, but any universalist solution will, of necessity, employ some general language. Localised solutions switch that uncertainty to a different form, creating local certainty, but removing the certainty of universalism. Moving away from a desire for universalism may remove pressure to seek some all-embracing legal definition, and provide management and dispute resolution mechanisms. It might substitute negotiation for "rights" language. The price to be paid might be a lack of uniformity bringing with it additional uncertainty. Whilst the Green Paper rejects the uncertainties of the localist approach, the provision for local by-laws, and the difficulties of land identification make it likely that it will be as difficult for the public to know their rights under the Green Paper proposals as under explicitly locally derived schemes. Uncertainty seems inevitable.

Challenging Property Rights

Given the vague nature of the land covered, the defeasibility of the public "right" by changes in land use and the lack of any right beyond immunity for trespass actions, it is difficult to see the Green Paper's "right" as anything more than a variant of "permissive access". It hardly merits the title "right to roam", indeed the Green Paper calls it a "freedom of access".[131] Within the limits of what Harris calls "situated justice",[132] the access movement has argued for localised reallocations of "rights". If the Green Paper is a fair guide to the scope for such reallocations, perhaps the time has come to move away from the language of rights altogether. The Green Paper could have avoided some of the problems highlighted in this essay, but some seem inherent in the continued reliance upon rights language in the access debate.

This poses a critical question: What is wrong with voluntarist agreements as opposed to a legal right to roam? If the only rights on offer are such minimalist residual ones, to be given only where voluntarism has failed, are they worth having? Opposition to voluntarism, as a second class form of access, can stem from concepts of lost ancient rights. Behind that however, lies the normal list of differences between a personal and a proprietary right: critically, defeasibility and the extent to which they bind successors in title. These give rise to fears of a lack of permanence undermining accessibility. Is it essential to confer a statutory, proprietary interest in land in order to overcome these? Is there no scope for statutory adjustments in the context of access to the countryside, which do not go so far as to confer an interest in the land: or at least which adopt a language which suggests they do not?

Both users and landowners have got into an increasingly self-referencing "rights" debate. What could sometimes look like a move towards a consensus may be merely the identification of a minimalist position, which gives nobody anything and will be deeply resented by "both sides". It proceeds on the basis that somewhere there is a logical solution to be found which will be accepted by all. This assumes that the use of "rights" within the language of landowner and user is based upon a logical analysis of property law. Yet in the writings of both landowners and users legal and emotional uses of the word "rights" are almost interchangeable. This is not an argument predicated on pure rationality. In this area, attitudes to proposals are based on emotion, tradition and history, rather than on the rationality of an idea. A different language is needed in order to move the debate forward.

The Green Paper refers to a "freedom of access". This may have potential, although the Green Paper itself too often reverts to the language of rights to free itself from the historical debate. An alternative is to look at the emerging debate about the "bundle of rights" concept itself. Theoretical critiques of the concept offer potential, but such analyses have not moved into the practical realm.[133] The most successful alternative to rights language at present would seem to be the environmental language of sustainable resource management. "Sustainability" language has been used, successfully, to justify strict restrictions upon landowners: in a context of wide public support, and little protest. The debate has been relatively rational, indeed landowners have themselves adopted the language of stewardship and sustainability. The debate has generally been about how to manage assets sustainability, not whether to do so. Landowners may or may not comply with the new requirements upon them, but the legislation has nonetheless happened. Owners of oilfields or minerals or holes in the ground accept the existence of legislation which regulates the extent to which they may exploit their assets.

The most pressurised commodity of all in England is land itself. Perhaps what is needed is a resource management strategy which seeks the maximum sustainable use of the land resource. The "right to roam" then becomes part of a duty to use land as a finite resource more effectively.

Access is not an infringement of an owner's freedom, but an opportunity to maximise the efficient use of resources.

Conclusion

This paper offers no solutions to the problems of increasing public access, but has identified some of the difficulties. Those who had expected proposals for a strongly worded statutory right of access which would be clear, simple and widely accessible in the Green Paper have been disappointed. In this paper I have sought to show that the disappointment is, perhaps, inherent in the pursuit of a "right to roam".

1   There is no clear definition of what is meant by a "right to roam". Rather it has been used as a phrase to cover a process of piecemeal and incremental change in public opportunities for access to the countryside.

2   It is easier to specify the character of the "right to roam" than to specify its precise content. To be of use a right to roam requires a degree of certainty such that the land affected can be readily identified, the scope of the public right to use is clear and sites are accessible.

3   Conferring a right to roam as any form of property right or restriction upon existing private ownership rights presents legal difficulties under the Human Rights Act 1998 and European Convention on Human Rights.

4   The Convention requires that any intervention with prior private property rights must be proportionate to the public benefit created. This is not necessarily easy to achieve without provision for compensation and requires the provision of public access to be carefully limited to the minimum necessary commensurate with differing forms of land use.

5   These are difficult to reconcile with the objectives of access set out at point 2 above.

6   Universality, as a proxy for certainty and accessibility, is unattainable, if the access conferred is to be sufficiently precise as to form a property law interest, whilst not infringing the proportionality test.

7   Compensation could offer a partial solution, but means a "right to roam" may encounter similar budgetary barriers to implementation as those limiting use of voluntarist solutions.

8   There is a risk of the gap between what can be offered by a legal "right to roam" and what can be provided by voluntarist solutions narrowing to the point that the resources required for dispute adjudication and compensation may make the achievement of a right to roam something of a Pyrrhic victory.

9   Fiscal, financial, voluntarist and ownership routes continue to offer opportunities for incremental change. More radical change needs to look for a language other than rights by which to assert a general freedom of access to open countryside.

Whatever the realities of the advances to be made from the current consultation, the language in which it needs to be phrased and the significance of compensation, will appear to move away from the "right to roam" concept as a property right. Unless there is a government willingness to invest public funds in a compensation scheme, the European Convention provides a real obstacle to stronger rights of access to open country framed within the tradition of the debate. Wider use of alternative mechanisms such as fiscal incentives offer less costly routes to persuade people along the voluntarist road, but still require state financial commitment. If a "right" to roam is to provide a less tenuous foothold on countryside access than those in the current proposal the debate must move on from the traditional assertions of moral entitlements to access into a language which carries more power.

The right to roam movement has not spent a century and a half in order to achieve a defeasible freedom from a trespass action in walking on pieces of land which the landowner chooses to enable us to use by his land management decisions. One suspects that is not quite what Octavia Hill and her contemporaries had in mind.

Notes

1   John Clare, "The Mores".
2   See for example Mattingly A (Director of the Ramblers Association) "Right to roam: legal options" (1995) RWLR section 11, p 37.
3   *Eg* Cocks R, "The Great Ashdown Forest Case", chapter 10, *Legal Record and Historical Reality: 8th British Legal History Conference* (1989).
4   The legal position in Scotland and historical position in Wales, distinguish them from England for the issues raised in this paper.

5   *Access to the Open Countryside in England and Wales: A Consultation Paper* February, 1998, DETR. This essay was produced for a conference in March 1998. It has not been revised to take account of the subsequent responses to the Green Paper.

6   See Moberly Bell E, *Octavia Hill* (1942, Constable & Co, London).

7   Whilst essentially middle class concern with the remote and wilderness countryside is often consistent with themes of open space as a requirement for the mass recreation of the poor, the two sometimes conflict. The former played an influential role in the national parks movement, the latter perhaps more directly influenced the Metropolitan Commons legislation.

8   The Pre-Raphaelite Brotherhood, and the Arts and Crafts Movement are reflections of this wider social romanticist movement. For practical examples of their involvement see Henderson P, *Letters of William Morris* (1950). It is also reflected in the socialist histories of Sidney and Beatrice Webb, *English Local Government: The Story of the King's Highway* (1913).

9   Earlier amenity and access groups had tended to be localised and tended to be footpath preservation bodies. The earliest seem to date from the 1820s.

10 See for example Henry George, *Our Land and Land Policy* (1871) an American publication translated into many languages which argued for taxation of unearned rents from land: and ultimately the 1910 Finance Act provisions.

11 The work of the Common Land Forum (see below) typifies this approach: a desire to find practical working compromises, which enable all involved to feel a sense of "victory" whilst making modest progress, owing more to pragmatism than to any attempt to establish a rationale within property law.

12 "Accessibility" as distinct from access connotes the ability of people to make use of such rights of access as exist: looking at factors such as waymarking, repair to routes, removal of obstructions, publication of maps and other information, to enable target groups to use the rights available.

13 See for example, Mattingly *op cit*. "Those who support proposed access to open country legislation believe that it will restore to the general public a freedom of which they should never have been deprived in the first place..." Sydney and Beatrice Webb, *The King's Highway, etc* must bear some of the responsibility for this simplistic and romantic picture.

14 Paragraph 1.2.

15 Shown by an August 1998 opinion poll commissioned by the Ramblers Association. This needs to be read in the context of earlier research which revealed a widespread misunderstanding of the current extent of public rights, by landowners and rural residents, as well as those less directly concerned. See research findings: *Access to the Countryside for Recreation and Sport* CCP217 (1986, Countryside Commission/Sports Council).

16 Enclosure involved converting common strip fields into enclosed fields in single occupation and privatisation of common rights which had enabled many residents of the parish to subsistence farm the same piece of land in parallel through stock grazing, taking of fuel, rights of warren and so on. These rights were attached to particular individuals and specified the level to which each could exploit the resource. They were not rights at liberty to be enjoyed freely by the public at large.

17 The demise of this notion seems to owe much to *Gale on Easements* (1st ed, 1839). See Sturley M, "Easements in Gross" (1980) 96 LQR 557.

18   *Schwinge v Dowell* (1862) 2 FF 845, where the court accepted there could be
      customary rights to wander in Waltham Forest, but if they existed they would be
      limited to the inhabitants.
19   *Fisons Horticulture Ltd v Bunting* [1976] 2 EGLR 120, Walton J.
20   See, for example, the work of John Clare.
21   Willmore C, "Enclosure Awards: public rights of way" (1990) RWLR section 9.3, p
      1.
22   *AG v Antrobus* [1905] 2 Ch 188 is the most common starting point for judicial denial
      of ·the existence of a *ius spatiendi* in English law. However that case asserts there is
      no such right (in the context of a dispute concerning public access to Stonehenge)
      without any authority except the argument of Sir Frances North in *Potter v North*
      (1669) 1 Vent 387. However North was dealing with the question of whether profits
      could exist in gross for the benefit of all: and p 397 makes clear his aim was to
      prevent the assertion of profits which would hinder enclosure or improvement. Whilst
      arguing that a profit in gross could not exist for policy reasons, North said that one
      could plead an easement stretching to all the inhabitants of a parish *ie* an easement in
      gross. This makes it, at best, dubious authority for the *Antrobus* denial of a *ius
      spatiendi.*
23   *Eg, Schwinge v Dowell* (1862) 2 FF 845; EP Thompson, *Customs in Common* (1991,
      London) pp 142-144.
24   Including extra-legal campaigning, such as the mass trespass on Kinder Scout in
      1932.
25   Metropolitan Commons Acts of 1866, 1869, 1898. The 1866 Act was limited to
      commons serving London.   These sought to ensure the commons remained
      unenclosed and provided for a scheme of management. Public use was a tacitly
      assumed incidental. The 1880 scheme of management for Clapham Common adopted
      under the 1866 Act, for example, included a requirement for public use and recreation
      see *de Morgan v Metropolitan Board of Works* (1880) 5 QBD 155.
26   The Metropolitan Commons 1876 Act only applies to the relatively few locations,
      where there was new enclosure after 1876: *egs* Blackdown Common, Somerset;
      Tebay Fell, Westmorland. Under that Act new enclosure could only take place if "of
      benefit to the neighbourhood", defined as a concern with the "health, comfort, and
      convenience of the inhabitants" of nearby communities, including expressly such
      things as access to viewpoints and recreation (s 7). No uniform solution was imposed,
      the Commissioners being required to make provision depending upon the local
      context. The Commons Act 1899, which could be applied to any common, adopted a
      similar approach but placed the power to determine the nature of the management
      scheme in the hands of local authorities and for the first time set out a prescribed form
      for schemes of management: as opposed to locally negotiated schemes *eg*
      Austenwood Common in the Chilterns. Whilst the original provisions of the 1876
      Act provided for recreation of the neighbourhood, the 1982 Commons (Schemes)
      Regulations acknowledge that this now applies to recreation by the public at large.
27   Section 193 Law of Property Act 1925 provides for public right of access to common
      land for air and exercise by reference primarily to whether the land was a common
      and fell within a particular local authority area in 1926. It covers manorial waste and
      commons which fell within urban districts or boroughs in 1926 and which carried
      commoners' rights at that date or land for which the owner executes a deed agreeing to

be bound by section 193. This can be a little misleading as unlikely places were covered by urban as opposed to rural district councils in 1926 and therefore, perhaps unexpectedly, carry access rights, *eg* much of the Lake District was covered by the Lakes UDC, Windermere UDC; Ilkley Moor was covered by Ilkley UDC. Between 1926 and 1988, 217 deeds under section 193 were entered - Ryan *op cit* - all relating to rural commons *eg* Painswick Commons, Gloucestershire.

28   The earliest example identified dates from 1593, 35 Eliza I c 6, which required land to be left open for the recreation of Londoners. See also Dartmoor Commons Act 1985, Malvern Hills Act 1884; Clifton and Durdham Down (Bristol) Act 1861.

29   The *Royal Commission on Common Land* (1958) recommendation for a right of access to all commons, subject to limited exceptions, with owners, commoners and local authorities agreeing the scheme of management for each common, was not implemented. See also CCP 215 Countryside Commission, *Report of the Common Land Forum* - a 1980s scheme to secure further access to commons, whose implementation was frustrated by the Moorland Association.

30   This Act was not bought into force. See also Access to the Mountains (Scotland) Bill and the Mountains, Rivers and Pathways (Wales) Bill in the 1880s.

31   See Harte J, "Land Development: the Role of Planning Law", in Howarth W and Rodgers C (eds) *Agriculture, Conservation and Land Use* (1992, Cardiff) p 108.

32   National Parks and Access to the Countryside Act ss 59-81.

33   For an analysis of existing access agreements see Woods A, "Access Agreements" (1995) RWLR section 11, p 41.

34   Written and edited by John Blunden and Nigel Curry with contributions from Theo Burrell, Gerald Smart, Roger Smith and Richard Steele, *A People's Charter?* (1990, London).

35   *Ibid*, p 141.

36   The 1998 Green Paper figures are more positive than the 1990 authors expected. Whether this is a sign of a desire by landowners to prove that the voluntary approach works and therefore that legislation is not needed or whether it a sign that the voluntary approach really works and would continue to work without the pressure of fear of legislation is not known. Surveys of landowner attitudes to such agreements are all over a decade old.

37   Agri-Environment Regulation Schemes, Countryside Stewardship and Tir Cymen are considered in Woods A, "Access Agreements" (1995) RWLR section 11, p 41.

38   Figures taken from Annex 2 to the Green Paper.

39   Open Spaces Act 1906.

40   Section 29 National Trust Act 1907, but note this does not include a duty to provide a right of access to the public, only to ensure the common land in its ownership is unenclosed and available as open space for the recreation and enjoyment of the public - which may be visual as opposed to physical.

41   Established in 1972, it now owns 492 woods covering 16,000 acres.

42   Section 7(2) Environment Act 1995. Subject to its other duties, the Agency must "have regard to the desirability of preserving for the public any freedom of access to areas of woodland, mountains, moor, health, down, cliff or foreshore and other places of natural beauty".

43   The Trust owns approximately 1% of the UK, including extensive upland areas, such as the Brecon Beacons, Exmoor, the Lake District, and most recently raising funds to

buy a large part of Snowdon. For consideration of its approach to access see: *Report of the National Trust Access Review Working Party* (April 1995).

44   A small number of philanthropic bodies have purchased land in order to make it available to the public: for example the City of London purchased Epping Forest in 1882 for public recreation, after a protracted access dispute between the public and the landowner.

45   See for example the Water Industry Act 1991 which requires the water and sewage companies to ensure so far as is reasonably practicable that the water and land they hold is available for recreational use (although not necessarily free and unrestricted use) and have regard to the desirability of preserving public access when exercising any of their functions.

46   Paragraph 2.1.

47   Written Answer by Gordon Cowie, Chief Executive, Forest Enterprise, to a Question from Joan Ruddock, 28th October, 1996. Of sites sold by the Forestry Commission between 1991 and 1995 only 6% of sites had access through agreement or sponsorship.

48   See research findings: *Access to the Countryside for Recreation and Sport* CCP217 (1986, Countryside Commission/Sports Council).

49   It remains to be seen how successful Access 2000 will be in addressing this unavailability of information. This project by the Country Landowner's Association in conjunction with the Countryside Commission is seeking to compile a database of access agreements. The register will not have statutory backing but will be available for consultation in local authority offices. Questions remain about the effectiveness of such dissemination unless it is denoted by posters on the site and by inclusion on the ordnance survey database.

50   Sections 30 *et seq*, Inheritance Tax Act 1984.

51   Perhaps the resulting limited use makes landowners more willing to enter such agreements than if faced by fears of mass access.

52   Whilst 24% of English woodland is owned by the Forestry Commission and the government asserts access to this is available, the Green Paper does not mention the 76% of woodland not owned by the Commission, which would provide a valuable recreational resource. These largely privately owned woodlands are smaller and may have management regimes less compatible with public access - but the lands are dismissed as access candidates without further consideration of the compatibility of activities or the extent to which such woodlands may fill gaps in existing access, particularly in central and eastern England where there is relatively little upland or low intensity agricultural land upon which access can readily be offered.

53   *England's Trees and Woods* (1993) (CCP408) in which the Countryside Commission expresses concern at losses of woodland access and declares it "vitally important" to maintain public access in perpetuity and urges improvements in existing mechanisms or their replacement.

54   For a critique see Penner J, *The Idea of Property in Law* (1996, Oxford).

55   The capacity of landowners to hinder access legislation should not be under-estimated. After the delays in the House of Lords during the passage of the Wildlife and Countryside Act 1981 the government indicated that it would not allocate parliamentary time for any further countryside legislation unless the Countryside Commission could demonstrate support from all relevant groups. Indeed the mere

threat of opposition from a new association of grouse moor owners was sufficient for the government to jettison any suggestion of giving parliamentary time to the recommendations of the Common Land Forum.

56 Possibly by a landowner relying upon Article 1 of the First Protocol, possibly by members of the Countryside Movement articulating a claim in terms of the rights of indigenous peoples and the right to family life. How far the latter would succeed is doubtful, although efforts have been made in the recent past, with some element of credibility, to convert planning law issues into question of the right to family life.

57 Article 1 of the First Protocol asserts the right "to peaceful enjoyment of his possessions. No one shall be deprived of his possessions except in the public interest and subject to the conditions provided for by law and by the general principles of international law. The preceding provision shall not, however, in any way impair the right of a state to enforce such laws as it deems necessary to control the use of property in accordance with the general interest or to secure the payment of taxes or other contributions or penalties."

58 *Marckx v Belgium* A 31 (1979). See Schermers HG, "The International Protection of the Right to Property", in Matscher F and Petzold H (eds) *Protecting Human Rights - the European Dimension: Essays in Honour of Gerard J Wiarda*, 2nd ed (Koln, 1990) p 565.

59 Defined under the Human Rights Act 1998 as including rights worded identically to Article 1 of the First Protocol.

60 The question has not been tested under the Convention, although see *Loizidou v Turkey* No 15318/89 (1993). Contractual rights can amount to possessions under Article 1, so rights under voluntary agreements may be covered in some circumstances.

61 See Robertson 28 BYIL 359 (1951); Peukert 2 HRLJ 37 (1981) for the difficulties of negotiating this provision.

62 Kingston, J "Rich People have Rights Too? The Status of Property as a Fundamental Human Right" in Heffernan L (ed) *Human Rights a European Perspective* (Dublin, Round Hall Press 1994) p 284.

63 The jurisprudence on this Article distinguishes between the expropriation of property and its control. The latter is a little more tightly controlled, in that a state must show the control is necessary in the general interest, but the court will accept the state's view of what is necessary, the court retaining a fairly loose scrutiny function. Cases have generally involved planning controls (*eg, Pine Valley Developments v Ireland* A 222 (1991)), but have also considered environmental controls, such as a requirement to plant trees in the interests of the environment (*Dene v Sweden* No 12570/86, 59 DR 127 (1989)). Whether a particular provision is seen as an expropriation or assertion of control, the critical issue for rights of access will be the one of public interest and distribution of the burden.

64 There is an inevitable shading of meaning between deprivation and control. The courts have sought to draw a distinction between these, but this would not seem to affect the way the ECHR would consider a right to roam. See *Sporrong and Lönnroth v Sweden* A 52 (1982).

65 For consideration of this generally see Van Dijk P and van Hoof GJH *Theory and Practice of the European Convention on Human Rights* 3rd ed (Deventer, 1997).

66 *Papanichalopoulos v Greece* A 260-B (1993).

67   *Eg* acceptance of leasehold enfranchisement as in the public interest in *James v UK* A 98 (1986). Policies to enhance social justice can be described as being "in the public interest".

68   " ... the provision finally adopted guarantees only a much qualified right, allowing the state a wide power to interfere with property" Harris D, O'Boyle M and Warbrick C, *Law of the European Convention on Human Rights* (Butterworths, 1995) p 516 re Article 1, First Protocol.

69   The Court of Human Rights pays little regard to environmental or aesthetic costs, *cf* *Rayner v UK* No 9210/81, 47 DR 5 (1986). Even some factors which would appear to have an economic effect are disregarded - see *S v France* N13728/88 65 DR 250 (1990) where noise pollution was not considered to be a relevant loss.

70   Either by direct adoption in English courts, or by cases being pursued to the Court of Human Rights itself.

71   *James v UK* A 98 (1986) and *Lithgow v UK* A 102 (1986). *Pine Valley Developments v Ireland* A 222 (1993).

72   Mattingly A, "Right to roam: legal options" (1995) RWLR section 11, p 37.

73   See above, "Lost Ancient Rights", p 16.

74   *James v UK* A 198 (1986) the Court of Human Rights said that where economic or social justice are the aim of the measure the payment may be less that the full market value of the loss.

75   The cost would need to relate to the loss of theoretical rights/use, not the actual loss. Compensation is payable for loss of rights to use which the landowner is not currently exercising.

76   Article 6 has been held to apply to disputes between private parties concerning real property *eg* landlord and tenant issues - *Langborger v Sweden* A 171 (1990): public law decisions by the state are also covered if the decision affects the state's relationship to that right *eg König v FRG* A 27 (1978).

77   Originally the National Parks and Access to the Countryside Act 1949, but now see sections 53-57 Wildlife and Countryside Act 1981.

78   Section 3d of the Green Paper.

79   Paragraph 5, Foreword to the Green Paper.

80   Paddy Tipping introduced a ten minute rule bill on 23rd July, 1997: Access to the Countryside Bill.

81   "Our policies include greater freedom for people to explore our open countryside. We will not, however, permit any abuse of a right to greater access".

82   Originally defined in section 59, National Parks and Access to the Countryside Act 1949, a phrase not without definitional problems. The government is consulting upon whether the definition needs revision or clarification. "Open" does not mean unenclosed: fencing and walls may occur.

83   Paragraph 2, Foreword to the Green Paper.

84   The Green Paper suggests 12% of England and Wales falls within the definition of "mountain, moor, heath, down and common". Annex 2 of the Paper makes some estimates of acreages already accessible but there are significant gaps, and the figures quoted are disputed.

85   Paragraph 3.16.

86   See for example the European Environmental Fifth Action Programme.

87   Section 2 of the Green Paper invites suggestions on how to increase voluntary access.

88 The provisions for creation orders in section 26, Highways Act 1980, have been little used because of the relatively high costs of compensation per mile; Countryside Commission studies of the lack of progress towards implementation of Recreation 2000 and the Milestones Approach to opening up existing public rights of way have emphasised the lack of funding being made available. A similar picture exists in relation to the acquisition of threatened SSSIs as Nature Reserves: although in the latter case the regime requires acquisition of an estate in the site, rather than merely payment for the creation of a right in relation to the land.

89 Even a "rights" based approach brings with it the need for a compensation scheme to satisfy the ECHR. The Green Paper rejects universal compensation, seeing existing grant and access agreement schemes as sufficient; coupled possibly with charging for ancillary facilities but not for use itself. See Section 3d of the Green Paper.

90 See Section 3d of the Green Paper.

91 Beyond "possibly - the reimbursement of some specific costs". Para 3.50.

92 Paragraphs 3.48-3.52. Under section 70 *et seq* National Parks and Access to the Countryside Act 1949, compensation was payable for depreciation in value as a result of access, based upon the actual experience of the first five years of operation of access.

93 Paragraphs 3.60-3.61; the Green Paper rejects charging walkers for access, but accepts the possibility of charging for incidental facilities such as parking.

94 The problem with defining the rights to be sought is not in defining the rights, but in securing agreement in relation to any definition. Unity of campaigning for improved access is easily fragmented when the question of which rights is raised: On foot only? With dogs? With horses? On mountain bikes?

95 Section 193.

96 Section 1(2).

97 Dartmoor Commons Act 1985 for example defined the area covered by reference to a map.

98 Section 59(2) defined "open country" as meaning "any area appearing to the authority with whom an access agreement is made or to the authority by whom an access order is made or by whom the area is acquired, as the case may be, to consist wholly or predominantly of mountain, moor, heath, down, cliff or foreshore (including any bank barrier, dune, beach, flat or other land adjacent to the foreshore)".

99 Section 61 National Parks and Access to the Countryside Act 1949. For a review of the provision and its implementation see Kempe P "Maps of open country" (1992) RWLR section 11.0, p 5. *Cf* the level of legal challenge to the Definitive Map process under the 1949 Act in relation to public rights of way, which was perceived (wrongly) as affecting status and (rightly) as affecting accessibility.

100 *Cf* 1949 National Parks and Access to the Countryside Act, Definitive Map process - still not completed more than 50 years later.

101 Paragraph 3.20.

102 Announcement by Michael Meacher at the DETR European Conference on Biodiversity and Sustainable Countryside 9th March, 1998. Whilst primarily aimed at assisting in implementation of the UK Biodiversity Action Plan, the database will also have implications for the habitat-defined elements of public access.

103 Paragraph 3.18 explains some of the problems with providing information: detailed mapping is expensive and given the definition of access land will at least partly

depend on the current use being made of the land and so the status of land will change; descriptions of vegetation can also be subject to different interpretation: will we need to call habitat experts to decide whether something does or does not have a species variety which amounts to a moor? OS is updated every three years and so could respond to changes; there is some experience of showing some access land on OS maps and some categories are easily identified (*eg* a mountain if defined as being anything over 600 m): the problems may only be around the edges.

104   See Wyatt *et al*, *Comparison of Land Cover Definitions* (1994, Department of the Environment) or the national Vegetation Classification. The Green Paper opts for less rigorous definitions than these. It characterises "moor" as including upland heath and grass, but it can also exist in lowlands. Moors "usually have a peaty top and are characterised by semi-natural vegetation used as rough grazing". "Down" is defined as being "characterised by semi-natural grassland on shallow, lime-rich soils associated with limestone escarpments". "Heath" has dwarf shrubs such as heather and gorse and may occur on uplands or lowlands.

105   The Green Paper includes maps estimating the areas to be covered by the provisions, derived from DETR data, but considerable further work will be required. The data submitted under the 1949 Act cannot be used even as a rough indicator of the land affected, because the definition of open space differs, the quality of reporting under the 1949 Act was so patchy as to be unreliable and changes to physical status or intensity of use will have occurred in the intervening period.

106   The Green Paper can be criticised for opting for a universalist solution, its separation of the definition of public usage from consideration of types of landowner activity and for being unnecessarily simplistic.

107   Proposal 15. It leaves open what is meant by "open-air recreation".

108   This narrow category of access might be a further effort to assuage landowner objections and Convention compensation claims, but is likely to be highly divisive within the access lobby. And note that in the Foreword the Minister of State for the Environment indicates he plans to consult "organisations representing walkers, the owners and occupiers of land, and others with an interest". This again appears to separate walkers from other user groups.

109   Paragraphs 3.35-3.36.

110   The Green Paper does not consider the context of this new negative "right". Will it supersede higher rights which already exist over some land covered by the proposals, such as access for air and exercise to commons covered by the 1925 Act? Unless explicitly protected, these could be inadvertently lost by implied repeal.

111   Section 60, National Parks and Access to the Countryside Act 1949.

112   Paragraph 3.31.

113   The latter is the model favoured in earlier access legislation, such as the Dartmoor Commons Act, as representing a flexible solution in which the particular needs of particular areas and agricultural practices can be identified and prohibitions minimised. There is no clear answer as to which offers the best solution. The latter gives less uniformity, but can offer direct discussion tailored to the site. It is possible that they provide a way for reducing exclusion to the minimum needed by particular local agricultural practices, although there is no evidence as to whether this is the case.

114   Paragraphs 3.15-3.17.

115 Is land lying fallow "access land"?

116 Paragraph 3.16.

117 Upland Britain bears the physical evidence of how ephemeral the extensive/intensive distinction can be: the remains of field walls and derelict buildings marking the limits of upland enclosure, from which activity has now retreated.

118 For example, access which is not acceptable during lambing may be compatible at other times of the year.

119 Paragraphs 3.25-3.28.

120 Paragraph 3.23.

121 Paragraph 3.17 excludes agricultural land from the access provisions, unless only extensively grazed. See above "*Defining the Land*" for consideration of the way the definition of open countryside by reference to species mix creates an incentive to change the character of the habitat. The provisions relating to user create a further incentive.

122 Paragraph 3.64.

123 See above "Creating New Rights to Roam".

124 See Dartmoor Commons Act 1985; *Recommendations of the Common Land Forum* (1985).

125 Proposal 18.

126 Proposal 26.

127 Paragraph 3.63.

128 The word "habitat" is used throughout this paper in reflection of the Habitats Directive 1992, although the Green Paper persists in using the older concept of "wildlife".

129 Mapping, a solution used in relation to commons (Commons Registration Act 1965) and public rights of way (Wildlife and Countryside Act 1981), has been rejected as a legal as opposed to practical aide.

130 See paragraphs 3.58-3.59.

131 Paragraph 4 of the Foreword.

132 Harris J, *Property and Justice* (1996, Oxford).

133 Penner J, *The Idea of Property in Law* (1997, Oxford).

3 Reforming Property Rights for Nature Conservation

CHRISTOPHER P RODGERS

Nature Conservation: Reconciling Property Rights and Public Policy

The protection of wildlife habitats has been a central feature of nature conservation law in the UK for the last fifty years - ever since the adoption of the recommendations of the Huxley Report in 1947.[1] Conferring protection on wildlife habitats has necessitated the imposition of legal controls on land use, and this has inevitably brought about conflict between the exploitative rights of individual property owners and the wider public interest in nature conservation. The law has sought to accommodate these competing interests by adopting a largely "voluntary" approach to the promotion of nature conservation, stressing the need for farmers, landowners and the government agencies charged with implementing conservation policy to work in partnership. The common law imposes selective restrictions on a landowner's property rights, but these are usually justified by reference to the protection of the rights of other property owners - the law of nuisance is perhaps the best example of this approach. The common law is concerned primarily with balancing the interests of competing private property owners, *eg* by preventing the use of land in a way which prejudices the legitimate expectations or quiet enjoyment of adjoining occupiers. Wildlife has no legal personality *per se* in English law, and birds or animals enjoy no legal rights or protection in their own right at common law. Conferring adequate legal protection on wildlife habitats is, therefore, heavily dependent on legislation reflecting the wider public interest in promoting nature conservation. In practice this has meant that the voluntary approach has had to be backed by the introduction of statutory measures, with legal sanctions to protect wildlife sites. The imposition of compulsory controls on land use has, however, hitherto been sparingly used.

The law currently uses two mechanisms to reconcile the

conflicting interests of private property and the wider public interest in nature conservation. The first is the process of site notification. Legal controls on land use are only imposed in defined areas - what may be termed a zonal policy. The primary wildlife habitat designation is the Site of Special Scientific Interest, of which there are over 5,800 notified sites in the United Kingdom.[2] The Wildlife and Countryside Act 1981[3] gives English Nature and the Countryside Council for Wales (CCW) power to notify areas of land as Sites of Special Scientific Interest (SSSIs) if certain criteria set out in the Act are satisfied (as to which see below). The primary legal effect of notification is to place enforceable restrictions on those operations which can be carried out on the land without the authorities notifying agency's permission. In practice, however, the legal controls are of limited utility, as the landowner can give notice of his intention to carry out proscribed operations and then wait four months before carrying them out. If this "waiting period" has elapsed the legal sanctions for breaking the terms of the notification cease to be binding. The penal sanctions in the 1981 Act are primarily a "lever" to persuade the property owner to enter into a management agreement with English Nature or the CCW, under which the protection of the site will be guaranteed by sympathetic management in return for the making of payments. This rather curious approach is illustrative of the fact that the Wildlife and Countryside Act 1981 is itself a compromise measure. The Act represents a carefully balanced compromise between the interests of property owners and (in particular) the agriculture industry on the one hand, and the wider public interest in environmental protection on the other. The limited use of compulsion in the legal regime for SSSIs was a considerable triumph for the agriculture policy community (particularly the National Farmers' Union and Country Landowners' Association), who devoted considerable resources to opposing the 1981 Act during its passage through Parliament.[4]

The second mechanism for resolving disputes is the management agreement. If a landowner wishes to carry out damaging operations, or otherwise change the nature of his land use in a way which will be detrimental to the environmental quality of the site, the conflict can be resolved by the conclusion of a management agreement with English Nature or the CCW. The landowner will agree to manage the land in a manner sympathetic to the conservation objectives of English Nature or the CCW, and in return will receive payments for the loss of income which flows from his having to restrict his commercial operations in the manner agreed. Payment may be made on one of several bases. The landowner is entitled to payments for net profits foregone by him as a consequence of the restrictions on land use imposed by the agreement, in accordance with the Financial Guidelines for Management Agreements under the Wildlife and Countryside Act 1981.[5] The Financial Guidelines have application, under section 50(1) of the Wildlife and Countryside Act, when a management agreement has been offered following the notification of a landowner's intention to carry out potentially damaging operations contrary to the SSSI notification. They also apply where a local authority offers a management agreement to a landowner, under general powers conferred by the 1981 Act.[6]

Although a landowner can insist on their use to quantify payments in these cases, the use of the Financial Guidelines is not mandatory in all cases. In practice, most new management agreements now involve incentive payments for positive land management, under which flat rate payments are made for capital works and conservation improvements. In recent years the conservation agencies have increasingly concentrated on introducing positive conservation management schemes, such as the Wildlife Enhancement Scheme in England and Tir Cymen in Wales. The Financial Guidelines have no application to management agreements concluded under these schemes. The current law governing the availability and negotiation of formal management agreements is contained in several statutes, principally the National Parks and Access to the Countryside Act 1949, the Countryside Act 1968, Part II of the Wildlife and Countryside Act 1981 (as amended) and regulation 16 of the Conservation (Natural Habitats *etc*) Regulations 1994[7] (in relation to European wildlife sites designated under the EU Habitats Directive).[8]

The current legal framework for the protection of wildlife habitats has proved deficient, and clearly needs reform. It has, in the first place, signally failed to deliver the level of protection intended for wildlife sites. The National Audit Office published a review of the operation of the Wildlife and Countryside Act in 1994. This found that over 20% of notified SSSIs had suffered serious degradation or damage during the six-year period from 1987 to 1993.[9] The latest statistics tell a similar story. There are 919 notified SSSIs in Wales. In the year to 31st March, 1997 there were 227 cases of damage, affecting 149 Welsh SSSIs.[10] The main culprit for both long term and short term damage was agriculture (and particularly overgrazing), with agricultural activities accounting for 133 cases of reported damage. The statistics for England tell a similar tale. In the year to 31st March, 1996 there were 163 cases of damage to SSSIs in

England, affecting 121 sites totalling 2,305 hectares.[11]   This figure represents damage to 4.2% of all notified sites in England.[12] Damage to many more sites undoubtedly goes undetected. The SSSI network is supposed to represent the pinnacle of legal protection for wildlife habitats in England and Wales, yet the law has demonstrably failed to deliver an adequate level of protection for these sites. At the same time, the legal mechanisms for resolving conflicts between property and conservation interests have failed to prevent a number of high profile disputes, some of which have exposed flaws and loopholes in the legislation. A new legal framework is needed, not only to guarantee the protection of valuable wildlife habitats, but to ensure that the property rights of private landowners affected by statutory wildlife designations can be properly accommodated. The balance between property rights and the public interest in nature conservation needs to be redrawn, and a new approach adopted which adequately balances the competing interests involved.

Notifying SSSIs: the Current Law

Notification of sites is currently governed by section 28 of the Wildlife and Countryside Act 1981.[13]   The criteria for the selection of sites for notification are primarily scientific. Section 28(1) provides that where English Nature or the CCW are of the opinion that an area of land is "of special interest by reason of any of its flora, fauna, or geological or physiographical features" the Council must notify that fact to the Planning Authority, the owner and occupier of the land concerned and to the Secretary of State. A notification made under section 28 must specify the features by reason of which the land is considered of special interest and, moreover, must specify any operations which the Council believes would be likely to damage the flora, fauna or other features of the site.[14] Agricultural operations, such as ploughing, re-seeding, or drainage work *etc* will commonly be operations specified as likely to damage notified SSSIs. There is currently no formal mechanism by which a property owner can appeal against notification of the site as an SSSI. The notification must, however, specify a period of not less than three months within which representations and objections can be made to the notifying agency.[15] Where objections are made by affected property owners, these will be considered by English Nature or the CCW, but no independent element of adjudication is (at present) involved. One issue considered below is whether a formal, independent, appeal procedure should be established.

Given the restrictions which notification as an SSSI will place upon a landowner's rights, the courts might have been expected to interpret the notification provisions strictly against the public agencies responsible for their implementation. The attitude of the judiciary has, however, been ambivalent. The courts have adopted a liberal interpretation of the notification provisions, recognising that the identification (and subsequent notification) of sites is primarily a scientific question which should be decided without undue interference from the courts. At the same time they have adopted a rather more restrictive interpretation of the legal effects of notification, once made. This attitude may be characterised as protective of private property rights, and the narrow interpretation given to some of the legal sanctions available to enforce land use restrictions in an SSSI have undoubtedly led to problems in implementing the legislation. The judges have sought to maintain a balance between the public interest in environmental protection and private property rights, by recognising the width of the statutory right to notify a site if the statutory criteria are met, while adopting a more restrictive interpretation of the legal restrictions which apply post-notification to potentially limit the property rights of affected landowners.

An important preliminary question concerns the freedom of action allowed to the Councils when deciding whether to notify. Section 28 imposes on English Nature and the CCW a "duty" to notify a site if they consider the area to be of special interest by reason of the criteria laid down in the 1981 Act. The precise ambit of the duty was considered in *R v Nature Conservancy Council ex parte London Brick Co Ltd*.[16] The court here held that the notification process involves two distinct and separate stages.

(i) First, section 28(1) imposes a duty on the Council to notify a site if it fulfils the scientific criteria set out in the 1981 Act. The initial notification is only provisional, however, as the 1981 Act gives parties affected by it three months in which to lodge objections to the notification, or make representations. It was held in *R v Nature Conservancy Council ex parte Bolton Metropolitan District Council*[17] that the Council must make the basis for the notification sufficiently clear to enable an affected landowner to make a full objection, should he wish to do so. If the notification is insufficiently clear as to the reasons for which the site is being notified as an SSSI, it may be quashed on judicial review.[18]

(ii) The second stage in the process involves the confirmation or withdrawal of the notification. By virtue of section 28(4A), following notification English Nature and the CCW have nine months, beginning on the date it was served on the Secretary of State, in which to give notice either withdrawing or confirming the notification. It was held in *ex parte London Brick Co Ltd* (*supra*) that the Council have a discretion at this second stage whether to confirm the notification, either with or without modifications.[19] A notification will cease to have effect upon notice of withdrawal being given, or on expiry of the nine-month period if no notice of withdrawal or confirmation is given within that time.[20]

The Councils currently have power, when confirming a notification, to do so with or without modifications. This power cannot be exercised, however, so as to add to the prohibited operations specified in the notification, or to extend the area to which it applies.[21] If the Council confirms the designation with modifications, it takes effect from the date of service of the Council's notice of confirmation, and has effect in its modified form to so much of the land originally notified which remains subject to it.[22] The wide interpretation of the Councils' powers in the *London Brick* case clearly gives English Nature and the CCW greater freedom of action at the second stage of the notification process, *ie* when considering the confirmation or modification of a notification. It says nothing, however, to the basis on which the discretion should be exercised, and leaves the decision in individual cases to the Councils to be decided on the merits.

The courts have also adopted a wide definition of the scientific criteria by reference to which a notification can be justified. In *Sweet v Secretary of State*[23] Schiemann J held that an area can be of "special interest", and hence validly subjected to notification under the 1981 Act, if it constitutes a "single environment" for flora or fauna, the protection of which is sought by the notification. It follows that areas of land which are scientifically interdependent with the land actually bearing the flora and/or fauna in question can be validly notified. It is clear from the ruling in *Sweet* that the primary reasons for notifying a site must remain scientific. Whether a site is of "special interest" is a scientific question, and the scientists are to have considerable latitude to decide this without interference from the courts. The courts will not interfere with a notification for technical legal reasons if the science underlying it is sound. Technical arguments against notification, based upon the fact that some of the land notified does not actually host the wildlife the SSSI seeks to protect, will not be viewed favourably by the courts. If land is integral to the site - in the sense that it is important for the sustenance, genetic exchange or migration of the species the notification is intended to protect - then it will be viewed as integral to the SSSI and validly subject to the notification provisions of the 1981 Act.

Property Rights Implications of Notification

Following notification of a site as an SSSI, the owner or occupier of land within the site must not carry out, or cause or permit to be carried out while the notification remains in force, any operation which is proscribed in the notification.[24] The SSSI notification must be served on every owner or occupier of land in the SSSI, as well as the local authority, and must notify them of the potentially damaging operations in question. It is a criminal offence to carry out any specified operations without the consent of English Nature or the CCW, unless certain conditions are met (see below).

The courts have adopted an ambivalent stance to the legal restrictions imposed by these provisions. The legal meaning of "operations" in this context was given a broad interpretation in *Sweet v Secretary of State*,[25] thus widening the scope of agricultural activities which can be notified as potentially damaging by an SSSI notification. The court here held that the phrase "operations" is not to be construed in the manner adopted under planning legislation, where the term carries an active connotation limiting it to the carrying out of development or engineering operations on land. In the context of the 1981 Act it has a wide meaning, and can encompass passive agricultural activities which have a potentially damaging effect on wildlife and habitats, such as the release of chemicals or seeds, and the grazing of livestock. On the other hand, only those operations "likely" to damage the conservation interest of the site can be notified. This has been construed restrictively in the courts. To be "likely" to damage the site, and therefore notifiable, there must be a probability that the operations concerned will cause damage to the conservation value of the site - and not merely a possibility that they might do so.[26]

Perhaps the most important issue for property rights is the scope of the bar on potentially damaging operations which can be imposed under section 28. The 1981 Act provides[27] that notified operations can only be carried out if both of the following conditions are satisfied:

(i)   the owner or occupier must give the Council written notice of his proposal to carry out the operation, including a specification of its nature and the land on which it is proposed to carry it out; and

(ii)   one of three additional specified conditions must be satisfied.[28] The operation must either be carried out with the Council's written consent, or be in accordance with a management agreement.[29] Alternatively, a period of four months must have expired from the giving of notice to the Council of the operation proposed. English Nature and the CCW have four months in which to respond to a notice proposing the carrying out of potentially damaging operations. If written agreement is reached between them and the owner/occupier that the four months condition is not to apply, then the operations proposed will only be lawful if carried out with their written consent or pursuant to a management agreement.[30] The land owner or occupier may subsequently terminate the agreement, in which event the carrying out of the operations is further prohibited for one month or such longer period as the owner or occupier himself specifies.[31]

It is in this key provision that the political compromise represented in the terms of the 1981 Act is most clearly seen. The Act imposes a statutory consultation procedure if a landowner wants to carry out a potentially damaging operation which has been notified as likely to damage the site's conservation interest. The four-month "waiting" period, during which notified operations cannot be carried out, enables the Council to enter into negotiations for the conclusion of a management agreement protecting the site. Once this period has expired without agreement, however, the criminal sanction ceases to apply and the proposed agricultural operations may be carried out. If a management agreement cannot be concluded, they can only be prohibited if the Secretary of State (after consultation with English Nature or the CCW) can be persuaded to make a Nature Conservation Order under section 29 of the 1981 Act. The effect of the making of a Nature Conservation Order will be to extend further the consultation period, during which the carrying out of agricultural operations contrary to the SSSI notification is prohibited, to twelve months. In practice the power to make Nature Conservation Orders is sparingly used.[32]

It will be immediately apparent that the protection afforded by the current regime under the 1981 Act is severely limited. It has, accordingly, been subjected to considerable criticism, not least from the judiciary:

> [I]t needs only a moment to see that this regime is toothless, for it demands no more from the owner or occupier of an SSSI than a little patience. Unless the council can convince the Secretary of State that the site is of sufficient national importance to justify an order under section 29 - ... a task rarely achieved - the owner will within months be free to disregard the notification and carry out the proscribed operations, no matter what the cost to the flora etc. on the site. In truth the Act does no more in the great majority of cases than give the council a breathing space within which to apply moral pressure, with a view to persuading the owner or occupier to make a voluntary agreement.[33]

Notification of land as an SSSI can be registered by the Council as a Local Land Charge.[34] This will ensure that a purchaser of affected land will have notice of the existence of the notification. It will not, however, protect the site where a new occupier is (perhaps) a tenant, contractor or grazier. Problems may arise, for example, where the land is subject to a farm tenancy, and there is a change of tenant without the knowledge of English Nature or the CCW. The initial SSSI notification will be served on the freehold owner and the current tenant of the land affected. If the tenant assigns or surrenders the tenancy, and is replaced by a new occupier, the latter may have no knowledge of the notification and its restrictions. In practice the protection of the site will usually depend on the landlord notifying a new tenant of the existence of the SSSI, and making observance of its restrictions a term of the tenancy agreement. There have been several well publicised cases in Wales[35] where SSSIs have been destroyed by tenants unaware of the notification, which will continuously have been made during the occupancy of a prior tenant or grazier. In this case the freeholder may be liable for "causing or permitting" the damage in question, but prosecutions will be difficult to mount successfully. They may in any event be counter-productive if the co-operation of large landowners in "policing" the SSSI network is to be maintained.

It will be appreciated that the Councils' role, as envisaged by the 1981 Act, is purely reactive. If a landowner notifies his intention to carry out a proscribed operation, in accordance with section 28(5), the Councils have several choices: to give consent to the operation because it will not damage the site, to offer a management agreement, or to risk damage to the site by allowing the notified operation(s) to proceed. Alternatively, they may object to an undesirable proposal and enter into dialogue on possible alternative solutions. This dialogue may lead to a management agreement, or (if the proposal remains unacceptable) the Council may seek a Nature Conservation Order under section 29 to protect the site.

Damage to SSSIs - the Scope of Legal Liability

Notwithstanding the wide interpretation given to the notification provisions (discussed above), the effectiveness of the legislation has been impaired by the adoption of a narrow judicial interpretation of the penal provisions in the 1981 Act. It is a criminal offence to carry out, without reasonable excuse, any operations specified as potentially damaging by the SSSI notification. It is also an offence to cause or permit to be carried out any operations proscribed in the notification. On summary conviction, this offence carries a fine not exceeding level 4 on the standard scale.[36] By virtue of section 28(5) of the 1981 Act, however, the prohibition on proscribed operations only extends to "the owner or occupier" of land which has been notified under the SSSI provisions. It follows that only the owner or occupier of the land in question can be criminally liable under section 28 for causing damage to an SSSI.

In the leading case of *Southern Water v Nature Conservancy Council*[37] the House of Lords adopted a restrictive interpretation of the scope of liability, limiting it to acts done by the freehold owner or an "occupier" with a legal right of occupation or some relationship of permanence with the land. An "occupier" is someone who, although lacking legal title to the land, nevertheless "stands in such a comprehensive and stable relationship with the land as to be, in company with the actual owner, someone to whom the [designation and notification procedures] could sensibly be made to apply. A stranger who enters the land for a few weeks solely to do some work on it does not fall into this category".[38] It follows that an independent contractor with no interest in the land will not be liable under this provision. Neither will (as in the *Southern Water* case itself) a statutory undertaker entering to carry out work under its statutory powers, even if the operations in question are prohibited by the SSSI notification. Liability would clearly extend to a tenant and to others farming the land under a legal relationship of long standing, such as commoners exercising registered rights of common. It is unlikely, however, that a grazier or licensee with short term contractual rights (grass keep *etc*), would be an "occupier" for this purpose. Although the owner or occupier will not be liable for damage caused by an independent agent, he may still be liable (quite independently) for causing or permitting the damage concerned, *eg* if independent contractors carry out proscribed operations at the owner's instigation. The *Southern Water* case highlighted a loophole in the protection afforded by the 1981 Act, and has been extensively criticised. In practice the greatest import of the decision may be to emphasise the need to frame prosecutions carefully, and to target them appropriately.

The practical efficacy of the statutory restrictions on land use are further weakened by the breadth of the statutory defences available to a landowner who damages an SSSI. No liability is engaged if a proscribed operation is carried out with "reasonable excuse", *viz* if either the operation was authorised by a grant of planning permission on an application under Part III of the Town and Country Planning Act 1990,[39] or the operation was an "emergency operation", details of which were notified to the relevant Council as soon as practicable after commencement of the operation.[40]

Where a damaging operation requires planning consent, the resolution of the dispute between the property rights of the landowner, and the environmental restrictions in the SSSI notification, will be shifted to the planning forum. If planning permission is granted, this gives the landowner a gateway through the legal restrictions otherwise applicable under the 1981 Act. Unfortunately, SSSIs are given an inadequately protected status under planning law. The conservation interest is only one out of a number of "material factors" which the planning committee will take into account when making a decision on a planning application in an SSSI.[41] Neither will the courts readily interfere with the decision of the local planning authority, *eg* as to whether to insist upon an environmental assessment in individual cases affecting wildlife sites.[42] The procedures for ensuring that consultation takes place with the conservation agencies before either planning consent is given, or the operation is subsequently carried out, are also insufficiently stringent. The 1981 Act does not require an owner or occupier of agricultural land to give the Council notice of an operation for which planning permission has been granted, prior to carrying it out. The Local Planning Authority is required, however, to notify English Nature or the CCW of any application for planning permission for development within a notified SSSI.[43]

The Councils are statutory consultees on all planning applications within an SSSI. They also have the right to designate "consultation areas" (or buffer zones) around notified SSSIs, and have the right to be consulted on all planning applications within these areas. Consultation areas can extend up to a maximum of 2 kilometres around the boundary of an SSSI, but planning guidance[44] indicates that they should not normally extend beyond 500 metres - except around sensitive sites of importance such as wetlands. The Council's views will be taken into account on the merits of the planning application, but are not determinative. Neither do they have any special status requiring the planning committee to place greater weight on them than on other material factors relevant to the application.

If planning permission is granted, the existence of planning consent is deemed to constitute a "reasonable excuse" relieving the owner or occupier of liability for carrying out a notified operation.[45] This means that the important policy issues for the environmental protection of the site will be taken in the planning forum, and not under the machinery of the 1981 Act. As a result, the dispute resolution mechanisms in the 1981 Act are only of relevance for restricting operations for which no planning permission is required. In practice this means agricultural operations - most of which are either outside the control of the Town and Country Planning Act 1990 altogether,[46] or are given automatic planning consent by the General Development Order.[47] The defence afforded by section 28(8) of the 1981 Act only applies where planning consent has been granted on application: it does not apply to operations carried out with permission under the General Development Order.

Where no planning application is required, the likelihood of damage to the site coming to the attention of English Nature or the CCW is largely dependent on the owner notifying them of his intention to carry out the operation, pursuant to section 28. If this is not done, or if the owner is simply ignorant of the need to do so, the damage may go unnoticed. This undoubtedly occurs in many cases. Local Planning Authorities are also required[48] to assist English Nature and the CCW by alerting them if they become aware of any other threat to the conservation interest of a site, *eg* changes in farming techniques and other matters not requiring planning permission. But in practice this may be of little utility in preventing damaging operations, or changes of use, which are outside the ambit of the planning legislation. If an operation does not require planning permission it may not come to the attention of either the local planning authority or the conservation agencies before irreparable damage has been done.

A second defence is afforded by section 28(8)(b), which provides that it is a reasonable excuse, exonerating damage to an SSSI, if the operation was an "emergency operation" particulars of which (including details of the emergency) were notified to the conservation agency as soon as practicable after commencement of the operation. No guidance is offered by the 1981 Act as to the scope of this provision, and no definition of "emergency" is given in the Act or case-law. The provision is intended to exonerate emergency agricultural operations in situations where it would be impossible/impractical to use the statutory consultation procedure required by the 1981 Act. Its inclusion in the 1981 Act, however, again emphasises the primacy of the agricultural imperative over nature conservation interests, and illustrates the compromise nature of the legal regime for SSSIs. Its most common use is where fire or flooding threatens livestock on farmland, and emergency restorative action is required to protect land, crops or animals from serious damage.

Notification: A Case for Reform?

The existing procedure following the notification of an SSSI, whereby the Council must consider representations before issuing confirmation (or modification) of the notification, falls short of conferring a formal right of appeal. Indeed, the current procedures involve English Nature or the CCW - the notifying bodies - in reconsidering the scientific basis of a notification they themselves have made. There is no right of appeal to an independent body, neither is there a right to have the notification reassessed periodically to ensure the site's conservation interest still merits notification. This is to be contrasted with the arrangements in Scotland, where there exists a right of appeal against notification to an independent committee, and where notifications can be periodically reviewed at the landowner's request. The introduction of an independent appeal procedure for England and Wales would undoubtedly introduce greater transparency into the operation of the notification provisions, and may provide a more effective mechanism for reconciling conflicts between the property and conservation interest.

Current perceptions of the notification process were recently tested in a research project undertaken by the Centre for Law in Rural Areas for the Royal Institution of Chartered Surveyors (RICS) Education Trust.[49] Interviews were conducted with farmers in four geographical areas, chosen because they contain both SSSIs and Environmentally Sensitive Areas designated under the Agriculture Act 1986.[50] Additionally, a postal survey of rural practitioners in the RICS Rural Practice Division was carried out, using a structured questionnaire. Of the rural practitioners who participated in the survey, 71% reported that the process of notifying SSSIs was not well understood by their farming clients. Only 29% of respondents felt that the process of notification, and the basis on which it was carried out, was reasonably well understood. Moreover, no fewer than 88% of participants thought that there should be an independent appeals procedure against notification. Many considered the notification process to be autocratic, leaving little room for the adjustment of the Councils' proposals in negotiation with the landowner. Whether this is the case or not, there was a clear perception of arbitrariness in the minds of many. A significant number of respondents stressed the need for a right of appeal for the purpose of de-notifying a site if the conservation interest no longer satisfies the criteria in the Wildlife and Countryside Act 1981. Another view canvassed was that there should be no notification without proof of a threat to the scientific interest of the site - though any change of this nature would require amendments to the 1981 Act itself.

It has already been noted that conservation policy is based on the voluntary principle, and relies heavily on co-operation between English Nature / the CCW and farmers and landowners in order to deliver the environmental management designed to protect SSSIs. It must therefore be a matter for concern that the overwhelming majority of rural property practitioners, and many of the farmers in the RICS survey, consider the notification procedures to be both arbitrary and poorly understood. This cannot assist in building co-operation and trust between the Councils, charged with overseeing the implementation of conservation policy, and the farmers and landowners who will be asked to deliver it on the ground. The implementation of conservation policy by English Nature and the CCW must be based on the twin principles of *transparency* and *trust*, if partnership with farmers and landowners is to be strengthened. This applies to the process of initial notification of SSSIs, as well as to the later negotiation of management agreements and payments. There is therefore a case for reform if the trust and co-operation of landowners and farmers is to be secured in implementing conservation policy.

Appeals - the Scottish Model

Provision is made under section 12 of the Natural Heritage (Scotland) Act 1991 for representations made by a landowner affected by an SSSI notification to be referred to an independent advisory committee. The advisory committee is independent of Scottish Natural Heritage (SNH), and its members must have appropriate scientific expertise and training. Its role is limited to considering the scientific basis for the notification, and it cannot (for example) consider the appropriateness or otherwise of the prohibitions contained in the notification of the site. SNH must consider its recommendations when deciding whether to confirm or vary the initial notification of the SSSI. Its findings are not binding on SNH however, though a decision to ratify which ignored the committee's clear recommendations may be open to judicial review in the courts.

The 1991 Act also gives the advisory committee a limited role in periodically reviewing SSSI notifications. An affected landowner may make representations to SNH that the original grounds for notification of the SSSI have ceased to be valid. In this event the matter is referred to the advisory committee for its view. Normally, a landowner can require a review only after 10 years, and thereafter at 10-yearly intervals. The only exception is where he made a relevant representation at the time of initial notification, in which case a reference can be made within the initial 10 years following notification. The committee's views must be taken into account before SNH decide to vary or revoke the notification.

Appeals Against Notification: A Model for England and Wales?

The Scottish arrangements have worked well since their inception in 1991-2. There have been a small number of cases, in all of which the SSSI notification was ratified with minor amendments. The overall result, therefore, has been to improve the transparency and fairness of the notification process without compromising the habitat protection delivered by SNH. Two related questions arose from our research survey of farmers/landowners, and of RICS rural practitioners, in England and Wales:

(i)   Should a model based on the Scottish one be adopted in England and Wales, and if so should the review body include representation from the farming or landowning organisations, *eg* the National Farmers Union or the Country Landowners' Association?

(ii)   Should the remit of any independent review body be limited to adjudicating on the scientific basis of the SSSI notification, as is the case in Scotland under the current arrangements? Or should there also be a right of appeal against the restrictions on land management imposed by the Councils in the SSSI notification? This would involve introducing an appeal mechanism going considerably beyond that currently used in Scotland.

The overwhelming majority of rural practitioners taking part in the survey strongly supported the adoption of a review body to which landowners could appeal against the notification of land as an SSSI. There was also considerable support for the inclusion of an independent farmer or landowner representative on any appeal body established. The experience of the Scottish appeal arrangements indicates that the existence of an appeal mechanism engenders trust and improves the transparency of the notification process, without imposing unreasonable administrative difficulties. There is therefore a case for the introduction of a similar right of appeal in England and Wales. There is, however, a compelling case for saying that appeals should be limited, as in Scotland, to a consideration of the scientific basis for the notification. Conferring an additional right of appeal - against the land management restrictions imposed by the Council to achieve its conservation objectives for the site - would generate a number of complex difficulties. The appeal committee would most appropriately comprise scientifically qualified individuals chosen and appointed by the Secretary of State. It may also be appropriate to include a representative of the farming or landowner organisations on the appeal panel. Another prominent response from both farmers and rural practitioners questioned in the project was that farmers often feel that their contribution, through long years of husbandry, towards the creation of an SSSI is not recognised by the Councils when notifying sites and imposing restrictions on damaging operations. The inclusion of a representative from the farming organisations could contribute a positive input, based on knowledge of the farming practices which have contributed to the past development of the site, as well as improving the perception among landowners of the transparency and independence of the notification and appeals processes.

How wide should the scope of an appeal process be, were one to be introduced? For the time being, there is a case for holding that any appeal process should be limited (as in Scotland) to reviewing the scientific basis for an SSSI notification. The value of this type of appeal system has been proven in Scotland, and it involves minimal additional cost and administrative difficulty in managing the current SSSI arrangements. In the longer term, however, there may be a case for introducing a mechanism allowing for appeals against restrictions and land management conditions imposed by the Councils. This could take several forms, and would probably require amendment to the primary legislation, principally the Wildlife and Countryside Act 1981, section 28. It could, for example, involve a two-stage notification process for potentially damaging operations. Under this model, if notified potentially damaging operations were minor an application to the Council for permission to carry them out would be granted forthwith. If the proposed operations were problematic, however, the landowner would be required to give further information as to his proposed plans for the site. These could be published, in the same manner as planning permission applications, and there could be a right of appeal against any refusal by the Council to grant consent. This would increase the transparency of the process. It would also deter the making of speculative and inappropriate applications for planning consent to carry out damaging operations in an SSSI.

A More Radical Option for Reform

Another model which might be considered is provided by the legislation on historic monuments.[51] There is no right of appeal, as such, against the listing of buildings under the Listed Buildings Act, nor is the Secretary of State required to consult with the owners or occupiers of affected buildings prior to listing. Under planning policy guidance revised in 1994,[52] however, the Secretary of State has indicated that he will in future engage in public consultation on all listing recommendations produced by English Heritage's survey programme of differing types of historic building. There is, moreover, a right of appeal against a refusal of listed building consent to carry out alterations or demolition of a listed building, and against the imposition of conditions on listed building consent.[53] The grounds of appeal can include a claim that the building is not of historic or architectural interest and should not, therefore, be listed.[54] This gives the owner a right to appeal against listing, albeit one which is only exercisable at the later stage when listed building consent has been refused. Although the Listed Buildings Act gives a right of appeal against listing, the *quid pro quo* is that no right to compensation accrues if an appeal is turned down. There has never been a right to compensation for listing *per se*. Until 1990, however, a limited right to compensation existed where the Secretary of State turned down an appeal against a refusal of listed building consent, or granted consent subject to conditions. The applicant had to show that the value of his interest in the property had been prejudiced by the decision. The right to compensation in this limited class of case was removed, however, by the Planning and Compensation Act 1990.[55]

The Listed Buildings Act therefore strikes a quite different balance between the conservation interest in the built environment and property rights to that in the Wildlife and Countryside Act 1981. There may be no compensation for listing, but the property owner is entitled to appeal to the Secretary of State against conditions imposed on his management of the building - via the listed building consent system - by English Heritage. This type of arrangement could, without undue difficulty, be adapted for the protection of important wildlife habitats. This would involve introducing public consultation prior to the notification of a site as an SSSI - a step which might be welcomed, in any event, as generating greater public awareness and involvement in the protection of wildlife sites. A right of appeal could be introduced enabling a landowner to challenge the restrictions on land use laid down by English Nature or the CCW, or their refusal of consent to the carrying out of proscribed operations. The grounds for appeal would need to be limited to the necessity of the restriction, or conditions attaching to a consent, for the protection of the conservation interest of the site. They could in appropriate cases be widened, however, to include a review of whether the site should continue to be notified under the 1981 Act, *viz* whether its conservation interest continues to warrant legislative notification. This would produce a more transparent system, and one which (through public consultation in notification issues) would engender greater public involvement in the protection of SSSIs.

Whichever model is considered the more appropriate, changes would be required to section 28 of the 1981 Act. For example, the four-month "waiting period" during which a landowner is prohibited from carrying out a damaging operation, after notifying English Nature or the CCW, would have to be amended. This would need to take account of the possibility of appeals against land management decisions which would take longer to adjudicate. If the listed buildings model were adopted, more radical changes would be required in the primary legislation. The right of the landowner to receive a management agreement and payment, if prevented from carrying out operations damaging to the site, would have to be removed. This would, however, enable English Nature and the CCW to concentrate their resources on the protection of key wildlife sites of

European or international importance, and on the wider implementation of positive management schemes to foster improvements to the rural environment. The government has recently initiated a wide ranging review of the operation of the Wildlife and Countryside Act 1981.[56] The current legal arrangements are clearly failing to deliver the level of habitat protection required, and involve considerable public expense in funding compensation and management agreement payments. Reform is long overdue.

Notes

1   Wildlife Conservation Special Committee, *Conservation of Nature in England and Wales*, Cmnd 7122 (1947).

2   As at March 1992 there were 5,852 notified SSSIs in the UK as a whole: see Pearce, D *Blue Print 3: Measuring Sustainable Development* (1993, Earth Scan) at p 109. At 31st March, 1996 there were 3,874 notified SSSIs in England (English Nature, *5th Annual Report*, 1996, at p 35. At 31st March, 1997 the total of notified SSSIs in Wales stood at 919 (Countryside Council for Wales, *Annual Report* 1996-7, Volume II).

3   Section 28.

4   See M Winter, *Rural Politics - Policies for Agriculture Forestry and the Environment* (1996, Routledge) at p 205*ff*. P Lowe *et al*, *Countryside Conflicts: The Politics of Farming Forestry and Conservation* (1986, Gower) at p 135*ff*.

5   DoE / Welsh Office Circular 4/83.

6   Section 39 empowers local authorities to enter into management agreements with any person "having an interest in the land" within their area of local government jurisdiction. Agreements can be concluded for the purpose of conserving or enhancing the natural beauty or amenity of any land which is within the countryside in their area. This provision is not widely used.

7   SI 1994/2716.

8   EC Directive 92/43.

9   National Audit Office *Protecting and Managing SSSIs* (1994, Stationery Office).

10   Countryside Council for Wales, *Annual Report 1996-97* Volume II pp 9-13.

11   English Nature, *5th Annual Report* 1st April, 1995 - 31st March, 1996 at pp 50-51.

12   *Ibid*, p 49.

13   These powers were formerly contained in section 23 National Parks and Access to the Countryside Act 1949.

14   Section 28(4) Wildlife and Countryside Act 1981.

15   The agencies have a duty to consider the objections within the time allowed: section 28(2) *ibid*, added by section 2 Wildlife and Countryside (Amendment) Act 1985.

16   [1996] Env LR1 (May J).

17   [1995] Env LR 237 (Popplewell J).

18   In *R v Nature Conservancy Council ex parte Bolton MBC* (*supra*) English Nature had considered the site both on its current state of conservation interest, and its possible

potential for future restoration. Bolton MBC (the recipients of the notification) had only made representations on its potential for restoration when objecting to the notification of the site. This was held to be a breach of natural justice in that the Council had not made the basis of the notification (*ie* the sites current conservation interest, as well as its potential) sufficiently clear to enable Bolton MBC to make a full response and objection. English Nature's confirmation of the notification was accordingly quashed.

19 It was accordingly held in *ex parte London Brick Co Ltd* that the policy of English Nature, which was to confirm all notifications unless there was likely to be unavoidable damage to the site and its conservation interest, was lawful and within the discretion vested in them at the second (*ie* the confirmation) stage by section 28(4A) of the 1981 Act.

20 Section 28(4A) *ibid*, added by Wildlife and Countryside (Amendment) Act 1985, section 2.

21 Section 28(4B) Wildlife and Countryside Act 1981.

22 Section 28(4C) *ibid*.

23 [1989] JPL 925 (decided under the parallel provisions in section 29 of the 1981 Act for the making of nature conservation orders).

24 Section 28(5) Wildlife and Countryside Act 1981.

25 [1989] JPL 925, *supra*.

26 *North Uist Fisheries v Secretary of State* (1992) JEL 241 (Court of Session).

27 Section 28(5).

28 See section 28(6) *ibid*.

29 Entered into under section 16 National Parks and Access to the Countryside Act 1949 or section 15 Countryside Act 1968.

30 Section 28(6A) Wildlife and Countryside Act 1981.

31 Section 28(6B) *ibid*.

32 See Withrington and Jones, "Enforcement of Conservation Legislation", ch 5 in (W Howarth and CP Rodgers eds) *Agriculture, Conservation and Land Use - Law and Policy Issues for Rural Areas* (University of Wales Press, 1992).

33 *Southern Water v Nature Conservancy Council* [1992] 1 WLR 775 (House of Lords) *per* Lord Mustill at 778B.

34 Section 28(11) Wildlife and Countryside Act 1981.

35 For example at Gwaun Cwm Conway SSSI, where the site was severely damaged by an incomer: see *Sites of Special Scientific Interest: Better Protection and Management* (DETR, 1998) at B.9.

36 Section 28(7) *ibid*. See currently Criminal Justice Act 1991, section 17, for the applicable maximum (£2,500).

37 [1992] 1 WLR 775, *supra*.

38 [1992] 1 WLR 775 at 782C *per* Lord Mustill.

39 Note that planning permission must be granted under Part III Town and Country Planning Act 1990 - deemed permission under the General Permitted Development Order 1995 will not suffice.

40 Section 28(8) Wildlife and Countryside Act 1981.

41 A good illustration of the weakness of protection in planning law is given by *R v Poole BC ex parte BeeBee* [1991] JPL 643 (Scheimann J).

42 See *R v Swale BC ex parte Royal Society for the Protection of Birds* [1991] 1 PLR 6.

43   Town and Country Planning (General Development Procedure) Order 1995, SI 1995/419.

44   Planning Policy Guidance Note 9 *Nature Conservation* (1994) para 31.

45   Section 28(8) Wildlife and Countryside Act 1981.

46   The use of land or existing buildings for agricultural purposes is not "development" requiring planning permission: section 55(2)(e) Town and Country Planning Act 1990. See further CP Rodgers, *Agricultural Law* (2nd ed, Butterworths, 1998) ch 12.

47   See Schedule 2 Part 6 Town and Country Planning (General Permitted Development) Order 1995 SI 1995/418.

48   PPG 9 *Nature Conservation* (1994) esp Annex A para A9, and see generally paras 30-33.

49   See CP Rodgers and J Bishop *Management Agreements for Promoting Nature Conservation* (1998 RICS London). See especially Annexe E (Selected Research Data).   The author acknowledges the generous financial support of the RICS Education Trust in supporting this research, and the co-operation of the staff of both English Nature and the Countryside Council for Wales who participated in the project. The research report (above) covers a wide range of issues in addition to notification procedures, including (for example) the legal arrangements for positive management agreements in SSSIs.

50   Discussion of Environmentally Sensitive Areas is beyond the scope of this paper. Designation is by the Minister of Agriculture under the Agriculture Act 1986, and management agreements are available to farmers in return for undertaking environmentally friendly farming practices stipulated by the Ministry. ESA policy is entirely based on the voluntary principle, and no residual compulsion is exercised along the lines of the regime in the Wildlife and Countryside Act 1981, discussed above.

51   See generally the Planning (Listed Buildings and Conservation Areas) Act 1990 (hereafter referred to as the "Listed Buildings Act").

52   See PPG 15 *Planning and the Historic Environment* (1994) paras 6.10-6.16.

53   Listed Buildings Act section 20(1).

54   *Ibid*, section 21(3).

55   Schedule 19, repealing Listed Buildings Act section 27.

56   *Sites of Special Scientific Interest: Better Protection and Management*   (DETR, September 1998). The consultation paper canvasses views on thirty-eight proposals for improving the legal regime for notifying and protecting SSSIs in England and Wales. The public consultation on the proposals closed on 21st December, 1998. It was, unfortunately, not possible to incorporate detailed discussion of the proposals in this paper, which states the law as at April 1998. Some of the proposals outlined in the DETR consultation document touch upon property rights issues which have been addressed in this paper. There is currently no intention to extend the Scottish appeals process on notification to England and Wales, for example, although the DETR recognises the need to encourage the countryside agencies to undertake "peer review" of their notification procedures. No suggestions are made, however, as to how this might be done, or the breadth of the "peer review" envisaged (see *Sites of Special Scientific Interest: Better Protection and Management, ibid* at B10, B11).

4   Reforming the Law on Charity Trading

PETER LUXTON

This year (1998) marks the fiftieth anniversary of the opening of the first Oxfam shop in Broad Street, Oxford - possibly the first charity shop in the UK.[1] Today, Oxfam has some 850 charity shops, and in 1997, they raised some £16.5 million, almost a quarter of that charity's annual income. Since the opening of that first charity shop, other charities have opened shops of their own. The next biggest operator after Oxfam is the Imperial Cancer Research Fund, which has more than 450 shops.[2] In the 1990s the number of charity shops has doubled. There are now more than 6,500 charity shops on our high streets, with a combined annual turnover of £312 million pounds, and combined profits of some £82 million. Charity shops proliferate, and they are favourably perceived by members of the public.[3] Charity shops are not the only means by which charities trade - there is also direct catalogue-mailing, and there is more specialised trading connected with the charity's purposes, such as the sale of equipment for the elderly or disabled. There may also be the supply of a service for a consideration, such as the arranging of funerals or the provision of home-helps.

Trading by charities, then, is big business; but it is a field which throws up complex problems of charity law and taxation, as well as giving rise to more general concerns. This paper concentrates on some specific problems relating to trading by charities: direct trading; the use by charities of subsidiary trading companies; and the broader issues concerning tax and rating exemptions, the competition which charity shops represent to the small commercial trader, and the potential for confusion between a charity and its trading subsidiary.

Problems of Direct Trading

The first problem is one of charity law: namely, that trading by a charity is not *per se* a charitable purpose,[4] and since a charity must be established for purposes which are wholly and exclusively charitable, the Charity Commission will not generally register as a charity a body whose purposes include the carrying on of a trade. There are exceptional instances where the carrying out of the charitable purposes itself involves trading, such as a university press which publishes and sells books in fulfilment of its educational purposes; but, outside these instances, the problem remains, and the scope for trading is narrow. The Charity Commissioners take the view that a charity is permitted to trade so far as the trading is merely ancillary to the carrying out of its wholly and exclusively charitable objects. This means that the activity in question must be carried out on a fairly limited scale, *eg* there will be no problem with the occasional jumble sale, or the sale of tickets for the odd fund-raising dinner; but if these activities are carried on regularly, they may be considered to comprise an independent, non-charitable, purpose.

The second problem - closely related to the first - is one of tax law. Unless a charity's trading falls within very limited exemptions, its profits will be liable to tax. The statutory definition of trade is rather unhelpful,[5] but guidance is obtainable from the so-called six "badges of trade" identified by the Radcliffe Commission. For present purposes, the third badge of trade - the frequency of the transaction - will often be an important factor. Thus in *British Legion Peterhead Branch Remembrance and Welcome Home Fund v IRC,*[6] the charity organised regular dances on Saturday nights, and this was held to be trading. The exceptions - where the legislation exempts a charity's trading profits from tax - are narrow: the profits must be applied solely to the purposes of the charity and either the trade must be exercised in the course of the actual carrying out of a primary purpose of the charity; or the work in connection with the trade must be mainly carried out by the beneficiaries of the charity.[7] The classic example of the latter is the charity for the blind which sells goods made by blind persons in workshops run by the charity.

Revenue practice is also important here. The Inland Revenue does not treat the sale of donated goods as trading.[8] The donation of funds to a charity is not trading (since there is no consideration by the charity), and the Inland Revenue takes the view that the sale of such goods is merely a way of realising their value. The Charity Commission takes the same views, at least where the sales are only incidental.[9] Secondly, by extra-statutory concession,[10] the Inland Revenue will not treat a charity raising funds by means of bazaars, jumble sales, carnivals and the like, as trading for tax purposes, provided that: the activities are not carried on regularly (by which the Revenue means in the same locality not more than three times a year),[11] they are not in competition with other traders; they are supported substantially because the public are aware that any profits will be devoted to charity; and the profits are applied for charitable purposes. These criteria suggest that there exists a fear that, were charities allowed to trade without being liable to tax, they would place other traders at a disadvantage. This rationale is unconvincing, since the tax laws do enable charities to trade freely by an indirect route - *via* a subsidiary trading company. [12] Outside the extra-statutory concession, the Inland Revenue also operates a *de minimis* exemption for charities whose charitable purposes involve the carrying out of a trade: the Revenue will not seek to raise a charge to tax on charities whose non-charitable trading activities are small in relation to their charitable trading activities, *ie* the charity's turnover from non-charitable trading activities must not exceed 10% of its combined turnover from charitable and non-charitable trading activities; and the turnover from the non-charitable trading must be small in itself, which in practice means generally less than £2,000.

What are the consequences if a charity's trading does not fall within the limits mentioned above? In practice, if the trading falls within the Inland Revenue concessions, the Charity Commissioners will treat the trading as merely ancillary to the carrying out of the charitable purposes, so there is no breach of charity law. If, however, the trading is carried on in such a way that income tax or corporation tax is payable, this will in practice be treated as a breach of the requirement that the charity must carry out wholly and exclusively charitable purposes, so there could be questions from the Charity Commissioners. Furthermore, since charity trustees are, as trustees, under a duty to act in the best interests of the charity, they may be in breach of trust if they fail to organise the trading activities in a way that minimises the tax payable. The Commissioners have, indeed, expressly stated that charity trustees may be personally liable to account for taxation liabilities which are unnecessarily incurred directly or indirectly as a result of the inefficient administration of the charity.[13] This is tantamount to saying that, in many cases, charity trustees will be effectively under a duty to have the trading carried out by a subsidiary trading company rather than by the charity itself.

A further difficulty of a charity itself carrying on a trade is that of liability to third parties. If the charity exists as an incorporated body, its directors will not incur personal liability in contract, as it will be the company itself which is carrying on the trade; but the charity's assets will still be at risk.[14] A substantial claim against the company in tort (*eg* where goods sold in the course of trade cause personal injury) could indeed be the cause of the charity's demise. If the charity exists in the form of a trust, the trading will be carried on by the trustees, who therefore run the risk of personal liability to third parties in contract or in tort (should the goods sold cause injury). The charity's assets are still at risk, however, since the charity trustees will generally have a right to be indemnified out of the charity's assets. Indeed, third parties may be able to proceed against a charitable trust's assets through subrogation to the trustee's right of indemnity, provided that there is evidence that any claim against the trustee directly is likely to prove fruitless.[15]

It is not clear to what extent the ordinary members of a charitable unincorporated association incur personal liability in respect of contracts entered into by its committee members. This is because it is unclear whether, when the committee members enter into contracts with third parties, they do so as agents (for the members) or as trustees. What case law there is on this area mostly concerns non-charitable associations, particularly members' clubs, where the contracts can more easily be construed as being entered into by the committee on behalf of the members. Even in the context of non-charitable associations, however, the law seems to have rejected any notion of members' liability flowing from the mere fact that the rules of association have vested the management of the association in a committee, and has decided that membership liability depends upon actual, not usual, authority.[16] Since members of a charitable association can have no proprietary interest, *qua* members, in the association's property, the concept of their being liable in contract through the agency of the committee members looks even less convincing.

The Use of Subsidiary Trading Companies

As a consequence of the combined effect of the foregoing considerations, many charities choose to trade through subsidiary trading companies. Indeed, both the Charity Commissioners and the Inland Revenue recognise and approve of charities establishing subsidiary trading companies. Thus the Charity Commissioners have stated:[17]

> Where a charity wishes to benefit substantially from permanent trading for the purpose of fund-raising, we advise that it does so through a separate non-charitable trading company, so that its charitable status is not endangered.

A charity trading company could be a general trading company, or a company created with a more specialised trading aim, *eg* to carry on a commercial activity which relates to the charity's own purposes and which will usually receive an endorsement by the charity. This could involve the sale of a product or a service in the area of the charity's operation (such as the supply of wheelchairs or motor cars for the disabled, or the provision of funeral arrangements) or it could be the marketing of a product (*eg* a drug) developed by the charity itself.

The legal niceties of setting up and funding a trading company are complex, and can only be touched upon here. [18] The trading subsidiary will be a commercial company limited by shares, in practice generally wholly owned by the charity itself. The charity will need a power to invest in its trading subsidiary; and, since the trading subsidiary will not be a company which is an authorised investment under the Trustee Investments Act 1961, a special power to invest must be contained in the governing instrument. If there is none initially, the Commissioners' approval to insert such a power must be obtained. There are also problems of funding the trading subsidiary: the charity is not permitted to fund its subsidiary by way of gift, since this would be an application of its funds for non-charitable purposes. The charity may be able to make a loan to its subsidiary, but only at a proper commercial rate of interest. If it guarantees a loan made to the subsidiary by a commercial lender, there can be problems of its providing any guarantee, since, from the charity's point of view, the guarantee is purely gratuitous. [19] In order to use the charity's name in its trading activities, the subsidiary will need to obtain a licence from the charity, which can be granted only at a proper market price.

There are also fiscal problems in profit-shedding, *ie* of ensuring that the trading company's profits are returned in a tax efficient manner to the charity itself. The usual method is by deed of covenant, whereby all the trading company's profits are covenanted to the charity. This results in the charity's receiving the profits as Schedule D Case III income, *ie* pure income profit, and income from this source is not liable to income or corporation tax in the charity's hands, provided it is applied to charitable purposes only. There are, however, other means by which the profits could be returned to the charity (*eg* Gift Aid, or by declaration of dividend). If the trading company is occupying the charity's premises, the rent might be geared to the trading company's profits; and the system works because rent is deductible in computing the trading company's profits, and the rental income, if applied to charitable purposes, will be free of tax in the charity's hands. There are, however, technical reasons why most charities prefer to use the covenant method - notably because the timetable for making returns to the Revenue means that the trading company's profits will not be capable of precise calculation, and an estimated payment to the charity will have to be made. It is easier to make adjustments to the figures through the deed of covenant method.

What is perhaps surprising is that the proportion of charities which are trading using a trading subsidiary is not larger than it is. A survey into trading by UK charities was conducted in 1994 by KPMG.[20] Out of 317 fund-raising charities which replied to the survey (which comprised about a third of those asked), 65% had no trading subsidiary at all, 26% had one such subsidiary, and between 1% and 3% had more than one. The survey also showed that only 60% of charities with a trading income of more than £10 million have a trading subsidiary; which reduces to 16% of charities with a trading income of less than £1 million. The authors of the survey expressed surprise at the high percentage of charities - particularly the larger charities - with no trading subsidiary, especially given that the survey was conducted among the country's leading charities. This may suggest ignorance of the advantages of the trading subsidiary method, and may also evidence some inefficiencies in charity management.

Conflicts of Interests

One particularly thorny problem with regard to trading subsidiaries is that of conflicts of interests. This can arise where the same, or some of the same, persons are both trustees of the charity and directors of the trading subsidiary. From a purely commercial point of view, the advantages of having one or more of the trustees on the board of directors of the subsidiary company are manifest. Indeed, since the trading subsidiary's shares will belong to the charity, it would seem that the trustees of the charity might be in breach of their duty to protect the charity's assets if they were not to ensure that they receive an adequate flow of information from the trading subsidiary.[21] Complying with such a duty might well encompass putting at least one of their own number, or perhaps a nominee, on the board of directors of the subsidiary. On the other hand, having the same persons as trustees and directors can give rise to difficulties. In their capacity as trustees, they owe fiduciary duties to the charity; yet, in their capacity as directors, they owe corresponding duties to the trading subsidiary. The Charity Commission has pointed out the risks a charity runs from one or more of its trustees being put into a position of conflict of interests:[22] namely, that the person occupying the dual role may be unable to separate the interests of the charity from those of the subsidiary. It might, for instance, be difficult to ascertain whether a trustee-director who, in his capacity of trustee, encourages his co-trustees to leave outstanding a loan which the charity has made to the trading company, is acting purely in the interests of the charity. The Commissioners recommend that there should be at least one person who is a trustee of the charity and not a director of the trading company, and *vice versa*.[23]

The fiduciary duties to which a charity trustee (including a director of a charitable company)[24] is subject are owed to the public at large,[25] and are enforceable by the Attorney-General or (to some extent) by the Charity Commissioners.[26] Since the trading subsidiary will be a commercial company, the fiduciary duties which the director owes *qua* director are owed to, and enforceable by, the trading subsidiary alone. As director of the subsidiary, he must act *bona fide* for the benefit of the company,[27] which means the interests of the company as a commercial enterprise. This largely means that he must act in the interests of the shareholders - which, in the case of a trading subsidiary, means in the interests of the charity. If the charity is itself a company, so that the relationship between it and the trading company is one of holding company and subsidiary, the directors of the latter are permitted to take into account the interests of the holding company and the subsidiary together, provided that an "intelligent and honest man" in their position could reasonably consider this to be in the interests of the subsidiary.[28] The directors must also have regard to the interests of the subsidiary company's employees in general.[29] If, however, the trading subsidiary is insolvent, or is facing insolvency, the interests of its creditors are paramount.[30]

The trading subsidiary itself will be a commercial company, and will be entitled to pay remuneration to its directors; but the "no conflicts" rule means that a trustee who becomes a director of the trading subsidiary cannot generally retain any fees paid to him in the latter capacity, since the directorship will usually flow from the trusteeship.[31] Payment to directors cannot, therefore, be used as a "back-door" method of remunerating charity trustees.[32] The Charity Commission is not generally willing to register bodies as charities which seek to restrict the "no conflicts" rule by permitting the trustees to retain any directors' fees which they might receive from a trading subsidiary, because they consider that this would be an application of the charity's assets to non-charitable purposes, and the body in question would therefore not satisfy the requirement that a charity's purposes must be wholly and exclusively charitable. Similarly, applying the decisions of the courts,[33] the Commissioners are not willing to authorise an amendment to the constitution of a registered charity to allow the trustees to retain fees which might be paid to them *qua* directors of a subsidiary. The Commissioners will be prepared to accept a provision in the charity's governing instrument permitting the retention of directors' fees only if the Commissioners are satisfied (and the onus of proof is on the trustees) that such remuneration is necessary from the point of view of the charity and that the level of remuneration received by the directors is reasonable having regard to the services which they actually render.[34] Since the Commissioners are strongly in favour of independent directors, these criteria are difficult for the trustees to meet.

Broader Issues

Competition With the Small Commercial Trader

In negotiating their leases with landlords, charities are in the market-place and in competition with other traders. Their leases are therefore usually on purely commercial terms, although some owners might generously permit a charity to occupy vacant premises without payment as a licensee for a short period, *eg* during the Christmas season, although such arrangements have become less common since the recession of the early 1990s. Some charities might be prepared to take a short-term lease during a void between commercial lettings until the landlord can re-let, with a corresponding reduction in the rent. Provided such a lease is for a period not exceeding six months, the lessee (whether the charity or its trading subsidiary) will not enjoy security of tenure as a business tenant.[35]

Charity shops which sell mainly donated goods enjoy a considerable fiscal advantage over the ordinary commercial trader, in that they are automatically entitled to relief from 80% of the business rate, and the local authority has a discretion (which some exercise) to extend this to 100%.[36] The relief is available only if the occupier of the property is a charity and the property is wholly or mainly used for charitable purposes;[37] but such user is stated to include the use of the property "wholly or mainly" for the sale of goods donated to a charity, provided the proceeds of sale (after deduction of expenses) are applied to the purposes of the charity.[38] "Wholly or mainly" is not defined in the statute, but it probably means "at least half."[39] No statutory relief is accorded where the occupier is a subsidiary trading company. A charity or its trading subsidiary also enjoys zero-rating on the sale of donated goods, provided (in the case of sale by a subsidiary) that it covenants all the profits of the supply to a charity.[40]

To these rating and tax concessions must be added the marketing advantages that charity shops enjoy: many of their goods are donated by the public rather than having to be bought in, and many of the staff in charity shops are volunteers, thus reducing the wages bill. The combined effect of these advantages is that charity shops enjoy a level of profitability that is the envy of many small independent traders. The average return for the largest chains of charity shops is 27 pence in the pound, the overheads being largely rent, heating and lighting, and the salary of a manager and perhaps an assistant.

Small traders, not surprisingly, consider that the law has created an uneven playing field, their particular objection being to the mandatory rate relief, especially because of the increased sales by charity shops of bought-in, as opposed to donated, goods. A recent survey by the Charities Advisory Trust, however, found that on average less than 8% of goods sold in charity shops are new[41] (which would easily satisfy the "wholly or mainly" requirement); and the removal of rate relief could reduce the net profits of such shops by a quarter.

The early 1990s, at the height of the recession, when many small traders were going out of business or were being driven into insolvency, was also a time of great expansion in the numbers of charity shops. Although the recession caused a decline in giving to charity generally, charity shops (with their tax and rating advantages) were better able to cope with the recession than small traders, especially since the demand for cheap second-hand goods increases in such periods. Indeed, the 1990s has been a period in which the charity shop has thrived. It is difficult to gauge whether, or to what extent, charity shops might be considered to have contributed to the decline of the small independent retailer during that period; but that they have done so is certainly the perception of many traders, who have seen charity shops taking over vacant premises.[42] The small commercial trader can do little to prevent this from happening: in the absence of express provision in its lease, a tenant-trader cannot prevent the landlord from letting nearby premises for use for a similar trade, even if the occupier will be a charity shop which might take away business from that tenant-trader.[43]

A key issue is whether charity shops should continue to benefit from business rate relief. To some extent this is a part of the broader question: why should charities obtain tax relief at all - a question which was raised in *Pemsel*'s case[44] itself, and where different views were expressed. It is not true that charitable status and fiscal privilege go hand in glove: charities do, for the most part, have to pay VAT. On the other hand, it is one thing not to grant a tax concession in the first place; to remove a tax concession already granted is quite another. The loss of business rate relief would seriously affect those charities which are especially dependent upon income from charity shops: some hospices, for instance, receive 40% of their income from charity shops. One possible solution would be to permit the business rate relief to continue, but to restrict the numbers of charity shops in any given area, which is not presently possible under the town and country planning legislation. This might, however, mean that some premises remain vacant when they might otherwise have been occupied.

The Treasury is presently reviewing the business rate discount for charity shops and the VAT exemption on the sale of donated goods. The review is expected to report in 1999, and the charitable sector has been warned that exemptions which give charities a competitive advantage will not be accepted.[45] The charity sector has additional fears that VAT harmonisation may lead to the withdrawal of the VAT exemption in any event.

Extension of Direct Charity Trading?

Many charities, not surprisingly, wish to see the fiscal restrictions on direct charity trading relaxed. A bold approach would be to grant charities a blanket exemption from tax on trading income. This would remove the fiscal need to use the device of a trading company. A bold recommendation of the Deakin report[46] is that the law should permit the trustees of all charities to authorise any trading activity which they consider to be in the best interests of the charity, which avoids unreasonable risk, and which represents a reasonably proportionate use of resources in relation to that charity's primary purposes. This would not itself overcome the problem of charity law that trading is not itself a charitable purpose; if such a change would mean that more than ancillary trading would be permitted, it would have to be accompanied by an abandonment of the requirement that a charity's purposes must be wholly and exclusively charitable. Deakin suggests that the solution lies in a broader interpretation of what is deemed "exclusively charitable", or in a tailor-made statutory provision. It is, however, difficult to see why the definition of what is charitable should be stretched to include commercial trading, which in itself is patently not a charitable purpose. In the event that its preferred recommendation were not to find favour, the Deakin report recommended, more modestly, that non-primary purpose income should be exempt up to a specified limit (such as £25,000), in order to ease the burden for smaller charities of having to run trading subsidiaries.[47] There may indeed be merit in raising the threshold of what effectively constitutes ancillary trading. It should, however, be borne in mind that there are other reasons (such as to safeguard its assets) why a charity might well prefer to trade by means of a trading subsidiary: the larger the scale of the trading activities, the greater the risk the charity takes, and the more desirable it generally becomes to use a trading subsidiary.

Scope for Confusion Between a Charity and its Trading Subsidiary

The use of trading subsidiaries has the potential to lead to confusion. It may confuse members of the public, who may assume that they are dealing with a charity, not with its commercial trading subsidiary. Many charity shops do not make it clear to those entering whether they are run by the charity or by a commercial company; if the trade is conducted by the latter, there should be a notice to this effect in the shop making this clear. If the charity permits the trading subsidiary to trade giving the impression that the subsidiary is in fact the charity, there is the risk that the charity may be treated as itself carrying on the trade through principles of agency.[48]

The distinction may also confuse third parties who supply goods or make loans to a trading subsidiary believing it to be the charity itself.[49] The Charity Commissioners strongly advise charities acting closely with an associated fund-raising company to ensure that all publicity material directed to fund-raising, and all contracts that such a company enters into with suppliers, make the status of the two bodies clear.[50]

It also appears that the distinction between a charity and a trading subsidiary confuses some local authorities into giving rate relief to trading subsidiaries, which are not entitled to it. Admittedly, it may not always be easy in practice to find out who the occupier is: as where the premises have been leased by a commercial lessor to the charity, the latter merely permitting its trading subsidiary to sell donated goods from the premises.

Even the legislature appears to have been unaware of the significant use of trading subsidiaries. The Charities Act 1992, section 59(2), makes it unlawful for a commercial participator to represent that charitable contributions are to be given to or applied for the benefit of a charity unless he does so in accordance with an agreement entered into with the charity which satisfies the prescribed requirements, these being laid down in regulations.[51] This ignores the fact that, where a charity has a trading subsidiary, the contract with the commercial participator will be made with the subsidiary, not with the charity itself. The problems have been overcome in practice by the use of tripartite agreements entered into by the commercial participator and the subsidiary, with the charity merely joining in (to comply with the statutory requirements) to indicate that it has no objection.[52] A further unsatisfactory aspect of the regulations made under the Charities Act 1992 is that they impose a criminal sanction on a commercial participator who does not pay to the charity any sums due to the charity within 28 days of receiving such sums.[53] Since the commercial participator will be paying sums it receives to the subsidiary trading company, whether it commits an offence is out of its hands - it depends on whether the trading subsidiary accounts for the sums to the charity within that period, and this is in practice quite unrealistic, since accounting will usually take place at less frequent intervals, such as quarterly.[54]

On the other hand, the use of subsidiary trading companies does, or at least should, distance the charity itself from the trading activities. The 1980s and 1990s have seen charities having to learn to adopt business techniques in order to raise funds and to compete with other charities and with commercial organisations. This has led to a fear that the traditional ethics of the voluntary sector are being, at least partially, supplanted by commercial considerations. There has, for instance, been some concern that some specialised trading companies which direct their activities at the charity's "beneficiaries" - such as the elderly or the disabled - may be putting undue pressure on vulnerable groups. Such activities might, for instance, involve the marketing of funeral or insurance services to the elderly. In an appropriate case, the Department of Trade, the Office of Fair Trading, or the Advertising Standards Authority, might become involved. There is clearly a difficult line to draw here; but it might be argued that to direct commercial and marketing activities towards a vulnerable group is worse if it is done under the cloak of charity. If this be so, any reform of the law of charity trading should be directed, not towards extending the legal ability of charities to trade directly, nor towards the broadening of the tax reliefs which presently discourage them from doing so; but rather towards ensuring that the public is made aware of the nature of the body (charity or trading company) with which it is dealing, and that the regulatory machinery is both adequate and used effectively to maintain ethical standards when trading is conducted in the name of charity.

Notes

1   See Henderson, "First Oxfam shop rings up 50 years", *The Times*, 23rd February, 1998.

2   The figures are taken from the annual Charity Shops' Survey by NGO Finance; and see Fanning, "A Charitable Undertaking", [1997] 34 EG 40.

3   See R Goodall and H Blume, *The Public Perception of Charity Shops: a National Survey*, Charities Advisory Trust (1997).

4   *Cf Oxfam v City of Birmingham District Council* [1976] AC 126 (HL); *Blackpool & Marton Rotary Club v Martin* [1988] STC 823, affd [1990] STC 1 (CA).

5   Income and Corporation Taxes Act 1988, ss 831, 832. Trade is statutorily defined to include "every trade, manufacture, adventure or concern in the nature of trade."

6   (1953) 3 STC 84.

7   Income and Corporation Taxes Act 1988, s 505(1)(e). See *Dean Leigh Temperance Canteen v IRC* (1958) 38 TC 315; *Grove v Young Men's Christian Association* (1903) 88 LT 696.

8   IR 75, para 4.

9   [1980] Ch Com Rep, para 8.

10   Inland Revenue, ESC C4.

11   Inland Revenue booklet, "Fund-raising for Charity".

12   J Hill and J De Souza, "Charities and Trading", (1989) 4 Trust Law and Practice 98.

13   See [1988] Ch Com Rep, para 44.

14   A salutary reminder of the dangers of a company entering into substantial contracts with third parties is the case of *Re ARMS (Multiple Sclerosis Research) Ltd, Alleyne v A-G* [1997] 1 WLR 877 (Ch), where the charity, a company limited by guarantee went first into administration and then into insolvent liquidation, owing nearly £1½ million in debts. It was held that simple legacies contained in the wills of testators who died after the date of the winding-up order but before the date of dissolution vested in the institution beneficially (on the principle of *Re Vernon's Will Trust* [1972] Ch 300n), and therefore effectively benefited the charity's creditors.

15   See generally, *Rights of Creditors Against Trustees and Trust Funds* (Consultation Paper by the Trust Law Committee, April 1997).

16   *Wise v Perpetual Trustee Co Ltd* [1903] AC 139. See generally HAJ Ford, *Unincorporated Non-Profit Associations* (Oxford University Press 1959); also T Cyprian Williams, "Club Trustees' Right to Indemnity: a Criticism of *Wise v Perpetual Trustee Co Ltd*", (1903) 19 LQR 386.

17   [1980] Ch Com Rep, para 10.

18   The technical difficulties are discussed in detail in S Lloyd, *Charities, Trading and the Law*, Charities Advisory Trust in association with the Directory of Social Change, 1995; and in P Framjee, *Charities and Trading: Law, Accounting and Tax Issues*, Charities Advisory Trust (1996). See also J Hill and J De Souza, "Charities and Trading", (1989) 4 Trust Law and Practice 98. The Charity Commission has produced its own leaflet: *Charities and Trading*, CC 35 (February 1997).

19   *Rosemary Simmons Memorial Housing Association Ltd v United Dominions Trust Ltd* [1986] 1 WLR 1440.

20   KPMG Tax Advisers, *Charities and Trading: a Recent Survey*, December 1994.

21   See the comments of Cross J in *Re Lucking's Will Trusts* [1968] 1 WLR 866.

22   (1994) 2 Decisions 20-21, and referring to the Commissioners' inquiries into War on Want and the Royal British Legion. The Commissioners' inquiry into War on Want reported grave deficiencies in the administration of the charity, including failure to recover sums owed to it by WOW Campaigns and War on Want Trading Ltd: see *Report on War on Want* (1991) HMSO, and [1992] Ch Com Rep 20-22 (paras 119-127). See also the Commissioners' inquiry into the affairs of the Royal British Legion: *Report on the Royal British Legion* (1992) HMSO, discussed [1992] Ch Com Rep 26 (paras 99-104), and (1993) 1 Decisions 24-25. The Royal British Legion (RBL) had made loans to the Legion Leasehold Housing Association (LLHA), which was not a charity. LLHA later went into liquidation owing debts of nearly £900,000 to the RBL. The Commissioners expressly criticised the overlap of membership of those controlling RBL and LLHA, and pointed out that this gave rise to a conflict of interests which caused particular problems when LLHA fell into financial difficulties: see (1993) 1 Decisions 25.

23   See *Charities and Trading*, CC 35 (February 1997), at p 17.

24   *Re French Protestant Hospital* [1951] Ch 567.

25   *Bray v Ford* [1896] AC 44 (HL).

26   Legal proceedings may now be instituted in certain instances by the Charity Commissioners themselves: see Charities Act 1993, s 32. Proceedings may be brought by individuals in certain instances, but such proceedings probably constitute "charity proceedings" and therefore require the consent of the Charity Commissioners or the High Court: Charities Act 1993, s 33.

27   *Re Smith & Fawcett Ltd* [1942] Ch 304, 306 (Lord Greene MR).

28   *Charterbridge Corporation Ltd v Lloyds Bank Ltd* [1970] Ch 72, 74.

29   Companies Act 1985, s 309.

30   *Lonrho Ltd v Shell Petroleum Ltd* [1980] 1 WLR 627, 634 (Lord Diplock); *Brady v Brady* [1989] AC 755 (HL).

31   *Re Macadam* [1946] Ch 73.

32   *Charities and Trading*, CC 35 (February 1997), at p 18.

33   Note particularly, in the context of charity, *Re Smallpiece Trust, Smallpiece v A-G*, unreported, but noted at [1990] Ch Com Rep 36 (Paul Baker QC, sitting as a judge of the Chancery Division). On trustee remuneration generally, see *Re Duke of Norfolk's Settlement Trusts* [1982] Ch 61 (CA); and, most recently, *Foster v Spencer* [1996] 2 All ER 672 (Paul Baker QC, sitting as a judge of the Chancery Division).

34   (1994) 2 Decisions 20-21, referring to *Re Smallpiece Trust, Smallpiece v A-G*, *supra*. See also [1988] Ch Com Rep 9 (paras 38-39).

35   Landlord and Tenant Act 1954, Part II, s 43(3).

36   Local Government Finance Act 1988, s 47. For an historical survey of rate relief for charities, see H Picarda, *The Law and Practice Relating to Charities*, (Butterworths, 2nd ed 1995), pp 740-741, and the sources there mentioned.

37   Local Government Finance Act 1988, s 43(6).

38   Local Government Finance Act 1988, s 64(10). The extension of rate relief to charity shops selling donated goods was originally introduced by the Rating (Charity Shops) Act 1976, following the decision of the House of Lords in *Oxfam v City of Birmingham District Council* [1976] AC 126, which had held that a charity shop selling donated goods was not in occupation for charitable purposes, and so was not entitled to rate relief.

39   *Cf Fawcett Properties v Buckingham* [1961] AC 636 (Lord Morton).

40   Value Added Tax Act 1994, Sch 8, Group 15, Item 1. Zero-rating is not given if the subsidiary sheds its profits to the charity by means other than a deed of covenant, *eg* by means of Gift Aid or dividend. This is one reason why the deed of covenant is the favoured method of profit-shedding.

41   R Goodall, *New Goods and Charity Shops: the Facts*, Charities Advisory Trust (1997). See also M Pountney, *Trading by Charities: a Statistical Analysis*, Charities Advisory Trust (1996).

42   A vignette of the period is to be found in *Chartered Trust plc v Davies* [1997] 2 EGLR 83 (CA).

43   *Port v Griffith* [1938] 1 All ER 295 (no breach of the landlord's implied covenant not to derogate from his grant); see also *Romulus Trading Co Ltd v Comet Properties Ltd* [1996] 2 EGLR 70.

44   [1891] AC 531 (HL).

45   See the address of Dawn Primarola MP, Financial Secretary to the Treasury, to the Annual Conference of the Charities Aid Foundation, 30th October, 1997: see Henderson, "Tax-break review threatens future of charity shops", *The Times*, 31st October, 1997.

46   *Meeting the Challenge of Change: Voluntary Action Into the 21st Century*, The Report of the Commission on the Future of the Voluntary Sector (chair: Nicholas Deakin), (1996), NCVO, at p 88 (para 3.6.12).

47   *Ibid*, at p 88 (paras 3.6.10 and 3.6.13).

48   *Cf Smith, Stone & Knight Ltd v Birmingham Corporation* [1939] 4 All ER 116.

49   See, *eg*, the problems relating to the insolvency of Sport for Sports Aid Ltd, a subsidiary trading company of the charity Sport Aid: discussed [1988] Ch Com Rep para 45. See further, Luxton, *Charity Fund-raising and the Public Interest*, (Avebury 1990), chapter 8.

50   [1988] Ch Com Rep 12 (para 48).

51   Charitable Institutions Fundraising Regulations 1994, reg 3.

52   See Hill, "Enter the Commercial Participator", (1995-6) 3 CL & PR 17.

53   Charitable Institutions Fundraising Regulations 1994, regs 6(2), 8.

54   See Hill, *ibid*.

PART II
COMMONHOLD

5 Is Apartment Ownership Genuine Ownership?

C G VAN DER MERWE

Introduction

According to Johannes Bärmann, one of the fathers of the German apartment ownership statute (*Wohnungseigentumsgesetz*), a person who purchases an apartment in an apartment ownership scheme enters into a threefold legal relationship.[1] Firstly, he becomes the individual owner or title-holder of the apartment; secondly, he becomes the joint or common owner in undivided shares of the land and common parts of the building like the foundations, roof, outside walls, corridors, stairways and lifts;[2] and thirdly, he becomes a member of the management body or unit owners' association which has to maintain the common property and manage the apartment ownership scheme. The legal rules concerning apartment ownership therefore straddle both the law of property and the law of associations.

Although the institution of apartment ownership is founded upon the traditional institutions of ownership (fee simple), co-ownership and membership of an association, these legal phenomena acquire special characteristics as a component part of the threefold unity embodied in apartment ownership. The joint or common ownership created in terms of an apartment ownership statute differs from traditional co-ownership in civil law jurisdictions in the sense that an apartment owner can demand partition of the scheme only in the special circumstances required for terminating a scheme. Secondly, the undivided share in the common property allocated to each owner proportionate to his participation quota, cannot be freely alienated or disposed of, but only together with the apartment to which it is inextricably linked. Thirdly, an apartment owner's undivided share in the common property entitles him to reasonable (and not ownership-like) use of the common property. Finally, the undivided share in the common property is not purely abstract as in the case of

87

ordinary co-ownership shares, but localised or materialised by being indivisibly linked to a specific apartment.[3]

The management body or unit owners' association, which could be incorporated or unincorporated, is also clearly distinct from a commercial company or a social club. Membership of the body corporate is inextricably linked to ownership of an apartment. Only persons to whom apartments are conveyed can be members of the management body. An owner automatically becomes a member thereof and he or she remains a member until the apartment is alienated or the management body dissolved. Membership of the unit owners' association is obligatory and not voluntary. Apartment owners are compelled to participate in the management and to share in the expenses of the scheme. No apartment owner can revoke his membership of the management association. Although apartment owners in principle have equal voting power, voting with regard to certain matters is loaded depending on how the voting power is allocated in the applicable statute or in the by-laws of the scheme.[4]

Unrestricted Ownership?

The purpose of this paper is to concentrate on the first and most important legal relationship the purchaser of an apartment enters into, namely the fact that he becomes the owner or holder in fee simple of the apartment which is conveyed to him.

The idea that an apartment owner obtains individual ownership of his apartment is conveyed not only by the designation of the institution as apartment ownership or flat ownership,[5] ownership of storeys or horizontal property,[6] condominium ownership or condominium property,[7] comparted ownership of buildings,[8] strata titles,[9] unit titles[10] and sectional titles[11] but also by the fact that most apartment ownership statutes contain express provisions to that effect.[12] One section of the South African Sectional Titles Act, for example, provides that separate ownership may be acquired in accordance with the provisions of the Act.[13] Another section states that the Registrar of Deeds may register a title deed whereby ownership in any section is acquired.[14] In similar vein the most recent English Commonhold Bill announces that provision is made for "a new kind of freehold ownership with special statutory attributes"[15] and provides further that a person can henceforth acquire "separate freehold title" to a unit.[16]

The crucial question is whether an apartment owner really acquires the same comprehensive powers of disposal, use and enjoyment in terms of apartment ownership statutes as a traditional landowner wields over his house on a separate parcel of land. In this regard the question can be posed whether an apartment owner genuinely has freedom to occupy, use and enjoy his apartment as he pleases, exclude other persons from interfering with his entitlements to his apartment, freely dispose of and sell his apartment, burden it with mortgages or other real and personal rights and ultimately retain a reversionary interest in the apartment if most of the legal interests therein have been burdened in favour of third parties.

More pointedly, the following questions spring to mind. May an apartment owner alter, redecorate and equip the inside of his apartment according to his own taste? Does he have the freedom to repair, repaint, retile and repanel his apartment at his discretion? May he drive nails into the walls to hang paintings? May he remove the inner walls and doors of his apartment or fashion a niche in the inner bearing wall to display a statuette of his favourite Greek goddess or god? May he put up a notice that no-one is allowed into his apartment under any circumstances and physically prevent anyone from entering? May he cook whatever smelly meals he likes and have parties on the balcony of his apartment until the small hours of the morning? Is he allowed to keep cats, dogs, rodents, canaries or crocodiles as pets in his apartment and if so, how many? May he exercise his profession as a dentist, a medical doctor or a conveyancer in his apartment? May he allow his daughter to practise her trade as a prostitute or his spouse to give piano or violin lessons in the apartment? May he rent out his apartment for short periods or invite a hippy colony to move into his apartment during the summer holidays when the family has left for their beach cottage? Does an apartment owner really acquire genuine ownership of his apartment, or does the fact that he is not entitled to perform some or most of the activities mentioned above degrade his entitlements with regard to his apartment to a "nebulous something" which cannot be designated ownership at all?[17]

Limitations on Apartment Ownership

In order to answer the questions posed, one must review the limitations placed on apartment ownership at common law as well as those contained in apartment ownership statutes.[18]

Most apartment ownership statutes limit an apartment owner's right freely to dispose of his apartment. The most common restriction is that an apartment owner is not allowed to dispose of his unit otherwise than as a whole, namely his apartment plus his undivided share in the common property which is inextricably linked thereto.[19] Again, many apartment ownership statutes contain restrictions on the alienation or lease of apartments to outsiders.[20] A very common restriction is to make the sale of an apartment subject to the approval of the owners' association. This allows executive boards to screen prospective purchasers and to keep unpleasant characters out of the apartment ownership community.

An owner's right of use and enjoyment of his apartment is curtailed first by the concurrent rights of other apartment owners. In accordance with the Roman law maxim *sic utere tuo ut alienum non laedas*, the owner can use and enjoy his apartment as he pleases as long as he does not infringe upon the rights of other apartment owners. In the interests of good neighbourliness, an apartment owner may not exercise his rights in a manner which inconveniences neighbouring apartment owners or in a way which constitutes an abuse of rights. Where an apartment owner acts with the sole purpose of injuring his neighbour without obtaining any benefit for himself or where his abnormal, unnatural or socially unacceptable practices cause unusual prejudice or inconvenience which a neighbour cannot be expected to tolerate, the prejudiced party would definitely have the ordinary remedies to redress his grievance. Examples of actionable nuisances would be where an apartment owner allows water from his bathroom or kitchen to overflow into the apartment below, where alterations endanger the structural soundness of the building or where an apartment owner is prejudiced by excessive smoke, noise or smell emanating from a neighbouring apartment.

Apart from limitations imposed by neighbour law most apartment ownership statutes contain one or more of the following general restrictions.[21] First, an apartment owner is obliged to repair his apartment and to maintain it in a state of good repair *inter alia* by replacing outdated improvements inside the apartment.[22] Secondly, an apartment owner is obliged to allow reasonable access to the management body to inspect his apartment, to replace and repair common facilities and to ensure that the provisions of the Act and the rules are being observed.[23] Thirdly, in terms of most of the United States and Canadian apartment ownership statutes, improvements or alterations inside an apartment may not impair the structural integrity or mechanical systems of the building or lessen the support of any portion of the apartment ownership buildings.[24] This corresponds to the reciprocal easements (servitudes) for subjacent and lateral support contained in some apartment ownership statutes.[25] Fourthly, the common law prohibition of nuisance is usually fortified in apartment ownership statutes by an express provision that an owner is not allowed to use his apartment or permit it to be used in such a manner or for such a purpose as will cause a nuisance to any occupant of any unit.[26]

Besides statutory limitations on unrestricted enjoyment of an apartment, such enjoyment is also curtailed by various rules and regulations contained in the document that constitutes an apartment ownership scheme,[27] the model by-laws and regulations that apply to schemes and the rules adopted by the general assembly of apartment owners or the executive board. These provisions usually place restrictions on the use and occupancy of an apartment, *inter alia* providing that an apartment may be used only for residential, professional or commercial purposes and that no apartment may be inhabited by more than two persons per bedroom. The model by-laws (usually in the schedules to the statutes) or the rules adopted by the general meeting or the executive board frequently contain restrictions on the keeping of pets, the holding of parties and the playing of musical instruments during certain periods of the day or night.[28]

Interesting provisions contained in the South African model rules are the following:[29] an owner shall not use his apartment or allow it to be used for any purpose injurious to the reputation of the building;[30] an owner shall not do anything to his apartment which is likely to prejudice the harmonious appearance of the building;[31] an owner shall not without the written consent of the executive board keep any animal, reptile or bird in his apartment;[32] an owner shall not place or do anything on his balcony or verandah which is aesthetically displeasing or undesirable when viewed from the outside of his apartment;[33] and an owner is obliged to eradicate pests in his apartment.[34] A peculiar Singapore rule is that parts of the floor of an apartment used for pounding chillies must be adequately covered so as not to cause a nuisance to neighbouring owners.[35] According to the New South Wales rules an owner must keep glass windows or doors forming boundaries of his apartment clean, must not hang any washing visible from the outside of the building in any part of his apartment and if an owner ventures on the common property, he must be adequately clothed and must not use language or behave in a manner likely to cause offence or embarrassment to the occupiers.[36] A Bavarian house rule prohibits occupiers of apartments from taking showers between 11pm and 5am.[37] The Spanish statute prohibits any activity which is immoral, irritating or dangerous to the health of fellow apartment owners.[38] Finally the model rules of Bolivia, Chile and Uruguay instruct apartment owners not to let their apartments to persons with bad reputations or notoriously bad habits.[39]

The tendency to regulate the lives of apartment owners in too detailed a fashion smacks of a landlord mentality. The notoriously detailed provisions of schedule 1 of the Strata Titles Act (NSW) of 1973 have been criticised for "nanny-ism".[40]

In conclusion a peculiar restriction contained in the German, Swiss, Austrian and Turkish apartment ownership statutes can be mentioned. These statutes provide that if an owner falls in arrears in the payment of the levies required to cover the cost of the maintenance and management of the common property, or if an owner makes such an intolerable nuisance of himself that the other occupants cannot be expected to continue living with him in the same community, a special resolution can be taken in general meeting forcing the offender to sell his apartment. If this does not happen within a prescribed period (usually three months), the apartment is sold by public auction.[41]

Conclusion

In conclusion the question might be raised whether apartment ownership can, in view of the severity of the above-mentioned restrictions still be regarded as genuine ownership or whether it would be more correct to say that the sectional owner obtains only a nebulous right which is a mere shadow of the extensive powers enjoyed by a conventional landowner. To answer this question one must first consider what is meant by genuine ownership. Secondly, one must enquire in how far the characteristics of the object of ownership in this case, namely an apartment in a multi-unit building, qualifies the answer to this question.

The well-known Roman-Dutch writer Hugo Grotius defines ownership as the right which entitles an owner to deal with the object of his ownership as he pleases within the boundaries of the law.[42] This fairly neutral concept was transformed into an absolutist concept by nineteenth century economic liberalism and German pandectism.[43] In an effort to free property from all kinds of state control, ownership is regarded as an absolute and indivisible right - absolute in the sense that it allows the owner the most comprehensive rights with regard to an object and indivisible in the sense that ownership is regarded as paramount and exclusive and in fact the mother of all real rights.[44] Contrary to this absolutist theory of ownership, modern property lawyers accept that the ownership of land and other immovables is extensively eroded and hollowed out by the restrictions placed on ownership by both private and public law. This is especially prevalent in the sphere of planning and environmental law.[45] Furthermore, the modern trend is to regard these restrictions not as external burdens which clog or hamper a potentially most comprehensive property right, but rather as immanent in and thus delimiting the content of ownership.[46] Then again constitutional recognition of property rights has emphasised the notion that property rights must be exercised in the interest of the general public. Thereby the comprehensive entitlements embodied in the ownership of land have been transformed into a sacred obligation to safeguard and cherish land and its attributes for future generations.[47] Consequently the modern owner is regarded as a custodian or trustee of the property under his control - he is no longer considered to have an unlimited freedom to use and enjoy his property as he pleases.[48]

Coupled with this reduced content of ownership, the basic features of apartment ownership not only warrant stricter limitations on the ownership of an apartment but also limitations different from those imposed on, or rather immanent in, the ownership of land. The characteristic features of apartment ownership are the following. First, the object of apartment ownership is not indestructible land as in the case of land ownership, but apartments which form part of a destructible building. Statutes on apartment ownership should therefore as far as possible endeavour to protect the physical structure of the building and the units themselves against destruction. For this reason, the positive obligation placed on apartment owners to maintain their apartments in a good state of repair is justified. Again, compulsory provisions on taking out a comprehensive insurance policy on the building financed by both the management body and the owners individually, is necessary to guarantee the reconstruction of the building and individual apartments in case of damage or partial destruction of the building.[49] Secondly, the apartments of an apartment ownership building are not structurally individualised but structurally interdependent.[50] To maintain the individuality of each unit, reciprocal easements (servitudes) of subjacent and lateral support must be considered a natural incident of all statutes on apartment ownership. The same is true about provisions in by-laws which prevent alterations inside an apartment which might affect the stability of the building or transfiguration of the outer limits of apartments (*eg* the conversion of a balcony into an extra bedroom) which might affect the architectural or aesthetical appearance of the building.[51] Thirdly, because of the close proximity of sectional owners, the community life in an apartment building is much more intensified than the community life of a group of neighbouring landowners.   To prevent apartment buildings becoming houses of dispute like their old Germanic counterparts, strict rules on the keeping of pets, the control of noise, the exercise of a profession and the conduct of practices that are prejudicial to the reputation of the building are indispensable.[52] Finally, the community of apartment owners is more or less permanent and is only terminated on dissolution of the apartment ownership scheme.

In my submission, these peculiar features of the object of apartment ownership justify more intensive limitations and restrictions on the powers and entitlements of an apartment owner and indeed demarcate the distinct content of apartment ownership.   Although this implies a special type of ownership coloured by the characteristic features of the institution, it still remains genuine ownership.   Apartment ownership should therefore not be degraded to a lesser limited real right or a "nebulous something", but should be placed on the same level as the ownership of land.

Finally, two reasons may be advanced why ownership of an apartment should be treated as genuine ownership and not as a limited real right. First, if considered genuine ownership, it would be easier for courts to invalidate Draconian provisions contained in the rules of a particular scheme.   German and Canadian courts have *inter alia* invalidated provisions containing an absolute prohibition on the keeping of pets, although they are prepared to allow a provision restricting pets to one dog, two cats or ten goldfish per apartment.[53] Secondly, one of the main reasons for introducing the concept of apartment ownership in post-war Europe which suffered from a severe housing shortage, was to satisfy the psychological and social need most persons have to own their own home.[54] The aim was to place apartment ownership and house ownership on the same footing and thus place the dream of home-ownership within reach of a greater segment of the population.[55] Precisely because of this, the public has to be convinced that they obtain something infinitely more than a lease when they buy an apartment.[56] In view of this, property developers and local building authorities should be encouraged to raise the technical standards of apartment ownership buildings to ensure that such apartments are adequately isolated and insulated.[57] Once it is possible to distinguish an apartment building at a glance from a mere rental building, an apartment owner would have no reservation in regarding his apartment as his castle and in affectionately calling it "home sweet home".

Notes

1   A detailed exposition of this idea appears in the first edition of J Bärmann *Kommentar zum Wohnungseigentumsgesetz* (ed 1, 1958) 152. See also the later editions of J Bärmann, E Pick and W Merle (ed 6, 1987) 45-52; CG Van der Merwe and DW Butler *Sectional Titles, Share Blocks and Time-sharing* Vol I *Sectional Titles* (1995) 2-3; CG Van der Merwe "Apartment Ownership" in U Drobnig *et al International Encyclopedia of Comparative Law* Vol VI *Property and Trust* chapter 5, s 47-49; Pérez Pascual *El derecho de propiedad horizontal, un ensayo sobre sa estructura y naturaleza jurídica* (Madrid 1974) 359.

2   In terms of ss 18(1) and 20 of the New South Wales Strata Titles Act of 1973 and cl 1(6) of the English Commonhold Bill of 1996, the common property does not vest in the apartment owners but in the management body (body corporate). See also *Commonhold: A Consultation Paper* (Lord Chancellor's Department) July 1996 para 2.5; M Aldridge and AA Van Velten (1997) 2 Notarius International 23.

3   See further CG Van der Merwe and DW Butler *Sectional Titles* 2-16/2-18; CG Van der Merwe "Apartment Ownership" s 57.

4   See further CG Van der Merwe and DW Butler *Sectional Titles* 2-19/2-24; CG Van der Merwe "Apartment Ownership" s 58.

5   See the equivalent German *Wohnungseigentum*, the Dutch *appartementeneigendom* and the Belgian *propriètè des appartements*. This term was also contained in the Model Condominium Law of 1962 suggested by the United States' Federal Housing Administration. Five state legislators of the United States favoured this term.

6   See the equivalent French *propriètè par étages* and the Spanish and Latin American *propiedad horizontal*. This term was apparently first employed in the Argentine statute of 1948 followed *inter alia* by the Cuban, Costa Rican and Peruvian statutes on apartment ownership. In addition 16 states of the United States, including the District of Columbia, followed the Puerto Rican lead in using the term horizontal property.

7   These terms were chosen by eight states of the United States as well as the Canadian provinces of Alberta and Saskatchewan.

8   This term was adopted by the Japanese statute of 1962.

9   This term was chosen by four Australian states as well as by the Canadian province of British Columbia.

10   Two Australian states and New Zealand favoured this designation.

11   This term was favoured by the South African legislator. The last three designations refer to ownership of strata, units or sections in a multi-unit building.

12   In terms of the German *Wohnungseigentumsgesetz* of 1951 s 13 para 1, a sectional owner has extensive powers with regard to his section in the sense that he can utilise it as he pleases and prevent others from encroaching on his entitlements (*"nach Belieben verfahren .... insbesondere dieses .... nutzen und andere von Einwirkungen ausschliessen"*). Section 2 paras 2 and 9 of the French statute on apartment ownership of 1965 (*Loi no 65-557 du 10 Julliet 1965*) describes apartments as the exclusive property of each apartment owner. Most of the Canadian and the United States' statutes (which are in this regard still modelled on s 2(b) of the Model Act of the Federal Housing Administration of 1962) contain similar provisions. Examples are s 6(2) of the Ontario Condominium Act of 1980, s 15(2) of the Nova Scotia Condominium Act of 1970 and s 7(2) of the Manitoba Condominium Act of 1980. S 115 of Singapore Land Titles (Strata) Act of 1968 provides that nothing in the Act shall affect or rescind any further rights or remedies that a subsidiary proprietor of a lot has.

13   Act 95 of 1986 s 2(b).

14   S 2(e).

15   Commonhold Bill of 1996 cl 1(1). See further the Quebec Civil Code art 1063: "Each co-owner has the disposal of his fraction; he has free use and enjoyment of his private portion....". Art 10 of the Albanian Law on Apartment Ownership (Law no 7688 of 13 March 1993 FZ 1993, 264) is even more comprehensive: "The apartment owner has the right to occupy, sell, lease, donate or burden his apartment according to principles pertaining to ownership and the general provisions in the Civil Code concerning the use and alienation of immovable property privately owned."

16   Cl 1(3) and (4). See also the Commonhold Consultation Paper of July 1996 para 1.3 and see ss 9(3) and 38(7) of the Singaporean Land Titles (Strata) Act of 1967. Alice Christudason "Subdivided Buildings - Developments in Australia, Singapore and England" (1996) 45 ICLQ 360 comments that this provision "confers a right as near as possible to that of a freeholder in respect of his property."

17   The criticism that an apartment owner only obtains a "nebulous something" (*"newelagtige iets"*) was levelled by JC De Wet and FS & GA Tatham, the most important South African legal academic and the most important legal practitioner at the time of the promulgation of the first Sectional Titles Act 66 of 1971. See JC De Wet and FS & GA Tatham *"Die Wet op Deeltitels"* 1972 *De Rebus* 205.

18   See in general CG Van der Merwe and DW Butler *Sectional Titles* 8-5/8-15; CG Van der Merwe "Apartment Ownership" s 183-s 200.

19   See *eg* s 2 of the Sectional Titles Act 95 of 1986 and art 10 of the Quebec Civil Code.

20   In terms of § 12 of the German *Wohnungseigentumsgesetz* the apartment owners can by a majority decide to make the alienation of a unit subject to the consent of the remaining apartment owners. In terms of art 1065 of the Quebec Civil Code an owner who leases his apartment must notify the unit owners' association (syndicate) and furnish it with the name of the lessee.

21   See in general for South Africa CG Van der Merwe and DW Butler *Sectional Titles* 8-6/8-12. See further Commonhold Consultation Paper of July 1996 para 2.2.

22   See *eg* the Sectional Titles Act 95 of 1986 s 44(1)(c). See also the Commonhold Bill of 1996 cl 6(2) and 7(1)(c).

23   See *eg* the Sectional Titles Act 95 of 1986 s 44(1)(a). See also art 1066 of the Quebec Civil Code: "No co-owner may interfere with the carrying out, even inside his private

portion, of work required for the conservation of the immovable decided upon by the syndicate or of urgent work". See also the Commonhold Bill of 1996 cl 25 dealing with the right of entry and repair under certain circumstances.

24   For the United States see the Model Act of the Federal Housing Administration of 1962 s 6(f) and the Uniform Condominium Act of 1980 which had been adopted by one third of the states of the United States, s 3-107(a) and s 2-111(1). For Canada see *inter alia* the Ontario Condominium Act of 1980 s 6(3) and (4), the Nova Scotia Condominium Act of 1970 s 15(3) and (4) and the Manitoba Condominium Act of 1970 s 7(3) and (4).

25   See *eg* the Sectional Titles Act 95 of 1986 s 28(1)(a)(i) and (b)(i). These servitudes are sometimes supplemented by a reciprocal servitude for the passage or provision of certain services such as water, electricity and sewerage pipes, wires, cables and ducts. See the Sectional Titles Act 95 of 1986 s 28(1)(a)(ii) and (b)(ii). See ss 16, 17, 18 and 21 of the Land Titles (Strata) Act of 1967 (cap 158 Rev Ed of Singapore Statutes 1988) for easements implied in terms of the Singaporean statute.

26   See *eg* the South African Sectional Titles Act 95 of 1986 s 44(1)(g).

27   In the United States and most of the Canadian states an apartment ownership scheme is established by a declaration of establishment usually supplemented by by-laws on the management of the scheme.

28   See further CG Van der Merwe and DW Butler *Sectional Titles* 8-12/8-15.

29   The South African model rules are contained in Annexures 8 and 9 of the Regulations published under s 55 of the Sectional Titles Act 95 of 1986. See Government Notice R664 in Government Gazette 11245 of 27th May, 1986 as amended.

30   Annexure 8 rule 68(1)(i).

31   Annexure 8 rule 68(1)(iv).

32   Annexure 9 rule 1(1).

33   Annexure 9 rule 5.

34   Annexure 9 rule 11.

35   First Schedule to the Land Titles (Strata) Act of 5 May 1968 by-law 19.

36   See Schedule 1 to the Strata Titles Act 68 of 1973 (NSW) cl 21, 23 and 27.

37   See the Higher Regional Court of Bavaria (Bay ObLG) NJW 1991, 1620.

38   See the Spanish Law of 1960 art 7 para 3: "*actividades .... inmorales, peligrosas, incómodas o insalubres*". See also art 6 of the Argentine Law of 1960.

39   See for Bolivia: Law of 1949 art 8; Chile: Law of 1963 art 51; Uruguay: Law of 1946 art 9.

40   See Alice Christudason "England" (1996) 45 ICLQ 361.

41   See for Germany the *Wohnungseigentumsgesetz* of 1951 s 18 19; for Austria the *Wohnungseigentumsgesetz* of 1975 s 22; for Switzerland the Swiss Civil Code ss 649b and 649c; for Turkey the Act of 1965 s 25. For a detailed discussion of the German provisions, see CG Van der Merwe "Sanctions in terms of the South African Sectional Titles Act and the German *Wohnungseigentumsgesetz*: Should the South African statute be given equally sharp teeth?" 1993 Comparative and International Law of Southern African (CILSA) 85-97. See also CG Van der Merwe "The Comparative Law of Apartment Ownership" 1996 Scottish Law and Practice Quarterly (SLPQ) 214-215. *Cf* the remark by CJ Berger "Condominium: Shelter on a Statutory Foundation" (1963) 63 Colum L Rev 987-1027 at 1012: "Furthermore, consumers may be chary of buying an estate that is forfeitable, and institutional lenders are

likely to treat a defeasible fee with greater caution. Although, at first, severe sanctions against the incorrigible unit owner may seem desirable, in the long run it is probably wiser for the condominium to depend upon financial and injunctive relief. The availability of injunction and the mediating role of the court, once relief is sought, should solve most serious problems that arise."

42   H Grotius *Inleidinge tot de Hollandsche Rechtgeleerdheid* 2.3.10 as translated by AFS Maasdorp *The Introduction to Dutch Jurisprudence of Hugo H Grotius* (ed 3 1903): "Full ownership is that whereby a person may, for his own benefit, do with a thing whatever he pleases, so long as it is not forbidden by the law". See also S Van Leeuwen *Censura Forensis* (Lugduni Batavorum 1662) 1.2.13.1 "*Proprietas autem, est ius de rebus nostris pro lubito disponendi ... nisi quatenus vi aut iure prohibeatur*".

43   For the idea that the Roman and Roman-Dutch law concept of ownership was not absolute and that the absolutist perception was a legacy from nineteenth century liberalism and pandectism, see PBH Birks "The Roman law concept of dominium and the idea of absolute ownership" 1985 *Acta Juridica* 1-37; DP Visser "The 'absoluteness' of ownership: the South African law in perspective" 1985 *Acta Juridica* 39-52; AJ Van der Walt: "*Bartolus se omskrywing van dominium en die interpretasies daarvan sedert die vyftiende eeu*" 1986 THRHR 305-321; *Idem* "*Gedagtes oor die Herkoms en Ontwikkeling van die Suid-Afrikaanse eiendomsbegrip*" 1988 *De Iure* 16-35, 306-325; AJ Van der Walt and DG Kleyn "Duplex domimium: the history and significance of the concept of divided ownership" in DP Visser (ed) *Essays on the History of Law* (1989), 212-260.

44   For a modern exposition of such an absolutist theory of ownership see Olzen "*Die geschichtliche Entwicklung des zivilrechtlichen Eigentumsbegrifts*" 1984 *Juristische Schulung* 328-335. The father of the absolutist theory was most probably J H Boehmer an exponent of the *Usus Modernus Pandectarum* who gave the following definition of ownership in his *Introductio in Ius Digestorum* 127: "*Dominium est ius in re corporali, quo haec ita nobis propria est, seu ad nos spectat, ut alio possimus excludere ab usu eius rei, atque illa disponere*".

45   See especially MA Rabie "The Impact of Environmental Conservation on Land Ownership" 1985 *Acta Juridica* 289-313; JRL Mitton "Planning and Property" 1985 *Acta Juridica* 267-288; AJ Van der Walt "The Effect of Environmental Conservation Measures on the Concept of Landownership" 1987 SALJ 469-479.

46   See in general DV Cohen *New Patterns of Landownership* (Trust Bank Series of Continuity Legal Education Lectures Law Students' Council University of the Witwatersrand 1984) 67-80; Carole Lewis "The Modern Concept of Ownership of Land" 1985 *Acta Juridica* 241 *et seq*; AJ Van der Walt "The Future of Common Law Landownership" in AJ Van der Walt (ed) *Land Reform and the Future of Landownership in South Africa* (1991) 26-28, 33-34; *Idem* "Unity and Pluralism in Property Theory - A Review of Property Theories and Debates in Recent Literature": Part I, II and III 1995 TSAR 15-41, 322-345, 493-526 especially 24, 514, 523-524. See also *King v Dykes* 1971 3 SA 540 (RA) 545-546.

47   Property rights are protected in terms of arts 14 and 15 of the German Basic Law and in terms of s 25 of the Constitution of the Republic of South Africa Act 108 of 1996. For the influence of the public law concept of ownership on the traditional concept of ownership see in general G Van Maanen "Ownership as a Constitutional Right in

South Africa" 1993 *Recht en Kritiek* 74-95 especially 78-80, 88-90; AJ Van der Walt "Towards a Theory of Rights in Property: Exploratory Observations on the Paradigm of Post-apartheid Property Law" 1995 SAPR/PL 298-345 especially 334-339; *Idem* 1995 TSAR 27.

48   German commentators, *eg*, *Münchener Kommentar zum BGB* (-FJ Säcker) Vol VI (ed 3) 1997 § 903 no 13 describes this idea as the *"Sozialplichtigkeit des Privateigentums"*.

49   See *inter alia* Alice Christudason (1996) 45 ICLQ 351: "In addition the very stability of the building depends on the proper maintenance and repair both of individual units and the common parts. If either falls into disrepair, there will be repercussions on the value of all the parts of the property and the continued enjoyment by the users of both individual units and the common parts."

50   See also DN Clarke "Commonhold - A Prospect of Promise" (1995) 58 MLR 487: "Any horizontal division leads inevitably to mutual interdependence" and Alice Christudason (1996) 45 ICLQ 344.

51   See also CG Van der Merwe 1996 SLPQ 213.

52   DN Clarke (1995) 58 MLR 504 has warned that apartment ownership (commonhold) as a concept is not the panacea for all the problems of communal living or co-operation between any occupants who share common facilities. He points out that the operation of any given apartment ownership scheme (commonhold) will still depend upon the willingness and enthusiasm of the unit owners. CJ Berger "Condominium: Shelter on a Statutory Foundation" (1963) 63 Colum L Rev 987-1026 states at 1010: "The well-being of a condominium venture requires the condominium owners both to support the common areas financially and to observe the decorum that communal life demands." Alice Christudason (1996) 45 ICLQ 346 mentions the "need to regulate the respective rights and obligations of interdependent owners which would perforce arise as a result of high-density living" and poses the following question at 361: "Or is it that a common code of civilised behaviour, consideration and decency simply has to be imposed due to the multiple occupancy and level of interdependence in a development?" At 364 she concludes: "There is of course, particularly in English outlook and thinking, a reluctance to regiment the affairs of citizens by introducing excessive legalism into even the mandanities of everyday existence. However, for productive co-existence in subdivided buildings, even commonplace matters cannot be left to the conscience or a sense of duty of the unit owners. Regulation may be a necessary evil."

53   For Germany see J Bärmann, E Pick and W Merle *Wohnungseigentumsgesetz* (ed 6 1987) s 13 no 53-66, s 15 para 7-13. For Canada see AH Oosterhoff and WB Rayner *Anger and Honsberger Law of Real Property II* (ed 2 1985) 1899-1902. The German Higher Regional Court (OLG) of Frankfurt (*Rechitspfleger* 1978, 414) drew a distinction between non-troublesome animals like birds, hamsters and goldfish the keeping of which can not be restricted and troublesome animals like cats and dogs the keeping of which can indeed be restricted.

54   See CG Van der Merwe and DW Butler *Sectional Titles* 1-11; CG Van der Merwe "Apartment Ownership" s 27.

55   See DN Clarke "Commonhold - A Prospect of Promise" (1995) 58 MLR 496 who points out that the Commonhold Bill creates commonhold as a subspecies of freehold rather than as a separate estate in its own right. He indicates that this was done to

allay the lay perception that commonhold would be "less valuable" than freehold. See also the 1984 Law Commission Report entitled *Transfer of Land - the Law of Positive and Restrictive Covenants* (Law Com No 127) which stated that "leasehold developments did nothing to cater for the psychological satisfaction of consumers who sought 'freehold' properties and resented continuing to pay a ground rent 'for nothing' under leasehold arrangements" (as paraphrased by Alice Christudason (1996) 45 ICLQ 355).

56   See DN Clarke "Commonhold - A Prospect of Promise" (1995) 58 MLR 486-890 for the uncertainties inherent in leasehold arrangement providing accommodation in multi-unit buildings. At 504 Clarke concludes: "Commonhold as a concept needs to escape and be disentangled from its close link with residential long leasehold flats. The field in which it will operate and the benefits it offers have a much wider compass." See further M Aldridge and AA Van Velten (1997) 2 Notarius International 26-27; Alice Christudason (1996) 45 ICLQ 345-346, 351-353.

57   The idea that apartment ownership buildings should be solidly built and adequately insulated was already advocated in the Draft Bill for the introduction of a German apartment ownership statute (*Wohnungseigentumsgesetz*) of 30th November, 1949. § 2 III reads as follows: "*Wohnungseigentum soll nur gebildet werden an Teilen von Gebäuden, die auf Grund neuzeitlicher, auf Abgeschlossenheit der einzelnen wohnungen gerichteter Bauweise die Gewähr für grösstmögliche ausschaltung aller gegenseitigen Störungen der Hausbewohner bieten*" ("Apartment ownership should be established only with regard to buildings constructed in accordance with modern building techniques aimed at insulating the individual apartments from each other in such a way that the virtual exclusion of mutual disturbances is guaranteed"). See Nils Thun *Die Rechtgeschichtliche Entwicklung des Stockwerkseigentum* (dissertation Hamburg 1997) 173.

6 Aspects of Condominium Law in The Bahamas

GILBERT KODILINYE

Background

The Commonwealth of The Bahamas is an archipelago of about 700 islands in the West Atlantic, south-east of Florida and north-east of Cuba, of which 30 are inhabited. The most important islands are New Providence (where the capital, Nassau, is situated) and Grand Bahama (where the city of Freeport is located). The resident population is 278,000. Tourism accounts for 50% of the GDP and 50% of employment. The Bahamas is one of the world's principal financial centres. Since 1717 there has been virtually no tax on individuals or companies; government revenue is raised through a range of excise duties and fees, including company registration fees and bank and trust company fees.

Condominium was introduced into The Bahamas in 1965 by the Law of Property and Conveyancing (Condominium) Act (Ch 124), and has proved to be a popular form of property ownership. This popularity is no doubt attributable to the close proximity of The Bahamas to the USA, and to the fact that the majority of visitors to The Bahamas are North Americans, to whom condominium is a familiar concept. There is a substantial body of case-law from the Bahamian Supreme Court.

The development of condominium in North America and Australia has been largely a response to the severe land shortages in the metropolitan areas and the "back-to-the-city" movement of many disenchanted suburb-dwellers. Condominium structures in these countries are often multi-storey, high-rise apartment buildings used by local residents as their only or principal home. By contrast, in most Caribbean countries condominium is primarily a creation of the tourism industry, whether it takes the form of residential accommodation for long-stay visitors, or commercial premises used by small businesses such as boutiques, beauty salons and souvenir shops in resort areas. The condominium concept is intended to incorporate all the economic advantages of co-operative apartment living with the economic and psychological advantages of home ownership, though the latter advantage may be less important in the Caribbean - because of the association of condominium with the tourism industry - than it would be in North America.

Ch 124 is based substantially on the Model Statute prepared in 1961 by the American Federal Housing Administration, which has been the model for much of the condominium legislation in the USA and Canada. Cap 224A (Barbados) is similar to Ch 124, and differs only in minor respects.

Nature of the Interest of the Unit Owner

In *Bank of Nova Scotia v GLT Corporation Ltd*[1] Smith J explained the genesis of the condominium concept in The Bahamas:

> Up until the coming into operation of the Law of Property and Conveyancing (Condominium) Act 1965, there was no provision in our law for the horizontal division-up of the fee simple estate in land. In other words, the fee simple estate in a part of a second or other storey of a building could not be in a totally different ownership than that of the ground floor of the same building. The Act was passed to make provision for the ownership in fee simple of units in multi-unit buildings, thus providing for horizontal division of a fee simple.

And in the words of Gonsalves-Sabola J in *Triple Ecstacy Ltd v Bay View Village Management Ltd*:[2]

> The Condominium Act, enacted in 1965, introduced in The Bahamas the condominium concept of ownership, whereby a building could be subdivided among several owners, each owner owning absolutely his compartmentalised unit, but yet having defined rights over other parts of the property, subject to his liability to make financial contributions towards the general maintenance of the condominium.

Under the Act, the purchaser of a condominium acquires a fee simple interest in the individual unit purchased, together with an individual share in the "common property". In *Southair (Bahamas) Ltd v Signet Bank (Bahamas) Ltd*[3] Strachan J stated that a unit owner's fee simple estate has "the maximum life-span that the law permits, and survives the destruction of the building". This seems to settle, for The Bahamas, the vexed question as to whether a unit owner's interest is confined to the tangible parts of the property (the earth, bricks and plaster) inside its boundary, or whether it includes the air space within the boundary. In the case of the former, where a building containing units is destroyed by fire or earthquake *etc*, the units will vanish; in the case of the latter, they will not be affected.

The legislation contemplates the use of individual mortgages for each unit, and the separate alienability of each. The provision in section 6(3) of Ch 124 to the effect that each unit together with the undivided share in the common property shall for all purposes constitute "an estate in real property" seems to have been intended to allay any fears on the part of mortgage lenders as to the nature of the security.

In common with most condominium legislation, Ch 124 and Cap 224A preclude the creation of a condominium on a leasehold. In the Caribbean, the Condominium Act 1981 of Trinidad and Tobago provides for the registration of both freehold and leasehold developments. The main disadvantage of leasehold condominiums is that the financial independence of individual unit owners from the other unit owners may be compromised.

The Definition of Unit

"Unit" is defined in Ch 124, section 3 as

> a part of the property to which a Declaration relates intended for any type of independent use, and which includes one or more floors or parts thereof in a building, and which has direct access to a street or to common property leading to a street, and may include any appurtenance such as a balcony, terrace or patio or any other structure such as a garage, store or parking place which may be situated in some other part of the property.

The requirement in the section that each unit must have a direct exit to a public street or common area leading to a public street is clearly intended to preclude the further subdividing of apartments into smaller units.

The Definition of Common Property

The Act defines "common property" somewhat unhelpfully as "so much of the property as is not contained within the boundaries of any unit". The FHA Model Act is much more specific, and states that the common property is to include *inter alia* (1) the land on which the building is located, (2) all structural members, bearing walls, lobbies, roofs, halls, corridors, stairways *etc*, (3) basements, yards, gardens, parking and storage space (4) caretakers' lodgings (5) central utilities such as power, water, air conditioning and (6) all other parts of the property normally in common use.

It is possible that, should the need arise, reference will be made to the Model Act for the purpose of defining common property in The Bahamas.   Preferably, however, each Declaration should contain a comprehensive definition of "common property".

The Method of Establishing a Condominium

The Act requires the following documents:
(1) Declaration;   (2) Bye-laws;   (3) Individual Unit Deeds.

The Declaration

Section 4(1) of the Act specifies what a Declaration must contain.   This includes:

(a)   a description of the property sufficient to identify it and its location precisely;

(b)   a description of the building (with number of storeys, basements, cellars and units, and the principal materials of which it is constructed);

(c)   a description of every unit by reference to its floor area, limits, boundaries, *etc*;

(d)   drawings and plans of the building;

(e)   a statement of covenants, conditions and restrictions affecting the use of the units;

(f)   the bye-laws applicable to the property;

(g)   the method of amendment of the Declaration by the unit owners.

In addition, a Declaration may contain any other matters (not inconsistent with the Act) which the person executing the instrument considers desirable.

In *Goodyear v Maynard*[4] the defendant declined to complete the purchase of a condominium apartment in Freeport on the ground that the Declaration did not comply with section 4(1).

By section 4(1)(l), a Declaration must provide for "the methods ...

to be observed and the conditions to be fulfilled for the amendment of the Declaration by the unit owners." The plaintiff vendor argued that clause 10 of the Declaration, which provided *inter alia* that the unit entitlement of each owner could be varied by the consents by deed of all the unit owners affected, satisfied section 4(1)(l). Henry J did not accept this argument. He pointed out that a variation within clause 10 of unit entitlements prescribed in the Schedule to the Declaration would certainly result in an amendment of the Declaration *pro tanto*, but it did not provide for the amendment of any other portion of the Declaration. But were the provisions of section 4(1)(l) mandatory, so that failure to comply with them would render the Declaration void? There was a conflict of authority on this question. In *Roberts Realty of The Bahamas Ltd v Innscinzi*,[5] Brice CJ had held that, although some of the particulars required by section 4(1) obviously had to "be included in order to carry out the purpose and intention of the Act", others, like section 4(1)(l), were "more in the nature of ancillary matters", so that a Declaration need contain provisions for the amendment only of those particulars which were contemplated as being capable of amendment. Henry J disagreed with this view and preferred the contrary view of da Costa J in *GLT Corporation Ltd v Bank of Nova Scotia*,[6] that the provisions of section 4(1)(l) were mandatory. Henry J pointed out that under section 6(4), the provisions of the Act, and the Declaration when recorded, were binding on the owners of all units in the building. The Act clearly recognised the necessity to empower the unit owners in appropriate cases to amend the Declaration and to this end it was necessary for the Declaration to contain provision for such amendment. Henry J concluded by emphasising that the "Declaration [was] the foundation stone on which the entire legal edifice in the Act [was] built," and "if the Declaration is defective, that edifice must fall." Accordingly, the Declaration in this case was void and the vendor was unable to show a good title in accordance with the contract of sale; so that the defendant was entitled to refuse to complete.

Who Must Execute Declaration

Under Ch 124 execution must be by "the person or persons having the legal and equitable title in fee simple absolute to the property to which the Declaration relates". This requirement has been in issue in the Bahamian courts, which have consistently held that the provisions of Ch 124 relating to Declarations of Condominium are mandatory, and failure to conform with them will result in the Declaration being invalid.

The facts of *Roberts v Albacore Developments Ltd*[7] were that in June 1978 an apartment in the Lucayan Towers Condominium was conveyed to the plaintiffs by B Ltd together with an undivided share of the common property. B Ltd had itself purchased the apartment from Albacore Ltd, the first defendant. In the course of selling the apartment, the plaintiffs' attorneys discovered that prior to the lodgement in the Registry of the Declaration of Condominium in July 1968, there had been lodged in the Registry in June 1968 an indenture of mortgage of the property by Albacore to a mortgagee. Issues thus arose as to the validity of the plaintiffs' title. In particular, the court was asked to determine whether the mortgagee ought to have executed the Declaration as the person having the legal estate to the property to which the Declaration related. Georges CJ answered that question in the affirmative, with the result that the Declaration was void and the Lucayan Towers Condominium had never become a property subject to the provisions of the Act. Accordingly, no title had passed from Albacore to B Ltd which, in turn, could convey no title to the plaintiffs. Nothing could pass under either conveyance because in fact the apartment and the undivided share in the common property had not become "land" under the Act. Georges CJ also rejected the possibility of imposing a constructive trust on either Albacore or B Ltd in favour of the plaintiffs on grounds of justice and good conscience. In the view of the learned Chief Justice, the difficulties which had arisen in the case were attributable to the failure to follow scrupulously the prescribed statutory procedure, which had created an unusual estate in the land not known to the common law. There would be

> no justification for introducing equitable principles to confer on one of the parties an estate completely different from that which was the subject-matter of the purchase and sale. The intervention of equity [was] aimed at creating an estate identical with that which would have been created at law, but existing in equity instead. This would be impossible in this case.

A number of further questions arose in *Glinton v Albacore Developments Ltd*,[8] which was a sequel to the first Albacore case. To rectify the situation concerning the void Declaration, Albacore, in which (the mortgage being redeemed) the legal and equitable title to the property was now vested, proposed to execute and lodge a new Declaration. The question which now came before the court was whether it was permissible to include in the new Declaration terms which differed from those of the original. One argument was that, the old Declaration being void, it was to be treated as if it had never existed in law, so there was no reason why the new Declaration should adhere to its terms.

On the other hand, it could be argued that although the original Declaration was invalid, it in fact constituted representations made by Albacore to prospective purchasers of condominiums, and such purchasers agreed to buy units on the faith of those representations. Now that it had been discovered that the Declaration was invalid, Albacore was under a duty to convey in keeping with the representations then made. If the terms of the Declaration were altered, this would amount to an alteration of the contractual terms, so that there was a danger of actions being brought against Albacore by aggrieved purchasers.

Georges CJ considered the counter-argument that the principle of *res extincta*, as illustrated in the familiar cases of *Coutourier v Hastie,*[9] *Strickland v Turner*[10] and *Bell v Lever Brothers,*[11] applied. The gist of this argument was that the original Declaration could not operate as a warranty because a warranty cannot exist independently of a contract, and if the subject-matter of the contracts of purchase - the condominiums - unknown to the parties did not exist, then there would be no contracts of which a warranty could be a term. Accordingly, there could be objection to altering the terms of the Declaration.

Ultimately, Georges CJ took the view that the principle in the *res extincta* cases was inapplicable. Unlike in *Coutourier v Hastie*, where the cargo of corn had fermented and been disposed of by the time the contract was made, or *Strickland v Turner*, where the person on whose life the annuity had been purchased was already dead, in this case the contracts of sale were still capable of fulfilment. The vendor could rectify matters by ensuring that the legal and equitable owner of the property executed and lodged a fresh Declaration. Georges CJ concluded by accepting the argument that the original Declaration constituted a contractual warranty which could not be varied, and the terms of the new Declaration should therefore not differ from those of the old.

Johnson v Wallace[12] was another case in which a Declaration was held void on the ground that a prior mortgagee (in this case the security was a charge by way of debenture) had not joined in its execution. Georges CJ accordingly set aside the conveyances of units to several purchasers on the ground that they had been based on a false assumption common to vendor and purchaser that the property being conveyed was in fact a condominium under the Act. These were instances of "common mistake" in which "equity would regard the contract as a nullity and set it aside notwithstanding that it has been executed; imposing terms if necessary to ensure justice between the parties."[13] It was also held that on the assumption that the developer executed and registered a new Declaration, it would be sufficient, in order to cure the defects in the purchasers' titles, to execute confirmatory conveyances reciting the facts which made such conveyances necessary.

In the recent case of *Grant v Francis*,[14] one issue was whether a wife who was entitled to dower rights in her husband's property was a person "having the legal and equitable title in fee simple absolute to the property to which the Declaration relates" within section 4(1) of the Act (Ch 124). If the answer were in the affirmative, then her concurrence in the execution of a Declaration of Condominium relating to her husband's property would be required by the section. Allen J briefly explored the history and nature of dower rights in The Bahamas. She pointed out that dower rights were made part of Bahamian law by the Declaratory Act of 1799, and such rights in The Bahamas today were identical to the common law dower rights which existed in England in 1799. Dower rights were an encumbrance upon the title. They were automatically acquired when the husband became the owner of land. Dower was a life estate in remainder in one third of the land of which the husband was sole owner. Dower was abolished altogether in England in 1925, but remained in effect in The Bahamas subject only to a wife renouncing her dower rights, or a widow formally releasing them in accordance with the prescribed statutory procedure. In the instant case, a husband had executed a Declaration without his wife's concurrence, and the question was whether her non-participation rendered the Declaration void. This depended upon whether the wife could be said to have a "legal or equitable title in fee simple absolute." Allen J answered this question in the negative. In her view, section 4 had to be construed as including (i) any person who has both the legal and the equitable title in fee simple absolute vested in him, or (ii) any persons who jointly or as tenants in common have such title vested in them. A wife entitled to dower rights did not come within either category. Her right to a life interest in one third of her husband's lands was, during her husband's life, only an incipient title, which was capable of being completed after his death by action in the Supreme Court. Until such right was asserted, and an assignment of the dower made, the wife had no title to any specific property; the right simply constituted a restriction on her husband's right to freely alienate his property.

Allen J also held that the execution of a Declaration under the Act did not amount to an alienation of property. The property made subject to the Act by the Declaration was simply deemed thereby to be divided into units. After execution of the Declaration, the plaintiff was still the owner of the property in fee simple, and there was no need for his wife to renounce her dower. However, Allen J did not consider the position where any of the units were sold to purchasers. That would certainly constitute alienation, and presumably it would be necessary for the wife to renounce her dower with respect to the units sold at that stage.

A third issue to be considered was whether the Declaration had the effect of extinguishing the plaintiff's wife's dower rights. Section 7(7) of the Act provided that "no right to dower shall accrue from the ownership in fee simple of any unit under the provisions of this Act or of the share in the common property appertaining to such unit." Allen J interpreted section 7(7) as precluding the vesting of dower rights in respect of the future ownership of the units - the words "shall accrue" meant "shall come into existence", or "shall vest". It did not affect dower rights already in existence before the division of the property into units. Accordingly, the plaintiff's wife's right to dower in the property existing prior to the Declaration of Condominium survived and was not extinguished by section 7(7) of the Act. In coming to this conclusion, Allen J emphasised that it was a well settled rule of construction that a statute ought not to be construed as taking away or extinguishing proprietary rights without compensation, unless the intention was manifested plainly, either by express words or by clear implication and beyond reasonable doubt.

Registration of Declaration

In Barbados, a Declaration must be registered in the Condominium Land Register which the Register of Titles is required to compile under section 12 of the Land Registration Act, Cap 229 (section 6 of Cap 224A). In The Bahamas, where there is no system of registration of title, the Declaration must be lodged for recording at the Registry of Records (section 6(1) of Ch 124).

Unit Entitlement

The Declaration must contain a schedule stating the "unit entitlement" of each unit in the scheme, expressed as a fraction or percentage of the aggregate estimated value of all the units taken together or of the aggregate floor area. This is a crucial factor in any condominium scheme because it determines (a) the voting rights of each unit owner in the body corporate and (b) the amount of contribution to the common expenses required of the unit owner. (Ch 124, section 4(4).)

Drawings and Plans

Cap 224A, section 4(1) and (6), and Ch 124, section 5(1)-(3) provide for a complete set of drawings and plans of the building to be annexed to the Declaration. Such plans must be accompanied by a certificate of a qualified architect (and under Cap 224A must also be approved by the Chief Town Planner) certifying that the drawings are accurate. In *Sawyer v Family Guardian Ins Co*[15] the question arose as to whether an architect's certificate submitted subsequently to an original void Declaration could be incorporated into a second valid Declaration without express words of incorporation. Strachan J was able to answer this question in the affirmative, following *Roberts v Albacore Developments Ltd*[16] and *Johnson v Wallace.*[17] Ch 124, section 5(2) also provides that where, at the date of recording of the Declaration, the building is not complete, the architect's statement is to be lodged for record in the Registry upon completion[18] of the building and before any unit is conveyed. It was also emphasised in *Sawyer* that the provisions of section 5 subsections (1) and (2) of Ch 124 are mandatory. On the other hand, it is arguable that the provisions of Cap 224A, section 4(1) and (6) are not mandatory, as the Act speaks of the annexation of such plans "as are deemed necessary or convenient".

Existing Mortgages

Ch 124, section 6(2) provides that where, before the first conveyance of any unit, there is in being any mortgage or charge affecting such unit, every such mortgage or charge must be satisfied, or the unit must be released from the encumbrance, or the mortgagee or chargee must join in the conveyance. In *Bank of Nova Scotia v GLT Ltd*[19] an argument to the effect that the execution of a Declaration of Condominium had the effect of extinguishing an existing mortgage over the building was rejected by the court.

No Partition of Common Property

The Acts provide that no share in the common property shall be disposed of, except as appurtenant to the unit to which it relates; and no unit owner may bring an action for partition of any interest in the common property. An exception to the latter is where the court orders the removal of the property from the provisions of the Act.

Bye-laws

In addition to the Declaration, every condominium scheme must have bye-laws containing rules concerning such matters as the composition of the board of management, procedure for election to and removal from the board, duties and powers of the board, voting procedures and the duties of unit owners. Some of these rules may be duplicated in the Declaration. In the absence of expressly drafted bye-laws, those set out in the Schedules to the Acts are deemed to apply.

The Body Corporate

Under Cap 224A, section 13(1) and Ch 124, section 13(1) and (2), as from the date of the recording of the Declaration, all the owners from time to time of the units constitute a "body corporate" in whom the operation of the property is vested. It is to be a non-profit making body, having perpetual succession and a common seal, and capable of suing and being sued in its corporate name. In many US jurisdictions, the equivalent body is not a company but an unincorporated association (*eg* in the Virgin Islands).

Duties of Body Corporate (Ch 124, section 14; Cap 224A, section 14)

The main duties of the body corporate under the sections are:

- (a)   to operate the property for the benefit of all unit owners and to be responsible for the enforcement of the bye-laws,
- (b)   to keep the common property in good repair,
- (c)   to insure the building to its replacement value against fire, hurricane and seawave.

Questions may arise as to the extent of the duty of a body corporate to enforce the bye-laws against defaulting unit owners; in the light of the provisions of section 14(1) and section 23(3) of Ch 124 and

Cap 224A. As stated above, section 14(1)(a) provides that the duties of the body corporate include responsibility for the enforcement of the bye-laws; and section 23(3) provides that an action to enforce compliance with the bye-laws "shall be maintainable by the body corporate acting on behalf of the unit owners, or by an aggrieved unit owner". The issue has not yet arisen in the courts of The Bahamas or Barbados, but there is a case from British Columbia which is apposite. In *Strachan v The Owners, Strata Corporation VR 574*[20] a unit owner applied under section 40 of the Condominium Act (BC) for an order requiring the strata corporation to enforce bye-laws prohibiting owners from making alterations to the exterior of the condominium structure without the written permission of the condominium council, and prohibiting use of strata lots for commercial purposes. Section 14 of the Condominium Act was similar in its terms to section 14 of the Bahamian and Barbadian Acts: "The strata corporation is responsible for the enforcement of the bye-laws, and the control, management and administration of the common property *etc*". On the other hand, the British Columbia statute contained a provision in section 40 which does not appear in the two Caribbean statutes; "Where a strata corporation fails to fulfil an obligation under this Act or bye-laws, the owner of a strata lot, or a registered mortgagee, may apply to the court for a mandatory injunction requiring the strata corporation to perform the obligation". Blair J held that the strata corporation had an obligation to enforce its own bye-laws (and indeed the defendant corporation admitted that it was under such a duty), and that failure to do so gave the petitioning lot owner the right to seek a mandatory injunction. It seems that, should the issue arise in The Bahamas or Barbados, the court should come to the same conclusion on the wording of section 14 of Ch 124 and Cap 224A for, despite the absence of any provision equivalent to section 40 of the British Columbia statute, section 23 of the Caribbean statutes, giving the aggrieved unit owner the right to enforce compliance with the by-laws, may ultimately have the same effect.

The duty of the body corporate to insure the property was in issue in *Meachem v Lucayan Towers South Condominium Association*[21] where Strachan J rejected an argument to the effect that there was no mandatory duty to insure because the body corporate was empowered to decide by unanimous resolution not to do so. In Strachan J's view, the Association had a duty under section 14(1)(c) to insure against the specified risks for the full replacement value of the building, unless the unit owners by resolution decided otherwise.

Liability for Negligent Management

In *Maillis v Town Court Ltd*[22] the plaintiff owner of an apartment in the Town Court Condominium in Nassau was shot by a masked bandit who held him up one night in the condominium car-park and robbed him of $3,000 in cash. The robber was never caught. The plaintiff brought an action against the defendant for breach of contract and negligence for its failure to provide adequate security and lighting in the parking area. The case was unusual in that the defendant vendor had contracted with each purchaser of units in the condominium to provide management services for which the unit owners were to pay in proportion to their entitlements. This arrangement was contrary to section 13 of the Act, under which all the owners from time to time of the units are to constitute a body corporate which is to be responsible for the management of the condominium. The contractual provisions for management in the *Maillis* case were intended to be transitional, as it was also agreed that when 44 units had been sold, the body corporate was to take over the management from the vendor. Gonsalves-Sabola J declined to decide the point as to whether the management agreement was valid in so far as it constituted a contracting out of the Act, but on the assumption that it was, the question to be decided was whether the defendant was in breach of its contractual duty and/or its duty of care in tort. The plaintiff's contention was that the defendant's failure to provide lighting and a security patrol in the area of the car-park amounted to a breach of an implied term that the defendant would exercise reasonable care in securing the common areas of the complex against the intrusion of trespassers and thieves. The evidence showed that on the night of the robbery there was only one female security guard on duty, and the level of lighting in the area of the car-park was appreciably lower than normal. However, Gonsalves-Sabola J took the view that "such deficiency as there was in the standard of illumination did not encourage or contribute to the attack on the plaintiff," and "perhaps nothing short of armed guards vested in suits of armour in the immediate presence of the plaintiff might have been an effective deterrent to the masked marauder who was determined to shoot the plaintiff and deprive him of his money."[23] Moreover, the main issue was whether the defendant was to be held liable in negligence for having failed to prevent a third party from causing damage to the plaintiff through the third party's deliberate wrongdoing - an issue which had been addressed in a number of well-known English cases such as *Stansbie v Troman*,[24] *Perl Ltd v London Borough of Camden*[25] and

Smith v Littlewoods Organisation Ltd.[26]   Gonsalves-Sabola J opined that
the scope of the duty owed by the defendant in this case to mount security
arrangements in the condominium was restricted by the financial resources
made available to the defendant through the contributions of the unit
owners, and in the circumstances the level of security and lighting
provided on the night in question was not so unreasonably low as to
amount to negligence.

Default in Payment of Contributions

As Gonsalves-Sabola J pointed out in *Triple Ecstacy Ltd v Bay View
Village Management Ltd,*[27] the success of the condominium idea depends
on the punctual discharge by the unit owners of their financial obligations.
To ensure this, the legislature has provided "machinery for effectively
protecting the rights of unit holders against breach by any of them of these
financial obligations."[28] Thus, where a unit owner is in default in payment
of contributions levied by the body corporate for common expenses, the
body corporate has two methods of recovery, which exist concurrently: (i)
to bring an action for debt in respect of the amount owed (Ch 124, section
18(2); Cap 224A, section 18(2)) (ii) to enforce a charge (Ch 124, section
21) or a lien (Cap 224A, section 21) against the unit of the offender. In the
Triple Ecstacy case, Gonsalves-Sabola J rejected an argument to the effect
that the charge created by section 21 was equitable only, holding that the
Act must be interpreted as providing for a legal charge, otherwise the body
corporate would only be able to put up for sale an inferior interest, and this
would defeat the purpose of the Act.

  An issue which arose on similar legislation in the US Virgin
Islands was whether the obligation to pay contributions (called "common
assessments") was independent of the condominium association's duty to
repair and maintain the units or common areas; and a further question was
whether the condominium had the authority to disconnect the water supply
to recalcitrant unit owners who had failed to pay their assessments.   In
Towers Condominium Association v Lawrence[29] the Territorial Court of the
Virgin Islands held that the alleged breaches of duty by the Association in
failing to maintain the buildings, facilities and common areas of the
condominium did not justify the unit owners' withholding of the common
charges payable by them. Meyers J emphasised that

> nowhere in the Declaration, the Bye-laws or the Condominium Act is a
> unit owner authorized or permitted to withhold the payment of common

assessments for any reason. This payment is mandatory without any exceptions.[30]

A unit owner's duty to pay assessments fees was conditional solely on his acquisition of title. Thus, a unit owner who was involved in a dispute with the Association concerning its services and operations was not entitled to "exert leverage in that controversy by withholding payment, but must seek other remedy."[31] The obligation to pay assessments was independent of the Association's obligation to carry out repairs; and it was further held in this case that the Association acted within the scope of its authority and was justified in disconnecting the water supply of delinquent unit owners, as the policy had been approved by the Board of Directors as a means of abating violations of the bye-laws, and in order to prevent the disconnection of the entire complex by the water authority because of the refusal of a few unit owners to pay their assessments.

Termination of Condominium Scheme

Property may be removed from the Acts by an Order of the Supreme Court (under Ch 124, section 31(1)) or the High Court (under Cap 224A, section 31(1)) where the Court is satisfied that either at least 90 per cent of the unit owners have resolved to terminate the scheme and all mortgagees have consented, or the building has been destroyed or damaged and is not to be reconstructed, or it is just and equitable to remove the property from the Act.

Upon dissolution, the building is deemed to be owned in common by all unit owners in undivided shares in the same proportions as they had originally been entitled to the common property.

Notes

1   (1986) Supreme Court, The Bahamas, no 112 of 1992 (unreported).
2   (1988-89) 1 Carib Comm LR 344, at 347.
3   (1993) Supreme Court, The Bahamas, no 112 of 1992 (unreported).
4   (1983) Supreme Court, The Bahamas, no 981 of 1982 (unreported).
5   E419/72 (unreported), cited in *Goodyear v Maynard*, n 4, *supra*.
6   E56/80 (unreported), cited in *Goodyear v Maynard*, n 4, *supra*.
7   (1988) Supreme Court, The Bahamas, no 488 of 1988 (unreported).
8   (1988) Supreme Court, The Bahamas, no 488 of 1988 (unreported).
9   (1856) 5 HLC 673.

10   (1852) 7 Exch 208.

11   [1932] AC 161.

12   (1988-89) 1 Carib Comm LR 49.

13   *Ibid*, at 59.

14   (1997) Supreme Court, The Bahamas, no 957 of 1996 (unreported).

15   (1992) Supreme Court, The Bahamas, no 503B of 1992 (unreported).

16   *Supra*.

17   *Supra*.

18   It is not clear whether "completion" in s 5(2) includes substantial completion.

19   (1986) Supreme Court, The Bahamas, no 795 of 1982 (unreported).

20   (1992) 28 RPR (2d) 279.

21   (1993) Supreme Court, The Bahamas, no 1581 of 1991 (unreported).

22   [1989-90] 1 LRB 184.

23   *Ibid*, at 189.

24   [1948] 2 KB 48.

25   [1984] QB 342.

26   [1987] AC 241.

27   (1988-89) 1 Carib Comm LR 344.

28   *Ibid*, at 347.

29   [1995] VIR 185.

30   *Ibid*, at 188.

31   *Ibid*, at 189, citing *Forest Villas Condominium Association Inc v Caneiro*, 422 SE 2d 884 (Ga App 1992), at 886.

7 *Caveat* Commonholds

PETER SMITH*

Introduction

Reforming any aspect of the law of private property can be a tortuous and difficult exercise. Take the fate of a Law Commission Report, praised as a *tour de force*,[1] that proposed legislation to introduce land obligations.[2] These proposals had been designed to overcome a nefarious rule,[3] which refuses to allow the enforcement of positive covenants against successors in title to freehold land, and which, despite the House of Lords having affirmed it recently,[4] has not improved with age,[5] and whose unreformed existence contrasts starkly with both legislative[6] and judicial[7] efforts to reform the rules applying to positive leasehold covenants. The land obligation proposals have however, for all their merits, been briskly confined to oblivion.[8]

Such was the story of the fate of good proposals which the Law Commission resisted the temptation to revise and which addressed a problem with few "political" overtones - being largely "lawyers' law". The current state of affairs with regard to reforming termination of tenancies is an object lesson in how not to go about things, showing the twin dangers of revising the reforms in the interests of expediency and in favour of one party alone. The original proposals[9] were generally welcomed.[10] They were balanced, proposing removing doctrines such as waiver and re-entry, which had become technical, and conferring on tenants a tenants' termination order scheme for the first time, for use against bad landlords. They were not enacted in this form. In 1994, the Law Commission decided to produce a draft Bill.[11] With that, they dropped or at best suspended the proposals for a tenant's termination order scheme, because "priority should be accorded to enacting the landlords' termination order scheme".[12] This decision appeared to have been based on considerations of expediency at the expense of justice and has been criticised for that reason.[13] After a further four years, there had been no reform but the Commission then carried out a low-key further consultation exercise. They expressed the view that the "commercial property industry has expressed concerns about the implications of the proposal to abolish physical re-entry".[14] If indeed the Commission decide further to revise their original proposals and to suggest legislation to permit the use of a remedy, even in a limited form, which Lord Templeman described as "dubious and dangerous"[15] we shall have come full circle in respect of a self-help remedy which had earlier been labelled by the Commission itself as being "at the heart of many difficulties".[16]

The triple set of proposals for commonhold tenure do not, at least, bear the marks of so radical a revision as those for termination of tenancies but they were made against a background of conflicting interests and to that extent the path of reform may be no smoother than is proving to be the case with forfeiture. One of the Law Commissioners has admitted that law reform in the present field is driven by political imperatives or by pressure from the public.[17] That being so, care is needed in relation to long-term proposals of this type. It is possible to infer from the long official silence of the government since the General Election of 1997 that it is not in any particular hurry to introduce commonhold legislation.

The fact that the latest set of commonhold proposals are stalled[18] is in fact welcome. The main thrust of this paper is to argue that the English commonhold proposals are not likely to promote the dual alleged objectives of allowing flat unit holders to own their dwellings while at the same time improving the running of the buildings in which the flats are contained. The proposals owe much to the French system of *copropriété des immeubles bâtis*, which are revisited. This system exists against a similar background of absolutist ownership ideas to that of English law. There is evidence that the French system is in some difficulty because flat owners are reluctant to make the unavoidable concessions to regulations or the collective interest, which experience shows must be made if any flat ownership scheme is to succeed.

Speedy action to legislate for commonholds would seem to be erroneous, if only because the current reforms have been rejected by the Scottish Law Commission.[19] We should not be pushed by the advocates of reform, into legislating in a hurry and then having time to criticise or regret the changes. We do not in any case share the confidence of some about the benefits of reform. One writer thinks that "the arguments in favour of enabling legislation for subdivided buildings cannot be resisted".[20] However, the current legislative models go rather further than providing a framework, and seem to aim at codification in places. Another reformer boldly claims that "lawyers need little convincing of the necessity of commonhold".[21] For reasons given, we form a dissenting minority with regard to the current sets of proposals. It has been regretted that lawyers would miss a good new chance for additional conveyancing business if commonholds were forgotten.[22] However, it is surely axiomatic that the legal profession does not exist merely for its own aggrandisement.

The 1996 commonhold proposals have been criticised by some of their supposed beneficiaries, noting the absence of any statutory protection against overcharging by the commonhold association of individual unit owners for services and maintenance.[23] The unease felt by such interest groups would not have been much appeased if they had thought about the fact that the commonhold proposals create a special regime of unlimited liability if a commonhold association fails, in contrast to the limited liability of long leaseholders. One writer has said that "to introduce a new variant of freehold and a new type of corporate body in tandem was bold indeed".[24] These tensions do not encourage one to think that relations between putative commonholders would be any easier than those between French unit owners,[25] or between freeholders and long lessees.

The case for not adopting the current commonhold models is strengthened by the fact that there is no clear or decisive evidence from the long leasehold system or in the French regime that the management problem sometimes associated with long leases would *ipso facto* disappear with the removal of a superior freehold title.[26] A flat ownership scheme, as the evidence seen by the present writer from France shows, would rely on the diligence of its members for its success. The focus of disputes about management might simply shift from the vertical to the horizontal, owing to difficulties in balancing the tensions between the "psychological satisfaction of consumers"[27] who wish to own freehold units and the need of all unit holders to live collectively in the common interest, for reasons which lie in the nature of all multi-occupied unit schemes.

There are no easy answers. General condemnations of principle of the idea of flat ownership[28] underplay the fact that some long leases may not be well drafted. As a matter of principle, moreover, if almost everyone else in the world has a flat owning system,[29] then it becomes hard to argue that England and Wales should not promote one. It is the means chosen for reform which are faulty. Moreover, the rejection on two occasions by the Scottish Law Commission, noted earlier,[30] of the English commonhold reform model, of itself casts real doubt on the wisdom of implementing the current set of commonhold proposals.

No Need to Rush into Commonholds

The perceived difficulties of the long leasehold system relate to tenure and management problems. It goes without saying that a long lease is a wasting asset. It is not possible for a long lessee whose term is reducing below a certain point to obtain mortgage funds[31] on the security of the lease, which then becomes unassignable. Worse, the freehold interest, until recent legislation,[32] could be sold on to anyone the freeholder pleased, to the possible detriment of long leaseholders who might find one absentee landlord replaced by another. If commonholds come about, the tenure problem is solved easily enough: a unit holder acquires a freehold in his unit. However, he would also, in recognition of a collective interest of all commonholders in the development, obtain a membership in the common parts of the relevant building.[33] A commonhold unit holder would acquire the benefit of nearly absolute freehold ownership but tied to it the burden of an individual liability to pay service charges to the commonhold association.[34] The resemblance to a well-run long leasehold system of the latter notion need not be stressed.[35]

Although an argument for commonholds is that management problems would be overcome by standardisation of management rules and practices,[36] so that one is not in the hands of the person drafting a long lease, this point is not conclusive. It does not address the fact that freehold unit holders under any scheme would not necessarily be any more diligent in running the property than would long leaseholders where the premises as a whole are to be repaired and maintained by a long lessees' management association.[37] French experience with *copropriété des immeubles bâtis* suggests that similar apathy problems exist across the Channel,[38] where in form, the general principle of absolute ownership of flat units is carried into the structure of the local legislative scheme.[39] It appears[40] that flat unit holders in France are not prepared to live collectively, which is not surprising, yet their co-ownership scheme can only operate where they do so. Apart from this manifestation of individualism at the expense of any collective interest, which, since commonholds are admitted to be "strongly similar" to other schemes in the world,[41] might affect commonholds, the tenure problem in the form faced by Aldridge[42] no longer exists. The legislature has reduced its significance by extending leasehold enfranchisement from houses to leasehold flats,[43] and by allowing long lessees the right to buy the freehold if the current freeholder decides to dispose of it.[44]

The trouble with these measures lies in their sheer complexity. The Court of Appeal has stigmatised the 1987 legislation as "complicated and confused".[45] The legislation promoting collective enfranchisement of flats has not yet earned judicial rebukes.[46] However, if the government promotes simplification of the collective enfranchisement system, this should ease any pressure for speedy legislation to promote commonholds.

If the tenure problem is not what it was, the management complaints about long leases must still be faced. These seem mainly founded on a notion that neglect of repairs and essential maintenance, is the result *ipso facto* of the leasehold system, which is so structured that the flat-lessees may have to deal with a neglectful landlord. The concept is of a mismatch between interest and obligation: of a long lessee who may not have control over whether repairs are done, or of how they are carried out, opposed by a lessor whose interest in the premises is not necessarily sufficient to induce him to behave responsibly. These are undeniable problems but they may not be confined to long leasehold tenure. There is no necessary reason to suppose that these difficulties would be solved merely by changing the tenure and control of the running of the buildings containing flats.

General Aspects of the French System

Introduction

Although the French rules have been set out elsewhere,[47] their genesis and principles are instructive, seeing that commonhold ownership is sometimes seen as a vehicle for widening freehold ownership, albeit in a necessarily limited form. An individualistic spirit still colours the French rules - much as it does our own.

Originally, only one article of the French Civil Code referred to co-ownership of storeys or *copropriété par étages*.[48] It was laconic,[49] although marking a shift from what has been assumed to be the refusal of Roman law to recognise apartment ownership in multi-occupied buildings.[50] Prior to the French Revolution, any regulation of apartment buildings outside the purely contractual or in residuary and minimal legislative form was based on *coutumes* of certain cities[51] where building in storeys was dictated by economic or social conditions.[52] Prompted by the shortage of housing in the post-1918 period, as well as by an increasing urbanisation of the population, it was felt that matters could no longer safely be left to private contract or custom: hence the passing of a law of 28th June, 1938. This was a cautious measure: for example, it did not impose a requirement of a constituent instrument or *règlement de copropriété* on common owners or developers. It continued to reflect the hostility of the *Napoleonic Code*, with its leanings to individual, absolute and even unlimited personal ownership and control, to *indivision*, shown by the retaining of a limiting principle that any decision of co-owners, such as to undertake repairs, had to be unanimous, and allowing the easy termination of the co-ownership by unconditional *partage* or severance at any time.

French Individualism

It seems appropriate, owing to the background to the French principles, to revisit the basis of traditional French individualism in the field of private property ownership. It affects the spirit of their thinking and so the interpretation and operation of the French legislation as to flat co-ownership. English law of "ownership", as it has evolved to be, seems often as absolutist as is French law.[53] This approach is supported by the "necessary evil" of regulation in the case of commonholds, having regard to the supposed reluctance of English tradition to accept regulation,[54] especially where spending money as opposed to observing negative restrictions is concerned. The following is therefore offered as some food for thought to common law reformers and others interested in commonhold schemes.

The absolutist French definition of ownership[55] may be ascribed to the narrowly individualistic attitude of those responsible, such as M Portalis,[56] for the drawing up of the *Napoleonic Code*.[57] To this day, some French *doctrine* (which unlike in England has an influence on the courts) believes that the French idea of individual and absolute, and so by all too ready inference, at least in private law relations, unlimited, ownership comes from the Roman notion of *dominium*.[58] The supposed principle adopted by the French Revolutionaries and still to some extent reflected in present concepts is that a Roman *dominus* was assumed to have had total and unrestricted power and control over the thing owned, or an "individualistic free-for-all"[59] over moveable or immovable goods. This view of the matter however, as has been observed,[60] is not a fault confined to French liberals.[61] Without going into the many details of the continuing debate as to the true understanding of Roman ownership, the French *Civil*

Code and its reflection in the co-ownership of flats law appear to have been based on at the least a selective reading of Roman law: in Jones' words, the ultra-liberals looked to Roman law for support "they were determined to find".[62] The expression *dominium*[63] was, it seems, little used in the texts,[64] and perhaps[65] the term merely, at least until Justinian, described that residual right remaining to an owner *ex jure Quiritium* who had failed to transfer land in the proper form.[66] What is more, seeing that there is no single "Roman law" of ownership but an evolving[67] and plastic system, especially with so wide a concept as ownership, it occasions few surprises to see that according to one reputed author, we cannot trace an ownership claim as opposed to an assertion to better possession of a thing back beyond the later Republic.[68] Moreover, even if the classical Roman law did recognise an absolutist concept of ownership over a thing such as land,[69] it does not follow that his powers over the thing were completely unlimited. Such an idea would be conceptually impossible in any system,[70] as the unlimited exercise of his theoretical powers[71] would inevitably risk conflict with the exercise by a neighbouring owner of his ownership, which may explain the existence of some basic private law limitations[72] affecting ownership which appear both in the *XII Tables* and in the *Digest*. These have been well explained elsewhere.[73] If then the French tradition, which also admits of rules to protect neighbouring owners, still continues to insist on the absolute and individual nature of ownership,[74] we would expect to find it facing problems when balancing the individual and the collective in the ownership of flats, and these are a warning to the English reformers, with similar absolutism to contend with. What appears to have happened in their system and in our proposed reforms is that there is a lot of regulation, but in France no sign and here no certainty that co-owners will behave any differently, owing to their respective traditions and expectations, than as a collection of physically proximate but factually independent owners.

Twin Legislative Pillars

Returning to co-ownership of flat units, the method of legislative regulation of most aspects of the relationship between flat unit holders (and unit holders in mixed and commercial developments, with which we are not concerned) was adopted by the twin pillars of a law of 10th July, 1965 and a decree of 17th March, 1967.[75] The cost of building in storeys on increasingly expensive urban land may have been one factor promoting the development of multiple-occupied premises.[76] Another factor was the growth after 1945 of rent control in France, which is said to have encouraged developers to build blocks for owner-occupation rather than to rent.[77] Mention may also be made of the predilection of French "consumers" with individual property ownership.[78] The French law has been said to apply to some four million unit owners.[79]

The French system is evidently dualist.[80] As noted in relation to apartment ownership systems of this type, a co-owner has a defined flat unit and with this a share in the common parts of the building housing it.[81] The *quote-part* or share allotted to each unit holder, calculated in fractions of a thousandth part, gives him weighted voting entitlement[82] in the general assembly of unit owners, the supreme decision-making body of the apartment scheme.[83]

The 1965 law is more interventionist than its predecessor. Thus the drawing up of a *règlement de copropriété* by the developer or, in default, the unit owners as a whole is compulsory.[84] The rule of unanimity for flat owner decisions has been preserved only where it relates to what are seen as fundamental matters, such as changes to the agreed basis of computation of service charges.[85] Owing to the need to try to promote effective decision-taking by the body or *syndicat* of co-owners, in their general assembly, decisions as to repairs may be taken by a simple majority of votes of owners voting at a general assembly meeting.[86] Assuming the building is in good repair and condition, improvements, the need for which may be opposed on financial or other grounds such as sentiment by some unit owners, do not need to be undertaken with the consent of all owners: but the respect for individual property rights is such that, as a rule, most improvements require a "re-enforced majority" of those owners whose votes represent two-thirds of the units, which may be hard to obtain.[87] One curious result of distinguishing between different kinds of work on the basis of classification rather than cost is that while potentially expensive repairing works such as re-roofing may be decided on by a small minority of active unit owners, a much larger majority is required for cheaper but useful work such as installing entry-phones to all flats.[88] This type of difficulty might affect commonholds. The latest English proposals permit the commonhold association to carry out improvements which are not repairs by a Class 1 resolution;[89] repairs, which they would be obliged to undertake,[90] require a simple majority vote.[91]

Comparing the French principles to the commonhold proposals, the commonhold system would, as is the French, be dualist, by making each unit holder an automatic member of a commonhold association with voting rights, and contains a similarly bold statement that his "ownership" is as near to freehold and thus to absolute ownership as possible.[92] There are detailed provisions for the rights and obligations of unit holders: for example, the commonhold association, of which unit holders are compulsorily a part, is subject to a long list of proposed statutory "general management functions".[93] The detail given in these obligations is if anything greater than in France. One striking feature of the latest commonhold proposals, is the ban on the granting of long leases.[94] If limited flat ownership is to mean anything, restrictions on the power of a unit holder to dispose as he thinks fit of a unit should be kept to a minimum, or the attractiveness of the scheme may be reduced. No comparable general ban exists either in France or in the proposed Scottish reforms to the Law of Tenement. To this aspect we return in due course.

More generally, it is the fact that the commonhold proposals put flat ownership into a detailed regulatory statutory framework governing and limiting the ownership of the flat unit holders and regulating in some detail the management of the premises which renders them so similar in approach to the detailed regulation apparent in France. Both systems carry the danger that the democracy and the ownership, albeit restricted, which they confer on flat owners may be difficult to reconcile with the inevitable demands of good property maintenance and preservation.

French Democracy

A virtue claimed for flat co-ownership schemes is that they are democratic. The Aldridge Committee referred to a "democratically run commonhold association".[95] They seemingly wished to meet complaints about presumably undemocratic long leasehold developments and the poor management resulting. That owners of units in a multi-unit ownership scheme are involuntarily bound together by purchase of a unit and a share in the common parts, by the medium of an association, incorporated or unincorporated, is also to overcome what Professor van der Merwe has called the "inevitable chaos caused by the lack of a central management body".[96] Unless a community of owners exists in both the formal legal and factual sense then many of the benefits said to flow from commonhold schemes are admitted by the proponents of these ideas to be imperilled.

There is some evidence as to the factual operation of the French system of *copropriété*. It is not very encouraging. French unit holders appear to remain individualist in their attitude.[97] Admittedly, the French system, for reasons to be explained, does not allow as much scope for day to day management by a manager as would the Scottish reform package. Nevertheless, it may be as risky in flat ownership schemes to place so much weight on a manager as it might be in long leasehold schemes. Thus it is pertinent to examine the basis of French individualism.

The right of ownership is embedded by article 2 of the French law of 1965 into *copropriété des immeubles bâtis*.[98] Although this right is limited to the confines of the flat of a unit owner or *copropriétaire*,[99] French unit holders tend to behave as individuals with no sense of any common identity.[100] This state of affairs, which is consistent with the spirit of French tradition,[101] carries the danger of domination by a small group of self-interested activists of a larger body of apartment owners, with the inherent risk of disputes. Professor Atias has claimed that there is no sense of community in multi-owned premises, so that absenteeism from the meetings of the general assembly of apartment owners (*assemblée générale des copropriétaires*) is commonplace.[102] In case it should be thought that such problems are confined to France, attached as some jurists remain to respect for individual ownership rights,[103] a Californian source is reported[104] as complaining of similar narrowly individualistic conduct in that state by apartment owners. Owing to the reliance of flat ownership schemes for their success on the active participation of unit holders in decision making,[105] it would be idle to imagine that similar individualism might not afflict commonhold developments.

The French rules, as well as the English and Scottish models, seek to overcome the apathy problem by assigning an important role to a manager. Some of the advantages and drawbacks to this type of approach are now examined.

The Role Assigned to Managers

The French 1965 law envisages that the *syndicat* (general body) of co-owners will appoint a *syndic* (or manager) to run the buildings on a routine daily basis.[106] Despite some appearances to the contrary,[107] a *syndic* is subject to the control of the general assembly, once again a reflection of the French reluctance to interfere, save where unavoidable, with individual rights. A management committee or *conseil syndicale* ought to exist,[108] apparently further to supervise the *syndic*[109] on behalf of all unit owners,[110] and also, it is said, to allow for representation of the views of co-owners during the intervals between general assembly meetings. Unhappily, it has been claimed that where there are divisions between three sets of factions of co-owners, *ie* between active, passive and litigious members, the *conseil syndicale* will only represent the interests and views of active members and so will, it seems, be useless.[111]

In relation to commonhold schemes, the problems might not be dissimilar. The Aldridge Committee recommended that there ought, save in the smallest developments, to be a management committee.[112] No manager would have to be appointed. Aldridge did not wish to discourage unit owner participation in management by imposing too high a standard of care, say by analogy with that imposed on fiduciaries, on committee members. In contrast to leaseholds, where the position has not, so far as is known, been considered,[113] the original commonhold proposals recommended that liability should be based on the exercise of the same degree of care and skill as the owner of a freehold house.[114] The latest set of proposals of 1996 are more interventionist: they suggest a universal requirement of a chairman and secretary and a mandatory managing committee, save with small developments.[115] They thus risk exposing commonholders to activist minority domination and leaning in favour of such persons as have been identified in France.

The Scottish Law Commission favour a streamlined approach. To them, executive power should rest with a manager rather than with a committee.[116] They reject the notion that a management committee should be required to be appointed.[117] In view of the inefficacy claimed for some French management committees, there is something to commend the lightness of touch of the Scottish proposals as compared to the latest commonhold proposals, on the ground that a good manager may go some way to overcoming the apathy problems which seem to have beset some French schemes and which pose a real risk in any commonhold developments. The Scottish Law Commission forcefully say; "Scheme B is unlikely to work efficiently unless one person - and one person alone - is charged with executive responsibility for the management of the tenement".[118] Perhaps what should be avoided is vesting much control other than in the general law on a manager: as an example perhaps of what to avoid, in France, if a manager undertakes emergency works, he risks subsequent disavowal by the general assembly.[119]

If good management is to be promoted, a question arises as to the term of office if any of a manager. In France, a rigid solution is imposed, in keeping with their detailed, over-regulatory approach.[120] Thanks to article 28 of the 1967 decree, a *syndic* is only able to hold office for a period of three years, and only recently has it been confirmed that this time-period is a rigid upper[121] limit.[122] The result of this rigid formalism has been that a unit holder in arrear with service charges had an unmeritorious defence to a recovery action by a *syndic* who had exceeded his term.[123] Any term of office, which one might think that unit owners should be entitled to fix if they think fit, should not necessarily need to be for so short a period as three years, provided the general body of unit owners are able to dismiss the manager.[124]

Service Charges Payments

The duties of a manager in flat co-ownership schemes may well, if only for the sake of convenience, include the responsibility for making arrangements to collect service charges and to enforce the liability of unit holders to pay them, in the common interest.[125] As Hill pointed out[126] in relation to the French system: "For the co-ownership system to operate efficiently, there must be some effective way of ensuring that the co-owners' obligations can be enforced".

The Aldridge Committee said similar things about the need for effective collection and enforcement systems in relation to service charges.[127] The commonhold proposals in their 1996 form would vest stringent powers in the commonhold association to terminate the freehold interest of a unit holder following service of one months' notice on the unit holder concerned.[128] The severity of these provisions may owe something to the fact that the liability of unit holders in a winding-up is not, it appears, limited to the same extent as that of long leaseholders, so exposing their personal assets to an enhanced degree of risk.[129] Failure to comply with the demand for service charges arrears could well trigger a sale of the unit concerned.[130] There are no provisions for relief against this power of determination of the unit holder's freehold interest. That the principal orientation of these provisions is the security of the commonhold association is confirmed by the general exclusion of the rights as to service charge information in relation to unit holders and their modifications in respect of unit tenants.[131]

The French system seems rather less drastic. As noted elsewhere,[132] it for example[133] allows for the sale of a unit to be blocked if no certificate has been presented from the manager that no service charges are owing. This and other remedies have been said to be inadequate, and a clause in the by-law obliging the purchaser of a unit to guarantee payment of charges in arrears may be a more effective means of pressure though it may have the effect of slowing sales of units.[134] The *syndic* has however a duty to bring a personal action against a defaulting owner, and is personally liable for failure to do so to the body of co-owners - presumably exposing him if the defaulter is insolvent.[135] This sort of risk factor might discourage any lay person from acting as a manager in this country.

The various systems of enforcement have in common the reliance they place on the quality, solvency and sense of obligation felt by unit holders to the payment of their contributions on a regular basis in the common interest. However, neither in France nor under the current commonhold proposals does there appear to be any way in which prospective unit purchasers can be screened and if need be vetoed in a similar fashion to the screening and possible refusal of consent to an assignment of a leasehold interest in English Law.[136] The French system has some safeguards against overcharging by the *syndicat* of co-owners. For example, it appears that liability to pay a service charge is governed by the utility of the service concerned to the particular unit holder's unit,[137] and if there is none to it, as with a ground-floor unit holder who makes by definition no use of a lift, then he does not have to pay any part of those costs.[138] Owing to the complexity and fruitful source of potential disputes of this doctrine, yet another example of the difficulties caused by the French exaggerated respect for individual property rights, the courts have limited its scope: the utility criterion is objective and not subjective. If in fact a unit owner could have made use of a service, but personally declines to do so, he must still pay for it - as with a second floor unit holder who uses the stairs and not the lift.[139]

There is no suggestion in any of the current commonhold proposals of any comparable restrictions or limitations on the liability of unit holders to pay service charges,[140] nor, seemingly, any formal recognition of any need in computing service charges that these should be fair and reasonable in amount, so as to protect against overcharging and extravagance[141] because the thrust of these proposals is the promotion of management efficiency in preference to unit holder security.[142] The courts might be prepared to imply such terms in the interests of business efficacy. However, the issue is one of balance: in France, it appears that the rights of the individual owner are given more weight than would be the case in England. Yet, following from what was mentioned at the beginning of this piece, "consumer groups" might prefer the safeguards of the French system to the efficiency and the risk of loss of one's home for perhaps minor default with no possibility of relief envisaged by the commonhold proposals currently on offer.[143]

Effects in France of Absolutist Ownership Concepts - Similar Poisoning of Commonholds?

We have seen that relations between French *copropriétaires* or unit holders are sometimes prickly.[144] It might well be no different in England and Wales with commonholders. Owing to the close physical proximity of commonhold units, there would be a continuing in-built tension between the claims of unit holders to deal as they think fit with "their" freehold units, and the pressures on unit holders to see to it that their development is properly safeguarded in character and protected against undesirable new unit holders.[145] Some compromises to the individualistic claims of unit holders to absolute ownership and so disposition rights in relation to their premises would be necessary, for reasons already explained, and getting the balance right is difficult.[146]

The French system makes only limited concessions to the collective interest, in respect of unit disposals and leasing and is both instructive and a warning to commonhold reforms, since the two systems both have an absolutist ownership tradition. The French bias in favour of private rights starts with a fact which bears repetition here: the 1965 law expressly confers on unit holders, in respect of the private part of each holder's unit, the right of ownership which is conferred by article 544 of the *Napoleonic Code* on all property owners. No matter that flat owners are physically interdependent, an individualistic bias colours the co-ownership of flats in French law not only in formal terms: it is perceived as such by many of the individuals concerned.[147] At a formal level, for example, a decision to change the intended use or *destination* of the development as a whole, as well as the intended use of the private units, requires unanimity of all *copropriétaires* which is not likely to happen in a large development where such changes may be most needed.

Notification of owners is a matter which cannot be neglected and in this respect the French law of 1965 is scrupulous, as would seem to be the Scottish reform proposals.[148] In France, a dissenting owner may contest in the Tribunal de Grande Instance decisions of a general assembly,[149] as for example dealing with repairs or the making of improvements, claiming that he had insufficient or no notification of the contested decision. It seems to be conceded that the risk of litigation is a price to pay for respect of individual rights, which could otherwise be overridden by an over-active minority of owners or an over-zealous manager.

Leanings to the Individual at Expense of Collective

A useful example of the way the French bias for individual property rights has affected their co-ownership rules is that of restrictions on sales. The flat owners are bound together by a *règlement de copropriété*.[150] This document is apparently contractual in nature and it should state the intended purpose or *destination* of the building. It has its counterpart in the commonhold declaration. It is not open to any *règlement* to limit the absolute right of sale conferred by law: hence, a clause requiring any sale of servants' quarters at the top of the building concerned to be only to any other co-owner was annulled.[151] Sanctity of contract accordingly yields to the principle of sanctity of ownership. Most commonholders would probably not have to worry about servants' quarters but they would benefit from a similar disapproval by the proponents of the scheme of any restrictions on sales of units, even where they might be aimed at giving the commonholders' association a power of veto over undesirable purchasers whose acquisition and use of their units might damage the development as a whole. The Aldridge Committee claimed that these would be inconsistent with the idea of freehold ownership[152] - but it is unclear as a matter of principle why the courts should be any less anxious not to enforce a voluntary restriction on sale entered into by a unit holder with all other commonholders than they have been in the case of contracts between co-owners limiting the power of one of their number to sell.[153]

Neither in France nor in our commonhold proposals is there any rule corresponding to that of the German law of 1951 aimed at preventing a sale of a unit to a person who is demonstrably undesirable.[154] This seems unfortunate since the success or failure of this type of co-ownership association (which cannot be ended by any one of the individuals belonging to it) may depend in part on the common commitment of all of its members to promote its success and preserve its general character. The idea of a power of the association to refuse consent to a proposed sale, of which it had to be notified, on an important ground,[155] would seem as much anathema in France as it might here.[156]

Protection of Character of Development

The protection of the character of the development as a whole by regulating any use to be made of units not envisaged at the date of the development taking place seems a good candidate for a concession to the collective interest, since importance may be attached by residents as a whole to preserving an exclusively residential character in the case of buildings containing flats. In France, the *règlement de copropriété* is likely to contain a statement of the *destination* of the premises, such as that the purpose of the development is solely residential.[157] The aim is no doubt to protect all co-owners against one of their number forcing a change of character in the premises on his neighbours by altering the use put to his flat, as from residential to trade. There is little unfairness in enforcing this type of limitation on a subsequent unit purchaser or lessee.[158] He was aware from the statement of the position when he acquired his premises from its appearance on the property register. However, the concept of *destination* has proved hard to apply: it seems that there are examples of poorly-drafted *règlements*.[159] Once the terms of this compulsory contract are settled, it is impossible to alter them, save in relation to the common parts, such is the respect for established private property rights that even a unanimous vote of all unit holders cannot alter the intended use and enjoyment of the private units.[160] If this is the case, there is a risk that the development of the property may be frozen and that small-scale changes of user, as by use of one room out of several for professional purposes, might not, at least in theory, be consistent with a by-law which specified exclusively residential use.[161]

One further problem which might affect co-owners is that, in keeping with a narrowly regulatory spirit not unfamiliar in some long leases, certain French by-laws contain terms about user which might be difficult or even impossible to enforce - one example being of a clause prohibiting moving house on Sundays.[162] This is the undesirable opposite of what the Scottish Law Commission said: "mandatory should mean modest".[163] The policy in relation to the question of protection of the character and use of commonholds is not particularly clear. The Aldridge Committee ducked the issue, referring it to regulations to be made once the Commonhold Act had been passed.[164] This is a pity. One of the seeming advantages of long leaseholds is the ability of the landlord to preserve the character and general uses permitted in the relevant development, even though the freedom of the lessees to act as they think fit is restricted.[165]

Although over-regulation is to be avoided, the present commonhold proposals seem deficient in not offering any convincing framework for this matter.

Powers of Leasing

By contrast with a need to respect the collective interest with regard to unit user, there is not necessarily any general interest requiring limits on a unit holder's power to lease his unit, provided that the leaseholder is bound to observe the rules applying to the development and not to alter its character from say residential to trading use. If so detailed a statute as the French law of 1965 raises no general difficulty about granting leases,[166] it is at first surprising that the 1996 version of the commonhold proposals,[167] in contrast to the original proposals,[168] suggest imposing a ban on the granting of any long lease by a commonholder. A long lease for this purpose would be a term exceeding 25 years. This proposal has been defended[169] on the ground that it is not desirable to reduce the unit holder to a shadowy figure. The justifications of so substantial a limit on disposition powers[170] perhaps need to be stronger than an assumption of irresponsibility by a spectral long lessee. Until now, restrictions on powers to grant long leases have been rarely imposed - as where a limited owner, such as a tenant for life,[171] might grant a lease for so long a term as to prejudice the interests of remaindermen entitled after the death of the life tenant to possession of the land concerned. Those are persons jointly interested in the same property.[172] The proposed commonhold restriction would seem to serve no obvious and unavoidable damage to the actual general interest. So far as is known, the relatively liberal French principle has not caused difficulties.[173] Leasing powers seem one candidate for following the French principles,[174] if only to avoid the inconsistency of commonholds being advertised as being a form of absolute ownership,[175] and then placing a controversial restriction on a fundamental disposition right inherent in such ownership. The case for rescinding the proposed ban on commonhold long leases is strengthened by the fact that in the current Scottish law of tenement it does not appear to exist,[176] and is not proposed in the Scottish Law Commission's reform package.[177]

Conclusion

Legislation would be essential if flat ownership is to be promoted in

England and Wales. The trouble with the commonhold proposals lies in their internal contradictions in attempting to reconcile individual ownership rights and the pressing needs of collective management from an absolutist standpoint.   The uneasy conflicts within the commonhold proposals may reflect the fact that, in contrast to Scotland, we have no background common law,[178] which the Scottish reform proposals were able to draw on.   Yet no set of general rules can specify the level of detail required by efficient tenement management.[179] A complaints-driven desire to promote detailed uniformity, which is seen from the commonhold proposals, could lead to an inability to adapt to changing circumstances, and to avoidable disputes. Such experience as is to hand of the operation of the complex French system[180] is not encouraging.   Luckily, the commonhold proposals have been overtaken by the recent proposals about tenements. This is one example of law reform by analogy benefiting from delays. A plea is therefore entered to do nothing more before looking at the Scottish reform model, which affords a contrast, by its minimalist approach to the excessive detail of the current commonhold proposals.

Delay in reform in the field may also be justified by the fact that the complaints about the long leasehold system seem to have been more narrowly based than appeared in the last decade, when these were publicised.   If the system for enfranchising long leasehold flats is simplified and extended, the case for any or any speedy commonhold legislation, certainly in its present proposed form, is much weakened.

More generally, French experience suggests that changing to a restricted system of freehold ownership[181] from a restricted system of long leasehold tenure might simply alter the focus of disputes, but not necessarily alleviate them.[182] As has been said, "we live in an increasingly litigious society".[183] We may even speculate that the fact that if English and Welsh "consumers" are yearning for the "freedom" of freehold as compared to the restrictions of a long lease, then French experience also suggests that they might be disappointed to obtain a restricted form of ownership, risking similarly nefarious effects to the management and enjoyment of commonhold flat schemes as are claimed for long leasehold developments.

These considerations do not amount to a claim that legislating for limited freehold ownership of flat developments is an inherently incorrect idea. That would fly in the face of the fact that in for example the states of countries such as Australia or Canada[184] commonhold schemes exist even though there had previously been long leases.

The English commonhold proposed reforms are, for reasons given, flawed. They are an uneasy mixture of absolute ownership and over-regulation of management. The Scottish Law Commission was right to have rejected them. Until better proposals are produced, the legislature should be encouraged to ease the path to the buying out of the freeholder by long lessees within the long leasehold system.[185]

Notes

*   I am grateful to Professor CG van der Merwe of Stellenbosch University and Professor Kenneth GC Reid of the Department of Private Law at Edinburgh University for commenting on an earlier draft of this piece. The opinions expressed and responsibility for them are my own. The financial assistance from The University of Reading, and the kindness of Mr T Finkelauer and Ms F Pieroth of The University of Trier, in connection with the obtaining of references in Germany for this piece, are gratefully acknowledged.

1   Alice Christaduson "Subdivided Buildings - Developments in Australia, Singapore and England" (1996) 46 ICLQ 343.

2   As originally advocated by the Wilberforce Committee Cmnd 2719 (1965) and later revisited by the Law Commission (Law Com No 127 (1984)).

3   Which despite the evasions listed in *eg* Megarry & Wade, *Law of Real Property*, 5th edn (1984) pp 767-770, render the tenure of freehold flats in England and Wales a perilous enterprise.

4   In *Rhone v Stephens* [1994] AC 310; see Snape [1994] Conv 477; and for an earlier controversy, see *eg* Bell "*Tulk v Moxhay* Revisited" [1983] Conv 55; Griffiths "*Tulk v Moxhay* Clarified" [1983] Conv 29.

5   Despite the lack of *locus standi* in the plaintiffs, the damaging consequences to the environment of the rule were shown by the refusal of the Norwich County Court in *Marlton v Turner* [1997] CLY No 453 to enforce an obligation by a freeholder to keep a boundary hedge in repair, which the owner proposed to cut into in connection with building plans.

6   In the Landlord and Tenant (Covenants) Act 1995, which however is flawed, as evidenced by the lengthy and technical analysis required of it in *eg* TM Fancourt, *Enforceability of Landlord and Tenant Covenants* (1997).

7   *Eg* in *P&A Swift Investments v Combined English Stores plc* [1989] AC 632; also *Friends' Provident Life Office v British Railways Board* [1996] 1 All ER 336, where the principles stated at p 351 (Sir C Slade) were treated as authoritative by Morritt LJ in *Beegas Nominees Ltd v BHP Petroleum Ltd* [1998] 2 EGLR 57 at p 59. See also *passim* S Bright "Variation of Leases and Tenant Liability" in *The Reform of Property Law*, P Jackson and DC Wilde eds (1997), ch 5.

8   See Hansard, Written Answers, 19th March, 1998, WA 214.

9   Law Com No 142 *Forfeiture of Tenancies* (1985): see PF Smith "Reform of the Law of Forfeiture" [1985] Conv 165; also *infra*.

10   See *eg* Cherryman (1887) 84 Law Soc Gaz 142; Adams (1991) 17 Law Soc Gaz 17;

Luxton [1991] JBL 42.

11 Law Com No 221 (1994) *Termination of Tenancies Bill.*

12 *Ibid*, para 1.7.

13 PF Smith "Termination of Tenancies by Tenants: A Just Cause?" in *The Reform of Property Law, supra.*

14 *Termination of Tenancies by Physical Re-Entry*, Consultative Document, January 1998. At the time of writing (August 1998) the results of consultation were not known.

15 In *Billson v Residential Apartments Ltd* [1992] 1 AC 494, 536F.

16 Law Com No 142, *supra*, para 3.3.

17 Charles Harpum "The Law Commission and Land Law", ch 6 in *Land Law - Themes and Perspectives* (1998) eds S Bright and J Dewar, p 162.

18 The 1996 Draft Bill was withdrawn from Parliament in the dying days of the Major administration: *The Times* 7th November, 1996. There is a useful review of the whole background to commonhold reform by DN Clarke "Occupying Cheek by Jowl" ch 15 in *Land Law - Themes and Perspectives, supra*. It now appears that the Lord Chancellor's Department will "in due course" further consult on commonhold: *Residential Leasehold Reform in England and Wales* DETR Consultation Paper (1998) para 1.12.

19 *Report on the Law of Tenement*, Scot Law Com No 162 (1998) esp para 2.3.

20 Alice Christaduson, *op cit, supra*, p 363.

21 DN Clarke, "Commonhold - A Prospect of Promise" (1995) 58 MLR 486, p 489.

22 L Charlebois "Commonhold - Lest We Forget" [1997] Conv 169, p 175.

23 *The Times* 28th October, 1996. According to this, "lenders and leaseholder support groups" condemned the 1996 proposals roundly as "hopelessly inadequate and fundamentally flawed and very dangerous".

24 L Crabb "The Commonhold Association - As You Like It?" [1998] Conv 283, at p 302. This is an exhaustive critique of the risky, when compared to long leases, unlimited liability regime proposed for commonholders.

25 Stigmatised by E Kischewsky-Broquisse, *La Copropriété des Immeubles Bâtis* 3rd edn no 3 as involving a "*voisinage de fer*".

26 The University of Reading College of Estate Management Report *Flats as a Way of Life* (1994) p 41 "ownership of the freehold ... does not appear to significantly affect the rating of management performance."

27 Alice Christudason, *op cit, supra*, p 355. The primacy of individual ownership and the need to satisfy the desire for it has a long progeny: see R von Jhering, *Geist des Römischen Rechts*, 6th edn (1907) Vol II, p 227; it appears in *Commonhold, Freehold Flats*, Cm 179 (1987), hereafter "Aldridge Committee", para 1.19; there are similar sentiments in *Copropriété and Commonhold*, by Union Internationale du Notoriat Latin (1996) p 11 (I am grateful to Professor W Mincke for supplying me with a copy of this Report).

28 See the matters set out by PH Kenny in "Commonhold Again" [1996] Conv 321.

29 The most comprehensive work analysing the world-wide position is that of CG van der Merwe, *Apartment Ownership*, ch 5 of Vol VI *Property and Trusts* in *International Encyclopaedia of Comparative Law* (1994).

30 Scot Law Com No 162, *supra*, para 2.3, repeating a rejection in an earlier Discussion Paper of 1991 (at paras 5.14-5.17). As to the current tenement law, see Kenneth GC

Reid *The Law of Property in Scotland* (1996) paras 227-51.

31   The Aldridge Committee, para 1.4 identified the "period of unmortgageability" as generally 40-45 years.

32   Part I of the Landlord and Tenant Act 1987 as amended by the Housing Act 1996 s 92 and Sched 6.

33   Draft Commonhold Bill 1996 cll 1 and 2.

34   Although cl 1(1) of the 1996 Draft Commonhold Bill reflects the desire for an absolute freehold, the true position is that adopted by van der Merwe, *op cit*, para 48, citing from J Bärmann's first commentary on the *Wohnungseigentumsgesetz* of 1951. Bärmann's view, repeated in the 7th edn (1997) p 87, of his commentary, is that flat *eigentum* has a threefold aspect: individual ownership of the unit, joint ownership of the land and membership of an association; and that none of these elements are separable. *Contra*, M Junker *Die Gesellschaft nach dem Wohnungseigentumsgesetz* (1993) pp 3-4, seemingly to the effect that a co-owner is cut off from ownership in the common parts. Bärmann's view has however been adopted judicially: Bay ObLG 9.2.1965; BGHZ 49 (1968) 250 at p 251.

35   The type of structure which may have triggered the setting up of the Nugee Committee may well have been that in which a landlord personally or through his own management company is responsible for repairs and maintenance to the common parts.

36   See *eg* the Aldridge Committee Report, para 1.14.

37   CEM Paper 1994, *supra*, ch 3 esp para 3.2.4.

38   In France, ownership attaches to the thing controlled by the person and not to an estate: hence, the difficulties experienced for common ownership in England from the abolition by s 34 of the Law of Property Act 1925 of legal but not equitable tenancies in common (and see *Bull v Bull* [1955] 1 QB 234) cannot exist in such systems, where estates are unheard of. See further CG van der Merwe and MJ de Waal, *The Law of Things and Servitudes* (1993) para 19.

39   By article 2 of the 1965 *loi*, incorporating by reference ("*sont privatives les parties des bâtiments ... réservées à l'usage exclusif d'un copropriétaire déterminé*") the terms of art 544 of the *Code Civil*.

40   *Le Monde*, 14-17th March, 1984, *Enquête Doyère*; also E Kischewsky-Broquisse, *La Copropriété des Immeubles Bâtis*, 4th edn (1989) no 596.

41   Alice Christudason, *op cit*, *supra*, p 354.

42   Committee Report, paras 1.19-1.20.

43   Part I of the Leasehold Reform, Housing and Urban Development Act 1993.

44   Part I of the Landlord and Tenant Act 1987.

45   *Denetower Ltd v Toop* [1991] 1 WLR 945 at p 952G (Sir Nicolas Browne-Wilkinson V-C) at p 668, which in *Belvedere Court Management v Frogmore Developments Ltd* [1997] QB 858 at p 881C, was described by Sir Thomas Bingham MR as an "understated criticism". That seems justified in the light of *eg* the poor drafting of s 4(2) of the Act, exposed in *Michaels v Harley House (Marylebone) Ltd* [1997] 1 WLR 967, and only partly plugged by the Housing Act 1996 s 90(1).

46   The length of the leading commentary, that of DN Clarke, *Leasehold Enfranchisement* (1994) suggests that the 1993 Act is not a simple measure.

47   By Hill "Freehold Flats in French Law" [1985] Conv 337 and, in a comparative context, by van der Merwe, *op cit, passim*.

48   Art 664, repealed by the law of 28th June, 1938.

49   It applied only if no contrary provision was made. The provision essentially gave common ownership to the roof and main walls, with separate titles to each floor owner. It had been adopted prior to 1900 in Baden-Baden and also, with modifications, in Bavaria (see *Redaktoren zum BGB*, *infra*, p 53; also Leyser, *infra*, pp 33-34).

50   See WW Buckland, *Main Institutions of Roman Law* (1931) ch XV no 105; also M Kaser, *Römisches Privatrecht* (1971) pp 410-412. Such is the "prevailing view", according to van der Merwe, *op cit*, no 2, noting that certain texts in the *Digest*, *eg* D.8.2.36; D.8.4.6.1., could be interpreted differently. JC van Oven, *Leerboek van Romeinsch Privatrecht* (1948) p 58, thinks that we do not have sufficient information on which to form a judgment one way or the other.

51   See Leyser "Ownership of Flats - A Comparative Survey" (1958) 7 ICLQ 31. Some *coutumes* were oral: Kischewsky-Broquisse, *op cit*, no 13, citing Nantes, Rennes and Grenoble. Not surprisingly, on the other side of the Rhine, especially where local law had been subject to French infusions, there were similar *Gewohnheitsrechten*: *eg* that of Würtemburg, noted in *Vorentwürfe*, *infra*, p 53.

52   There seems some uncertainty as to which cities had such customs. HL Mazeaud, J Mazeaud and F Chabas, *Leçons de Droit Civil* 8th edn (1994), no 1324: "*avant la Révolution la copropriété par étages n'était en usage qu'à Grenoble et à Rennes*"; but van der Merwe, *op cit*, no 3, gives more details and mentions also Orléans and Lyons and the adoption in "many French customs" of the Rennes scheme of 1720.

53   See *eg* Challis, *Law of Real Property* 3rd edn (1911) p 218; *Bradford Corporation v Pickles* [1895] AC 587; *Stephens v Anglian Water Authority* [1987] 1 WLR 1381, esp at p 1387 (Slade LJ).

54   See Alice Christaduson, *op cit*, *supra*, p 364.

55   By art 544 of the *Civil Code*, "*la propriété est le droit de jouir et disposer des choses de la manière la plus absolue...*" which is only qualified, in a phrase inserted as a last-minute thought, by the need to observe any laws and regulations.

56   "The Tribonian of Napoleon's commission" (*pace Justinian's Institutes*, Birks and McCleod (1987), p 23), cited in G Marty and P Reynaud, *Droit Civil, Biens*, 2nd edn (1980) no 35 thus: "*on a toujours tenu pour maxime libérale que la propriété individuelle du Code Civil est considérée comme faisant partie de l'ordre naturel et même divin, que des domaines des particuliers sont des propriétés sacrées qui doivent être respectées par le souverain lui-même*". The confusion between hostility to confiscation of private property by the State, causing a blending of absolute and unlimited rights is clear, and might be said to be only of reduced modern importance, having regard to their planning law. However, an absolutist spirit underpins art 2 of the *Déclaration des Droits de l'Homme et du Citoyen*.

57   See Robert, n to Cass civ 3e 9 mars 1994, D 1994 somm 162.

58   J Carbonnier, *Droit Civil*, Vol 3, p 122; G Marty and P Reynaud, *Droit Civil, Biens*, 3rd edn (1995) no 33; *cf* however HL Mazeaud, J Mazeaud and F Chabas, *op cit*, nos 1335 and 1338. P Malaurie and L Aynès, *Droit Civil, Les Biens*, (1990) no 405 is more reserved and draws attention to the historical evolution of Roman conceptions, as well as to restrictions on private owners' rights in the public and in neighbouring owners' interests.

59   A Rodger, *Owners and Neighbours in Roman Law*, (1972) p 3.

60 A Rodger, *op cit*, ch 1 *passim*: thus at p 1 reference is made to the "intensely individualistic spirit" of the nineteenth-century German authors cited in the next note. There is of course contemporary evidence to suggest that at the close of the twentieth century we have re-entered that rugged spirit. Thus Mrs M Thatcher commented in relation to s 1 of the Housing Act 1980 (conferring a right to buy on council tenants) that it created a "compulsory right" (see PF Smith, *Housing Act 1980*, (1981) p 83).

61 A similar rigorous individualism pervades FK von Savigny, *System des Heutigen Römischen Rechts* (1840) Vol 1, esp p 367; and Pandektists such as B Windscheid, *Lehrbuch des Pandektenrechts*, 4th edn (1875) no 167 (repeated unaltered *eg* the 7th and 9th editions; see also J Baron, *Pandekten* (1897) Book II, p 234*ff*) and it prevailed, with some modifications, noted by Jones, *infra*, in the 1900 German civil code in preference to the supposedly more socially-oriented native German view, which is examined in O Gierke's *Deutches Genossenshaftsrecht* (1879) and indeed to his horror: see O Gierke, *Zur Entwurf eines Bürgerlichen Gesetzbuches* (1889) esp pp 281-282. Jones "Expropriation in Roman Law" (1929) XLV LQR 512, examines restrictions on owners' rights in the public interest, some of which, *eg* in relation to road-buildings, went beyond mere balancing of neighbourly relations.

62 *Op cit, supra*, p 520.

63 As to the derivation of which see notably M Kaser, *Eigentum und Besitz im Alterem Römischen Recht* 2nd edn (1956), pp 308-309.

64 WW Buckland, *Main Institutions of Roman Law* (1931) ch VI no 32.

65 For other possible explanations of the expression see Getzler "Roman Ideas of Ownership", ch 3 in *Land Law - Themes and Perspectives, supra*.

66 WW Buckland, *Textbook of Roman Law* (1963, ed Stein) LXVIII. A different explanation is that of HR Hagemann (*Handwörterbuch des Deutches Rechtgeschichte* (1971) Vol 1, p 886) at least in relation to Justinian, *viz*, that the expression was solely to do with inheritance.

67 It appears that Vulgar law reverted to the pre-Classical, less individualistic and less abstract view of ownership: M Kaser, *Eigentum und Besitz, supra*, p 247.

68 M Kaser, *Eigentum und Besitz, supra*, p 3*ff*. He claims that *vindicatio rei* was until then not a demand for a thing. The position in Ancient Greek law, is examined by M Kaser, *Der Altgriechische Eigentumsschutz* ZSS (1944), 134, basing his arguments on their personal procedure to reclaim possession; also H Wieling, "The History of the Ownership of Land", in *The Public Concept of Land Ownership* (1996) Vol 43, pp 14-17; as to some possible reasons for the non-proprietary claim in ancient Roman law, see O Karlowa, *Römische Rechtsgeschichte* (1901) Vol II, pp 345-360, including *eg* the fact that in early times the tribe held most land and allowed a *paterfamilias* to have a house and strip of land surrounding it which his family could inherit.

69 Indeed the misconception about Roman ownership under the Republic or the Empire may be thanks to the thirteenth century glossators: see *eg Handwörterbuch, supra*, p 886. It may be that the Vulgar law, under Christian influence, which regarded the ultimate owner of all property as God, would not have adopted an absolutist view in any case, but *cf* the moral justification for private property given by St Thomas Aquinas, cited by JM Kelly, *A Short History of Western Legal Theory*, (1992) p 152.

70 See Buckland, *Main Institutions, supra*, ch VI no 35 "that a man can do as he will with his own has never been true of any system of law".

71 It seems that in this period we cannot speak of rights: see HF Jolowicz, *Roman*

Foundations of Modern Law (1957) p 67; also F Schulz, *Classical Roman Law* (1951) p 336.

72   Not to mention those existing in public law, as to which see Jones, *op cit, supra*; also de Fresquet *"Principes de l'Expropriation pour Cause d'Utilité Publique à Rome et à Constantinople"* (1860) 6 Revue Historique du Droit Français et Etranger 97, citing *eg* the requirement that riparian owners allow navigation (p 97) and taxing those who cut back fruiting trees to avoid tax to the same extent as if they had not done so (p 124).

73   Even Windscheid admits these: see *Lehrbuch, supra,* no 169; a clear statement is that of P Gérard, *Manuel Elémentaire de Droit Romain* (1929) 8th edn no II, pp 276-279 (*eg* noting the fact that a neighbour could enter land adjoining his to collect fruit falling from his trees) and see *passim* Rodger, *op cit,* notably as to *aquae pluviae arcendae*; Kaser, *Römisches Privatrecht, supra,* nos 135*ff* and 404*ff.*

74   It is curious how at the same time French jurisprudence recognises the principle of abuse of rights (rejected by English law see, *eg, Bradford Corporation v Pickles, supra*): see, *eg,* Req 15 août 1915, S 1920 1 300; Pau 30 9 1986, D 1989, somm 32, obs Robert. *Cf* also Mazeaud, Mazeaud and Chabas, no 1338, citing an *arrêt* of the Parlement of Aix of 1 2 1577.

75   There is a review of the original 48-article *Loi* of 1965 by Esmein, Gaz Pal 1968 2 Doctr 38. For a full list of amendments to July 1992 of the law, see van der Merwe, *op cit,* pp 214-215.

76   Mazeaud, Mazeaud and Chabas, no 1324.

77   Kischewsky-Broquisse, *op cit,* nos 6 and 7.

78   Noted by Mazeaud, Mazeaud and Chabas, no 1324; also in England and Wales by College of Estate Management Paper *Is the Cure Worse than the Disease?* (1990) para 4.4.2.

79   According to F Givord and C Giverdon, *La Copropriété,* 4th edn (1992) no 1. The *Enquête Doyère, supra,* claims that no-one is really sure as to exact numbers. There is little doubt about the popularity of this form of apartment ownership in Germany: thus in Bärmann *et al, op cit* (7th edn) p 31, it is said that by 1987 there were some 1,827,856 unit holders.

80   See van der Merwe, *op cit,* p 25; Kischewsky-Broquisse, *op cit,* no 93; Mazeaud, Mazeaud and Chabas, *op cit,* no 1326; Bournias, *"Les Formes Juridiques de la Propriété d'Etage ou d'Appartement en Droit Comparé"* Revue Internationale de Droit Comparé, 1979, 583-601.

81   Law of 1965, arts 1, 2 and 3. Therefore, the unit holder cannot dispose of his share in the common parts separately from his unit, so emphasising, in theory, the integration of his unit with the whole: *cf* C Atias, *La Copropriété Immobilière,* (1995) p 10.

82   Law of 1965, art 22.

83   These matters are discussed in *eg* Hill, *supra,* pp 337-338.

84   Law of 1965, art 8; see *eg* TGI Grenoble 24 2 1967, D 1967 352; the description by law of the nature of the *règlement* is, however, that it is contractual.

85   Law of 1965, art 11 and 26.

86   Law of 1965 art 24.

87   Law of 1965 art 26c, as amended by *Loi* no 92-653 of 13th July, 1992. See *passim* Kischewsky-Broquisse, *op cit,* no 598*ff.* As a concession to reality, certain essential improvements, *eg* installation of energy consumption measuring facilities, may be passed by a simple majority vote: art 25g, excepted from art 26c. Hill, *op cit,* pp 347-

349, notes a familiar problem at common law (*cf* cases such as *Pearlman v Keepers and Governors of Harrow School* [1979] 1 All ER 365 at pp 369j-370a (Lord Denning MR): there is no clear line between repairs (*entretien*) and improvements: also Givord and Giverdon, no 633. The respect for individual rights is confirmed by the right of a co-owner to apply to a Tribunal de Grande Instance for a declaration that in Hill's words, he is to be exempted from having to contribute towards the cost of the improvement, as to which see Kischewsky-Broquisse, *op cit*, nos 664-667. It seems consistent with the French exaltation of private rights that an owner who is declared not liable to contribute to a "sumptuous" improvement, *eg* unnecessary garden embellishments, may still benefit from it, free of charge, in contrast to those who voted for it, who must contribute to the cost of the work.

88   The difficulties of classification are discussed by Morand, Gaz Pal 1968 29. See also TGI Nice, 7 6 1967 D 1968 441.

89   As defined in 1996 Draft Bill cl 15(9).

90   The French *Loi* of 1965 provides no detailed list of duties, beyond saying that the *syndicat* (body as a whole) of co-owners has as one object that of maintaining the building (art 14). There is an obvious contrast to detail of the commonhold proposals.

91   1996 Draft Bill Sched 5 paras 1 and 2.

92   See *eg* 1996 Draft Commonhold Bill cll 1 and 2.

93   Draft Bill of 1996, Sched 5. These include a duty to keep the common parts in repair, to decorate them, to provide cleaning and lighting thereto (para 1).

94   1996 Draft Bill cl 2(3).

95   Report, para 1.21.

96   *Apartment Ownership, supra,* para 332.

97   "*Nombreux sont les copropriétaires qui, ayant acheté un apartement, n'ont pas eu conscience qu'ils entraient dans un univers de relations et de décisions collectives*": *Enquête Doyère, Le Monde,* 14th March, 1984. Also Atias, "*Propriété et Communauté dans la Copropriété des Immeubles Bâtis*" JCP 1980 I 2971 no 4.

98   Also by *ibid,* art 9; "*chaque copropriétaire dispose des parties privatives comprises dans son lot; il use et jouit librement des parties privatives*".

99   As opposed to his share or quote-part in the parties communes, which he cannot alienate separately from the unit itself (law of 1965 art 4).

100   *Enquête Doyère, Le Monde,* 14th March, 1984 "*les gens ne sont pas prêts à vivre cette démocracie de fait*".

101   In contrast to that of Germany: the 1951 law is based on a community of unit holders and not as in France and as proposed in England, an association: Bärmann "*Das Wohnungseigentumsgesetz*" 1951 NJW 292. The psychological difference is indefinable but real.

102   Atias, "*Propriété et Communauté dans la Copropriété des Immeubles Bâtis*", JCP 1980 I 2971 no 4.

103   In addition to matters already mentioned, see *eg* Mazeaud Mazeaud and Chabas, *op cit, supra,* no 1329, stigmatising art 30 of the 1965 law, allowing for making certain useful improvements (such as installing new gas central heating: TGI Bobigny 18 6 1986 JCP 1987 II 2084) against the opposition of a recalcitrant minority of *copropriétaires,* as "*une atteinte grave aux droits des copropriétaires*".

104   College of Estate Management Study, *Is the Cure Worse than the Disease?* (1990) para 5.4. Under "Apathy reigns supreme", it is said "most owners want some unpaid

volunteer to make decisions for them rather than attend Board or annual membership meetings". As to the current state of condominium legislation in the USA, see van der Merwe, para 14, pp 9-10; R Cunningham, W Stoebuck and D Whitman, *Law of Property*, (1993) pp 32-33.

105   The Scottish Law Commission mention that "the enemy of good management is apathy" and that "experience shows that owners of flats are often reluctant to attend meetings or otherwise to play an active part in the management of the building" (Scot Law Com No 162 para 6.11).

106   The most concise, recent and useful analysis of the duties and liabilities of a *syndic* is that of M Weismann, *Copropriété*, 15th edn (1995) pp 89-108.

107   *Eg* that he may engage and dismiss personnel to carry out works: decree of 17th March, 1967 art 31: in the teeth of objections from the *syndicat* of co-owners; Civ 3e 3 10 1969 D 1970 202, n Givord.

108   Law of 1965 art 21, inserted by *Loi* no 85-1470 of 31st December, 1985, art 4, which in most cases is compulsory, in contrast to the pre-1985 position. Members of this body are selected from the members of the general assembly of owners. The best treatment of the whole area is that of Kischewsky-Broquisse, *op cit*, nos 519-535. She questions the usefulness of these *conseils* in relation to developments with less than six units and thinks them essential with larger (over 60 unit) developments.

109   The success of this measure may be questioned since the Reform Commission which has put forward proposals for technical rather then fundamental changes to the French rules, and whose proposals are set out in Weismann, *op cit*, Annex, suggested reforms of the detailed presentation and content of annual accounts to be presented by a *syndic* to the general assembly meeting.

110   *Eg* by presenting an annual report to the general assembly, which is not obligatory: Givord and Giverdon no 544.

111   Atias, *Copropriété*, p 53. However, this point does not seem to be made in the extensive analysis of Givord and Giverdon, nos 533-545.

112   Para 8.48. Their measure of the smallest developments was a maximum of six units.

113   Perhaps because leasehold and presumably also commonhold management committee members would not be remunerated and have to have an essentially consultative role.

114   Aldridge Committee Report, para 8.48.

115   Draft Bill 1996 Sched 2 paras 2 and 3.

116   At least in relation to Tenement Scheme B, which seems the nearest to *copropriété* or the commonhold proposals: Scot Law Com No 162 para 6.16.

117   Report, *supra*, para 6.17, even in relation to larger Scheme B.

118   Report (1998) para 6.11. In contrast it seems to the commonhold proposals, a Scottish manager would be paid and his duties would be listed.

119   Givord and Giverdon no 518 citing *eg* Civ 3e 30 11 1971, JCP IV 11. However, it is easier to see why it is open to a general assembly to reject an annual plan which provides for works beyond maintenance (as required to be submitted by law of 1965 art 18) though the difference between say repairs and work beyond that has been explored by litigation, see *eg* Versailles 28 6 1988, D 1988 IR 263 (one test being the time it takes to finish the work); also Paris 12 10 1974, D 1974 IR 72 (replacing boiler equals a running repair); Paris 1 6 1981, D 1982 IR 146 (same result for replacing boiler). See Kischewsky-Broquisse, Gaz Pal 1994 I doctr 455.

120   Which continues, as shown by *eg* the recommendations of their Reform Commission

as to Co-ownership, as to the allocation of central heating charges, cited in Weismann, *op cit*, pp 272-275.

121 It is not clear what might happen if a *syndic* were appointed for a shorter period.

122 Aix-en-Provence 31 10 1996 D 1998 somm 119, n Atias, noting that the formal limit applies even if the whole *syndicat* of owners has acquiesced to informal management without a formal three-year appointment.

123 Civ 3e 30 11 1971 JCP IV 11; seemingly, the machinery for appointing a provisional administrator of art 46 of the decree of 1967 had not been operated.

124 However, the Scots Law Commission, in their Report, *supra*, just stop short of suggesting a mandatory fixed period of office for a Scheme B manager: para 6.14.

125 The problem of collecting arrears of charges has been labelled as an obsession for French managers by Kischewsky-Broquisse, *op cit*, no 177, suggesting the existence of a fresh source of problems in that country; see also Calfan, "*Les risques d'impayés dans la copropriété*" Gaz Pal 1983 II doctr 436.

126 "Freehold Flats in French Law" [1985] Conv 337 at p 349. Also van der Merwe, *op cit*, no 332.

127 Report, para 9.1.

128 1996 Draft Bill cl 22(1)-(3) and Sched 6.

129 As to this, see *passim* L Crabb *op cit, supra*.

130 1996 Draft Bill Sched 6 paras 5-11.

131 1996 Draft Bill Sched 6 paras 14-20.

132 Hill *op cit*, p 350; Mazeaud Mazeaud and Chabas, no 1330.

133 For other remedies, including the legal hypothec of the association on all debts owed to it by an owner for the last five years see *eg* Kischewsky-Broquisse, *op cit*, nos 178-182 and 199-200.

134 See *passim* Souleau, n to Paris 16 2 1976, D 1977 637; also Hill, *loc cit*, p 350.

135 See *passim* Givord and Giverdon no 328; Cass Civ 3e 20 6 1972, JCP 1972 II 17202.

136 As where a lessor covenants not to withhold his consent to the assignment or sub-letting of a leasehold interest, such consent not to be unreasonably withheld, where financial security of a proposed assignee is an obvious ground of concern to the landlord: see L Crabb, *Leases Covenants and Consents* (1991) pp 88-94.

137 Law of 10th July 1965 art 10. As a further safeguard to unit holders, each item of service for which a charge is payable should be set out in the *règlement de copropriété*: Lyon 12 2 1976, JCP 1976 II 18437, n Guillot.

138 Cass Civ 3e 17 3 1971, D 1971 somm 133 (lift not used by ground floor owner); Civ 3e 18 7 1979 D 1980 IR 238 and Paris 26 5 1989 D 1990 somm 131 (wages of concierge in different building to that of co-owner not chargeable to latter). This *jurisprudence* seems to be consistent: *eg* Cass Civ 3e 19 2 1976, D 1976 543; Cass Civ 29 11 1977, D 1978 522, n Souleau; Cass Civ 8 11 1991, JCP 1994 IV 590. For *doctrine* see *eg* Morand Gaz Pal 1966, doctr 81; Givord and Giverdon, nos 271 and 275.

139 Paris 5 7 1977, D 1978 IR 294, n Giverdon (stairs and hall cleaning); also Cass Civ 28 10 1983, D 1984 313.

140 Despite the fact that such exist at common law in the field of landlord and tenant, where the interest of the lessee may be less substantial than that of a freehold unit holder: see *Pole Properties Ltd v Fineberg* (1981) 43 P&CR 121.

141 See *Finchbourne v Rodrigues* [1976] 3 All ER 581, esp at pp 586-587 (Cairns LJ)

(service charges payable by 125 year lessee of flat in respect of maintenance).

142   See *eg* Aldridge Committee, paras 9.5-9.7.

143   Commonhold unit holders would have less protection in respect of information and loss of their units than that awarded to lessees, *eg* by Landlord and Tenant Act 1985 ss 18-30 (information); Law of Property Act 1925 s 146(2) (relief against forfeiture); Housing Act 1996 ss 81-82 (prevention of abuse of powers to collect service charges from long leaseholders whose former landlord had failed to build up a sinking fund for maintenance).

144   "*Les divergences d'intérêts entrainent entre les copropriétaires une mésentente qui ... est beaucoup plus sensible qu'entre propriétaires autonomes*": Kischewsky-Broquisse, *op cit*, no 15.

145   The absence from the commonhold proposals of a general right in the owners' association to exclude an undesirable unit holder from the scheme such as exists in the *Wohnunseigentumsgesetz* (art 18) - explained by H Weitnauer, *Wohnungseig-entumsgesetz*, 8th ed (1995), p 352 as necessary precisely because the relationship between unit owners is indissoluble, and with a view to avoiding the endless unbearable conflicts associated with *Stockwerkeigentum* - is a serious lacuna best explicable by English attachment to absolute ownership.

146   But not impossible, as the schemes mentioned throughout van der Merwe's book, *supra*, seem to show. However, it should not be forgotten the drafters of the 1900 German Civil Code rejected *Stockwerkeigentum* schemes, a primitive form of commonhold, as inconsistent with ownership and as productive, by reason of the indissoluble nature of the relations between owners, of many unhappy disputes: *Vorentwürfe der Redaktoren zum BGB* Vol I (1982) ed R Johow pp 52-54.

147   In addition to the *Enquête Doyère*, *supra*, see *passim* the 73rd Rapport des Notaires de France (1976).

148   See *eg* the proposals in Scot Law Com No 162 in relation to Scheme A tenements, paras 5.33-5.39, which are claimed to be relatively simple, a view supported by the fact that a distinction is drawn between a need to notify an owner, formally or otherwise, and an ability to make decisions without a full meeting of owners.

149   The problem is compounded by the narrow interpretation of art 42 of the 1965 *Loi*. A two-month time-limit to challenges applies, apparently to prevent paralysis of decision-making (Notaires' Report, *supra*, p 87); but it has no application to assembly decisions which interfere with private rights: Bayonne 4 11 1974, JCP 1975 II 17951.

150   Which must be drawn up by the developer or in default the general assembly: 1965 *Loi* art 8. See as to the contents of the *règlement*, Hill, *supra*, pp 338-339.

151   Such a limitation is taken by jurisprudence to be contrary to the property rights of art 2 of the 1965 *Loi*: Civ 11 3 1971, D 1971 427; also *eg* Cass Civ 3e 6 3 1973, Gaz Pal 1973 2 427; Paris, 30 11 1979, D 1980 IR 128.

152   Report, para 7.20; also Draft Bill of 1996, cl 7.

153   As in *Re Buchanan-Wollaston's Conveyance* [1939] Ch 738.

154   *Wohnungseigentumsgesetz*, 1950, art 12; see further Weitnauer, *op cit*, pp 266-277.

155   It is conceded that this would raise difficult questions of fact (*cf* Bay Ob LG NJW 1973 152) and risk conflict with the traditional principle of making conveyancing easier.

156   Thus the Aldridge Committee para 6.3, "A unit holder is entirely free to sell the complete commonhold unit", and they contrast the position of leaseholders, where the

landlord's consent may be requisite.

157 See further *eg* Hill "Freehold Flats in French Law" [1985] Conv 337, pp 338-339.

158 As to the binding effect of the *règlement* on purchasers in due course, see law of 1965 art 13; Givord and Giverdon, nos 388-390; Civ 3e 14 11 1985, D 1986 368. It is assumed that a unit tenant would be bound by a use clause in the *règlement de copropriété*, but for doubts see Dagot, JCP 1967 I 2108.

159 Report of 73 Congress of Notaries (1976), p 154.

160 Law of 1965, art 26; Givord and Giverdon no 363; Civ le 7 5 1962, JCP 1962, II 12829; even in the case of changes to the use *etc* of common parts, a qualified majority vote of all unit holders is required.

161 A further complication in the French system is that some *règlements* apparently do not contain any statement as to the *destination* of the property, whereupon this must be discovered *aluinde*, *eg* from the description of the premises, as to which see further Hill, *supra*, p 343, or by inference (as in Bastia 3 4 1979, D 1980 IR 446).

162 Example of the Congress of Notaires, *supra*, p 178.

163 Scot Law Com No 162, *Report on the Law of Tenement* (1998) para 5.3. - although in the context of their proposed tenement Scheme A, this point seems of general value.

164 Report, para 7.3; likewise 1996 Draft Bill, cll 6 and 7.

165 There are provisions in Chapter IV ss 69-75 of Part I of the Leasehold Reform *etc* Act 1993 to reflect the importance of this point; see P Matthews and D Millichap's *A Guide to the Leasehold Reform, Housing and Urban Development Act 1993*, (1993) ch 6; also the commentary of PH Kenny in Current Law Statutes.

166 The 1965 law does not outlaw any leasing, and Kischewsky-Broquisse, *op cit*, no 277 considers the issue hardly worth discussing, although she cites an unreported decision of the Cour d'Appel de Lyon of 22 1 1969 which annulled a clause in a by-law which required any lease to be submitted to the *conseil syndicale*. According to Weismann, *op cit*, p 15, a lease should be in conformity with the general character or *destination* of the building.

167 Draft Bill 1996 cl 2(3).

168 Aldridge Committee, para 6.6.

169 DN Clarke "Commonhold - A Prospect of Promise" *supra*, p 500.

170 As opposed to the giving of notice to the commonhold association, as suggested by Aldridge, para 6.6.

171 Settled Land Act 1925 s 41.

172 The protection conferred by the restrictions was strictly limited having regard to Settled Land Act 1925 s 110 in favour of "purchasers"; see *Cheshire & Burn's Modern Law of Real Property* 15th edn (1994) pp 815-817.

173 There seems to be nothing in the Report of the 73rd Congress of Notaries on this point nor in the Reform Commission of Co-ownership, *supra*.

174 And for that matter the German principles, except that according to Bärmann *et al*, *op cit*, p 372, a lease of a residential apartment cannot in principle be for non-residential purposes, unless these are "quiet or not injurious". This affords a further example of the community-minded spirit of German law. Wieling, *op cit*, refers at p 34 to the fact that Germany is a social state, as laid down by arts 24 and 28 of the German Basic Law.

175 For other solutions to leasing problems, see van der Merwe, *loc cit*, para 87, citing *eg* the Condominium Act 1979 (BC) s 30, allowing adoption of a by-law limiting the

number of flats which may be leased, with protection of owners caused hardship thereby. The voluntary approach will be noticed: it is the compulsion of the 1996 commonhold proposals to which objection is taken.

176   D Cuisine, in "Copropriété and Commonhold", *supra*, Appendix B, no 17.

177   Scot Law Com No 162 (1998) para 3.6., favouring leaving as much of the current law of tenement undisturbed as possible.

178   Albeit suffering from some difficulties, as to which see Kenneth CG Reid, *The Law of Property in Scotland*, *supra*; also Scottish Law Commission Report on the Law of Tenement, *supra*, paras 2.13-2.19.

179   Scottish Law Commission Report, *supra*, para 3.8.

180   It is worth noting the frequency with which the 1965 regime has needed amendment, as discussed by van der Merwe, *passim*. We may cite *eg* the amendments of art 22 by décret No 86-768 (provisions for a *conseil syndicale*); art 29, by *ibid*, in relation to fees payable to a *syndic*.

181   *Cf Becker Properties Ltd v Garden Court NW8 Property Co Ltd* [1998] 1 EGLR 121, at p 124H (Lands Tribunal, Judge Marder QC): "the house tenant [enfranchising] gains complete control ... the flat tenant ... gains one vote in 13 in the management of the block and remains liable for contributions".

182   Especially, if the German evidence is to be believed, in relation to developments with 60 units or more: Diester, "*Zwanzig Jahre Wohnungseigentum*" 1971 NJW 1153, p 1156.

183   Ian Ferrier, Tax Editors' Notes, [1998] Conv 153 (in the context of professional negligence claims). In France many of the cases reported under Co-Ownership are about the 1965 law; there are specialist journals dealing mainly with such matters both in France and in Germany; Diester, *op cit*, *supra*, p 1154 notes a steady if not rapid increase in litigation on the *Wohnungseigentumsgesetz*. It may be that litigiousness is a feature of co-owned property: this was the view of St Thomas Aquinas, cited in Kelly, *op cit*, *supra*, p 152; it was also, as noted earlier, the reason for the rejection by the drafters of the 1900 German Civil Code of *Stockwerkeigentum* schemes.

184   The principles as to states in both countries are considered throughout van der Merwe, *supra*, mainly under "Anglo-American" rubrics.

185   It seems from the DETR Consultation Paper, *supra*, that the government, at a stage not yet fixed, intends to proceed with this reform "path", *eg* by easing the qualifying rules for enfranchisement (para 2.6-7), more or less in parallel with introducing commonholds.

8 The Proposed Commonhold Association - A Company Law Perspective

LETITIA CRABB

The relative merits of leasehold and commonhold from the point of view of property lawyers and property professionals have already been addressed by official bodies, interest groups and academics far better qualified than the writer.[1] The relative merits of leasehold and commonhold from the point of view of a company lawyer have received less attention. They are however the subject of this paper. From a company law perspective, do the current commonhold proposals represent an improvement on the existing leasehold mechanism?[2] The proposals are interesting because they involve a new corporate form: the commonhold association. New forms of incorporation are rare - not as rare as a tenure spawning a sub-tenure[3] - but rare all the same. A proposal involving both of these is surprisingly bold. The easier thing to do would have been to use an existing form of incorporation as the vehicle of commonhold. This paper focuses first of all upon the rejection of the registered company, then upon the brief for its replacement, and then upon the 1996 Bill. Finally a conclusion will be expressed as to the adequacy of the commonhold association as a vehicle for strata title.

Reasons for the Rejection of the Registered Company

The Aldridge Report concluded that the registered company was inappropriate.[4] In the first place a registered company is at the mercy of its creditors who can execute judgments against its assets (in the case of a leasehold flat management company, the freehold reversion and the common parts) and petition for a winding-up under section 122(1)(f) of the Insolvency Act 1986 on the ground that the company is unable to pay its debts.[5] It was hoped that commonholds could be protected from such inconvenient or unpredictable creditor intervention: in particular it should be impossible for a commonhold association to be wound up while the commonhold continues.[6]   In the second place the "detailed regulatory provisions" applicable to registered companies were thought to be unnecessary for a non-trading entity[7] and were the cause of much irritation to property managers who fell foul of them.[8]   The obligation to file an annual return[9] and the provisions relating to accounts and audit[10] caused particular resentment.

The Commonhold Association Brief

A reduction both in creditors' remedies and annual disclosure was therefore central to the commonhold association brief. It was however recognised that a price had to be paid for this reduction. The price was to be paid by the unit owners. The shield of limited liability was to be withdrawn and instead the members of a commonhold association were to have something between limited liability and unlimited liability which was termed "restricted liability".[11]   Other features were specified - the association was to be registered at the Land Registry rather than the Companies Registry so issues of title and compliance were united under one roof.[12]   The legislation was also to offer a "high level" of constitutional standardisation to avoid the variety and inadequacy of the provisions currently governing leasehold flat management companies.[13]   Such was the brief.

The Bill[14]

The Bill deals with all these areas and yet it seems to have been a disappointment. One[15] reason for this is the large volume of the insolvency provisions. A number of issues need to be addressed here:

1   Why are the insolvency provisions in the Commonhold Bill rather than somewhere else?
2   Are they needed at all?
3   Why are they so long?
4   What do they do?

1 Why Are the Insolvency Provisions in the Commonhold Bill?

Why not just incorporate the Insolvency Act 1986 by reference? This has been done where possible, but mostly it not possible because the commonhold association provisions, in accordance with the brief, forge a completely new relationship between the association, its members and its creditors. Many provisions are unique to the commonhold association - in particular those which restrict the remedies of the creditor over the commonhold association assets, withdraw the right to petition for a winding-up and introduce restricted liability.[16] Such novel concepts mean that other established insolvency mechanisms, like the administration order and the winding-up provisions, need substantial modification. The position of the creditors of a commonhold association is fundamentally different from the position of the creditors of a registered company. They cannot share the same insolvency regime. In any event the property sector wanted self-standing legislation.[17]

2 Are They Needed At All?

Insolvency would be rare because there are powerful provisions which minimise the risk to creditors. The association would normally meet its liabilities by levying service charges on the unit owners.[18] It can deal with defaulters by selling the unit, a power which has priority over mortgages whenever created.[19] Normally the threat of this would suffice to cause the unit owner to pay, but if not the proceeds of sale would usually be more than enough to cover arrears. In the rare case where they were not, the unit owner would remain personally liable to the association for the balance.[20] The unit itself is discharged.[21] However the operation of these mechanisms depends on effective management and it is widely acknowledged that the commonhold scheme cannot guarantee effective management. As noted in the 1990 College of Estate Management Research Paper[22] successful management depends not on the legal structure but the enthusiasm and ability of the individuals concerned. Commonhold schemes are not going to be immune from poor management and it is out of poor management that problems of non-payment will arise. In the event of non-payment, the Bill enables the creditor to sue the association but, in accordance with the brief, remedies are restricted. A judgment against the commonhold association cannot be executed against its land (the common parts) nor may such land be the subject of sequestration or a charging order.[23] No receiver may be appointed in respect of *any* commonhold association property.[24] Creditors who have extended credit for a reserve purpose[25] can be paid out of the relevant reserve fund: indeed their claim must be met from that source so far as is possible.[26] Where it is not so met, the fund can be the subject of execution,[27] attachment or sequestration in their favour.[28] Regulations will define reserve purposes[29] but they are expected to relate to major items of expenditure like renewal of a lift or boiler. While many large liabilities will fall into the reserve category, the provisions relating to the level and maintenance of the reserve fund are as yet too unspecific to enable one to predict the level of security that such funds would afford, especially if the association is caught in the vice of poor management. Other types of creditor, supplying more routine services (*eg* cleaning the common parts or maintaining the grounds) or involuntary creditors with a claim in tort against the association, cannot execute judgments against the reserve fund.[30] They may claim payment out of the general fund and in the event of non-payment levy execution against that fund if it has a balance. In a badly run commonhold it is quite likely that these limited remedies will prove inadequate. Then the unpaid creditor needs access to the protected commonhold assets (its land, and in the case of non-reserve purpose creditors, any surplus in the reserve fund) and to the restricted liability of the unit owners. The insolvency regime provides that access. It is therefore vital.

3 Why Are the Insolvency Provisions So Long?

In part this has already been answered: they redefine creditors' remedies against solvent associations and they constitute a self-standing insolvency regime. This cannot be done in a nutshell. A number of insolvency mechanisms have been stripped out of the commonhold regime - there is no voluntary arrangement, no receivership and, at the moment, no wrongful trading liability.[31] The scope for more pruning must be limited. Much detail has already been relegated to the Rules. In other jurisdictions the insolvency regime does seem to have a lower profile but there could be a number of reasons for this. If a form of association already recognised in that jurisdiction has been employed as the vehicle of the strata title scheme then the insolvency regime appropriate to that form may have been incorporated by reference. Less regulation may be required where creditors are subject to less risk as where, for example, non-payment of service charges is a criminal offence punishable by a daily fine[32] or where units owners have unlimited liability.[33] Finally it may be the case that the strata title scheme was introduced before the enactment of insolvency reforms comparable to the UK reforms of the mid-1980s. These are simply suggestions. One thing is clear: for a commonhold association to be acceptable here, it must fit into our insolvency regime. The fact that it does that is a plus not a minus.

4 What Do the Insolvency Provisions Do?

They provide creditors with access to the protected commonhold assets (its land, and in the case of non-reserve purpose creditors, surpluses in the reserve fund) and to restricted liability. Access is via the narrow gate of a commonhold administration order.[34] No creditor has a right to petition for a winding-up by the court,[35] but he can apply for a commonhold administration order. This, like its mainstream equivalent,[36] is a rescue procedure and as such particularly valuable in the context of a poorly managed commonhold.[37] A creditor has to show either that the association is falling down on its duties in relation to collection of service charges or that it is not paying its debts.[38] The court can make the order if satisfied that the application is well-founded and that the order would be likely to achieve either of the statutory purposes, namely -

(a) securing that the affairs of the association are put on a sound basis and that satisfactory arrangements are made for the future management of the association; and

(b) safeguarding the interests of the association's creditors and members pending determination by the commonhold administrator whether there is any reasonable prospect of achieving the purpose mentioned in paragraph (a).[39]

While the order is in force the association is run by the commonhold administrator.[40] If it appears to the administrator that the purpose of the order has been achieved he must apply for the order to be discharged,[41] and the court can make any order it thinks fit.[42] In a "type (a)" case, if the association has been put on a sound basis for the future, the court will doubtless order a discharge and the association will operate henceforth on the basis of service charge levies as intended. In a "type (b)" case, if the administrator determines that there is a reasonable prospect of putting the association on a sound basis, the court can vary the order to specify purpose (a). If however the administrator determines that there is no such reasonable prospect, the court may make some other order; perhaps, initially, adjourning for meetings of unit owners or creditors. If the commonhold association is irretrievably insolvent[43] the administrator must[44] apply for a winding-up order.[45] Creditors have no right to petition for winding-up.[46] They can only apply for a commonhold administration order which may result in a petition by the administrator. This restriction, coupled with the restrictions on executions,[47] represents a major concession to the commonhold lobby. It insulates commonhold schemes from the inconveniences occasioned by arbitrary action on the part of creditors. A price, namely "restricted liability", has to be paid for this concession.

Under the existing law applicable to flat management companies, in the event of insolvency, limited liability ensures that leaseholders have no liability to contribute to the assets of the company beyond the nominal value of their shares[48] or, in the case of a company limited by guarantee, the amount of their guarantee (usually £100).[49] Leaseholders have no direct liability for the debts of the management company, and their personal assets, including their lease, are safe from the claims of creditors.[50] The freehold reversion on the units and the ownership of the common parts may pass from their management company to some third party with perhaps unfortunate consequences in relation to the anticipated granting of new leases. This would put pressure upon the unit owners to meet the debts of the management company but they are under no liability to do so. Under the commonhold proposals limited liability is replaced with restricted liability. This means that while unit owners have no direct liability for the debts of the association, their personal assets, in particular the value of their unit, are exposed to creditors. In the event of an insolvent liquidation the value of the unit becomes available to creditors to the extent of the unit's allocated proportion of the liabilities.[51] Unit owners will know that proportion from the start; the actual amount, which could exceed the full value of the unit, only becomes apparent in the course of the winding-up. To the extent that some unit owners fail to satisfy their proportion of the liability, the loss falls on creditors[52] not other unit owners. This situation has been described as "a half way house between limited and unlimited liability".[53] In the case of unlimited liability calls can be made on members until the deficiency is covered. While advantageous to creditors, from a member's point of view this may well result in greater calls on those with greater resources. In the case of restricted liability calls cannot be made against a former unit owner once that unit owner has paid his or her due proportion of the deficiency.[54] The concept of restricted liability is therefore a unique compromise between the needs of creditors and unit owners.[55]

Conclusion

Viewing the commonhold association provisions broadly, they provide a number of important advantages over the current leasehold system. The disclosure and audit concessions are welcomed (though the concessions already in place for small registered companies may have been under appreciated).[56] There are real advantages in restricting creditors' rights against the commonhold property and in interposing the administration procedure between creditors and the winding-up remedy. There are other valuable features in the Aldridge proposals: the association is established and operated under the Land Registry[57] rather than the Companies Registry thus avoiding the necessity of dealing with two agencies and also avoiding what some would judge to be the contaminating effect of company law.[58] The commonhold association provisions also offer a standard constitution, and a "high level of standardisation" is an important aim of the commonhold scheme[59] in view of the current diversity and the difficulties to which it gives rise.[60]

The major disadvantage, it is submitted, is restricted liability. From a company law point of view the most significant feature of the commonhold association is the absence of limited liability. The reduction in public disclosure and in creditors' rights more than justifies its withdrawal but it remains to be seen whether the absence of such a popular device has a deterrent effect: restricted liability puts personal assets, including the value of the unit, at risk. The Aldridge rationalisation that restricted liability brings

> the ownership of a commonhold unit more into line with ownership of an
> ordinary freehold property, by protecting the unit owner from liability
> which ought, in fairness, be borne by his neighbour, while placing on him
> the responsibility for the whole of his fair share of liability just like any
> other freehold property owner.[61]

seems to underplay the realities of living in horizontally divided property. Such living involves constitutional arrangements[62] which necessarily deprive individual unit owners of full control over the running of the building.[63] Classifying the tenure as a type of freehold does not *per se* justify the imposition of freehold burdens. The risk faced by a unit owner is greater than that faced by ordinary freeholders: his fate is in the hands of others whose fraud or incompetence may cause him to lose his home.[64] The state of the common parts may give rise to claims in tort.[65] The imposition of a duty to insure[66] does not guarantee compliance. Specifying the qualifications of, and the indemnity to be provided by, members of the management committee will minimise but not eliminate the risk.[67] The plain fact is that, under these proposals, unit owners are exposed to a liability of an uncertain amount and that is not the case under the leasehold system.   This may not concern developers and funders, some of whom have advocated reform of the leasehold system:[68] from their point of view the other advantages of the scheme may outweigh what may be seen as a remote risk.   But while the proposals seem to be stalled it is perhaps useful to recall that the current leasehold scheme does at least afford limited liability and that one of its major disadvantages, the wasting character of the lease, has already been addressed.[69] If it is felt that restricted liability, and the necessarily lengthy and complex provisions to which it has given rise, can be sold to developers, funders, property lawyers and the public and piloted through Parliament, then so be it.   If there are doubts about this, and perhaps other features of the scheme which have not been examined here,[70] then there is no point in going ahead.   Other models should be sought based upon the familiar concepts of limited[71] or unlimited liability.[72]

Notes

1   Law Commission, *Commonhold: Freehold Flats and Freehold Ownership of Other Interdependent Buildings*. Report of a Working Group (Chairman Mr TM Aldridge) Cm 179 (1987) ("Aldridge Report"); *Commonhold: A Consultation Paper*, (with draft Bill attached), Cm 1345 (1990) ("1990 Consultation Paper"); *Commonhold: A Consultation Paper*, Lord Chancellor's Department, July 1996 ("1996 Consultation Paper"); DN Clarke, "A Prospect of Promise" (1995) 58 MLR 486; *Commonhold: Is the Cure Worse than the Complaint?*   Reading University College of Estate Management Research Paper No 90/93 ("CEM Paper 1990"); Reading University College of Estate Management Research Paper (1994), *Flats as a Way Of Life: Flat Management Companies in England and Wales*: A research project funded by the Joseph Rowntree Foundation ("CEM Paper 1994").

2   Leasehold flat management companies are examined in Plant, "Management Companies: How and Why?" (1991) Law Soc Gaz vol 88 no 21 p 24.

3   See Clarke (*supra* n 1), at p 496.

4   (*Supra* n 1): see para 8.12.

5   A state of affairs defined in s 123.

6   Aldridge Report (*supra* n 1), para 8.12.

7   *Ibid.*

8   See CEM Paper 1994 (*supra* n 1), at pp 65-66.

9   See Companies Act 1985, ss 363-365.

10   See Companies Act 1985, Part VII.

11   See 1990 Consultation Paper (*supra* n 1), para 3.14. See also Aldridge Report (*supra* n 1), paras 8.10-8.11; 1996 Consultation Paper (*supra* n 1), paras 4.2-4.3 (see also cl 38 and Sched 10 of the Bill).

12 See 1990 Consultation Paper (*supra* n 1), para 3.9.
13 *Ibid.*
14 In the version attached to 1996 Consultation Paper (*supra* n 1).
15 A fuller critique of the proposals can be found in DN Clarke, "A Prospect of Promise" (1995) 58 MLR 486.
16 See *infra*.
17 "[A] self-contained scheme for the establishment, conduct and dissolution of the commonhold association" (1990 Consultation Paper, *supra* n 1, para 3.9).
18 Cl 1(7)(b), cl 21 and cl 22.
19 Cl 22(9) and Sched 6 para 5.
20 Sched 6 para 9(5).
21 See Sched 6 para 9(4). It seems to be envisaged that irrecoverable arrears would fall on continuing unit owners in the form of higher service charges in the future: see cl 21(2)(c).
22 *Supra* n 1, para 1.6.
23 Cl 27(1) and (4).
24 Cl 27(5).
25 See cl 6(1)(b).
26 Cl 23(2). Other types of payment out cannot be made except by an order of the court under cl 24(7) which applies where there is a surplus.
27 Including the making of a charging order under the Charging Orders Act 1979, cl 27(4).
28 Cl 27(2) and (3).
29 Cl 6(1)(b).
30 Cl 27(2).
31 Cl 41(2)(d) facilitates the incorporation into the commonhold association regime by regulation of further provisions relating to insolvency and dissolution. The 1990 Consultation Paper (*supra* n 1, paras 3.15 and 3.17) envisages liability for fraudulent trading (compare s 213 Insolvency Act 1986 and s 458 Companies Act 1985). Imposition of liability for wrongful trading (see s 214 Insolvency Act 1986) may deter unit owners from active participation in management and would perhaps be an undue burden to impose on amateur managers.
32 Land Titles (Strata Title) Act Cap 158, s 42(11) (Singapore). See generally, NK Khublall, *Strata Titles* (Butterworths Asia, 1995).
33 As is proposed by the Scottish Law Commission: *Report on the Law of Tenement* (1998) (Scot Law Com No 162). Under Scheme B creditors have a right of direct recourse against members. This is achieved by allowing the creditor to impose a levy on the members as if he were the manager. In the event of a member being insolvent a further levy could be imposed upon the remaining members thus ensuring that the creditor is paid in full. See paras 6.47-6.54 and clause 10. Unlimited liability is also a feature of condominium liability in some jurisdictions of the USA (*Ruoff v Harbour Creek Community Association* 10 Cal App 4th 1624 (Calif, 1992)) and is a common feature world-wide (see CG van der Merwe, *International Encyclopaedia of Comparative Law*, Volume VI, *Property and Trust*, chapter 5, "Apartment Ownership", section 58.
34 Cls 29 and 30.
35 See cl 32(2).

36   See Insolvency Act 1986 Pt II.

37   The administration order procedure has been under-employed and to some extent misused in the context of trading companies. The reasons for this are complex and may need to be addressed as part of a reform of the general law. Some of them would be less applicable in the context of a commonhold association. (See Ian F Fletcher, *The Law of Insolvency* (2nd ed, 1996) chapter 16, especially pp 478-481).

38   Cls 29 and 30. The Secretary of State can apply on any of the grounds stated. Unit owners can apply on the more general ground of unfair prejudice. (Compare Companies Act 1985, s 459.)

39   Cl 30 (4) and (5). The relevant purpose must be stated in the order.

40   Cl 29(4); who must be qualified to act as an insolvency practitioner, see Sched 11 Pt III para 14.

41   Under cl 31(2).

42   Cl 31(3).

43   See cl 32(3).

44   Sched 8 Pt II para 11.

45   Under cl 32(2)(b). Any undischarged administration order ceases to have effect once the commonhold association goes into liquidation.

46   In extreme cases the Secretary of State can petition on the ground that it is expedient in the public interest (cl 32(2)(a)). Members can wind up voluntarily by unanimous resolution or with court approval (cl 32(1) and Sched 8 Pt I para 3(5)). Such a voluntary winding-up would be appropriate in the case of irreconcilable differences. It would also be open to a member to apply to the court for an unfair prejudice remedy under cl 43.

47   In cl 27.

48   Which liability has normally been cleared well in advance of winding-up.

49   See Companies (Tables A to F) Regulations 1985, Table C (SI 1985/802).

50   Other than in exceptional circumstances, *eg* if, as directors, they are liable for wrongful trading: see s 214 Companies Act 1985.

51   See cl 33(1). The fee simple in each unit vests in the commonhold association. The unit owner becomes entitled to the commonhold share which the liquidator must first apply in accordance with Sched 10 and the principles of restricted liability: cl 38.

52   Some creditors have priority: those owed winding-up expenses and reserve liabilities. Mortgages secured on the unit owner's commonhold share rank next.

53   See 1990 Consultation Paper (*supra* n 1), para 3.14.

54   See 1996 Consultation Paper (*supra* n 1), para 4.2-4.3 and cl 38 and Sched 10.

55   The detailed consequences are set out in Part III and Sched 8-11 of the Bill.

56   These relate to the introduction of a "shuttle" system for the filing of the annual return (see *Palmer's Company Law*, Vol 2, paras 9.001-9.008) and amendments to ss 246-249 of the Companies Act 1985 (see *Company Law Review: the Law Applicable to Private Companies*: DTI Consultative Document, November 1994 (URN 94/529); *Accounting Simplifications: Re-arrangements to Companies Act Schedule on Small Company Accounts*: DTI Consultative Document, July 1996 (URN 96/755) implemented in SI 1997 no 220; The Companies Act 1985 (Audit Exemption) (Amendment) Regulations (SI 1997/936)).

57   See cls 1(6), 8, 12.

58   CEM Paper 1994 (*supra* n 1), p 71.

59   1990 Consultation Paper (*supra* n 1), para 3.9.

60   1990 Consultation Paper (*supra* n 1), paras 3.18 3.19, and cls 6 and 7 of the Bill.

61   1990 Consultation Paper (*supra* n 1), para 3.14.

62   See cl 15 and Sched 2.

63   Requirements for unanimity or qualified unanimity (defined respectively in cls 53(4)(a) and 15(8)) only affect constitutional changes like variation of the commonhold declaration (cl 17(3)) and voluntary winding-up (cl 32).

64   And other personal assets: see Sched 10 para 12.

65   Including for breach of statutory duty: see *Sedan v "Tyalla" Court* [1978] Qd R 53 and compare cl 20(4) and Sched 5 para 1. The fact that the resources of the association include the value of the unit may encourage such claims by improving the prospects of recovery: see 1990 Consultation Paper (*supra* n 1), para 3.43.

66   See cl 20(4) and Sched 5 para 7 and also Sched 2 para 20.

67   These issues will be covered in commonhold association regulations: see Sched 2 para 16(d), (e) and (l).

68   For example the Building Societies Association: see *Leaseholds: A Time for Change* (London, 1984).

69   See the Landlord and Tenant Act 1987 and the Leasehold Reform and Urban Development Act 1993. These Acts have been criticised (S Bright and G Gilbert, *Landlord and Tenant Law: The Nature of Tenancies* (1995) para 12.4.3; PF Smith, [1994] 12 PM 34) but the present government is committed to improvements (Labour Party Manifesto, *New Labour: Because Britain Deserves Better*).

70   See Clarke, *supra* n 1.

71   For example a limited company registered under the Companies Act 1985 and subject to the ordinary creditor protection and winding up regime but with specialised constitutional provisions in place of The Companies (Tables A to F) Regulations 1985 and, in view of the restriction on trading, disclosure and audit concessions. While such a company would be registered at the Companies Registry, there would have to be Land Registry involvement in many aspects of the establishment and operation of the company.

72   Using perhaps the proposals of the Scottish Law Commission (*supra* n 33) as a guide.

PART III

COMPARATIVE AND INTERNATIONAL PROPERTY LAW

9 Are Property Rights So Simple In Europe?

GEOFFREY SAMUEL

An English law professor has recently noted that one will find in any Continental civil code "a succinct and informative account of what can be owned, how you know who owns it, how ownership is transmitted or hypothecated, the permissible *iura in re aliena* which can subsist in it, and how you recover your thing when someone else has got it".[1] Although few would wish to dispute in any way this comment, it does nevertheless help consolidate the impression that the approach of the Romanists to private law is particularly rational and structured compared with the thinking of English lawyers. It is the purpose of this paper to examine this rationality in more depth not just for European harmonisation purposes, but equally for property thinking - and rights thinking - in general. It will be suggested that the theoretical (epistemological) foundation of property rights in civilian thinking is much more ambiguous than it might at first appear. Part of this ambiguity comes from conceptual confusion. However, another cause of confusion is that the structural underpinning of property concepts in the civil law is now so complex that the traditional two-dimensional rule model through which this structure finds expression is no longer adequate. What is needed is something of a "revolution" in the way that legal structures are understood at the conceptual level.

Introduction: Owning and Owing

One of the fundamental distinctions in the structural make-up of the codes is the dichotomy between property and obligations. Owning is to be sharply distinguished from owing. In German law the distinction is fundamental to legal science, but in Roman law itself it was more ambiguous.[2] Certainly the Romans maintained a rigid distinction between real and personal actions and they never allowed property relations to become confused with personal obligations.[3] But in classifying both property and obligations under "things" they also recognised that the law

161

of obligations was an adjunct to the law of property. This ambiguity is important in as much as it indicates that there is nothing inevitable about the Roman scheme.[4]

The political structures of the Middle Ages - the period when Roman law was being rediscovered - did not think in terms of a sharp division between property and obligations or between the public and the private.[5] Feudalism was more realistic in some ways. It made a distinction between land and chattels with the result that different legal categories developed which did not harmonise easily with the learned Roman law of the universities.[6] Accordingly the common law, which is feudal in origin, is much more ambiguous about the Roman distinctions even if it does share with the Roman law of the *Digest* a certain empirical frame of mind. However, for the common lawyer to appreciate the ambiguity in the area of property ideas it is important to be familiar with some of the theoretical issues underpinning the civilian ideas.[7] Yet the civilian position is, at the theoretical level, more complex than it might at first appear and this complexity can, in its turn, endow the ambiguity in English law with a certain *raison d'être*.[8]

At all events, the law of property in Europe as a whole (including the UK) is complex for several reasons. First, because the terms and notions to be found in the Roman sources have over the centuries been subjected to intense analysis and theoretical speculation. This analysis and speculation has of course refined the Roman concepts. Yet it has done more than this in as much as the history of the second life of Roman law is a history of differing intellectual methods and schemes of intelligibility.[9] Ownership and obligations have therefore to be understood not just within an ever more structured and refined view of private law. They have to be appreciated within rather different theoretical conceptions of law itself. Secondly, because the notion of property, particularly in more recent times, has not been static; new types of property have appeared and these new kinds of property have in their own ways contributed to further speculation about the nature of proprietary relationships. Thirdly, because the common law has always maintained a property regime that is quite different to the one to be found in the Roman sources. This does not mean that common lawyers have not adopted some civilian ideas. However the distinction between law and equity in England has resulted in a more multi-dimensional system than is to be found in the codified countries. Developments have attached as much to the power of independent legal remedies than to coherent and refined notions of ownership and possession. The result is that property thinking probably provides one of the greatest obstacles to harmonisation of private law between the civil law and common law traditions.[10]

Before looking at these civilian ideas it might be useful to recall very briefly the different developments within the two traditions. The rediscovery of Roman law in the eleventh century and its subsequent study over the following centuries was to have a major impact on the customary laws that were to be found in the societies of the late Middle Ages. These societies were, until the end of the fourteenth century, largely feudal in organisation, a political structure that was unknown to Roman law. Gradually the customary law gave way to Romanisation.[11] However in England the position was quite different. The customary legal system, consolidated by the Normans, was able to resist the learned Roman law with the result that a quite separate legal mentality survived into the modern era.[12] The common law tradition is thus an independent one from the *ius civile* family on the continent. It was, and to some extent remains, a law of remedies rather than rationalised subjective rights.[13] Nevertheless the work of the medieval university doctors and the concepts to be found in Roman law itself were not completely without influence on the common law. And thus it has to be said at once that Roman ideas have a general relevance for every jurist within the EU. These ideas often seem to be detached from history in as much as they are contained as succinct linguistic propositions in codes of private law. Yet such propositional succinctness is misleading. The structural foundation of civilian legal thought is, when viewed from the position of the history of legal science, extremely rich in both conceptual subtlety and conceptual ambiguity.

The Middle Ages

The starting point for the modern civil law is the late Middle Ages rather than the Roman law of the Roman Empire.[14] It was the medieval lawyers, in particular the Post-glossators, who constructed the framework upon which modern legal and political theory in Continental Europe is based.[15] Nonetheless, the Romans must be credited with providing the conceptual foundations and vocabulary upon which this framework was built. In particular the notions of ownership (*dominium, proprietas*) and possession (*possessio*) were the two central features of the Roman law of property and the sophisticated nature of Roman thinking is particularly evident in the ability to take legal thought to abstract levels. The dichotomy between tangible (*res corporales*) and intangible property (*res incorporales*), together with a range of other sophisticated ideas, facilitated the move from an agricultural model of law towards one capable of supporting a relatively advanced monetary and commercial economy. These ideas might well have been lost had it not been for the Emperor Justinian. He wanted to make available the whole of Roman law and in order to achieve this he appointed a commission in 527 charged with collecting together and editing the writings of the classical jurists.[16] This work was combined with a similar collection of imperial legislation and an updated edition of a third-century student textbook called the *Institutiones*. This whole collection subsequently became known as the *Corpus Iuris Civilis*. Roman law entered the modern world simply because copies of the *Corpus Iuris* survived the fall and disappearance of the Roman world to become the foundation of all legal knowledge in the first universities of Europe.[17]

The Roman ideas to be found in the *Corpus Iuris Civilis* had little direct relevance to the feudal structures which actually dominated the society of the late Middle Ages. The rediscovered Roman law was the learned law largely confined until the fourteenth century to the Law faculties and feudal customary law was the reality outside of the universities.[18] This feudal law had a quite different view of property in that the idea of an exclusive and absolute legal relationship between *persona* and *res* simply did not apply to the most important form of property in medieval society, namely land.[19] Several different people could have entitlements in a single piece of land. The medieval Roman lawyers tried to reconcile the feudal practice with the Roman notions of *dominium* and *iura in re* and this had the effect of reducing all entitlements in land to *iura*.[20] The Roman idea of a direct relationship between *persona* and *res corporalis* disappeared in that all property entitlements, including *dominium*, became an entitlement to a "right".[21] As one French historian puts it:

> In the late Middle Ages, the words *proprietas, dominium* are always used by the scribes who were mechanically reproducing a dead Roman vocabulary; many are the texts which mention "ownership". But the word no longer meant the physical mastery of matter, but only the enjoyment of its interests.... "Ownership" is no longer sovereignty, it is only, and pragmatically, the legitimate possibility to draw profit from land. It no longer is confused with the matter, it is only the exploitation of matter. Practice called it "seisin", but right from the 13th century the jurists of Roman law erased this term from the vocabulary of property and replaced

it with the Roman terms *proprietas* and *dominium* to mean a polymorphic appropriation technique which had no point in common with Roman ownership except the name.[22]

Nevertheless the later medieval Roman lawyers (Glossators and Post-glossators),[23] being scholars of Roman law, went to great lengths to distinguish *dominium* (the *ius domini*) from other property rights, the *iura in re*.[24] These rights, which could be granted to others by an owner, were, so the Glossators gleaned from the Roman texts, the right to use property belonging to another or the right to take the fruits. The Post-glossators arrived at the position where the *ius domini* must consist of the right to use, enjoy and dispose of a thing (*ius utendi, ius fruendi, ius abutendi*) in the most absolute manner.[25]

Feudalism was, then, able to survive in outline in France up until the Revolution primarily because of the detailed theoretical work of the Roman lawyers. They Romanised the customary law. Their constructions accorded well with practice and they underpinned the landed classes with a legal foundation that was to allow them to continue until the eighteenth century.[26] At another level, however, the power of the feudal landowners was being drained by the strengthening power of the king. Roman ideas were proving more useful than those of the feudal lawyers in that they promoted *imperium* (sovereignty) and independent power.[27] *Quod principi placuit legis habet vigorem* (what pleases the prince has force of law).[28] The reduction of feudal (customary) law to writing and the extension of legislation favoured the Roman structures rather than the more local customary ideas. The political vocabulary was also developing along Roman lines; the notions of *respublica* and of *potestas* were leading inexorably towards an independent idea of the state which, although primarily concerned with public law, started to intervene in commercial and private law. The development of economic regulation went hand-in-hand with the first attempts at codification by Louis XIV's minister, Colbert.[29]

Political and legal philosophy itself was also changing. In the Roman world the idea of the individual as a political focal point found expression neither in law nor in Latin.[30] In the fourteenth century, however, the philosopher William of Ockham is credited as being the catalyst for a revolution against the holistic view of the world. In posing questions about the existence of things - do men or forests exist as realities or do only individual humans and trees exist? - he, and like-minded thinkers, created an epistemological revolution in which universals were seen simply as names having no ontological (real) existence in the world. The starting point of all social and political thinking was no longer the *persona* and the *universitas* but the *individuum*.[31] When translated into legal thinking, *ius* (right) was a legal bond that attached to the individual. The individual had his natural right to own property since God had given man the power to acquire and dispose of goods on earth according to the modes dictated by natural reason.[32] Thus with the decline of feudalism and the rise of individualism from the sixteenth century the original Roman notion of ownership re-established itself as an absolute power (*potestas*) belonging to the individual.

However ownership re-established itself, thanks to the Post-glossators, as a *ius* (right) and not, as in Roman law, a power relation in a physical thing separate from a *ius* in the thing.[33] Thus one arrives at the modern famous definition of ownership as "the right to enjoy and to dispose of things in the most absolute manner".[34] Thanks to the Roman jurists there are in law both *res corporales* and *res incorporales*, but thanks to the Post-glossators, there are in law only *iura* (rights) which are *res incorporales*. The later civilians (Natural Lawyers) tried to escape from this feudal view by re-introducing the physical thing back into the law of property. Man is the master of his physical body and all his possessions and this, in turn, meant that each man had an exclusive power over a thing in his control and not just an entitlement to rights in property shared with others.[35] Modern writers are able to exploit this confusion by imposing upon the notion of a right (*ius*) the idea of an absolute power (*ius domini*) to something which can be conceived of as a "thing", even if it is not actually physical.[36] Having conceived of this "thing" it can, following the Romanist structure, be vindicated. The modern notion of a right (*droit subjectif*) is thus a concept constructed out of the Roman property relations. It is to apply the language of property to other areas of law. This can create difficulties when applied to the *in rem* and *in personam* dichotomy.

The end of the medieval world was marked by another revolution. In place of the scholastic methodology of the medieval university doctors, a new type of intellectual methodology was developed by a group of teachers who attracted the name "Humanists".[37] Humanism was a powerful intellectual movement which sought to escape the rigid and casuistic methods which were dominating the medieval faculties. It was a movement in which "there was both a return to philosophical and moral conceptions of the ancient classical world, an exaltation of human nature ignored by medieval Christianity, and a return to the texts".[38] In legal studies, it sought "to simplify the law, to make it accessible to any honest man, to wrench it away from the Law faculty pedants, the Bartolist technicians, the specialist lawyers".[39] It was the Humanists who started to rationalise the law in terms of grand systems. Whereas the medieval jurists - the Glossators and the Post-glossators - had concentrated on the *Digest* and its practical examples, the Humanists turned to the *Institutes*. They developed the institutional system into its modern form;[40] and thus the "work of humanism ended in modern codifications".[41]

Res

The codifications are all framed around institutions which acted as the starting point of what is called the "institutional system".[42] Law is about *persona*, *res* and *actiones*.[43] *Res* can loosely be translated as "thing" - although the Latin word is rather amorphous - and, like *persona*, represents another focal point around which legal propositions can be grouped. That is to say, things, like people, exist both in the real world and the legal world and thus *res* acts as a bridge between social fact and legal conceptualisation.[44] "Things" (*res*) also act as a counterpoint to "person" (*persona*) and, accordingly, the law of things cannot be understood divorced from persons. *Persona* and *res* represent a legal structure upon which almost the whole of substantive private law is founded. Indeed it has been noted that in the *Code civil* persons are dealt with only from the angle of potential subjects of the law of property.[45] That said, the law of things was, and arguably remains (in some systems at least), wedded to the law of actions; and so the distinction between a personal and a real action lies at the heart of the distinction between property and obligations.[46] Moreover the varying structural patterns of these interrelationships are the key to the different comparative models. In civil law, ownership (*dominium*) is the paradigm relationship between person and thing,[47] but the feudal tradition of English law has resulted in a more complex picture where ownership as a relationship has much less practical importance than possession and its associated remedies.[48]

   Res might be a difficult word to define or to translate, but within the institutional model it was a key institution in that it had meaning in both the empirical and the legal worlds. As Gaius himself implied, tangible things (*res corporales*) are things that can be touched (*quae tangi possunt*) such as land, a man, clothes, gold and the like.[49]   These things exist both in fact and in law. However Gaius goes on to explain that *res* also encompasses intangible things (*res incorporales*) which exist only in law (*quae iure consistunt*);[50] here it is, in effect, the institutional system itself that is creating the *res*. A right to a debt is a *res* - a form of property - even although the legal asset consists only of an entitlement to a legal action (*actio in personam*).

This idea of debt as a *res* is also to be found in English private law. Appropriately a debt is a termed a "chose in action" which reflects the Roman law idea that the relationship is as much between *persona* and *actio* as between person and thing. A chose in action, in turn, is a form of property.[51] In Roman law, however, a debt might have been a *res* but it was not something that could be claimed directly through an *actio in rem*. It was a personal claim that could be recovered only through an action directed at the debtor. English law, in contrast, has not been so formal. The Court of Chancery has allowed trustees and beneficiaries to trace wrongfully appropriated money into the bank account of all but the *bona fide* purchaser for value;[52] and this idea of a right *in rem* to a debt has been adopted by the common law.   In cases of unjustified enrichment, a common law claim in debt, in the absence of a contractual obligation, can be founded upon the proprietary relationship between creditor and debt.[53]

In fact *res* has always been interpreted widely by the courts of equity.   A deliberate interference with the plaintiff's property will be restrained by an injunction and for this purpose "property" has been held to include a whole range of intangible "things" including a live musical performance.[54]   In effect it is sometimes difficult to distinguish between "property" and "rights" in some of these injunction cases and this results in a situation where, from point of view of a law of remedies, it is the injunction rather than the *res* itself which is the defining vehicle.[55] In some ways this is reminiscent of the Roman method in as much as it was the *actio in rem* rather than *dominium* which determined property rights.[56] But the Romans nevertheless found it difficult to escape from the idea that property relations were based upon a relationship between *persona* and *res* and they were reluctant to venture beyond a fairly traditional view of things. The paradigm *res* was always physical.[57]

Corporeal and Incorporeal Property

This paradigm of ownership of a physical thing might be said to be the starting point of the civilian law of property.[58] Nevertheless, despite its conceptual simplicity, the Roman notion of *dominium*, particularly when related to other legal notions, can be problematic. The Romans did not, it seems, conceive of ownership as a right (*ius*), but as a direct power relationship with a physical thing (*res corporalis*) and thus the thing itself became, so to speak, confused with the notion of ownership.[59] The action to recover a physical thing, the *actio in rem*, was, as the name suggests, originally an action against the thing itself and thus the name of the defendant was not mentioned in the action.[60] Furthermore the thing itself (or something representing it) had to be in court.[61] If D took wrongful possession of P's chalice and would not return it to P, the latter would, in effect, bring an action against the chalice itself. If the judge found P to be the owner he had to order the chalice to be handed back to P.[62] The power of *dominium* was thus located in the "duty" of the judge to order repossession. Such a law of actions "duty" could then be extended to a thing of which the plaintiff was not the actual owner.[63] In this situation the power (*potestas*) of ownership was in effect being extended simply by recognising that the plaintiff could bring an action against the *res*. The Romans were getting very close to the idea that ownership was a "right" (power) over a thing.

With regard to lesser property rights, for example a right to quarry on someone else's land, the theoretical position was ambiguous.[64] Such "rights" were, on the one hand, legal relations between *persona* and *res* and thus there had to be a tangible physical object.[65] On the other hand they were also *res incorporales* and thus existed only in law as, so to speak, a "right" (*ius in re*, as the later civilians called it).[66] Equally, it is almost impossible to envisage this kind of intangible thing without a *persona* and thus the object of such a property right is as much the relationship (*ius*) between *persona* and *res* as the *res* to which the *ius* attaches. A *décalage* therefore begins to emerge between the ownership of physical things (*res corporales*) and the ownership of intangible things (*res incorporales*).

Matters became more complicated in the later civil law when the medieval Roman lawyers amalgamated *ius* with *dominium*: ownership then became a right (*ius*) and a kind of *res incorporalis* in itself.[67] In order to avoid this confusion the medieval Romanists concluded that ownership was to be found in the physical thing whereas all other real rights were *res incorporales*; one talked of "my thing" as opposed to "my right".[68] One arrives at a situation, bearing in mind that "goods" (*bona*) are "things" (*res*) which have been appropriated by a person (*persona*),[69] where "goods are things, but things are goods only by the rights of which the things form the object; thus it is the rights which are in reality the goods".[70] All goods are goods only because they are rights. One can then reverse the situation in saying that all rights are goods of a sort (a right to something). But the problem with this analysis is that there are, according to the structure of the codes, rights which are not property rights, that is to say rights which are not goods. A contractual right is, for example, a right against some other person; it is a right which is *in personam*.[71] That is to say, it is a right whose object is another person (*persona*) rather than a thing (*res*). The *Code civil*, like the *Institutes of Gaius*, is, however, ambiguous because, although it does distinguish between property and obligation rights, it places the law of obligations (personal rather than real rights) under the general heading of "things". This suggests that behind every right there is in fact a "thing". However, at the same time, the *Code* retains the Roman notion that ownership devours the *res*; ownership (*la propriété*) is the thing itself.[72] Theorists on the continent are still trying to escape from this paradox.[73] Is ownership simply a right or is it something more?

　　If it is only a right then this has the effect of reducing it to the level of all rights. It becomes a patrimonial right like any other right. Now, if contractual rights are extended through the gradual abolition of the relative effect of contractual rights (the rule of privity of contract as English lawyers would call it) this will have the effect of endowing them with an *in rem* flavour. That is to say they will become effective against third parties. Contractual rights become more like rights good against the whole world. This may not actually destroy the distinction between owing and owning, but it certainly weakens the boundary in as much as it interferes with the symmetrical dichotomy between relations between person and person (personal rights) and relations between person and thing (real rights).

Proprietary Remedies

The Romans themselves were little interested in theorising at an abstract level about the distinction between property and obligations. They, seemingly, provided no definition of *dominium* and gave legal expression to the idea only through the law of actions.[74] It was the *actio in rem* which functioned as the vehicle for ownership and other real rights (*iura in re aliena*) and these claims were alternatively called vindication actions (*rei vindicatio*). They were about asserting a relationship directly against a thing and thus they attached to the thing itself with the result that once the thing disappeared so did the *vindicatio*.[75] Of course, in order to bring the *actio in rem* the plaintiff had to show that he was either the owner or had some *ius* in the thing;[76] and thus, to this extent, it could be said that the remedy was founded upon a legal "right". But title was often tested via the question of who had the *vindicatio* remedy.[77] In contrast, it was the *actio in personam* that gave expression to an obligation relationship, although an obligation was defined by Justinian as a legal chain (*vinculum iuris*) binding two people to perform something.[78] As Gaius observed, one would not use an *actio in personam* to recover one's property "for what is ours cannot be conveyed to us".[79] Property "rights" thus tended to be expressed as matters attaching to the *actio* (and then to the *res* itself) and not as substantive matters concerning ownership.

In the later civil law, when categories were no longer being defined in terms of actions, the idea of a vindication remedy was nevertheless retained. Owners deserved the full protection of the law and they ought thus to be able to claim physical restitution of the things which they owned.[80] In the modern civilian systems, then, a distinction is still made at the level of legal remedies between real and personal actions. Real rights are expressed through the idea that one is asserting a right in a thing rather than against a person and this allows a plaintiff owner in theory to follow (trace) his thing into the hands of others.[81] It is the *res* and not the *persona* that is the subject-matter of the remedy and the right.[82] All the same, such a structure, it should be noted, continues to emphasise the distinction between physical things and real rights since the vindication action presumes the existence of a thing. The *actio in rem* has by definition the need for a *res* and thus was developed in relation to *res corporales*. It can extend to certain types of *res incorporales*, but only where there is some kind of "thing" that can support the conceptual structure.

Possession

The *rei vindicatio* was a remedy allowing a dispossessed owner to recover possession of his thing. At first sight, therefore, it might appear that the *actio in rem* was a remedy protecting both the legal relation with a thing and the factual relation. The medieval jurists discovered, however, that the two kinds of relationship were sharply distinguished in Roman law. Possession was protected by its own set of quite separate public law (*imperium*) remedies called interdicts. And it was a relationship with a thing that endowed the possessor - even the unworthy possessor - with certain "rights" *in rem*.[83]   As the Roman sources themselves (rather misleadingly) state, possession has nothing in common with ownership.[84] One can be owner without possessing and one can possess without owning.

The distinction was originally seen as being one of fact and law.[85] Possession gave expression to factual detention of a thing[86] - thus there could only ever be one possessor at any given moment[87] - whereas ownership gave expression to a legal relation with the *res*. However the moment that possession itself was given its own separate regime of protection in the law of actions, then possession as a concept no longer expressed a pure situation of fact. Possession became a more subtle notion.[88]   Thus someone who was ejected from possession was still considered to be in possession since he could recover the *res* through the inderdict remedies (*interdicta*).[89] Moreover, with respect to the possession of an inheritance that might contain no corporeal property, one could talk of legal rather than factual possession.[90] As well as expressing a situation of fact, it was also, then, a notion giving expression to a legal relationship between *persona* and *res*. Person A, although not owner of a thing, might nevertheless have a better "right" to possess (*ius possessionis*) it than person B and could seek a possessory remedy giving expression to this "right".

In addition to this ambiguity, actually defining possession has not been easy and has given rise to much controversy and literature over the centuries.[91]   In Roman law possession was distinguished from *detentio* which meant that the mere transfer of a *res* under say a contract of deposit would not pass possession.[92]   At the level of definition, one could not possess without both physical control (*corpus*) and mental intent (*animus*) to control[93] and thus Roman possession continued to emphasise the distinction between *res corporales* and *res incorporales*. This distinction became blurred when the later civilians started to see ownership (*dominium*) as a right (*ius*); what one possessed was a right (*ius*) and what one exercised was a right (to possession).[94] If the *actio in rem* was an action giving the owner a right to possession (*ius possessionis*), what kind of right was being protected by an interdict? Roman law provided some help in answering this question since the sources stated clearly that in cases of disputed ownership the possessor was in the stronger position.[95] Possession and possessory remedies could thus be seen as some kind of procedural prelude to a *vindicatio* action.[96] Another way of viewing the possessory interdicts is through the public and private divide; the protection of possession can be seen as a series of public law remedies designed to keep the peace and to discourage self-help.[97] It is an example of public law protecting private interests for the sake of the general interest.

The problem for the later civilians, however, is that these Roman techniques did not accord with the feudal structure of the late Middle Ages. Land was possessed rather than owned in the Roman sense. Remedies protecting "possession" could effectively be seen as protecting actual property "rights". Each "right" in its turn could be seen as a form of *dominium*.[98] Possession, in other words, acquired the capacity to become a complex and subtle legal relation in itself. With the decline of feudalism and the ascendancy of Roman law throughout Europe the emphasis was once again on the sharp distinction between *dominium* and *possessio*. However the confusion between *ius possessionis* and the object of such a *ius*, namely the possibility of possessing a right (*ius*), was ingrained in legal thought.[99] One could it seems have a right to possess (*ius possessionis*), that is to say a *ius in re*. All rights are, in this scheme of thought, capable of being possessed. Yet modern French law actually defines possession as "the detention or the enjoyment of a *thing or a right* that we hold or that we exercise ourselves or through another who holds it or exercises it in our name".[100] This seems to be continuing the distinction between physical property and rights.[101]

In fact one of the main functions of possession is to confer ownership either through a long period of uninterrupted possession[102] or through the appearance of being an owner *vis-à-vis* a third party *bona fide* purchaser for value.[103] In truth, then, possession does, after all, have important connections both with ownership and with physical objects (for example consumer goods). This impacts upon the theory of possession. Is possession simply an adjunct of the law of ownership or is it an independent notion with its own theoretical and social basis? No doubt both theories have their relevance, but two points in particular can be noted. First, possession acts as an essential bridge between the worlds of social fact and legal relation; accordingly possession as a legal notion has the capacity of turning raw fact (long possession) into legal title (ownership by prescription).[104] Secondly, the distinction between possession and ownership remains rooted as much in the law of actions as in legal theory. Possessory remedies, even in the modern civil law, are distinct both from revindication claims and from personal actions.[105]

Possession therefore assumes an interesting conceptual status. It started life as a descriptive notion but became increasingly normative as it attracted its own remedies and became thought of as a right (*ius*). In relation to the concept of a right it has a tendency to retain its descriptive identity. It is a situation of fact that ought to be maintained by public law remedies probably designed to ensure the keeping of the peace. However the moment that one brings together the law of actions and possession under the rubric of a "right" complexity sets in around the notion of the right itself. Is it a right to the *res*? Is it an entitlement to an abstract "thing" (*ius*), that is to say a "right" detached from the *res*? Or is possession itself a relationship now endowed with a normative dimension? This may all seem academic if not scholastic.[106] Yet it represents a confusion of ideas that itself is a cause of serious complexity at the heart of "rights" talk. In the area of time-share does one own a right to possession for a limited period every year? And can one possess the right to possession? If D takes possession of an apartment during the period when P has his or her exclusive possession, has D taken possession of the *res* or of the *ius*?

Universals

The Roman emphasis on the physical thing gave rise to another problem.[107] What exactly was owned and (or) possessed where the physical thing consisted of, or contained, other things? If one owned a house did one own, as well, all the things in the house? If one possessed a library or a flock what exactly did one possess: the thing as a whole or its individual parts? The Romans recognised the problem and thus distinguished between three types of physical things (*corpora*): a single unitary thing such as a branch or stone; a constructed thing such as a house or a ship; and a thing consisting of individual things such as a flock or a legion.[108] The problem was more complex where *res corporales* became mixed with *res incorporales* within a single mass which itself was viewed as an independent "thing". That is to say the two types of property formed part of a person's "goods" (*bona*)[109] which in turn was seen as an asset which could be valued in terms of money[110] and described as a person's patrimony (*patrimonium*).[111] In Roman law the classic example of such a universality was the estate of a dead person (*hereditas*); this was a distinct "thing" (*universitas*) protected by its own *actio in rem* which would be applicable even with respect to the personal obligations contained in the estate.[112] A marriage dowry and slave's *peculium* were conceived of in a similar way:

each was a *universitas*, a kind of mini patrimony (*patrimonium pusillum*).[113]

This form of abstract thinking was to prove fundamental to commercial property law in that it established the idea not just of a general asset or "thing" made up of other things but of a patrimony that remained constant while the individual things within it came and went. The Romans drew an analogy with a boat or a legion where every plank or every soldier changes over a long period but one still had the same "thing"[114] since one thing could be substituted (subrogated) for another.[115] The commercial aspect to this conceptual structure becomes clearer when one views a slave and his *peculium* as an independent "company" with an independent patrimony. One is getting very close to the idea of an independent trading patrimony which can be born, grow and die[116] and which provided a limited liability for the master.[117] The notion of a patrimony became even more commercially creative when associated with a *universitas personarum*, that is to say a group of persons viewed as a single *persona*. Colleges and towns, for example, were treated as if they were a single person in the legal plan and thus could sue and be sued as an entity.[118] The medieval jurists developed these Roman ideas into a *corpus fictum* since universals did not exist according to the late medieval philosophers; what existed were only the individual things. Thus the separation between the *universitas* and the individual things was complete: things could come and go with ease but the *universitas* would remain the same. When the same intellectual thinking was applied to groups of people, the medieval jurists developed, to accompany the *universitas rerum*, a *persona ficta*; the elements of the modern commercial trading and property company were now becoming even clearer.[119]

Subrogation

The structural idea that one *res* can be substituted for another within a *universitas rerum* can also be applied to the notion of a *res* itself. That is to say, if a thing is envisaged not as a physical object but as an intangible idea (*res incorporalis*) there is no reason in principle why one physical thing cannot be substituted for another. Such substitution need not destroy the existing *persona* and *res* proprietary relationship. For example, O is the owner of a gold chalice which he swaps for an ornate silver one of similar value: could it not be envisaged that the actual legal relationship between O and "chalice" remains unchanged? That is to say, can the idea of a "chalice" be divorced from the physical object? In a commercial context such a possibility has very real advantages since for example it means that a creditor can take out a real security right (*in rem*) over a commercial asset without immobilising the asset itself. A business can continue to trade while its creditors continue to enjoy rights *in rem* over the stock-in-trade. The Romans themselves never reached this level of sophistication and the actual development of real subrogation was the work of the medieval Roman lawyers who formulated the maxim *res succedit pretio et pretium rei* (the thing succeeds the price and the price the thing).[120] However Roman law certainly provided the conceptual building blocks for such ideas.[121] The original contribution of the Post-glossators was to hold that the second *res* not only replaced the first but also took on its nature: *subrogatum capit naturam subrogati*.[122]

By way of analogy, a similar substitution can be made at the other end of the proprietary relationship so to speak. One *persona* can be substituted for another. If one person pays a debt secured by a right *in rem* on behalf of another person it is conceptually possible to allow the person who has paid off the creditor to be subrogated to the relationship *in rem*. Such a substitution will have the effect of giving the person who has paid off the debt the security enjoyed by the original creditor. This type of subrogation was originally based upon a contract and thus there had to be an *in personam* relationship between the original debtor and the payer stipulating that the latter would take over the security.[123] Later civilians allowed such a substitution by operation of law.[124] Personal subrogation thus became an important personal right outside of the law of contract.

Subrogation, particularly real subrogation, is, however, more complex than it might at first seem since it raises the question of what is being revindicated. Is it the physical *res* itself or is it the right, the *res incorporalis*? Such a question comes close to undermining the whole dichotomy between rights *in rem* and *in personam* in that the moment one says that it is the *res incorporalis* (the right to security) that is being revindicated one is coming close to allowing a real action for the debt itself.[125] Real subrogation, when applied to a sum of money that has replaced a piece of property in a patrimony, becomes in effect an *actio in rem* for a debt. One theory, in other words, undermines another.

Towards a Theoretical Structure of Civilian Private Law

Such theoretical contradiction illustrates how the internal structure of modern continental private law is, on closer examination, rather more complex than the general categories of persons, things and obligations might at first suggest. Ideas that were basically rather straightforward in Roman law itself became distorted through the theoretical contortions of the later civilians. These civilians were keen not only to adapt Roman structures to the quite different social conditions of the late Middle Ages, but to discover the supposed truths hidden beneath the institutions of the classical world. One major structural distortion was the movement away from the law of actions; for the *actio* actually provided the basic institution by which the Roman scheme made sense. Once one tried to explain *dominium, possessio, obligatio* and *iura in re* uniquely through the substantive idea of a *ius* itself problems were bound to occur since the theorists were investing the universal notion of *ius* with the *dominium* idea of power (*potestas*). All rights became things to be revindicated.

Matters were made even more complex when the word *ius* (right) was injected with a more subjective meaning by the Enlightenment and post-Enlightenment philosophers. Attempts to analyse institutional relationships like possession in terms of subjective right were bound to cause theoretical difficulties and they continue to do so.[126] For, the subjective right - itself traceable back to the merging of *ius* with *dominium*[127] - had transcended the law of property to become a general normative concept applicable throughout private law. In other words, all law had become "property" law since all law concerned "rights" (*iura*) and all rights were founded ultimately on the notion of *dominium*.

Nevertheless the structural contribution of both Roman law and the modern Romanists to the internal plan of private law must never be underestimated. It is not so much the rules as the institutional structure that is important. The distinctions between ownership and possession, between property and obligations, between the universal and the singular, between rights and remedies and so on are part of a structural framework. And this structural framework is vital for understanding not just the organisation of legal rules and principles but equally, and perhaps more importantly, the organisation of facts. Property, obligations and rights are notions for understanding the social world and it was the civilians that sought to impose this world-view on a non-Roman Europe. The codes and their structure are a measure of their success.

The question, however, for the new millennium is whether this success is too great. Rights-talk, as this paper has tried to show, has the effect ultimately of reducing all legal issues to property-talk. A right is a right to something. It is law expressed as power without obligation. One response of civil lawyers has, of course, been to develop a theory of abuse of rights which has the effect of re-introducing the notion of an obligation into the power relationship of a right.   This, however, runs the risk of turning all property rights into obligational relationships.   The point to note for the English lawyer is that the seemingly clear separation between real and personal rights is not in fact as simple or consistent as it might at first seem.   Or, put another way, the institutional model which endows the codes with their form and symmetry can be much more flexible in the hands of a legal reasoner able to manipulate the model of institutions and relationships to form quite different patterns within particular factual situations.   Some in the EU might dream of imposing via a European Code the strict dichotomy between owning and owing on the chaos of English law.[128]   If that were to happen, what the common lawyer might do is to expose, at the level of reasoning, the Achilles' heel of the model itself. Gaius' *Institutes* is actually quite subversive.

Rethinking the Symmetry

Yet perhaps the weakness is not to be found in Gaius' system as such but in the way the modern lawyer conceives of legal knowledge.   Knowledge of law is knowledge of rules and principles, that is to say knowledge of normative propositions.   The difficulty with this "rule model" of legal knowledge is that it is strictly two-dimensional.   It envisages law as a "flat" hierarchy of norms where contradiction and complexity are avoided only by the assigning of elements of knowledge to different categories functioning in strictly independent spheres and at different levels within the structure.   Yet such categories and levels are quite incapable of giving full expression to legal knowledge because the concepts themselves are, in the end, incapable of being comprehensively rationalised within a two-dimensional model.   This is the lesson that arises out of the history of the law of property in Europe.   The idea that coherent scheme of rights (*iura*) can give expression to all the various types of conceptual relations flowing between *persona*, *res* and *actiones* is nothing but a myth.   And it is a myth not just because the reduction of legal knowledge to axioms and mathematical equations is itself a myth when measured against the social objectives of a legal system;[129] but equally because the legal conceptions themselves cannot be reduced to a two-dimensional structural model where all ambiguity and contradiction are avoided.   Thus the notion of a "right" is, as this paper has endeavoured to show, a notion that itself functions at one and the same time at two levels in the hierarchy. It developed out of the notion of ownership (*dominium*) and the vindication claim (*actio in rem*) and as such forms part of the law of property. Yet it has risen above the law of property to become a "meta-legal" concept capable of explaining all legal entitlements including those *in personam* entitlements that are strictly to be separated from the law of property. The logical contradiction here is evident.[130]

These contradictions are exacerbated by the ambiguity of the concepts themselves. The confusion of *dominium* with *res* gives rise to a situation where it is logically possible to say that one can have a *ius in rem* in an obligation since an obligation is a *res*.[131] One way, seemingly, out of this contradiction is to restrict the object of ownership to a *res corporalis*. Yet this relies upon the assumption that the structural nature of ownership is the *vinculum iuris* between person and thing, which itself raises conceptual difficulties. The first difficulty, as we have seen, is that the *Code civil* quite simply does not make this restriction. Yet even if, like the German model, it did, there would be a second difficulty arising out of the ambiguous nature of both ownership and corporality themselves.[132] If things such as electricity are to be treated as corporeal things,[133] how are they to be owned? The physically fluid nature of the *res* helps undermine the thesis that ownership is the relation between person and thing. Ownership begins to look like a power *vis-à-vis* another person and this change of image goes far in undermining the model and making ownership appear like any other "right". This confusion is again exacerbated both by the historical existence of, and by the later disappearance of, the law of actions. In Roman law the distinction between property and obligations was one that primarily found expression in terms of the *actio*. *Dominium* itself found expression via the *actio in rem*. With the disappearance of the law of actions from substantive law, it was, and is, no longer possible to distinguish real rights from personal rights via the object of a legal claim. That is to say via the *res* against which an action was aimed and which thus had to be in court. Equally it is no longer easy to retain the idea of ownership without supporting it by its own type of claim.

Of course this is not to suggest that the Romans were more "logical" than the modern civil lawyer. They were not interested in two-dimensional logical coherence and used the institutional system for educational rather than inference purposes. When it came to problem-solving the law of actions was used primarily to make sense of the facts and one worked back from actions to more substantive ideas only in terms of particular factual situations.[134]   Now facts are not two-dimensional and that is, arguably, why the Roman jurists felt little need to locate the foundation of legal knowledge in the rule-model (*regulae iuris*).[135]   Facts are three-dimensional and in order to model them in a way that captures their full complexity one needs a legal knowledge model that functions in three dimensions. This, arguably, is exactly what the original Gaian model of persons, things and actions did. It allowed a range of legal relations to flow between person and person, person and thing and person and action in dimensions that were on the same level but independent.[136]   Thus, to give just one example, a *municipium* could not as such own or possess property since it was not possible in the law of things to envisage the necessary mental intent.[137]   However, in the law of actions, the town could make use of remedies designed to protect possession and so had power to recover things . wrongfully appropriated by another.[138]   The logical conclusion flowing from this is that such "public" property was not actually public since towns were considered as private legal subjects;[139] they were *personae* capable of having private legal relations with their things.[140]   Yet, when viewed from the status of the *res* itself, such "public" property was both public and *extra commercium* (incapable of being owned).[141]   Modern theories envisage the corporate body as a legal person capable of having a mind of its own.   But to the Romans it was all a matter of relations attaching to the *actio* functioning independently from relations attaching to human individuals and their things.[142]   Relations were constructed and deconstructed within differing dimensions of the institutional model and thus property could be both "public" and "private" at one and the same time.   Town lands were outside private ownership (*extra commercium*) in the law of things,[143] but were later protected as if they were capable of being owned in the law of actions.[144]

Conclusion: Towards a New Model of Legal Knowledge

The dimensional richness of this kind of thinking was lost with the *mos geometricus* of the Enlightenment.   Law was a logically closed system in which "the ultimate basis for decision was a synthetic legal concept which could be traced back to ultimate higher principles in a manner consonant with the system".[145]   Law was not a matter of construction of facts out of which law arises, but deduction from a hierarchical system of axioms. Contradiction was not possible in such a system, as Wieacker explains: if A is there, B cannot be there at the same time.[146]   This rationality did not, evidently, lack rigour. What it lacked was the dimensional structure to make sense of the social world - a world in which concepts were not fixed in rigid hierarchies but were fluid and changing as social ideas and notions changed. The complexities of the feudal world bear witness to the multi-dimensional structure of property thinking and this structural richness remains evident in a world of time-shares and, in English law, of legal and equitable rights and remedies. The two-dimensional symmetry of the civil codes (law as propositional axioms) is, in short, incapable of giving expression to the multi-dimensional world of complex factual situations and thus what is needed is a new epistemological model for envisaging property (and indeed other) rights.

In order to give substance to a new epistemological model in which the complexities of property law might find expression perhaps one can use an example from the history of science and the philosophy of time. Before Albert Einstein's revolutionary theory of relativity, time was envisaged in terms of an arrow.[147] It was a *res* in as much as it could be described as a linear dimension (arrow) consisting of a past, present and future. This view of time was essentially one-dimensional in structure and absolute in as much as it represented a standard clock throughout the universe. Einstein's theory of time as relative to the observer overthrew this one-dimensional view of time as an arrow. The notion of an absolute distinction between past and future was incompatible with the complexities of a universe where the dimensions of time are circular and closed upon themselves.[148] Future and past have a sense relative only to isolated sets of observers.[149] The one-dimensional structure of an arrow of time is quite inadequate to give expression to this changed view of time and space. Time is part of the multi-dimensional structure of the universe itself and cannot be disassociated from the complexities of this universe.[150] In short, the one-dimensional view of time is now an utterly inadequate knowledge model to give expression to the time and space of the universe.

By way of analogy one might say that the two-dimensional civil code is equally inadequate as a knowledge model when it comes to expressing the complexity of law. Notions such as "rights" cannot act as both the objects of legal science and the science itself without contradiction, at least in the two-dimensional world of propositions (rules and principles). Legal concepts, like time, are part of the universe of social facts and cannot be divorced from the dimensions of these facts; they are not in themselves a *res* which exists in an empty hierarchical form abstracted from the complexities of the actual world.[151] Certainly the two-dimensional view of property notions is inadequate for the common lawyer. Such notions must be seen as part of the social world and thus they must be envisaged as functioning within at least a three-dimensional model. In this model real rights might, for example, be seen as acting as the basis for personal remedies and where equitable remedies might be seen as contradicting, but living alongside, legal rights. What this paper has tried to show is that the same complexity is to be found in the civil law. The history of property notions in the Romanist systems might seem like a progression from the descriptive to the axiomatic passing through the inductive and the deductive respectively.[152] But one has now moved, in legal science if not in all of the natural sciences, to a stage beyond the axiomatic. Such a stage does not necessarily mean that codes are no longer relevant or of help in orientating legal knowledge. What it means is that the propositions themselves can no longer act as a model of understanding legal knowledge in all its complexity and all its historical richness. One needs to go deeper and to re-think the dimensional symmetry of the institutional structure that underpins such codes.

Notes

1   A Tettenborn, book review (1997) 56 CLJ 653.

2   CG van der Merwe and MJ de Waal, *The Law of Things and Servitudes* (Butterworths, Durban, 1993), n° 14. (Hereinafter cited van der Merwe and de Waal. The author would like to thank Professor CG van der Merwe for kindly supplying a copy of his co-authored book.)

3   D.44.7.3pr.

4   HF Jolowicz, *Roman Foundations of Modern Law* (Oxford, 1957), pp 61-62.

5   J-P Lévy, *Histoire de la propriété* (Presses Universitaires de France, 1972), pp 35-36.

6   *Ibid*, pp 44-46.

7   See *eg* SFC Milsom, *Historical Foundations of the Common Law* (Butterworths, 2nd ed, 1981), pp 6, 99, 263.

8   *Cf* FH Lawson, *The Rational Strength of English Law* (Stevens, 1951).

9   G Samuel, *The Foundations of Legal Reasoning* (Maklu, 1994), pp 33-62.

10   *Cf* AS Hartkamp *et al* (eds), *Towards a European Civil Code* (Ars Aequi Libri, 1994).

11   P Stein, *Legal Institutions: The Development of Dispute Settlement* (Butterworths, 1984), pp 77-79; RC van Caenegem, *An Historical Introduction to Private Law* (Cambridge, 1992; trans DEL Johnston), pp 35-38.

12   RC van Caenegem, *The Birth of the English Common Law* (Cambridge, 2nd ed, 1988), pp 88-93.

13   OF Robinson, TD Fergus and WM Gordon, *European Legal History* (Butterworths, 2nd ed, 1994), pp 149-152.

14 See generally HJ Berman, *Law and Revolution: The Formation of the Western Legal Tradition* (Harvard, 1983).

15 See generally W Ullmann, *Law and Politics in the Middle Ages* (Sources of History, 1975). For a brief introduction to the Glossators and Post-glossators (or Commentators) see A Borkowski, *Textbook on Roman Law* (Blackstone, 2nd ed, 1997), pp 366-372.

16 See Ullmann, *op cit*, p 55.

17 P Vinogradoff, *Roman Law in Medieval Europe* (Cambridge, 1968 edition), pp 43-70.

18 There was also political opposition to Romanisation: van Caenegem, *Private Law, op cit*, pp 80-83.

19 A-M Patault, *Introduction historique au droit des biens* (Presses Universitaires de France, 1989), pp 21-23. (Hereinafter cited Patault.)

20 F Zenati and T Revet, *Les biens* (Presses Universitaires de France, 1997), pp 133-135, 245-246. (Hereinafter cited Zenati and Revet.)

21 "If Gaius had known of customary law seisin he would have classed it under incorporeal things, jura": Patault, p 22.

22 Patault, p 19.

23 See generally Ullmann, *op cit*, pp 83-116; JW Jones, *Historical Introduction to the Theory of Law* (Oxford, 1940), pp 11-21. For an excellent and up-to-date overview: Borkowski, *op cit*, pp 366-379.

24 P Ourliac and J De Malafosse *Histoire du Droit privé 2/Les Biens* (Presses Universitaires de France, 2nd ed, 1971), pp 156-162. (Hereinafter cited Ourliac and De Malafosse.)

25 Pataut, pp 110-111.

26 Ourliac and De Malafosse, p 159.

27 H Legohérel, *Histoire du droit public français* (Presses Universitaires de France, 3rd ed, 1994), pp 48-63.

28 D.1.4.1pr.

29 J Hilaire, *Introduction historique au droit commercial* (Presses Universitaires de France, 1986), p 16.

30 A Laurant, *Histoire de l'individualisme* (Presses Universitaires de France, 1993), p 19.

31 *Ibid*, pp 21-24.

32 *Ibid*, p 24.

33 D.39.2.19.

34 *Code civil* art 544.

35 Patault, pp 142-143.

36 M Villey, *La formation de la pensée juridique moderne* (Montchrestien, 4th ed, 1975), pp 671-672.

37 See generally DR Kelley, "Law", in JH Burns (ed), *The Cambridge History of Political Thought 1450-1700* (Cambridge, 1991), pp 66-94.

38 J-B Duroselle and J-M Mayeur, *Histoire du catholicisme* (Presses Universitaires de France, 8th ed, 1996), p 78.

39 Villey, *op cit*, p 516.

40 P Stein, *The Character and Influence of the Roman Civil Law* (Hambledon, 1988), pp 73-82.

41 Villey, *op cit*, p 540.

42   Stein, *Legal Institutions, op cit*, pp 126-129; G Samuel, "Classification of Obligations and the Impact of Constructivist Epistemologies" (1997) 17 Legal Studies 483, 456-461.
43   G.1.8; J.1.2.12; D.1.5.1.
44   Samuel, *Foundations of Legal Reasoning, op cit*, pp 172-173.
45   J-L Halpérin, *Histoire du droit privé français depuis 1804* (Presses Universitaires de France, 1996), p 25.
46   G.4.4.
47   *Code civil* art 544.
48   *Waverley BC v Fletcher* [1996] QB 334.
49   G.2.13.
50   G.2.14.
51   Law of Property Act 1925 s 205(1)(xx).
52   FH Lawson, *Remedies of English Law* (Butterworths, 2nd ed, 1980), pp 147-160.
53   *Lipkin Gorman v Karpnale Ltd* [1991] 2 AC 548.
54   *Ex parte Island Records* [1978] Ch 122.
55   *Kingdom of Spain v Christie, Mason & Woods Ltd* [1986] 1 WLR 1120.
56   See *eg* D.6.3.1.1.
57   This view has been bequeathed to German law: van der Merwe and de Waal, n° 14.
58   Van der Merwe and de Waal, n° 103.
59   Patault, pp 17-18; Zenati and Revet, pp 133-135.
60   Jolowicz, *op cit*, pp 73-74. The action was against the possessor of the *res* claimed: D.4.7.4.2; 6.1.42.
61   G.4.16-17.
62   D.6.1.9.
63   See D.6.3.1.1.
64   Van der Merwe and de Waal, n°s 42-43.
65   D.7.1.2 (*ius in corpore*).
66   *Usus fructus est ius alienis rebus utendi fruendi*: D.7.1.1. See also D.39.2.19pr.
67   See generally Villey, *op cit*, pp 381-382, 672.
68   Zenati and Revet, pp 58-59.
69   *Cf* D.50.16.49.
70   Zenati and Revet, p 19.
71   Van der Merwe and de Waal, n° 43.
72   See *eg CC* art 644.
73   Zenati and Revet, pp 133-142.
74   See in particular D.6.3.1.1.
75   J.2.1.26; D.5.3.16.8.
76   D.7.6.5pr.
77   See *eg* D.39.6.29.
78   J.3.13pr.
79   G.4.4.
80   Zenati and Revet, pp 201-230.
81   *Cf CC* art 2279.
82   See *eg CC* art 644.
83   D.41.2.53; D.43.17.2.
84   D.41.2.12.1.

85   Van der Merwe and de Waal, n° 53.
86   *Possessio pluimum facti habet*: D.4.6.19.
87   D.41.2.3.5.
88   Van der Merwe and de Waal, n° 53.
89   D.41.2.17.
90   D.37.1.3.1.
91   Definition may in truth be impossible: van der Merwe and de Waal, n° 63.
92   D.16.3.17.1; D.41.2.3.18.
93   D.41.2.3.1.
94   Van der Merwe and de Waal, n° 53.
95   D.50.17.128pr.
96   Ourliac and De Malafosse, p 226.
97   See *eg* D.43.16.1.1.
98   Ourliac and De Malafosse, p 240.
99   Van der Merwe and de Waal, n° 53.
100   *CC* art 2228 emphasis added.
101   Zenati and Revet, p 336.
102   *CC* art 2229.
103   *CC* art 2279.
104   D.41.3.3.
105   *CC* art 2283; *Nouveau Code de Procédure Civile* art 1265.
106   Van der Merwe and de Waal, n° 53.
107   Van der Merwe and de Waal, n° 30.
108   D.41.3.30pr.
109   D.50.16.49.
110   D.50.16.5.
111   D.27.1.30.1.
112   D.5.3.25.18.
113   D.15.1.5.3.
114   D.5.1.76.
115   D.15.1.32.1.
116   D.15.1.40.
117   D.15.1.41.
118   D.50.16.16.
119   Ourliac and De Malafosse, pp 63-66.
120   Zenati and Revet, pp 107-108.
121   See *eg* D.4.2.18.
122   Zenati and Revet, p 108.
123   C.8.19.1.
124   P Ourliac and J De Malafosse, *Histoire du Droit privé 1/Les Obligations* (Presses Universitaires de France, 2nd ed, 1969), pp 241-242.
125   Zenati and Revet, p 223.
126   Zenati and Revet, p 337.
127   R Tuck, *Natural Rights Theories* (Cambridge, 1979), pp 5-31.
128   See *eg* Hartkamp *et al*, *op cit*.
129   J-L Bergel, *Théorie générale du droit* (Dalloz, 3rd ed, 1999), n° 252.
130   Van der Merwe and de Waal, n° 14.

131   *Ibid.*
132   Van der Merwe and de Waal, n° 16.
133   *Ibid.*
134   T Weir, "Contracts in Rome and England" (1992) 66 Tulane Law Review 1615.
135   D.50.17.1.
136   Samuel, *Foundations, op cit*, pp 243-258.
137   D.41.2.1.22.
138   D.41.2.22.
139   D.50.16.15-17.
140   D.1.8.6.1.
141   G.2.11.
142   D.41.2.3.5.
143   D.20.3.1.2.
144   D.6.3.1.1.
145   F Wieacker, *A History of Private Law in Europe* (Oxford, 1995; trans. T Weir), p 255.
146   *Ibid*, p 344.
147   H Barreau, *Le temps* (Presses Universitaires de France, 1996), p 105.
148   B Piettre, *Philosophie et science du temps* (Presses Universitaires de France, 1994), pp 70-72.
149   *Ibid*, p 71.
150   *Ibid*, pp 117-125; P Davies, *The Mind of God* (Penguin, 1992), pp 62-69.
151   *Cf* Piettre, *op cit*, p 124.
152   R Blanché, *L'épistémologie* (Presses Universitaires de France, 3rd ed, 1983), p 65.

10 Limitations on Constitutional Property Rights

TOM ALLEN

Introduction

Most Commonwealth constitutions contain a bill of rights with an express right to property.[1] While these constitutions provide that compensation should be paid for the compulsory acquisition of property, they do not require compensation for every form of interference with property. Hence, losses from injurious affection or regulation are not normally compensatable under constitutional law. As a result, while a great many persons may be adversely affected by a law affecting property, only a small number are entitled to compensation. However, the number that do receive compensation are generally treated quite generously. Accordingly, it is plainly of the greatest importance to determine whether a given interference with property gives rise to a right to compensation. The search for a just and workable distinction between compensatable and non-compensatable interferences with property rights has occupied the attention of many courts and scholars in this century, especially as it has become apparent that the regulation of property can cause economic loss of the same magnitude as an outright acquisition of part or even all of the property. In such circumstances, the justice of awarding compensation to one person and not to another is difficult to see.

In the Commonwealth, constitutional framers and courts have developed several types of limitations on the right to compensation. The first type is based on the characterisation of the interest or rights that are affected by state action. For example, all Commonwealth constitutions limit the right to property to property itself; that is, there is a rule that corresponds to the tort rule limiting recovery for negligence in cases of pure economic loss. All courts have taken this a step further, by holding that compensation is only payable when the rights that are affected are sufficiently important to constitute a "property" bundle of rights.

The second and third types of limitation concentrate on the reasons for the state action. The second concentrates on the state's immediate purpose, by distinguishing between the deprivation and acquisition of property. Deprivation is broader; for example, most courts would agree that the extinction of a debt owed by the state to an individual is a deprivation of property, but some courts have stated that it is not an acquisition of property and hence it does not give rise to a right to compensation.

The third type relates to the motives of the state in acting against the property owner. It is often framed in terms of the power exercised by the state. For example, compulsory acquisition is treated as a distinct power from the power of taxation or powers relating to the regulation of land use. Of the various powers over property, only the power of compulsory acquisition gives rise to a right to compensation.

This paper reviews these three methods and examines some of the difficult cases on each method. It then contrasts these tests with a more general limitation based on the proportionality of state action. A "pure" proportionality limitation would extend the right to property to any interference with property-like interests; that is, it would not accept the three limitations set out above. Instead, in each case, the court would ask whether the public and private interests are fairly balanced. The provision of compensation would be one factor to be weighed in the balance. The paper outlines how a proportionality limitation would differ from the limitations currently used. In particular, there would be a shift from a system where a loss of property is either compensated fully or not at all, as proportionality would raise the possibility of partial compensation for a partial "taking".

Limitations Based on the Nature of the Affected Interest

In the Commonwealth, constitutional protection applies to property rather than all vested, contractual or economic rights. The judicial conception of "property" is therefore a primary limitation on the right to compensation, and hence the distinction between compensatable and non-compensatable acts turns on whether the affected interest is property.[2] Accordingly, there has never been any difficulty with the idea that the compulsory acquisition of part of a parcel of land is compensatable. The fact that the owner remains an owner of something is clearly not enough to defeat the entitlement to compensation; it is enough that the state has acquired property. Since most courts regard property as a bundle of rights over a thing, it seems possible that an acquisition of some of the rights over a thing could be an acquisition of property. As in the case of the severance of the land, the fact that the owner of property retains a property interest of some sort should be immaterial. But, while the severance of the thing itself poses no difficulties for the courts, the severance of the bundle of rights does. Arguably, every right in the bundle of rights is a property right and hence any acquisition of any right in the bundle is a compensatable act. Richard Epstein puts it as follows:

> No matter how the basic entitlements contained within the bundle of ownership rights are divided and no matter how many times the division takes place, all of the pieces together, and each of them individually, fall within the scope of the eminent domain clause.[3]

This view of property would recognise a *prima facie* right to compensation in respect of any type of regulation that imposes a restriction on the exercise of an existing property right. Potentially, virtually all forms of land use regulation or consumer protection would be caught.[4]

Commonwealth courts are unwilling to push the right to property to this extreme, although they still apply the bundle-of-rights conception of property. Most courts distinguish between the rights that constitute the bundle of rights and property itself. In the leading case, *Belfast v OD Cars*, Viscount Simonds stated that

> ...anyone using the English language in its ordinary signification would ... agree that "property" is a word of very wide import, including intangible and tangible property. But he would surely deny that any one of those rights which in the aggregate constituted ownership of property could itself and by itself aptly be called "property" and to come to the instant case, he would deny that the right to use property in a particular way was itself property.[5]

Accordingly, regulations prohibiting a landowner from erecting buildings did not constitute a taking of "property" under section 5 of the Government of Ireland Act, 1920.

Belfast v OD Cars has been widely cited throughout the Commonwealth,[6] but it still requires the courts to distinguish between bundles of rights that constitute property and bundles of property rights that do not. In fact, although the courts accept the *dicta* in *Belfast v OD Cars*, they are also fond of saying that "property", as used in the constitutions, is an all-encompassing term: it "must receive the widest interpretation and must be held to refer to property of every kind";[7] it is "indicative and descriptive of every possible interest which a party can have";[8] and it is a "*nomen generalissimum* and extends to every species of valuable right and interest".[9] Not only does this seem to contradict *Belfast v OD Cars*, but it skirts around the difficulty that property can take on different meanings in different contexts.[10]

As most Commonwealth courts claim to interpret constitutions purposively, it suggests that they would wish to determine whether property exists in the light of some identified purpose of the right to property. For example, since Commonwealth courts tend to follow the liberal view of constitutional rights, they might argue that the purpose of the bill of rights generally is to protect the individual from the state; hence, the right to property should, at the very least, protect property interests that are closely tied to personal security and autonomy. From this, they might conclude that possessory rights to tangible property must always be treated as property under constitutional law. This is the position in the United States: the Supreme Court has stated that the right to possession is so important that any restriction on it must constitute a taking under the Fifth Amendment.[11] This could be described as a type of purposive analysis, as it invites the courts to associate some rights, such as the right to possession, with the purpose of the right to property.

In the Commonwealth, no such "bright-line" tests seem to apply, even where possessory rights are affected. A permanent loss of some possessory rights and a temporary loss of all possessory rights would probably amount to acquisitions of property, but there are no clear boundaries.[12] From *Belfast v OD Cars*, it would seem that neither a permanent but relatively trivial loss of possession nor a fleeting loss of all possession is a taking of property. It is a question of degree; the difficult point is that there are very few judicial guidelines to these questions. This is illustrated by two cases on controls imposed on the rights of company shareholders.

In *A-G v Lawrence* the Court of Appeal of St Christopher and Nevis held that the shareholders' right to manage the company through the power to appoint directors is constitutionally protected because it is "an important incident of property".[13] Hence, legislation that gave the Minister of Finance the power to appoint the majority of directors on the board of the St Kitts/Nevis/Anguilla National Bank amounted to a taking of a shareholder's property. By contrast, in *Government of Mauritius v Union Flacq Sugar Estates Co Ltd*,[14] the Privy Council held that legislation that barred companies from exercising voting rights attached to shares held in associated companies was not a taking of property. According to Lord Templeman, "[t]he Act did not deprive the company or any ordinary shareholder of property or any interests in or right over property. The company and its property are unaffected by the Act. Each ordinary shareholder remains entitled to his property namely his share and the dividends and capital to which he was entitled by virtue of his shareholding before the Act came into force."[15]

A further argument might identify the primary purpose of property with its social functions. In a sense, Commonwealth courts have done so, but only to the extent that property is associated with wealth. Accordingly, a law that effectively takes a substantial portion of the wealth associated with the ownership of a particular thing may be treated as taking of property. The classic formulation of this position is that of Holmes J in the leading American case, *Pennsylvania Coal Co v Mahon*:

> Government hardly could go on if to some extent values incident to property could not be diminished without paying for every such change in the general law. As long recognised, some values are enjoyed under an implied limitation and must yield to the police power. But obviously the implied limitation must have its limits, or the contract and due process clauses are gone. One fact for consideration in determining such limits is the extent of the diminution. When it reaches a certain magnitude, in most if not in all cases there must be an exercise of eminent domain and compensation to sustain the act.[16]

While Holmes J recognised that there are circumstances where the value of property may be diminished without giving rise to a right to compensation, "[t]he general rule at least is, that while property may be regulated to a certain extent, if regulation goes too far it will be recognised as a taking."[17]

Pennsylvania Coal has received widespread approval in the Commonwealth, although there is no consensus regarding the point at which a diminution of value becomes so serious that a compensatable act has occurred.[18] In *Manitoba Fisheries*, Ritchie J suggested that only an "obliteration of the appellant's entire business" would be compensatable.[19] By contrast, in *La Compagnie Sucriere de Bel Ombre Ltee v The Government of Mauritius*, the Privy Council stated that it was not necessary to reduce a business to a "valueless shell".[20] Moreover, it is not clear how the test works in combination with the bundle-of-rights conception of property. For example, in *Manitoba Fisheries* and several other cases, compensation claims have been made for the loss of goodwill caused by regulations that prohibit private companies from carrying on a particular type of business. Such cases arise where governments seek to create a state monopoly in an industry.[21] Where no assets are acquired from the private companies, or where assets are acquired but no compensation is paid for goodwill, the loss of goodwill can represent a significant economic loss. In terms of the diminution of value test, should the courts treat the loss as a total loss of value in a single asset (*ie* the goodwill), or as a partial loss of value in the business as a whole? In *Manitoba Fisheries*, the Canadian Supreme Court required a complete loss of value, it only applied the test to the value of the company's goodwill; in *Selangor Pilot Association (1946) v Government of Malaysia & Anor*, however, it appeared that the Privy Council treated a similar loss as only a partial loss in the value of the business as a whole.[22]

The position on the severance of the bundle of rights is therefore quite vague. It seems that it is not necessary to take every right in the bundle to demonstrate that a taking of property has occurred, but it is not clear just how many rights, or which rights, must be taken. It seems, at present, to involve a vague sort of balancing between public and private interests in the resources, but it is not possible to be more precise than that.

Limitations Based on the Purpose of the State's Actions

Plainly, there are circumstances where the degree of interference with property rights has no bearing on the question of compensation. For example, the state does not owe a duty to compensate when it seizes property to satisfy a tax or when it destroys property that puts public health or safety at risk. It makes no difference in such cases whether the interference with property is partial or total.[23] Commonwealth constitutions adopt two methods of ensuring that such actions are not compensatable. Some constitutions concentrate on the immediate purpose of the state's action, by requiring compensation only where property is acquired. Where the owner is merely deprived of property, there is no duty to compensate. This test would exclude a duty to compensate in cases involving the destruction or regulation of property, since neither destruction nor regulation normally involves the transfer of rights to the state or another party.[24] The second method concentrates on the motive or long-term purpose of the state's action, in that it identifies certain purposes where the public interest is sufficiently important that no compensation is required. For example, some constitutions state expressly that the compensation guarantee does not extend to property taken in satisfaction of a tax or a civil judgment, although it is quite clear that there has been an acquisition of property.

The Immediate Purpose of State Action and the Acquisition-Deprivation Distinction

Where the compensation guarantee is limited to the acquisition of property, two questions arise. The first concerns the nature of the test: is it a formal test, in the sense that it requires a movement of rights to the state, or is it sufficient merely to find that the state benefits in some way from the detriment suffered by the owner? Plainly, the different tests that might be adopted reflect the different views of property outlined above, and the choice of test should reflect the court's perception of the purpose of the right to property. In terms of acquisitions of property, the difference is most easily illustrated in relation to the extinction of debts owed by the state. In such cases, the courts accept quite readily that the creditor is deprived of property in the debt, but there is greater doubt over the acquisition of property by the state. Some courts have taken a highly formal approach and hold that no acquisition of property occurs because the state cannot become its own creditor.[25] Other courts hold that an acquisition occurs if the state realises a financial benefit by extinguishing the debt.[26]

The second question is whether the courts should seek to minimise the importance of the test by interpreting the right to property in a manner that extends it to deprivations of property. There have been several cases where this has happened. This first occurred with the Indian Supreme Court in relation to Article 31 of the Constitution. As originally drafted, Article 31(1) stated that "[n]o person shall be *deprived* of property save in accordance with law", but without guaranteeing compensation. Article 31(2) stated that "[n]o property ... shall be taken possession of or acquired for public purposes" unless compensation was paid. It therefore appears that only Article 31(2) guaranteed compensation, and only where possession was taken or property was acquired. However, in *Dwarkadas Shrinivas v Sholapur Spinning and Weaving Co Ltd*, Mahajan J stated that only a "close and literal construction" of Article 31 could justify limiting the duty to compensate to an acquisition of property, since "[i]t is immaterial to the person who is deprived of property as to what use the

State makes of his property or what title it acquires in it. The protection is against loss of property to the owner..."[27] The Supreme Court therefore held that the legislature could not deprive an individual of property without adequate compensation.[28]

Several decades later, in *Selangor Pilot Association (1946) v Government of Malaysia & Anor*,[29] the same question arose under provisions of the Malaysian Constitution that were similar to the original Article 31 of the Indian Constitution. The Privy Council explicitly rejected the reasoning of *Dwarkadas*. However, in 1985, just seven years after *Selangor Pilot Association*, the Privy Council appeared to reverse its position. In *Société United Docks and Others v Government of Mauritius; Marine Workers Union and Others v Mauritius Marine Authority*,[30] the extinction of a debt was challenged under the Constitution of Mauritius, which protects against the "compulsory acquisition" of property. Lord Templeman, who delivered the decision in *Société United Docks*, assumed that the extinction of the debt was no more than a deprivation of property but, like Mahajan J in *Dwarkadas*, he doubted that the distinction between acquisitions and deprivations should determine whether the duty to compensate should apply. Although Lord Templeman did not refer to *Dwarkadas* (or *Selangor Pilot Association*), his position was very close to that of Mahajan J, as he stated that deprivation should be compensatable because "[l]oss caused by deprivation and destruction is the same in quality and effect as loss caused by compulsory acquisition".[31]

The reasoning in *Société United Docks* involves an activist construction of the opening provision of the fundamental rights chapter of the Mauritian Constitution. The opening provision provides that:

> 3. It is hereby recognised and declared that in Mauritius there have existed and shall continue to exist without discrimination by reason of race, place of origin, political opinions, colour, creed or sex, but subject to respect for the rights and freedoms of others and for the public interest, each and all of the following human rights and fundamental freedoms, namely - . . .
> (c) the right of the individual to protection for the privacy of his home and other property and from deprivation of property without compensation...

A number of specific provisions follow, including section 8, which states that:

> 8. No property of any description shall be compulsorily taken possession of, and no interest in or right over property of any description shall be

compulsorily acquired, except where...

(c) provision is made by a law applicable to that taking of possession or acquisition -

(i) for the prompt payment of adequate compensation...

On its face, the effect of section 3 is unclear. There are similar provisions in many other Commonwealth constitutions; prior to *Société United Docks*, a number of courts stated that these provisions are merely preambular with no independent effect, but Lord Templeman held that it must be given effect; otherwise, the "inexplicable inconsistency" that only an acquisition of property would be protected would result.

Lord Templeman's approach is somewhat surprising, as he took a formal view of acquisition and property, but much less formal view of interpretation itself. It is quite clear that he accepts the liberal view that the primary purpose of a right to property is the protection of the individual from the state, and that the Constitution of Mauritius protects property as it is traditionally understood from any form of interference.[32] Hence, constitutional interpretation must take this purpose into account. By contrast, the Zimbabwean courts also profess to interpret purposively and also adopt a traditional view of property, but do not give themselves the freedom to extend the express protection of property from acquisitions to deprivations of property.[33]

A further contrast is provided by the Australian courts, which do not share Lord Templeman's belief that acquisition and deprivation should not be treated differently.[34] Their reasons are very close to the position taken by Joseph Sax in his 1964 article, "Takings and the Police Power".[35] Sax argues that the purpose of a constitutional guarantee of compensation for takings is not merely to protect individuals against loss, as Lord Templeman seems to assume. The real purpose, argues Sax, is the prevention of arbitrary acts of government. The duty to compensate provides a check on the arbitrary action by removing the potential for profit in those situations where the risk of arbitrary action arises from the possibility of profit; that is, when the state acquires resources for its own account. Arbitrary action is not as likely to arise when the state merely arbitrates between competing private claims to resources, and hence compensation is not normally required in such circumstances.[36] Arbitrating between competing claims often results in the deprivation of one person's property, but there is no corresponding acquisition by the state.

Sax's theory is consistent with the approach taken by the Australian High Court in *Mutual Pools and Staff Pty Ltd v The*

Commonwealth of Australia[37] and *Georgiadis v Australian and Overseas Telecommunications Corporation.*[38] *Mutual Pools* arose over legislation concerning the refund of an improperly collected tax on the construction of swimming-pools. The builders remitted the tax, but many of the builders had collected the tax from their customers. In such cases, the legislation provided that the tax would be refunded directly to the customers. The builders challenged direct refunds, on the basis that they had a restitutionary claim to the tax, which had been acquired by the Commonwealth as a consequence of the decision not to refund the tax to them. The High Court upheld the legislation, for reasons that come quite close to Sax's theory. Mason CJ stated that, although the loss of a restitutionary claim could amount to an acquisition of property by the Commonwealth, no compensation was payable in this case. The general principle could be derived from the existing body of cases, where it was apparent that compensation would not be payable where the acquisition of property by the Commonwealth "was subservient and incidental to or consequential upon the principal purpose and effect sought to be achieved by the law so that the provision respecting property had no recognisable independent character." In these cases, "the relevant statute provided a means of resolving or adjusting competing claims, obligations or property rights of individuals as an incident of the regulation of their relationship".[39] Here, the legislation merely determined which one of two competing private claims to the refund should succeed.

In *Georgiadis*, it was held that the Commonwealth extinguished the common law claims of the applicants in order to enhance its resources and, for this reason, compensation should have been paid. Some members of the court relied partly on the fact that the legislation only extinguished the claims of Commonwealth employees. If the legislation had applied to all employees, public or private, it may have survived scrutiny under section 51(xxxi), as the purpose of the legislation would not have been to enhance the Commonwealth's resources but to adjust competing private claims to resources. This is borne out by Australian cases holding that laws providing for the price controls,[40] land use restrictions[41] and the sequestration of the property of bankrupts do not fall under section 51(xxxi).[42] In such cases, the state does not acquire resources for its own account. Indeed, even a direct transfer of property from a private person to the Commonwealth may fall outside section 51(xxxi) if the primary objective of the Commonwealth is something other than the enhancement of its resources.[43]

From the Zimbabwean and Australian cases, it is clear that the "inexplicable inconsistency" of compensating for acquisitions of property but not deprivations of property, identified by Lord Templeman in *Société United Docks*, is only inexplicable if one views the purpose of the right to property as purely a protection for the individual. If one takes the position of the Zimbabwean courts, the language of the provisions makes the intentions of the constitution-makers very clear; absent some ambiguity in the provisions, there is no justification for looking behind them. The word "acquisition" is clear enough; at least, it is clear that it is not the same as "deprivation". While this may not satisfy courts that interpret constitutions purposively, the perspective of the Australian courts and Joseph Sax does provide an alternative purpose to the right to property as prevention of arbitrary government; not every case of individual loss raises such doubts about government motives that it requires compensation in order to prevent arbitrary or corrupt action.

The Motives of State Action and the Powers Over Property

The Australian approach suggests that it is the ends of state action that are important. That is, the reason for acquiring property is the determining factor in deciding whether compensation should be paid. Elsewhere in the Commonwealth, there is little doubt that the state may at least interfere with private property for some purposes without payment of compensation, irrespective of the degree of interference or the receipt of the property by the state.

The Commonwealth constitutions based on the Nigerian model include relatively detailed derogation clauses that set out certain purposes for which property can be taken without compensation. These clauses typically state that compensation is not payable to the extent that the taking of property is necessary because the property endangers public health or safety; or that the taking is a penalty or forfeiture for breach of any law; or if the taking relates to certain aspects of private law and civil proceedings, such as the enforcement of contracts, the execution of judgments and the limitation of actions. Most of these derogation clauses also provide that any such exception is not available if the taking "is shown not to be reasonably justifiable in a democratic society."

The closing proviso to the derogations clause incorporates the idea of proportionality. Although the proviso has been analysed in only a small number of property cases, similar language is found in derogations to other rights in the Nigerian-model constitutions and in the European Convention on Human Rights,[44] as well as the general derogation clauses of the Canadian Charter of Rights and Freedoms[45] and the South African Constitution.[46] The proportionality test is described in *Nyambirai v National Social Security Authority*, where Gubbay CJ stated that, in judging whether a compulsory acquisition of property without compensation for a compulsory savings scheme was permissible, the court

> ...will ask itself whether: (i) the legislative objective is sufficiently important to justify limiting a fundamental right; (ii) the measures designed to meet the legislative objective are rationally connected to it; and (iii) the means used to impair the right or freedom are no more than is necessary to accomplish the objective.[47]

The first part of the *Nyambirai* test has not raised difficulties and it is unlikely that it would do so, as it is a general principle that an expropriation must serve a public purpose. It therefore seems unlikely that the public purpose that justifies expropriation would not satisfy the test.

The second part of the test provided grounds for challenge in *Commissioner of Taxes v CW (Pvt) Ltd.* On whether the tax would not be "reasonably justifiable in a democratic society", Gubbay JA (as he then was) stated that the issue was whether it was "arbitrary or irrational", in the following sense:

> The test ... is whether the particular classification challenged by the taxpayer rests upon some ground of difference having a fair, equitable and substantial relation to the achievement of a valid legislative objective, so that all persons similarly circumstanced shall be treated alike. If the classification lacks these attributes the legislative action must be taken to be irrational. Accordingly, the question to be posed in this case is whether there is some ground that rationally explains the different treatment...[48]

The ground of difference rested solely on the fact that the taxpayers had challenged the constitutionality of an expropriation of property in separate proceedings.[49] For this reason, Gubbay JA concluded that "no acceptable rationale immediately appears"; indeed, the legislation was "irrational and arbitrary"[50] and failed to bear "a fair, equitable and substantial relation to the achievement of a valid legislative objective"[51] because it was intended to punish those who had challenged its constitutionality. This was especially difficult to justify in a democratic society.

Part (iii) of the *Nyambirai* test has not been discussed at any length in property cases, although in *Nyambirai* itself, the Zimbabwean Supreme Court was content to observe that similar pension schemes operated in other countries. This suggests that the court did not think that the overall impact on the contributor was significant enough to call the constitutionality of the programme into question.

Limitations Based on Proportionality

While the derogation clause of the Nigerian-model constitutions allows the courts to invoke proportionality as the basis for developing limitations on the right to property, the influence of the idea of proportionality has been relatively modest in relation to property cases to date. Arguably, greater use of a proportionality test would reduce the need to rely on the other types of limitation to the right to compensation. Determining the meaning of "property", "acquisition", "deprivation" and "compensation" would be less important than striking a balance between individual and state based on a broad test of proportionality.

To some extent, the balancing process of the proportionality test is already part of the other tests for determining compensatability. As discussed above, determining whether property has been taken often involves a balancing between public and private interests. Similarly, elements of proportionality tests are evident in cases where compensatability is said to depend on the nature or purpose of the power that is exercised. In Australia, the Commonwealth may acquire property without just terms only if the acquisition is "reasonably incidental" to some other head of power reserved to the Commonwealth.[52] Some judges maintain that an acquisition of property is reasonably incidental only if it is both a rational and proportionate means of pursuing an objective under the relevant head of power.[53] Similarly, as mentioned above, most constitutions state that property may only be taken for a public purpose or in the public interest; in this sense, the rationality aspect of proportionality is already incorporated into the right to property. In addition, the compensation guarantee incorporates the balancing aspect of the proportionality test. However, there is no flexibility in the balancing; both courts and constitutional framers in the Commonwealth seem to have assumed that the guarantee of compensation is a guarantee of full compensation.

The importance of proportionality may change if Commonwealth courts follow the guidance given in a recent case from Mauritius, *La Compagnie Sucriere de Bel Ombre Ltee v The Government of Mauritius*.[54] In this case, the Privy Council upheld legislation that provided tenant farmers with greater security of tenure, but at the cost of depriving landowners of certain rights over land. From the discussion in this paper, it is apparent that there were several possible arguments for upholding the legislation. For example, the Mauritian court stated that, although some property rights were taken from the landowners, those rights were not sufficiently important to constitute "property" under the right to property; and, in any case, a compensatable deprivation would occur only if property was reduced to a "valueless shell".[55] However, in the Privy Council, Lord Woolf felt that this was too narrow: "to refer to a "valueless shell" is to overstate the situation which needs to exist before there is a constructive deprivation".[56]

Under some constitutions, it could be argued that the legislation merely deprived the landowners of rights. However, in *Bel Ombre*, this argument would have required a review of the decision in *Société United Docks*. As explained above, the Privy Council decided in *Société United Docks* that section 3 of the Constitution protects against the deprivation of property without compensation. Lord Woolf indicated that Lord Templeman's construction of sections 3 and 8 was not without difficulty; however, he did not suggest that section 3 was a mere preamble without independent force.

Finally, it might have been argued that the purpose of the legislation was such that no compensation was payable, irrespective of the impact on the landowners. One can compare with the American case, *Midkiff v Hawaii Housing Authority*,[57] where the Supreme Court of the United States held that Hawaii's leasehold enfranchisement legislation was enacted under the police power.[58] This possibility was not raised.

Lord Woolf drew on the jurisprudence of the European Court of Human Rights. Article 1, Protocol 1 protects property in the following terms:

> Every natural or legal person is entitled to the peaceful enjoyment of his possessions. No one shall be deprived of his possessions except in the public interest and subject to the conditions provided for by law and by the general principles of international law. The preceding provisions shall not, however, in any way impair the right of a state to enforce such laws as it deems necessary to control the use of property in accordance with the general interest or to secure the payment of taxes or other contributions or

penalties.

In *Sporrong and Lönnroth*, the European Court stated that Article 1 of the Protocol sets out three rules regarding rights to property.

The first rule, which is of general nature, enounces the principle of peaceful enjoyment of property; it is set out in the first sentence of the paragraph. The second rule covers deprivation of possessions and subjects it to certain conditions; it appears in the second sentence of the same paragraph. The third rule recognises the States are entitled, amongst other things, to control the use of property in accordance with the general interest, by enforcing such laws as they deem necessary to that purpose; it is contained in the second paragraph.[59]

These rules overlap, in that all three rules require a "fair balance" between "the demands of the general interest of the community and the requirements of the protection of the individual's fundamental rights."[60] However, the method of achieving of a "fair balance" under each may differ. Compensation would normally be required to achieve a fair balance under the second rule, but it is merely one factor in achieving a fair balance under the first and third rules. Furthermore, even though a formal acquisition of title normally requires some compensation, it may not be necessary to provide full compensation to achieve a fair balance in every case. For example, in *Lithgow v UK*, the court held that the measure of compensation for the nationalisation of property need not be the same as it is for the typical compulsory purchase of land.[61] Similarly, in *James v UK*, the court stated that, where the state seeks to achieve greater economic or social justice by re-allocating property rights, compensation need not be given at full market value.[62] In these cases, it appears that a greater public gain justifies the imposition of a greater individual loss.

Prior to *La Compagnie Sucriere de Bel Ombre Ltee*, the Protocol had little influence on Commonwealth jurisprudence, primarily because it refers to the "enjoyment of possessions" rather than "property" and it does not expressly require compensation for a deprivation of property.[63] However, in *Bel Ombre*, Lord Woolf stated that the three rules of Article 1 of Protocol 1, as set out in *Sporrong and Lönnroth*, provide a guide on the interpretation of the Mauritius Constitution. Section 3 corresponds to the first rule of *Sporrong and Lönnroth*, section 8 corresponds to the second rule and the derogations clause of section 8 corresponds to the third rule. Hence, although section 3 of the Constitution, as construed in *Société United Docks*, protects against the deprivation of property without compensation, it does not guarantee compensation in every case:[64]

> ...[regulations] would only contravene the protection provided by section 3 if, because of the lack of any provision for compensation, they do not achieve a fair balance between the interests of the community and the rights of the individuals whose property interests are adversely affected.

On the facts of the case, Lord Woolf concluded that a fair balance was achieved, even though no compensation was paid.

Bel Ombre goes further than merely resolving the difficulties that were created by the *Société United Docks* decision, which could have been interpreted as requiring compensation in a great many situations. Lord Woolf's reasoning would allow the courts considerably greater flexibility in deciding property cases. Prior to *Bel Ombre*, property cases presented the courts with two choices: either require full compensation or no compensation.[65] It is not surprising that Commonwealth constitutional framers and courts would regard the balancing process in this way. One can see close parallels with common law of negligence: pure economic loss is not generally recoverable, even if the loss was foreseeable and degree of loss seems just as significant as a loss to property. Moreover, as in negligence (and tort law generally), the ordinary measure of compensation is full compensation. The result is that a small number of people who are affected by a careless act are able to recover for the losses caused by it. Limiting recoverable losses to property losses can produce distinctions that seem arbitrary, but as long as full compensation is promised, limitations are necessary to avoid an undue financial burden on the potential payer, whether it is the class of potential tortfeasors or the public treasury. In fact, the effects of a pure proportionality test on the compensation burden resulting from equal levels of state action cannot be predicted. More cases might be treated as requiring a balance, but the balance might be struck at a lower level of compensation in many cases now requiring full compensation.

Conclusions

The more general application of a proportionality test would permit some flexibility in the tests themselves. That is, as long as it is not necessary to require full compensation in every case where an acquisition (or deprivation) of property (or property rights) has occurred, the emphasis can shift to a more general question of whether an adequate balance has been struck. Inviting the courts to engage in a more flexible balancing process may produce greater justice in the individual case, but some have argued that it challenges the judicial conception of its role. It has been argued, both in relation to tort and takings law, that a more open balancing process would endanger the rule of law by creating tremendous uncertainty in the law.[66] This seems doubtful. Neither the reasoning in *Bel Ombre* nor the jurisprudence of the European Court of Human Rights seem so indefinite that the cases can be said to have been decided on judicial whim. The real change in judicial style would be a movement away from "trying to identify the linguistic core of some very general and ill-defined word or phrase,"[67] such as "property", "acquisition", "deprivation". Perhaps a general proportionality test, and the balancing process, would not be more certain than the linguistic, conceptual analysis that now dominates the Commonwealth analysis of the right to property, but it is equally possible that the balancing process would be more easily accessible and understood.

Notes

1   For a general review, see T Allen, "Commonwealth Constitutions and the Right not to be Deprived of Property," (1993) 42 ICLQ 523.

2   S 299 of the Government of India Act, 1935, went even further, by limiting the right to property to land and commercial and industrial undertakings. This was done because the British found it impossible to arrive at a wording for provisions protecting personal property without endangering the power to tax; see Sir Thomas Inskip, the Attorney-General: "It is practically impossible - I think quite impossible - to devise words which will prevent [the state] from taking personal property without compensation unless we do that which is absurd, namely, make it illegal to tax people." 300 HC Debs 5s (1934-1935), 1071-90.

3   Richard A Epstein, *Takings: Private Property and the Power of Eminent Domain* (Harvard University Press: 1985), p 57.

4   For a criticism of Epstein's position, see Margaret Jane Radin, "The Liberal Conception of Property: Cross Currents in the Jurisprudence of Takings" (1988) 88 Colum LR 1667, pp 1674-78.

5   [1960] AC 490, p 517.

6   See, *eg, Dwarkadas Shrinivas v Sholapur Spinning and Weaving Co Ltd*, AIR [1954] SC 119, p 136 *per* Das J. But *cf Saghir Ahmad v The State of Uttar Pradesh* [1955] SCR 707, p 728, *per* Mukherjea J; *Smith, Kline & French Laboratories Ltd et al v Attorney-General of Canada* (1986) 34 DLR (4th) 584 (FCA), (1985) 24 DLR (4th) 321 (FTD), *per* Strayer J p 356 (TD).

7   *Madan Mohan Pathak v Union of India*, AIR [1978] SC 803, p 820, *per* Bhagwati J, following Shah J in *RC Cooper v Union of India* AIR [1970] SC 564.

8　　*Zimbabwe Township Developers (Pvt) Ltd v Lou's Shoes (Pvt) Ltd* (1983) 2 ZLR 376 (SC Zim), p 384, *per* Georges CJ.

9　　*Minister of State for the Army v Dalziel* (1944) 68 CLR 261 (HC Aust), at 290, *per* Starke J.

10　　See Thomas C Grey, "The Disintegration of Property," in J Roland Pennock and John W Chapman, eds, *Property: Nomos XXII* (New York University Press: 1980).

11　　*Loretto v Teleprompter Manhattan CATV Corp* 458 US 419 (1982), *Nollan v California Coastal Commission* 483 US 825 (1987).

12　　See, *eg*, *D'Aguiar v Attorney-General* (1962), 4 WIR 481 (SC British Guiana) and *Minister of State for the Army v Dalziel* (1944) 68 CLR 261 (HC Aust).

13　　[1985] LRC (Const) 921, p 930, *per* Peterkin CJ.

14　　[1992] 1 WLR 903 (PC-Mauritius); see also *Dwarkadas Shrinivas v Sholapur Spinning and Weaving Co Ltd*, AIR [1954] SC 119, where the Supreme Court held that voting rights, and management itself, do not constitute property.

15　　[1992] 1 WLR 903, p 911.

16　　260 US 393, p 413 (1922).

17　　*Ibid*, p 415.

18　　See, *eg*, *Belfast v OD Cars* [1960] AC 490, p 519, *per* Viscount Simonds; *Selangor Pilot Association (1946) v Government of Malaysia & Anor* [1978] AC 337 (PC-Malaysia), p 358, *per* Lord Salmon (diss); *Revere Jamaica Alumina, Ltd v Attorney General* (1977) 26 WIR 486 (SC Jam), p 497; *State of West Bengal v Subodh Gopal Bose* [1954] SCR 587, p 618 *per* Patanjali Sastri CJ; *La Compagnie Sucriere de Bel Ombre Ltee v The Government of Mauritius* [1995] 3 LRC 494 (PC), 502-506. Note that the relevance of the diminution of value test has been doubted by some Commonwealth judges; see, *eg*, *Mutual Pools and Staff Pty Ltd v The Commonwealth of Australia* (1994) 179 CLR 155, pp 195-196, 201-202, *per* Dawson and Toohey JJ; *Georgiadis v Australian and Overseas Telecommunications Corporation* (1994) 179 CLR 297, p 315 *per* Dawson J, pp 319-320 *per* Toohey J.

19　　*Manitoba Fisheries v The Queen* (1978) 88 DLR (3d) 462 (SCC), p 471.

20　　[1995] 3 LRC 494.

21　　See also *Selangor Pilot Association (1946) v Government of Malaysia & Anor* [1978] AC 337 (PC-Malaysia); *Saghir Ahmad v The State of Uttar Pradesh* [1955] SCR 707; *RC Cooper v Union of India* AIR [1970] SC 564; *cf Société United Docks and Others v Government of Mauritius; Marine Workers Union and Others v Mauritius Marine Authority* [1985] 1 AC 585; [1985] 2 WLR 114; [1985] LRC (Const) 801 (PC-Mauritius).

22　　*Ibid*. See generally Frank I Michelman, "Property, Utility, and Fairness: Comments on the Ethical Foundations of 'Just Compensation' Law," (1967) 80 Harv LR 1165, pp 1192, 1232-33; Carol Rose, "*Mahon* Reconstructed: Why the Takings Issue Is Still a Muddle," (1984) 57 South Calif Rev 561, pp 566-569.

23　　Holmes J acknowledges this point in *Pennsylvania Coal* where he states that, "[a]s long recognised, some values are enjoyed under an implied limitation and must yield to the police power." 260 US 393, p 413 (1922). In *Belfast v OD Cars* [1960] AC 490, Lord Radcliffe's reasoning follows this line of argument, rather than the severance argument of Viscount Simonds.

24　　*Davies and Others v Minister of Lands, Agriculture and Water Development* 1996 (9) BCLR 1209 (ZS); 1996 SACLR LEXIS 29.

25   See, *eg, Hewlett v Minister of Finance and Another* [1982] 1 SA 490, [1981] ZLR
      571 (SC Zim); but *cf Mhora v Minister of Home Affairs* [1990] 2 ZLR 236 (HC),
      Chairman of the Public Service Commission v Zimbabwe Teachers Association
      [1997] 1 LRC 479.

26   *Georgiadis v Australian and Overseas Telecommunications Corporation* (1994) 179
      CLR 297. Mason CJ stated that it is sufficient that the extinction of the obligation
      "results in a direct benefit or financial gain" to the Commonwealth (p 305); Brennan J
      stated that there is an acquisition if the release from liability is the "correlative" of the
      plaintiff's claim (p 311).

27   AIR [1954] SC 119, p 128.

28   In *Dwarkadas*, it meant that legislation that allowed the state to appoint a company's
      board of directors, without compensation, infringed Art 31(2), although in formal
      terms only a deprivation of the shareholders' rights had occurred. See also *The State
      of West Bengal v Subodh Gopal Bose* [1954] SCR 587. In response to *Dwarkadas*,
      Parliament passed the Constitution (Fourth Amendment) Act, 1955, which added cl
      31(2A) to Art 31; it provided that "where a law does not provide for the transfer of the
      ownership or right to possession of any property ... it shall not be deemed to provide
      for the compulsory acquisition or requisitioning of property, notwithstanding that it
      deprives any person of his property."

29   [1978] AC 337.

30   [1985] 1 AC 585; [1985] LRC (Const) 801 (PC-Mauritius).

31   [1985] AC 585, 600A; [1985] LRC (Const) 801, 841.

32   More recently, in *La Compagnie Sucriere de Bel Ombre Ltee v The Government of
      Mauritius* [1995] 3 LRC 494, the Privy Council expressed some concern at the
      apparent breadth of Lord Templeman's opinion. As explained below, they further
      modified his views by holding that s 3 did not guarantee full compensation in every
      case of deprivation.

33   See especially *Hewlett v Minister of Finance and Another* [1982] 1 SA 490, [1981]
      ZLR 571 (SC Zim); *Davies and Others v Minister of Lands, Agriculture and Water
      Development* 1996 (9) BCLR 1209 (ZS); 1996 SACLR LEXIS 29.

34   See, *eg, The Commonwealth v Tasmania (The Tasmanian Dam Case)* (1983) 158
      CLR 1, p 145, *per* Mason J; *Georgiadis v Australian and Overseas
      Telecommunications Corporation* (1994) 179 CLR 297, pp 304-305, *per* Mason CJ,
      Deane and Gaudron, JJ.

35   (1964) 74 Yale LJ 36.

36   Sax argues that there are several reasons why the risk of arbitrariness is greater when
      governments acquire resources for their own account than when they arbitrate
      between competing private interests: (i) the risk of corruption is greater; (ii) there is,
      in every case, a conflict of interest between governmental and private interests when
      the compulsory powers are used to acquire resources; and (iii) the acquisition of
      resources is far more likely to have an unequal impact on individuals (*ibid*, p 64
      passim).

37   (1994) 179 CLR 155.

38   (1994) 179 CLR 297.

39   *Mutual Pools and Staff Pty Ltd v The Commonwealth of Australia* (1994) 179 CLR
      155, p 171; see also Deane and Gaudron JJ, pp 189-190: s 51(xxxi) does not apply to
      "...laws which provide for the creation, modification, extinguishment or transfer of

rights and liabilities as an incident of, or a means for enforcing, some general regulation of the conduct, rights and obligations of citizens in relationships or areas which need to be regulated in the common interest."

40   *British Medical Association v The Commonwealth* (1949) 79 CLR 201.

41   *The Tasmanian Dam Case* (1983) 158 CLR 1; see also *The Queen in Right of British Columbia v Tener* (1985) 17 DLR (4th) 1 (SC Can), p 17, where Estey J distinguished between restrictions on land use imposed to "enhance the value of a public park" and "the imposition of zoning regulation and the regulation of activities on lands, fire regulation limits and so on [which] add nothing to the value of public property."

42   *Attorney-General (Cth) v Schmidt* (1961) 105 CLR 361, p 372.

43   For example, in *Re Director of Public Prosecutions; ex parte Lawler* (1994) 179 CLR 270, where the court held that the forfeiture of property used for illegal activity cannot be characterised as an "acquisition of property" under s 51(xxxi), because forfeiture is intended to impose a penalty and not to enhance Commonwealth resources.

44   Although the right to peaceful enjoyment of possessions does not contain the proviso.

45   S 1.

46   S 36.

47   [1996] 1 LRC 64, p 75.

48   1989 (3) ZLR 361, pp 372-373.

49   *May v Reserve Bank of Zimbabwe* [1986] 3 SA 107 (Zim SC).

50   1989 (3) ZLR 361, p 373. Gubbay JA, also referred, with approval, to the following statement from *Chintaman Rao v Madhya Pradesh* [1950] SCR 759, p 763, *per* Mahajan J: "the word 'reasonable' implies intelligent care and deliberation - the choice of a course which reason dictates, and that legislation which arbitrarily or excessively invades the enjoyment of a substantive right does not possess the quality of reasonableness".

51   *Ibid*, p 373.

52   The Commonwealth has the power to acquire property under s 51(xxxi), but only on "just terms"; hence, if it can acquire property under some other head of power reserved to it under the Constitution, it need not do so on "just terms".

53   Others maintain that it is merely a test of rationality. Contrast Deane and Dawson JJ in *Re Director of Public Prosecutions; ex parte Lawler* (1994) 179 CLR 270: Deane J stated (at p 286, Gaudron J agreeing) determining whether legislation is reasonably incidental "will usually involve a consideration of whether it is reasonably capable of being seen as appropriate and adapted to achieving, or, as reasonably proportionate to some object or purpose within power". Dawson J stated (at p 291) that "The question is, of course, one of connection, not whether the means adopted to achieve the end are appropriate or desirable in the view of the Court. And notwithstanding the immediate operation of the law, if its end lies within the scope of the power, then there will ordinarily be a sufficient connection to support the law." See also *Nationwide News Pty Ltd v Wills* (1992) 177 CLR 1, pp 26-34, 39-40, 68-69, 92-94, 100-101.

54   [1995] 3 LRC 494.

55   *Cf Belfast v OD Cars* [1960] AC 490.

56   Although he also remarked that "[e]ven in the case of section 3 there is difficulty in bringing the increased control of land which [the legislation] involves within its language."

57   467 US 229, 104 SCt 2321 (1984).

58   The legislation was intended to attack the concentration of land holding in Hawaii; no compensation was required because "[r]egulating oligopoly and the evils associated with it is a classic example of a State's police powers." 467 US 229, p 242.

59   *Sporrong and Lönnroth*, A 52 (1982), para 61.

60   *Ibid*, para 69.

61   A 102 (1986), para 120.

62   A 98 (1986), para 54.

63   See *Bickle & Others v Minister of Home Affairs; Minister of Home Affairs v Bickle & Others* (1983) (Zim SC), Korsah J, p 421.

64   [1995] 3 LRC 494, pp 504-505.

65   The meaning of "full compensation" is controversial; there are difficult questions over matters such as the determination of market value and the relevance of the value to the taker, but in general compensation is quite generous. One recent and interesting development, contrary to the general trend, is the enactment of s 25 of the South African Constitution, as it breaks from the Commonwealth tradition of guaranteeing full compensation.

66   *Cf* Radin, *op cit*.

67   David Beatty, "Human Rights and the Rules of Law," in D Beatty, ed, *Human Rights and Judicial Review: A Comparative Perspective* (Kluwer: Dordrecht, 1994), p 51.

11 The Constitutional Property Clause and Police Power Regulation of Intangible Commercial Property - A Comparative Analysis of Case Law

AJ VAN DER WALT*

Introduction

Comparative constitutional case law presents the analyst with a quite bewildering array of precedents regarding the validity, in terms of a constitutional property guarantee, of state interferences with private property interests. The reported cases cover a diversity of topics, ranging from the content and meaning of "property" to the calculation of just and equitable compensation in cases where the property in question is expropriated. In addition to the cases, there is an equally extensive volume of academic commentary, often accompanied by an apology for the confusing state of learning in this field. The purpose of this paper is to suggest an avenue for avoiding at least some of the confusions in this field, by introducing a number of distinctions that highlight the dangers of using decisions in one area as authority for cases in another. I focus on a limited category of cases, defined by three considerations: first, the property in question consists of some kind of intangible commercial right or interest; secondly, the purpose of the state interference with the said property is to regulate, in terms of the state's police power, the use and exploitation of that property in some way or another; and, thirdly, the effect of the regulation in question is so harsh or extreme that the property interest is lost, destroyed or rendered worthless in the process.

The first consideration narrows the analysis down to cases regarding intangible property, and particularly intangible property with some form of commercial interest or value. Included in this category are business enterprises in general; the goodwill of a business concern; shares in a company; debts; a business interest in a commercial licence, permit or quota; immaterial property interests deriving from or connected with patents, copyrights, trademarks and confidential commercial information; and so forth. Occasionally, reference will be made to a case where the property in question was held individually rather than commercially, but in these cases the question whether the property was owned individually or commercially will usually not make much difference. However, because of the focus on commercial interests certain related issues are ignored – for example, rent control regulation cases are ignored because they normally affect private residential rather than commercial property, and interesting as housing regulation and rent control cases are, they involve unique characteristics and problems all their own that cannot be addressed here. This analysis will not attempt to describe or investigate the constitutional nature and content of intangible commercial rights in any detail either; the nature of the property interest is used as a demarcation criterion here but does not constitute the focus of the investigation.[1]

The second consideration narrows the analysis down to instances of state regulation of commercial enterprises and property interests, based on the police power and aimed at the promotion of the public interest. The intention of the state actions and statutes in this category is always to control and regulate the use, enjoyment and exploitation of the property involved, in the public interest. It will be necessary, in the course of the analysis, to refer to wider issues such as the constitutional validity of limitations of entrenched rights and the distinction between deprivations and expropriations of property, but once again the police power nature of regulations features here as a demarcation criterion and not as a central concern. Moreover, cases dealing with land-use regulation, while arguably satisfying this criterion, will be ignored because land-use regulation cases are determined by unique and specific factors[2] not necessarily germane to the regulation of intangible property as such.

The third consideration narrows the analysis down to situations where the regulation in question, although it is aimed at police power control over the use and exploitation of property, results in infringements that practically destroy the property rights, thereby raising questions about the nature of the limitation imposed[3] and its general validity.[4] The regulation can have extraordinarily harsh effects because the business is taken over by the state, or because a state monopoly is created at the cost of the private enterprise, or because the state interferes with the management of a commercial enterprise, or because the business that loses its permit or licence cannot function, or for any similar reason. In some cases the loss is caused by a statute that cancels a state debt. Again, the intention here is to analyse cases dealing with regulations that have the defined kind of effect, and not to discuss the wider issues surrounding this category of regulations and their justifiability or validity in general. Some general remarks about the nature of regulation and the public interest it serves are included in the conclusion.

While these demarcation principles may seem artificial or arbitrary, they have the advantage of isolating a relatively clear field of investigation and thereby reducing the scope of the inquiry to manageable proportions. Some of the implications of this inquiry could be suitable for extension to other areas in the broader field of constitutional property, and perhaps they can even be used to construct a rudimentary basis for a methodology of comparative constitutional property rights. My aim here is more modest, though, and I make no claims in this regard. The main reasons for selecting a topic defined by these rather narrow criteria are that it epitomises some of the most intriguing difficulties that confront a student of constitutional property law, and that the case law on this topic is so interesting and confusing that it deserves special attention anyway. To demonstrate my awareness of the fact that my selection is as significant in its exclusions as in its inclusions, I start the discussion off with a case that does not satisfy the criteria I have identified: *Harksen v Lane NO and Another*.[5] This is the first case in which the South African Constitutional Court was offered an opportunity to say something substantial about the property clause in section 28[6] of the interim Constitution of 1993,[7] and it does not really fit into the framework of this discussion because it concerns all the property of the applicant and not just her (individually held) intangible assets. However, patriotism demands that I should start off with a discussion of a South African case, and besides, the *Harksen* decision offers an opportunity to segue into a discussion of a number of decisions of the Zimbabwe Supreme Court that do satisfy my selection criteria, and that illustrate the problem I had in mind when selecting this topic.

In the next section of this paper I discuss the *Harksen* decision by way of a case study that highlights some of the problems raised by the regulation of intangible commercial property and the case law on that topic. In the case study, I propose that the problems raised by the regulation of intangible commercial property are often exacerbated by the fact that precedent in this area is considered and used very loosely, and not in terms of the distinctive context of different issues and problems. The case study is followed by an analysis of cases in a number of categories that I propose for this purpose: cases dealing with the cancellation of state debts; regulation that creates state monopolies; regulation that interferes with the management of a business enterprise; regulation by way of licences, permits and quotas; and the regulation of immaterial property rights. In each category, I consider a number of cases that may be classified under that heading, and the effect of the classification for the problems and solutions on offer. Finally, I consider the implications and possible value of the classification for the problem of regulation of intangible commercial property as a whole. It should be stated clearly at the outset that my analysis is not a comprehensive survey of the relevant case law; for that the issues are simply too complex and the cases too numerous. The cases I refer to can be no more than a fairly representative selection of examples in each category.

A South African Case Study

Harksen v Lane NO and Others[8] concerns an attack on the validity of section 21[9] of the South African Insolvency Act 24 of 1936. Section 21(1) of the Insolvency Act provides that, upon the sequestration of the estate of an insolvent spouse, the property of the solvent spouse shall vest in the master of the Supreme Court[10] and, once one has been appointed, in the trustee of the insolvent estate; and that the solvent spouse's property shall be dealt with by the master and trustee as if it were property of the sequestrated estate. In *De Villiers NO v Delta Cables (Pty) Ltd*[11] the former Appellate Division of the Supreme Court[12] stated *obiter* that the effect of the vesting of the solvent spouse's property is to transfer full ownership (*dominium*) of the property from the spouse to the master or trustee.[13] Under the terms of section 21, the solvent spouse's property will vest in the master or trustee of the insolvent estate even if it is clear and accepted by the master or trustee that the property in question belongs to the solvent spouse, that the insolvent estate has no claim to it and that there is no question of collusion between the spouses with regard to ownership of the property.[14] Sections 64(2) and 65(1) respectively provide that the officer presiding at meetings of the creditors of the insolvent estate can summon all persons who may be able to provide information relating to the business, affairs or property of the insolvent or of the solvent spouse, and that the presiding officer at such a meeting, as well as the trustee and the creditors of the insolvent estate, may interrogate persons so summoned concerning all matters relating to the business, affairs and property of the insolvent and of the solvent spouse.[15]

The applicant's husband's estate was sequestrated, and subsequently her property was attached by the trustees of the insolvent estate, and she was summoned to appear and be interrogated at a meeting of her husband's creditors. The applicant challenged the constitutional validity of sections 21, 64 and 65 of the Act to the extent that they affect the property and affairs of the solvent spouse. She claimed that section 21 is in conflict with section 28(3) of the 1993 Constitution in that it effects an expropriation of her property without compensation; that section 21 is in conflict with section 8 of the 1993 Constitution in that it subjects her to interference and loss of property and that in doing so it violates the equality guarantee and amounts to unfair discrimination; and that sections 64 and 65 are unconstitutional for related reasons. The Cape Supreme Court[16] referred the constitutional challenge to the Constitutional Court, where the majority[17] decided that the provisions of section 21 and the impugned parts of sections 64 and 65 of the Insolvency Act are not inconsistent with the interim Constitution of 1993. The minority[18] agreed with the majority finding on the property question[19] and part of the equality question,[20] but disagreed with the majority decision on the main aspect of the equality issue.[21]

For present purposes we are interested in the property issue: the charge that section 21 of the Insolvency Act is inconsistent with section 28(3) of the 1993 Constitution[22] in that section 21 of the Act constitutes an expropriation of the property of the solvent spouse without provision for compensation as required by section 28(3) of the interim Constitution. The basis for this argument is that the vesting of the solvent spouse's property under section 21 amounts to a transfer of the solvent spouse's rights in property to the master and (upon appointment) the trustee of the insolvent estate,[23] while making no provision for compensation.

In his judgment for the majority Goldstone J pointed out that the distinction between deprivation and expropriation of property, as set out in section 28(2) and 28(3) of the interim Constitution,[24] is recognised in South African law and in many foreign jurisdictions. The main difference, as the court described it,[25] is that a deprivation falls short of the "acquisition of rights in property by a public authority for a public purpose" (and usually with compensation) that characterises an expropriation. The court referred to a decision of the Transvaal Supreme Court[26] and two decisions of the Zimbabwe Supreme Court[27] to support the statement that an expropriation amounts to more than a "mere dispossession", that it in fact requires the expropriator to appropriate or acquire or become the owner of the property or right in question.[28] On the basis of the considerations mentioned above, Goldstone J decided[29] that the effect of section 21 of the Act, even if it does amount to a transfer of ownership in the solvent spouse's property to the master or trustee of the insolvent estate, is of a temporary nature and not permanent, and that the purpose is not for the state to acquire the property but to ensure that the insolvent estate is not deprived of property that actually belongs to it, so that this vesting process cannot be described as an expropriation. Consequently it was decided that the effect of section 21 of the Act is not to constitute an expropriation and that the section is therefore not inconsistent with section 28(3) of the Constitution.

One may or may not agree with this decision, and in a sense the main problem is not whether this finding is correct, but rather that the constitutional validity of section 21 was tested with reference to section 28(3) only, and not with reference to the requirements for a deprivation of property in terms of section 28(2) of the interim Constitution. This is of course the result of the applicant's rather limited attack, but that is not the focal point of my interest in the decision. For the purposes of this paper, the interesting point is the court's assumption that the question whether section 21 constitutes an expropriation turns upon the further question whether the state acquired something, and the authority that is offered for this proposition. The assumption that the term "expropriation" in section 28(3) of the interim Constitution had to be interpreted with reference to the actual acquisition by the state of the property was justified with reference to the Transvaal *Beckenstrater* decision[30] and the Zimbabwean *Hewlett*[31] and *Davies*[32] decisions. In my view, the court's reliance on these decisions[33] is problematic, since there are fundamental differences between the decisions cited by the court and the case in hand: *Hewlett* dealt with a law that cancelled an existing state debt to an individual; *Davies* concerned a law that "designates" certain land for possible future expropriation for purposes of land reform; and *Harksen* involved the vesting of a solvent spouse's property to prevent fraudulent dealings to the detriment of innocent creditors. It does not take an overactive imagination to see that the three situations differ in what must surely be essential characteristics. A truly contextual interpretation of any constitutional expropriation provision must take note of and account for these differences between cases. This makes it necessary to consider the comparative authority of similar-looking cases very carefully: in actual fact, the *Davies* case should not even be mentioned in the same breath as the *Hewlett* case, even though both are decisions of the Zimbabwe Supreme Court. Both provide authority for the validity of the distinction between deprivations and expropriations, but *Davies* dealt with regulations that notify the state's intention to consider the expropriation of the property in future, without acquiring any rights in it for the time being. In *Hewlett* the law in question cancelled a state debt, thereby destroying the creditor's right to claim the debt and relieving the state of the duty to pay. The statement that a certain state action does not constitute an expropriation because it does not cause the state to acquire any rights in the property is perfectly acceptable in the context of *Davies*, but it simply makes no sense in the context of *Hewlett*, because it is clear that the plaintiff in *Davies* did not lose anything, while the plaintiff in *Hewlett* probably did. The same question assumes a different aspect in *Harksen*, where the nature of the state action that interfered with the plaintiff's property is of a completely different order. In the Australian cases that are discussed below,[34] it would probably have been said that the issue in *Harksen* was not whether property was taken away or acquired, but under what head of power it was done; if it was under a head of power that was not primarily concerned with the acquisition of property (as it clearly was) the expropriation issue does not come up. To take the point one step further: the more recent Zimbabwean decision in *Chairman, Public Service Commission and Others v Zimbabwe Teachers' Association and Others*[35] should also be distinguished carefully from *Hewlett*, although both dealt with money debts. In *Teachers' Association* the *ratio decidendi* was not[36] (as in *Hewlett*) that a cancellation of a state debt does not constitute an acquisition and therefore also not an expropriation, but rather that the debt in question (teachers' annual bonus) was not a vested right and that the law in question could therefore amend or abolish the annual bonus without thereby affecting an existing property right. While the two issues are closely related, as is indicated below, they have to be distinguished to avoid confusion.

Apart from ignoring the differences between various kinds of property, the reasoning of the *Harksen* court (and the Zimbabwean Supreme Court in the cases referred to) is too simplistic in its analysis of the effects of the regulation concerned. Although there is no clear approach in case law,[37] a comparative analysis suggests that, as far as constitutional property guarantees are concerned, the scope of the term "expropriation" or "compulsory acquisition" cannot simply be restricted to physical dispossessions or actual acquisitions by the state – the distinction between deprivations and expropriations is clearly more complex than that. More particularly, there are instances, especially in the range of intangible property rights, where a complete destruction of a property right by the state could arguably be regarded as an expropriation even though the state "acquires nothing". Both *Hewlett*, which deals with laws that purport to "cancel" an existing state debt, and *Harksen*, which concerns a law that transfers property to an officer of the court to protect the interests of creditors, illustrate the danger of distinguishing between deprivation (by way of regulation) and expropriation of property on the basis of the question whether the state acquires anything in the process. However difficult the distinction between deprivation and expropriation of property may be to make, courts ought to follow a more sophisticated approach than is evident from *Hewlett* or *Harksen*.

The considerations set out in the previous paragraphs indicate that academic and judicial discourse on the problem of regulation of intangible commercial property has not come to terms yet with the fact that contemporary property law, especially in the constitutional area, has moved away from its pre-modern roots in the social and economic appreciation of tangible things and the ways in which they are regulated by the modern state. The insistent focus on the classic image of expropriation as a physical taking away and concomitant state acquisition of tangible things (especially land) seems to suggest a lack of theoretical insight in the fundamental changes that characterise property law (and law in general) since the advent of modern society, and particularly in the changes that result from the social and economic (not to mention political) importance of state control over the use and exploitation of intangible (and commercial) property in modern society. There is also a lack of awareness of what "context" really means in the adjudication of constitutional cases: the broader the brush with which different cases are painted into a single category, the less chance of taking full account of the unique features and circumstances that surround each case in fact. This paper is an attempt to move towards greater awareness of these changes, differences and their implications, especially in the analysis of constitutional case law.

The case study of *Harksen* and its reference to the Zimbabwean decisions in *Hewlett* and *Davies* illustrates some of the problems surrounding the regulation of intangible commercial property rights: unless the characteristics and unique features of different cases in the field of regulation of intangible property are distinguished and accounted for quite carefully, decisions and the reasoning behind them will suffer from unnecessary inconsistency and lack of clarity. This means not only that injustice is done to the individual rights in question, but also that there is insufficient attention to the social, economic and political importance and implications of control and regulation of (intangible) property rights. In the rest of this paper I propose to analyse cases dealing with the regulation of intangible commercial property by distinguishing between a number of situations where this problem assumes different forms and requires different approaches and solutions. In each category I discuss a number of cases to illustrate some of the characteristic features of the problem and the possible solutions that might or might not suit those features.

Regulatory Cancellation of State Debts

One of the most controversial areas where the regulation of intangible commercial property produces claims that the results of regulation are expropriatory or confiscatory, is the regulatory cancellation of state debts. Some of the cases that feature in this category involve private rather than commercial property (debts), but these cases are nevertheless often confused with some of the other categories discussed below, and although the cases involve private property there is nothing in the principles evolved below that prevents them from also applying to commercial property of the same nature. What is involved in these cases is a state debt of some kind and a law that cancels that state debt, ostensibly for a regulatory purpose. The question usually is whether the effects of the cancellation are really regulatory in nature or whether the state action amounts to an expropriation.

The most controversial decision in this area was handed down by the Zimbabwe Supreme Court in *Hewlett v Minister of Finance and Another*,[38] which was decided under the original 1980 version of section 16 of the Zimbabwean Constitution, prior to the amendment of 1990.[39] The applicant was a farmer to whom a sum of money was awarded in respect of losses suffered as a result of "acts of terrorism" as defined in the Victims of Terrorism (Compensation) Act.[40] Subsequent to the award being made, the Emergency Powers (Stay of Compensation Claims) Regulations 1980 froze all proceedings for compensation and the payment of claims, and shortly thereafter the War Victims Compensation Act 22 of 1980 repealed the initial Compensation Act and provided[41] that no further compensation was to be paid under the repealed Act or pursuant to any award, judgment, or court order made under that law. The applicant claimed that the regulations and section 38 of the new Compensation Act are unconstitutional on the ground that they violate section 16 of the Constitution. The first part of the decision is uncontroversial. The court favoured a wide interpretation of the undefined term "property" in section 11,[42] the ordinary meaning of which was said to include a money debt.[43] The major part of the judgment focused on the phrase "property of any description or any interest or right therein" in section 16. The court made it clear that this phrase, as used in section 16, must "embrace the widest possible range of property", and particularly a money debt.[44] The term was explicitly stated to include both movable and immovable property, and both tangible and intangible property.[45] This approach to the scope of the property concept in a constitutional property clause is in line with decisions, such as *Attorney-General v Lawrence*[46] and *Shah v Attorney-General (No 2)*,[47] from other Commonwealth jurisdictions. The most important part of the judgment, for present purposes, is the finding[48] that, whatever the position of unresolved claims for compensation may be, an award of compensation once made constitutes a debt which is property for the purposes of section 16. In response to the state's averment that the compensation payment was of a gratuitous nature as the product of a "bounty law",[49] and that it could be cancelled by the state without compensation, the court came to the conclusion that, even if "bounty" payments can be recalled by the state without compensation, "they do not ... establish the principle that the State can withdraw its undertaking to pay a debt which has crystallised".[50] Given the fact that the compensation payment in question has "crystallised" once the award was made, it has become property which cannot be cancelled without compensation. In other words, the court confirmed the widely established principle that a right will be considered and protected as property once it has vested in the beneficiary, one way of vesting being the confirmation of a debt by court order.[51]

The first part of the *Hewlett* decision is uncontroversial, but the second part, which deals with the nature and validity of the regulation in question, is not. Initially the court's approach to the regulation issue looks acceptable. The term "deprivation" does not appear in the Zimbabwean property clause, but the court nevertheless decided that the distinction[52] between deprivations[53] and expropriations[54] forms part of Zimbabwean law, and that the nature and validity of the Compensation Act had to be judged against the background of this distinction. This approach translates the question before the court to the well-known inquiry whether the law in question constitutes a deprivation of property or a compulsory acquisition. The finding is that the state, in promulgating the law and cancelling the debt created by an existing compensation award, did not "acquire anything" even though it destroyed the beneficiary's claim. Therefore, so the court's argument goes, the cancellation of the debt amounts to a deprivation of property rather than a compulsory acquisition. In arriving at this conclusion the court accepted an extremely limited and narrow interpretation of "compulsory acquisition", which means that the cancellation of a state debt, which admittedly constitutes property, is not regarded as a compulsory acquisition.[55]

Generally speaking, the court's analysis[56] of the distinction between non-compensable, non-acquisitive regulation (deprivations) of property in the terms of section 11 and compensable compulsory acquisitions of property in the terms of section 16 is clear and convincing, but the application of the distinction to the facts of the case is questionable. In accepting the narrow interpretation that restricts "compulsory acquisitions" to situations where the state actually acquires something, the court allowed itself to be misled by conceptual thinking and (poorly argued) private-law dogma, unable to distance itself from the classic perception of expropriation as a process whereby the state physically takes something (particularly land) from someone and uses it for a public purpose. Given the extremely wide interpretation which is (correctly) given to the term "property" in the constitutional context, a similarly wide interpretation should also have been given to the term "acquisition". To argue that an "acquisition" only takes place, as is the case with tangible property, when that which is lost by the one party actually "goes over to" or is transferred to the recipient is simply wrong, even in traditional private-law dogma. Moreover, this narrow interpretation is flawed by reasoning which does not account for the fact that, in cancelling the debt, the state actually did "acquire something" in the form of a saving or release from the duty to pay.

In view of the nature of intangible property which is included in constitutional property guarantees, and given the public-law nature of the constitutional relation between state and citizen, the court's approach is even less acceptable. In a situation where the state is in a position to use its state power to make a law that benefits itself by nullifying an existing and "crystallised" debt, and thereby deprive a citizen of property, the inequality of the relationship between the state as lawmaker and the citizen as creditor should suffice to indicate that a more sympathetic interpretation of the acquisition requirement is needed. To acknowledge the deprivation of the plaintiff and the simultaneous benefit of the state and still refuse to regard the action as an acquisition amounts to sophistry.

A completely different approach was followed by the Uganda High Court in *Shah v Attorney-General (No 2)*.[57] The plaintiff concluded a contract with the former government of Buganda by the terms of which, once he fulfilled his obligations under the contract, he was entitled to a money payment from the government. Shortly afterwards the kingdom of Buganda ceased to exist and the government of Uganda took over the assets, rights and liabilities of the former administration in terms of the Local Administrations Act 1967. The government refused to pay the amount still outstanding to the plaintiff and the plaintiff obtained judgment against the government. The government did not appeal but failed to pay the judgement debt. The plaintiff applied for a *mandamus* on the officials responsible for payment. The attorney-general applied for a dismissal of the plaintiff's application on grounds of section 2(1) of the Local Administrations (Amendment) (No 2) Act 1969 which had been passed subsequent to the judgment and which made all contracts with the former Buganda government unenforceable except insofar as they had been ratified by the minister. The Act also made provision for the dismissal of any proceedings based on an unratified contract regardless of any judgment already given in such proceedings. The plaintiff challenged the relevant provisions of the Act on the grounds that they were unconstitutional as they amounted to a deprivation of property without compensation. There are differences between this case and the Zimbabwean *Hewlett* case, mostly due to differences in the structure of the "double" guarantee in each of the relevant constitutions.[58] The most important difference is that the Ugandan property clause, because of the way in which it is structured, guarantees compensation for both compulsory acquisitions and deprivations of property. However, these differences are not fundamental, and the cases remain comparable, mainly because the Ugandan Constitution allows the question of compensation to be raised with regard to deprivations of property as well as compulsory acquisitions. Like the Zimbabwe Supreme Court, the Uganda High Court also decided that "property" as referred to in the Ugandan Constitution must be interpreted widely to include any form of property whatsoever, and that a judgment debt establishes a form of personal property which is protected by the general, introductory guarantee against deprivations in section 8(2)(c).[59] Moreover, the court decided that a deprivation in the form of a cancellation of a judgment debt against the state entails enrichment for the state in the form of absolvement from the duty to pay, and therefore rejected the argument that the state acquired nothing in the process.[60]

A similar approach was followed by the Australian Federal Court in *Peverill v Health Insurance Commission*.[61] Peverill was a specialist pathologist who rendered certain pathology services to the state. He sued the Health Insurance Commission for medicare benefits due to him for these services under the Health Insurance Act 1973. The Health Insurance (Pathology Services) Amendment Act 1991 effected certain retrospective changes to the Health Insurance Act, with the result that Peverill's right to payment by the Commonwealth was extinguished. Peverill claimed that the Amendment Act was *ultra vires* and beyond the power of the parliament of the Commonwealth on the grounds that it amounted to an acquisition of property other than on just terms, contrary to section 51(xxxi) of the Commonwealth Constitution 1900. The Federal Court concluded that the right which the plaintiff had to payment of the statutory debt in question was property within the meaning of section 51(xxxi) of the Commonwealth Constitution.[62] Since the Amendment Act not only extinguished the debt, but resulted in a clear and direct benefit accruing to the state, it is clear that this property was acquired by the state as meant in section 51(xxxi).[63] The right acquired by the state consists in the benefit of not having to pay the debt. Although it may be possible to acquire property without compensation legitimately in some cases, this was not such a case, and therefore the property was acquired without just terms, in conflict with the property guarantee. As will appear below, this decision was later overturned on appeal on the basis that the debt was, in fact, not a vested right but a claim to a gratuitous payment. This does not change the principle established or illustrated in the Federal Court: a vested debt is regarded as property and a cancellation of such a debt amounts to an acquisition of property because the state derives a direct benefit from it in being freed from the duty to pay.

The principles deriving from the Ugandan *Shah* decision and the Australian *Peverill* decision clearly contradict the Zimbabwean *Hewlett* decision, and in my view they present the better arguments and authority for cases of this nature. They have been confirmed in a number of other cases dealing with the salaries of state employees[64] and with a statutory freeze of public servants' wages.[65] The principles that have been evolved so far can be summarised as follows:

(i)   A money debt, once vested according to the normal principles of law, constitutes property for purposes of the protection of a constitutional property clause. Such a debt can vest by contract, or by court order, or by legislation, depending on the nature of the debt.

(ii)   A statutory cancellation of such a vested debt that benefits the state by absolving it from the duty to pay constitutes a compulsory acquisition of property, which may be subject to payment of compensation in terms of the relevant property clause.

An interesting variation on the question of cancellation of state debts appears in the decision of the Zimbabwe Supreme Court in *Chairman, Public Service Commission, and Others v Zimbabwe Teachers' Association and Others*.[66] Public servants in Zimbabwe had been paid an annual bonus since 1974. In September 1995 it was announced by regulation that the annual bonus for 1995 would not be paid. The Zimbabwe Teachers' Association attacked this decision on behalf of all public servants, averring that it was unlawful and unconstitutional to withhold the bonus. The High Court declared the regulation unlawful, and the Public Service Commission appealed against this decision. The question was whether the regulation amounted to a compulsory acquisition of property in conflict with the property clause in the Zimbabwean Constitution.[67] The majority of the Supreme Court[68] decided that an annual bonus is part of a public servant's remuneration, but distinct from and not part of the salary as such, and that a bonus could consequently be reduced or eliminated lawfully, provided it was done in proper form and that there was no provision in the Constitution or elsewhere that forbade such action. This decision was based on the finding[69] that a bonus does not become a vested right before the year in question is completed. This part of the decision, based as it was on a finding on the facts, seems acceptable, although the minority[70] disagreed, arguing that the bonus was a vested right and therefore property that was protected by section 16. However, the majority chose to proceed beyond the factual finding and make a further ruling on the possibility that the bonus was property. In such a case, the majority decided,[71] even though the law in question extinguishes a state debt, and although the state gains a corresponding benefit, the state does not acquire any right or interest which it did not possess before, and therefore the cancellation of the bonus does not amount to a compulsory acquisition that was affected by section 16. This finding is in line with the Supreme Court's earlier finding in the *Hewlett* case,[72] and in conflict with the other decisions referred to above.

However, regardless of one's evaluation of the Zimbabwean decision in the *Teachers' Association* case, the facts of the case sound a warning that the principles set out earlier are perhaps too simplistic, and that further analysis is required. This impression was substantiated by a series of fairly recent decisions in the High Court of Australia, where a number of finer distinctions and qualifications were added to the general principles set out above. The most striking of these decisions is *Health Insurance Commission v Peverill*,[73] in which the earlier *Peverill* decision discussed above was overturned on the facts. The High Court held that Peverill's claim, being based on medicare benefits, was not a vested debt (as was assumed by Burchett J in the Federal Court), in that it originated in legislation and was always open for legislative amendment, reduction and even extinguishment. Of course, on the facts of the case this decision actually confirms the general principles enunciated earlier, but the position of debts created by legislation requires further attention. Debts and claims sounding in money are described in the decision as choses in action that qualify as property, but the decision of the court is eventually couched in terms that focus more strongly on the finding that the state did not acquire anything when medicare benefits were reduced or extinguished. A moment's reflection will show that the effect of the decision is in fact that a debt or claim sounding in money can only qualify as property for the purposes of the constitutional guarantee if it is not open to legislative amendment or extinguishment, which means that the property issue is perhaps more important in the decision than the acquisition issue. This is an important point, because it illustrates the fact that many decisions that are ostensibly based on the finding that no property was acquired when a debt was extinguished in fact mean that there was no property in the constitutional sense present to start out with; usually because the debts or claims were open to legislative interference and therefore not vested.

This in turn means that welfare benefits or "the new property", in so far as it is open to legislative reduction or extinguishment, does not really qualify as constitutional property: the so-called "due process" protection it is said to enjoy under the constitutional property clause is not really a function of its being regarded as property, because it would probably enjoy the same protection even in the absence of a property clause. On the other hand, the fact that it is not protected for the purposes of compensation suggests that this kind of interest is not really recognised as constitutional property. The exception, in German law, is welfare or social security rights that are not based exclusively on gratuitous legislative grants, but on substantial own effort or input, in which case it is arguable that the debt or claim is no longer a gratuity but a vested debt that assumes the character of property.[74]

In the *Health Insurance Commission* case, Brennan J gave the most convincing and clear explanation of the distinction between a claim to a gratuitous payment of money (which is not recognised as property for the purposes of the property clause) and a vested debt sounding in money (which is recognised as property for the purposes of the property clause): the claim to a gratuitous payment not only originates in legislation,[75] but in cases where it is susceptible to legislative amendment, reduction or even extinguishment,[76] it lacks the required "stability and permanence" that have been described as vital characteristics of property.[77] The principle laid down in this decision is that money or a right to receive money can qualify as property for the purposes of the property guarantee, provided the debt or claim is a vested right with the necessary stability and permanence that results from its not being susceptible to legislative reduction or extinguishment (because it is a gratuity).[78] This was confirmed and applied in *Georgiadis v Australian and Overseas Telecommunications Corporation*,[79] where it was held that a legislative extinguishment of a common law claim for damages based on negligence was an interference with a vested right, which did not originate in and was not restricted to legislation, and consequently the law in question was declared in conflict with the property guarantee because it (obviously) did not provide just terms. In this case, the claim originated outside of or was "recognised in general law", which means that it was not a gratuity created by legislation, and therefore not open to legislative amendment or extinguishment.

However, the Australian cases indicate that the principle has to be qualified and specified even further. Even though it is acknowledged that a debt or claim sounding in money can be recognised as property for the purposes of the property clause if it is a vested right that originates in or is recognised by "general law" outside of legislation, not every reduction or extinguishment of such a debt will be recognised as a compulsory acquisition of property. Playing on the difference between an *acquisition* of property and a *taking* of property, the High Court of Australia assumed the position that an actual acquisition was required before the just terms guarantee in section 51(xxxi) was activated. Apart from a minority,[80] who insist that an acquisition is only present when the acquirer actually acquires what the plaintiff loses,[81] the majority of the High Court accepted in recent decisions that an acquisition will be present when the acquirer[82] gains any benefit or advantage, however slight or insubstantial, and regardless of whether what is gained is exactly the same as what was lost.[83] However, without such benefit there is no acquisition of property and the property guarantee is not activated. In a sense, this position is similar to the result in *Health Insurance Commission v Peverill*, where it was said that nothing was acquired by the state because there was no stable and vested right to the medicare benefits in the first place. The result is, in any event, that compulsory acquisitions by way of the cancellation of state debts are restricted to instances where some benefit or advantage that the state derives from the cancellation can be identified. This restriction obviously only applies to jurisdictions where the property clause refers to "acquisitions" of property, and not to jurisdictions where the property clause refers to "takings". It is arguable that "expropriation" is an equally limited term that refers to actual acquisitions, in which case the same argument would be possible.

However, that is still not all. The Australian decisions suggest that yet another qualification is required before one gets the whole picture. The cancellation of state debts or money claims can only qualify as a compulsory acquisition if the debt was sufficiently stable and vested, and if there was an actual acquisition of some advantage or benefit; but even then not every acquisition will attract the just terms guarantee in the property clause. In some cases, according to the High Court of Australia, an acquisition of a debt that is recognised as property may be effected under a different "head of power", and then the property clause does not apply at all. This qualification refers to the exclusions from the property clause that are recognised by the Australian courts, in other words cases where the state can acquire property in the course of exercising another category of state power, without activating the compensation guarantee. In a sense this is nothing else than the fact, which is also recognised in other jurisdictions, that some acquisitions of property (often referred to as "deprivations" of property) that are effected in terms of the state's police power do not attract compensation. At least three categories of this nature are identified in recent Australian case law: (a) Some powers, like the taxation power, are simply and clearly distinct from and not "abstracted" by the property clause, and the property clause simply does not apply to "acquisitions" of property effected in terms of these powers.[84] (b) The exercise of some powers cause losses of property that, although they may even involve an actual acquisition of property by the state, simply do not "permit of" compensation. The most obvious example here is laws that declare property forfeit as a penalty for its being used in committing a crime, even if the property belongs to an innocent third party.[85] Most jurisdictions recognise that laws involving the state acquisition of property by way of penalties or for purposes of administering the property of insolvents and people with legal incapacities fall into this category. (c) A third category involves acquisitions that were incidental to the exercise of another state power, especially the police power, for example when property has to be acquired from one person in order to ensure or promote the public interest in the proper administration of competing claims, rights and interests. The best Australian example here is *Mutual Pools & Staff Pty Ltd v The Commonwealth of Australia*,[86] where a contractual claim for a tax refund (which satisfied all the requirements for a vested property right) was extinguished by law to ensure that the tax refund would be paid to the people who carried the tax burden. In this case, builders of swimming-pools had a contractual claim to receive tax refunds, but the legislature wanted to ensure that the refund would be paid to the clients in cases where the builders had passed the tax burden on to the clients. The purpose was, therefore, to manage the competing claims and interests of citizens and not to acquire property, even though it was necessary to extinguish some contractual debts in the process.

In a sense, the third category of exclusions is the most interesting one. It is said that this exclusion would only exempt an acquisition of property from the compensation guarantee if the acquisition is justified in terms of the exercise of a different power.[87] This means that the state must have been exercising powers that are authorised under a different heading in the Constitution; the acquisition of property must have been an incidental result and not the sole or main purpose of the action; the action taken must be appropriate and proper for the (other) purpose it serves; and the result must be reasonably proportionate to the (other) purpose served.

This proportionality test can be applied to test whether it is justified to exempt an acquisition of property from the compensation guarantee, and if the answer is negative for any reason,[88] the authority of the other head of power falls away and the acquisition can be judged in terms of the compensation guarantee in the property clause.

These Australian cases introduce a number of really important and relevant qualifications and specifications into the debate about the cancellation of state debts in the context of the constitutional property guarantee. Not only is the principle confirmed that a debt must be a vested right to qualify, it is also made clear that the question whether a debt is a vested right must be determined with reference to the stability and permanence of the claim to receive money, and more specifically the question whether the debt originates in and is restricted to legislation with the result that it remains open to legislative amendment. Furthermore, it is made clear that, at least in some jurisdictions, it might be reasonable to require that the cancellation of a state debt be accompanied by the actual acquisition of some benefit or advantage before the compensation duty is triggered; even if the benefit or advantage is not the same thing as what was lost. And, finally, the extremely important point is made that not all acquisitions of property (by way of the cancellation of a state debt) need attract the property guarantee, especially when the acquisition was an incidental side-effect of reasonable, appropriate and proportionate measures taken to serve a purpose other than to acquire property.

On the basis of the analysis above it seems reasonably clear that a state action that cancels or destroys a vested state debt and transfers some benefit to the state could, depending on the structure and phraseology of the relevant constitutional property clause and the head of power under which the result was reached, be regarded as an expropriation rather than a mere regulation of the property in question and should, therefore, either be in conflict with or require compensation in terms of the property clause. However, this cannot be proposed as a general and absolute rule. There might be cases where the cancellation of the debt in question, without "compensation", could be reasonable and justifiable in terms of the constitutional provisions concerned. This would, arguably, especially be the case when the debt was open to legislative amendment or acquired under a different head of power, as was pointed out with reference to Australian case law, or where the debt originated in circumstances where the creation or existence of the debt or the payment of compensation is or would be morally or politically objectionable. It can be argued that this might have been a reason for not upholding the debt in the Zimbabwean *Hewlett* case, seeing that the debt was created by the white government to benefit white farmers.[89] A similar situation arose in Namibia in the case of *Cultura 2000 and Another v Government of the Republic of Namibia and Others*.[90] The first applicant was a non-profit association, incorporated prior to the independence of Namibia, for the purpose of co-ordinating the activities and interests of cultural organisations aimed at promoting Western European cultural activities in Namibia. In 1989 the association bought a farm from the then representative authority for whites (RAW), and later the RAW donated a substantial sum of money to the association, subject to the condition that it should be seen as "a donation for founding purposes to promote, develop and extend the cultures of the Afrikaner, German, English and Portuguese or other communities of European descent". On the same day the RAW lent another sum to the association on very lenient terms. A short time before Namibia's independence, the loan was converted to a donation by the Administrator-General. The new government of Namibia promulgated the State Repudiation (Cultura 2000) Act 32 of 1991 (Nm), section 2(1) of which repudiated any sale, donation or other alienation of movable or immovable property to or in respect of the association, under laws in force prior to the independence of Namibia, by the government or an official of the Republic of South Africa. The Act was stated to have been promulgated in terms of article 140(3) of the Namibian Constitution, which states that anything done under laws in force prior to independence by the government or an official of the Republic of South Africa shall be deemed to have been done by the government or an official of the Republic of Namibia, unless repudiated by an Act of Parliament. The applicants challenged the constitutionality of the Act on the grounds that it was contrary to article 16 of the Constitution. The High Court accepted that the property guarantee in article 16(1) of the Namibian Constitution includes both tangible and intangible property (in this case farms and money),[91] but the court held that the expropriation provision in article 16(2) cannot apply with regard to money, since it would be "completely and utterly nonsensical"[92] to expropriate money against payment of just compensation in the form of (the same amount of) money. On the basis of this finding the expropriatory part of the Act was held to be unconstitutional, and declared *ultra vires* and invalid by the High Court.[93]

On appeal, the Supreme Court of Namibia was not willing actually to decide that a cancellation of the debt was constitutionally in order because of moral objections to the way in which it was created and vested in the organisation, but the decision did make it possible for the new Namibian government to distance itself from the obligation without releasing them from paying the debt.[94] The interesting part of the decision *a quo*, in terms of which the essential section 2(2) of the Act was declared *ultra vires* and invalid, was not under discussion in the appeal, and the only question was whether the repudiatory section 2(1) of the Act was valid. The Supreme Court decided that section 2(1) does not invade the property rights or other rights of the respondent, because the only effect of this section was that the Namibian government restored the real state of affairs, namely that the action by which the property was given to the respondent was an action of the former administration, and not of the Namibian government. The effect of sections 2(2) and 3 of the Act was to declare the donation of the property to the respondent null and void, but these sections were already declared invalid by the court *a quo* and were not in issue on appeal.[95] The end result was, therefore, that the debt was upheld but in terms of a framework that at least allowed the new Namibian government to distance itself from the moral obligations it involved. Because of the restricted nature of the appeal the Supreme Court was not asked to decide on the validity of the section of the Act that declared the debt subject to repudiation. In my view, the really interesting question is whether a debt of this nature, coloured by moral objections to the way in which it was created and vested by a former regime, can be cancelled by a new regime without falling foul of the compulsory acquisition provisions in the property clause. It seems possible, if there is sufficient contextual (social, economic and political) justification, that such a cancellation could be reasonable and justifiable in terms of a constitutional property clause, and that would amount to a truly (and legitimate) regulatory cancellation of a state debt. The Australian *Mutual Pools* decision illustrates the fact that such a position is not at all uncommon, and that a proportionality approach could make it easier to judge the legitimacy and justification of such a case.

"Regulatory" Creation of State Monopolies

A second category of cases where the regulation of commercial property often results in claims that the effects of the regulation are expropriatory or confiscatory, concerns the situation where the regulation in question, usually in the form of production, trade or import/export regulations pertaining to a certain commercial branch, simultaneously destroys or prohibits the continued existence of a private enterprise and establishes a state monopoly in the same area. The question is whether this regulation is legitimate and whether it does not constitute a compulsory acquisition of (some of) the property in question, in which case the action would either require compensation or be unconstitutional and invalid.

A good example of this kind of situation appears from the widely-cited Malaysian case of *Government of Malaysia & Another v Selangor Pilot Association*.[96] The respondents provided private pilotage services and had an effective monopoly on the business in certain pilotage districts. The Port Authorities (Amendment) Act 1972 prohibited the respondents from carrying on their business within the relevant pilotage districts. The physical assets of the respondents were sold voluntarily to the second appellant, who paid compensation for them to the respondents. The respondents asked for additional compensation for loss of future profits and loss of goodwill, but this was denied. They then applied for a declaration that they were entitled to compensation for loss of goodwill, and in the alternative that the relevant section in the Act was unconstitutional as it was in conflict with section 13 (the property guarantee) of the Federal Constitution of Malaysia 1957.[97] The High Court dismissed the action and the pilots' association appealed to the Federal Court, which allowed the appeal.[98] The government then appealed to the Privy Council. The question was, first, whether the licences of the plaintiffs and their right to employ pilots, or alternatively the goodwill of their business, could be regarded as property for purposes of section 13; and, secondly, whether any part of that property was acquired by the state. Even if the licences or the goodwill were regarded as property, the Privy Council was not willing to accept that it was acquired by the state as a result of the legislation in question. The Privy Council agreed that a person might be deprived of property by a "mere negative or restrictive provision", but that does not necessarily imply that the deprivation also results in a compulsory acquisition or use. The term "compulsory acquisition or use" in section 13(2) was, therefore, interpreted strictly, which means that the state should not merely deprive the plaintiff of property but also acquire or use it. This means that the Privy Council recognised, for purposes of section 13 of the Constitution, the existence of deprivations of private property that completely destroy the affected person's property but still do not amount to compulsory acquisitions or use of such property by the state. This is in line with the constitutional provision that, while all deprivations of private property must be in accordance with a law,[99] only those deprivations which also involve the compulsory acquisition or use of the property by the state need to be compensated.[100]   Lord Salmon, in a dissenting opinion, agreed that the licences did not constitute property, but in his view the property which the pilots had in the business (the goodwill) was indirectly acquired through the legislation, and therefore compensation should have been paid. Lord Salmon's dissenting opinion was based on the same premises as the majority decision, but he argued that the effect of the law in question was that the plaintiffs' goodwill was actually acquired by the state, which means that compensation had to be paid for that part of the property that was not merely destroyed by the regulation but actually taken over by the state.

The same argument was used in the Canadian case of *Manitoba Fisheries Ltd v The Queen*.[101] The plaintiffs were the owners of a private fish exporting business until 1969, when the Fresh Water Fish Marketing Act 1970 was promulgated. This Act gave a statutory corporation an effective monopoly in the business of exporting fish, except if the corporation were to grant a licence to or exempt anyone from the prohibition on continuing their business. No licences were issued and no exemptions made. The Act provided for payment of compensation, but no compensation was paid to the plaintiffs.   The plaintiffs claimed compensation for the loss of their business, including loss of goodwill.[102] The decision was based on the distinction between a "mere" deprivation and a so-called "regulatory taking", and the Canadian court referred to the Malaysian decision in *Government of Malaysia v Selangor Pilot Association* for authority on this point.[103] However, the Canadian court distinguished the decision of the Privy Council in *Selangor Pilot Association*, and decided that the Act did effect an expropriation, because it did not merely regulate the conditions under which the plaintiffs might continue their business, but actually deprived them of it and effectively transferred their business to the statutory corporation. This is an expropriation and not a regulation, even if the law was intended to function as a regulation.[104]

The comparison between the Canadian *Manitoba* decision and the Malaysian *Selangor* decision raises the question whether it is necessary that intangible commercial property must actually be acquired or used by the state to constitute a taking. The Canadian court was satisfied that the property in question (the goodwill) was actually taken or acquired by the state, because the plaintiff's customers were actually forced to trade with the state corporation, which suggests that there might be a taking if the state somehow acquires or uses the property, for example by acquiring the benefit of the former private enterprise's goodwill. Lord Salmond's dissenting opinion in *Selangor Pilot Association* suggests that the same might have been true in that case, which would mean that the majority decision in *Selangor Pilot Association* was wrong. The implication seems to be that a regulation should be regarded as a compulsory acquisition (and compensated) when its effect is not merely to control (which may include closing down) private enterprises, but actually to take over their business for the benefit of the state (through the creation of a state monopoly). On the other hand, a regulation that does not amount to a taking over of the business should not be regarded as a compulsory acquisition merely because it resulted in the closing down of a private enterprise: there is probably room for the possibility that truly (and legitimate) regulatory measures can close down a commercial enterprise, for a valid public purpose, without acquiring the business or benefiting from its closing down in any way. In such a case there could be no question of compensation. Partial support for this position is provided by the Mauritian case of *Société United Docks and Others v Government of Mauritius; Marine Workers Union and Others v Mauritius Marine Authority and Others*.[105]

The appellant companies were engaged in the business of storing and loading sugar for export by means of manual labour by dockers and stevedores. New developments changed the method of loading sugar from the manual loading of bags to mechanised bulk loading. Following this development, the Mauritius Sugar Terminal Corporation Act 1979 established the Mauritius Sugar Terminal Corporation, which had a monopoly on the storing and loading of sugar for export (except insofar as the Minister might authorise other persons to do so). As a result of the implementation of this Act, the appellants' businesses became redundant. The Act makes provision for compensation to be paid to the employees of the affected companies, but not to the companies themselves. The appellant companies instituted proceedings claiming compensation on the grounds that the Act amounted to a compulsory acquisition of their property in their businesses, without compensation, in conflict with the property clause in sections 3(c) and 8 of the Constitution of Mauritius. The Privy Council refused to award compensation. A strong indication that the relevant statute in this case was actually supposed to regulate and control the sugar industry and not to take over the business of private enterprises appears from the fact that the government of Mauritius was protecting its main source of commerce, the sugar industry, by promoting technological progress in the establishment of a new loading facility. In principle, this could mean that the regulation in question should be regarded as a "proper" exercise of the police power, with the result that any deprivation of property resulting from it does not require compensation. In a sense, this conclusion is similar to the result reached by the Australian High Court in decisions concerning the cancellation of debts, as discussed above. However, the situation is slightly more complicated than it seems at first sight, and at least two further questions remain.

First, the fact that the Mauritian government was clearly exercising its police power in this case does not necessarily mean, as the Privy Council seems to have thought, that its actions cannot attract a compensation award. The mere fact that the state clearly exercises its police power in a legitimate situation and for the public interest does not dispose of the matter completely: the question remains whether the promotion of technological progress also requires the state to get involved in the business as a competitor, especially by way of setting up a state monopoly.[106] This question involves the distinction between the various roles of the state as regulator and as competitor in business:[107] as soon as the state assumes the role of competitor (for instance by establishing a state monopoly) the "purely" regulatory nature of its exercise of the police power is placed in question. In *Société United Docks*, the fact that the state went beyond regulation of the sugar industry and set up a state monopoly could mean that it crossed the line from a regulation to a compulsory acquisition. However, this result is not necessarily the only explanation, and Allen offers an alternative perspective on the facts.[108] In his view, the decision implies that a company that wishes to claim compensation for loss as a result of state action which destroyed the business in question needs to prove that (a) it was subject to a coercive action, and (b) that the coercive action was the actual cause of the owner's loss. Although coercive action was present in the form of the statute which created the state monopoly, this monopoly was not the effective cause of the appellants' loss. The loss was caused by the technological advance in the storage and loading industry, and the appellants would have been unable to compete with the new bulk loading terminal even in the absence of a statutory monopoly. This means, in Allen's view, that the establishment of the state monopoly does not automatically point towards a compulsory acquisition and compensation. While this approach has the advantage, in Allen's judgement, of being clear and certain (and it does present the facts in an interesting contextual perspective), it leaves the state free to attack rights indirectly where a direct attack would have been unconstitutional.

However, even though Allen's criticism of the decision seems reasonable, he (like the Privy Council) fails to take into account a second major factor that influences the situation in the Mauritian case. Both the Privy Council's decision and Allen's discussion of the *Société United Docks* case fail to pay sufficient attention to the fact that the Mauritian property clause is different from, for example, the Malaysian property clause in one essential aspect: being a "standard" variation of the "double" property clause found in a number of post-colonial constitutions, it requires compensation for both compulsory acquisitions and deprivations of property.[109] So, even if the court should decide that the regulation in question constituted a deprivation of property in terms of the police power and not a compulsory acquisition, it is still possible that section 3 of the Mauritian Constitution could require compensation for that deprivation. This is due to a structural and phraseological quirk of some post-colonial constitutions, and should not be seen as a fundamental problem that undermines the general conclusions of this part of the article, namely that the destruction of a private enterprise, combined with the creation of a state monopoly, might indicate that the state acquired certain property from the private enterprise in the process. The possible conclusion that the closing down of the enterprise in this case could be regarded as a deprivation of property rather than a compulsory acquisition of property does not, in other words, exclude the further possibility that compensation might nevertheless have been required under the Mauritian Constitution. The question whether the closing down of the private sugar loading businesses amounted to a deprivation or a compulsory acquisition had to be answered with reference to other considerations, such as the fact that the state monopoly acquired benefits from the closing down of the private enterprises and that the technological advances promoted by the Act rendered the private enterprises redundant regardless of any benefit to the state monopoly. In the final analysis, this is a judgement call that has to be made with full recognition of the unique facts and circumstances of the case. This kind of value judgement may become slightly easier in view of a more recent Mauritian case, *La Compagnie Sucriere de Bel Ombre Ltee v The Government of Mauritius*,[110] where it was indicated that a proportionality approach, based on the jurisprudence of the European Court of Human Rights,[111] might provide a suitable approach for judging the effect of a law that deprives someone of property under circumstances where it is alleged that the deprivation amounts to a compulsory acquisition that should be subject to compensation. One implication of this approach is, as in the recent jurisprudence of the High Court of Australia discussed above, that not every deprivation of property is subject to the duty to compensate. The application of a proportionality test could not only help the courts decide when it would be suitable to require compensation, but also the amount of compensation.

The importance of the individual facts also appears from the decision of the Indian Supreme Court in *Saghir Ahmad v The State of Uttar Pradesh and Others*.[112] The appellant was a private entrepreneur who provided transport on the Bulandshahr-Delhi route. Section 42(3) of the Motor Vehicles Act 1939 exempted government-owned transport vehicles from the requirement of obtaining permits. The government of the state of Uttar Pradesh decided to operate their own buses on the public thoroughfares as competitors with the private operators. They later decided to exclude all private bus owners and create a state monopoly in road transport. To this end, the transport authorities began cancelling the permits issued to private bus owners and refusing new permits to private operators. Several private bus owners instituted proceedings complaining of the illegal use by the government of Uttar Pradesh of the provisions of the Motor Vehicles Act 1939. The court held that it was not possible to nationalise an industry without appropriate legislation which would have to be justified under article 19(6) of the Constitution. The state government promulgated the Uttar Pradesh Road Transport Act 2 of 1951, authorising the creation of a state monopoly in road transport services where the state is satisfied that this would be in the public interest. The state issued a notification under this Act to the effect that road transport services on the Bulandshahr-Delhi route, among others, were to be operated exclusively by the state government. The constitutionality of the Act was challenged, *inter alia* on the ground that it amounted to an uncompensated acquisition of the appellant's interest in a commercial undertaking, contrary to article 31(2) of the Constitution. The action was dismissed and the appellant appealed to the Supreme Court. The point raised for decision was whether the prohibition of a trade or business amounts to a deprivation of property in a commercial undertaking within the meaning of article 31(2) of the Constitution, and whether the absence of provision for compensation meant that the Uttar Pradesh Road Transport Act 2 of 1951 was unconstitutional.

The High Court decided that the mere prohibition of the business ventures in question did not amount to a compensable acquisition in terms of article 31(2), because no property was taken over by the state, although it was clear that the prohibition was aimed at instituting a state monopoly. With reference to the majority decision in *State of West Bengal v Subodh Gopal Bose*[113] the Supreme Court overturned this decision, and held that the effect of the law was to deprive the plaintiffs of their interests in the business venture, and that the absence of provision for compensation rendered the law unconstitutional for being in conflict with the property clause in article 31(2).[114]

The general trend in decisions in this category seems to be that a regulatory control measure does not necessarily constitute a compulsory acquisition of commercial property and require compensation simply because it destroys or prohibits the continued existence of a private business enterprise; but on the other hand the simultaneous destruction or prohibition of a private enterprise and establishment of a competing state monopoly could be an indication that part of the private property (such as the goodwill of the enterprise) was taken over by the state and should be compensated. These principles correspond nicely with the notion, discussed in the previous section on the cancellation of state debts, that not every deprivation of property qualifies for compensation: there has to be an indication of some benefit or advantage accruing to the state, even if it is not exactly the same as what has been lost by the plaintiff. Moreover, there are indications that not every acquisition of property by the state should attract the compensation duty, since at least some acquisitions are incidental side-effects that result from otherwise constitutionally authorised, reasonable and appropriate steps taken in pursuit of some other state objective. The proportionality test should be used to indicate whether it is reasonable and justifiable to authorise the acquisition, without compensation, in terms of the other power (such as the police power) and whether compensation should not be considered.

Regulatory Interference with the Management of Businesses

In some instances, the regulation of commercial property also interferes with a private commercial enterprise in a manner that seems to threaten its continued existence, but without setting up a state monopoly or competing state enterprise. The relatively obvious "taking over" element that pointed in the direction of a compulsory acquisition in the previous category is therefore absent in this case, and claims that a regulation of this nature constitutes a taking is restricted to arguments based on its extreme nature or on the harshness of its effects for the affected property owners. The cases discussed below have been selected because of their common feature that the property owner's right to manage the property was taken over or substantially interfered with in each case. To distinguish this category from the next one, cases dealing with the cancellation of or interferences with licences, permits and quotas are not considered here.

A decision of the Grand Bench of the Supreme Court of Japan[115] illustrates the importance of the right to manage a business in the context of constitutional property. In November 1946 the workers in a metal factory went on a "production control" strike, which means that the workers took over the management of the factory and continued with production. In December 1946 the workers sold steel plate belonging to the company in order to obtain money to cover operating expenses and to pay the workers' wages, and subsequently the leaders of the strike were charged with and convicted of theft of company property and were sentenced to six months' imprisonment. Their appeal against this conviction was unsuccessful and they proceeded with their case in the Supreme Court. The Supreme Court confirmed that the property rights of employers are not absolute, and that they are limited *inter alia* to accommodate labour rights, but on the other hand it is "not permissible" to "oppress the free will of the employer and to obstruct his control over his property".[116] In the final analysis the management, administration, supervision and direction of an enterprise (the property) remain in the hands of the owner, even though the rights of labour have to be and are recognised and protected. The rights of labour include the right to strike, and this right "also produces an infringement on the right to property", but that is still different from taking over the management of the property itself from the owner.[117] The court therefore upheld the management rights of the property holder against the (recognised) labour rights of labourers. This gives an indication that the right to manage is considered an important aspect of property in commercial enterprises.[118]

Two decisions of the Indian Supreme Court deal with almost the exact opposite situation under comparable circumstances: in these cases, the state took over the management of private companies to ensure continued production. In *Charanjit Lal Chowdhury v The Union of India and Others*,[119] the applicant was a shareholder in one of the principal producers of cotton textiles. Due to labour disputes between employees and management, the mills were temporarily closed in 1949 and production ceased. In order to ensure continued production of an essential commodity and to prevent serious unemployment, the Governor-General intervened, promulgating the Sholapur Spinning and Weaving Company (Emergency Provisions) Ordinance 2 of 1950, which authorised the government to take over the management of the company. The government of Bombay exercised these powers by appointing directors to manage and administer the property and affairs of the company. The ordinance was later replaced by the Sholapur Spinning and Weaving Company (Emergency Provisions) Act 28 of 1950, which contained similar provisions. The applicant contended that the effect of the Act was to take possession of property and other interests in the undertaking away from the shareholders and the company and vest them in persons appointed by the state. The applicant alleged that the taking of property was uncompensated and not for a public purpose and therefore violated the property clause in article 31 of the Constitution.

The majority of the Supreme Court dismissed the application. The main arguments for this decision are set out in the judgment of Mukherjea J, who restricted the scope of the investigation by arguing[120] that the petition should have been brought by the company itself if it concerned the property of the company, and that the court in the present case could merely ask whether the law in question infringed the individual applicant's property (as opposed to the company's property). Furthermore, Mukherjea J argued that the question of expropriation should be narrowed down to the question whether the state took possession of the petitioner's property, since it was clear that it could not be said that his property (in the sense of "the whole bundle" of his rights) was taken over and passed to the state, leaving nothing vested in the petitioner.[121] On this basis, it could not be said that the petitioner was dispossessed of his shares, even though some of his rights as shareholder were restricted.[122] Mukherjea J was not convinced that the law in question constituted an improper discrimination against the petitioner either.[123] Patanjali Sastri J and Das J were of the opinion that the petition should have succeeded, because they thought that the law in question constituted an improper discrimination against one specific company.[124] Das J concurred with the majority that the acquisition issue had to be decided with reference to the applicant's property, in other words the shares, and not the company as such. From this perspective he concluded that the law in question did not amount to an acquisition of the petitioner's property: a law deprives someone of his property when it takes away "the substantial bulk of the rights constituting his 'property'",[125] but in this case the rights which the petitioner retained were "the most important of the rights constituting his 'property'",[126] even though some of his rights were undeniably taken away. Das J therefore concluded that the petitioner's rights were not taken away as meant in article 31 or article 19, and that the "curtailment of the incidental privileges, namely, the right to elect directors, to pass resolutions and to apply for the winding up may well be supported as a reasonable restraint on the exercise and enjoyment of the shareholder's right of property imposed in the interests of the general public...", in other words, as a regulatory non-compensable deprivation.[127] The rights that were taken away or restricted were described as "privileges incidental to the ownership of the share which itself is property", but in themselves and on their own they did not constitute property.[128]

. The view taken in this case was coloured by the fact that the applicant was a shareholder in the affected company and not the company itself, and the *ratio* of the decision is therefore that the state's interference with the management of the company did not take over any property from the shareholders as such. A different position was assumed in *Dwarkadas Shrinivas v The Sholapur Spinning and Weaving Co Ltd and Others*,[129] which dealt with the same Sholapur Spinning and Weaving Company (Emergency Provisions) Ordinance 2 of 1950 and Sholapur Spinning and Weaving Company (Emergency Provisions) Act 28 of 1950. In this case, the new directors appointed by the terms of the Act passed a resolution making a contribution call for a certain amount on each preferent share, payable on a certain date. The applicant instituted an action on behalf of himself and all other preferent shareholders, challenging the validity of the ordinance on the grounds that it violated section 299(2) of the Government of India Act 1935. The action was dismissed and this decision was confirmed by the High Court on appeal. The applicant appealed to the Supreme Court on the grounds that the provisions of the ordinance authorising the taking over of the management and administration of the company were contrary to article 31(2) of the Constitution of India 1950. In this case Das J concluded[130] that a law which transfers management of a company to the state "has far overstepped the limits of police power and is, in substance, nothing short of expropriation by way of the exercise of the power of eminent domain", even though neither the shares of the shareholders nor the actual property of the company was acquired by the state. Bose J agreed that property includes any interest in any commercial and industrial undertaking, as well as any interest in a company with an interest in a commercial or industrial undertaking, which means that the law in question did not involve acquiring property for the purposes of article 31(2) by taking over the management of the company.

The decisions in these two Indian cases seem somewhat inconsistent, considering that the applicant in *Dwarkadas Shrinivas* was also an individual shareholder and not the company itself, so that there was no obvious reason to depart from the restricted approach in *Charanjit Lal Chowdhury* and decide this case with reference to the property of the company as such. The inconsistencies must, however, probably be seen as a result of a constitutional wrangle between the courts and the legislature about the interpretation of the property clause and a consequent difference of opinion between some of the judges (particularly Sastri J and Das J) about the relationship between articles 19 and 31, and between article 31(1) and 31(2).[131] The decision in the influential case of *State of West Bengal v Subodh Gopal Bose and Others*,[132] in which the Supreme Court set out the Sastri vision of the structure, meaning and scope of the property guarantee contained in articles 19(1)(f) and 31, and which was followed by the majority in *Dwarkadas Shrinivas*, tended to restrict the power of the state to introduce non-compensable regulatory limitations of property while increasing the scope of compensable deprivations of property. The result was that the right to manage commercial property was considered such an important aspect of the property that a material interference with that right by the state was regarded as a compulsory acquisition of the property. However, this result (and the different approaches of particularly Das J in *Dwarkadas Shrinivas* and *Charanjit Lal Chowdhury*) cannot be explained exclusively in terms of the reactionary mood of the Sastri court. Even before this development took place Das J was already willing to recognise the importance of the right to manage property and to protect it against state interference. In *Kameshwar Singh v Province of Bihar*[133] the Supreme Court had to decide on the constitutional validity of the Bihar State Management of Estates and Tenures Act 21 of 1949, which provided that the management of certain estates and tenures in land would be placed in the hands of civil servants for a certain period of time. Shearer J (for the majority) concluded that the law does not take away rights in property, but merely restricts powers incident to ownership.[134] However, in this case Das J[135] thought that the law did indeed amount to an acquisition of property, because "certain very important rights of, and incidental to ownership are taken away...." Even though "the entire bundle of rights of a proprietor or tenure holder" was not taken away, the fact that several rights in land were in fact acquired was sufficient to qualify the Act in question as acquisitive.[136] There is, therefore, a certain measure of inconsistency in the various opinions of Das J on the question whether state interference with the management of a private company amounts to an expropriation of the property or not. These inconsistencies are due partly to the courts' constitutional wrangle with the legislature and partly to different features and contexts of the various cases involved. It should not detract from the general impression that, in the view of the Indian courts, state interference with the management of a private company can be (and more often than not is) so serious an infringement of the owners' rights that it amounts to an expropriation rather than a regulation, even if it is recognised that the intention was to protect a legitimate and important aspect of the public interest.[137]

Three cases that concerned the complete or partial nationalisation of private banks also illustrate the constitutional importance of the right to manage a private business enterprise. In *RC Cooper v Union of India (Bank Nationalisation* case)[138] the Indian Supreme Court had the opportunity to consider the validity of a 1968 amendment of the Banking Companies Act 1949 that was intended to give effect to the policy of social control over commercial banks. In July 1969, an ordinance transferred the undertaking of 14 commercial banks to 14 new banks established under the ordinance. The post of chairperson and director of each bank was deemed to have been vacated. Provision was made for the payment of compensation to the named banks. The ordinance was replaced by the Banking Companies (Acquisition and Transfer of Undertaking) Act 22 of 1969, the declared aim of which was to serve the needs of the development of the economy in accordance with national policy and objectives, and which provided for the taking over of the affected banks' banking business, but left their non-banking business to be carried out within certain restrictions. The petitioner was a shareholder in several banks and had accounts with those banks. He was also a director of the Central Bank of India. He challenged the validity of the ordinance and the Act on the ground that it infringed his fundamental rights under articles 19(1)(f) and 31(2) of the Constitution. The majority of the court declared the Banking Companies (Acquisition and Transfer of Undertakings) Act 22 of 1969 unconstitutional and void. In reaching this judgment the court followed the reasoning of the decisions in *Kochuni v States of Madras and Kerala*[139] and *Vajravelu Mudaliar v The Special Deputy Collector for Land Acquisition, West Madras and Another*:[140] a law may only deprive a person of property without compensation if it does not impair the fundamental rights as such; articles 19 and 31 must be read together and not disjunctively; the validity of the state action in acquiring or restricting property rights must be determined in the light of its effects on the right, and not just with reference to the object of the law in question or the power of the state; because articles 19 and 31 have to be read together, the fact that an acquisition of property is for a public purpose creates a presumption of reasonableness, but that does not preclude an investigation into the reasonableness of the procedural provisions; accordingly, an acquisition of property is tested not only against the requirements of article 31(2) but also against the requirements of article 19. In view of this line of argument, the court investigated the Act, and decided that it would not pronounce on or investigate the advisability of taking over the banks, but it could and did investigate the effect of the provisions on the rights of those affected by the take-over. The restrictions imposed on the carrying on of the non-banking business were found to be so stringent that the business could not in practice be carried on, and were therefore unreasonable. In following the *Vajravelu* decision the court considered itself justified in asking whether the compensation provided for or the principles laid down for its determination were relevant. In this case the principles were irrelevant, because they were aimed at the acquisition of and compensation for the whole business concern, but in fact related to the value of certain of its assets only. The Act was, therefore, declared void in its entirety.

Attorney-General v Lawrence[141] was decided in terms of the old Constitution of St Christopher, Nevis and Anguilla 1967, prior to promulgation of the Constitution of Saint Christopher and Nevis 1983.[142] The St Kitts/Nevis/Anguilla National Bank Ltd (Special Provisions) Act 1982 was promulgated to remove the directors of the bank from office and to install a new management. The respondent claimed that the Act constituted a contravention of section 6 of the Constitution, which protects property rights. The court held that section 6, which refers to "any interest in or right over property of any description", applies equally to "concrete as well as abstract right[s] of property", and that management is an important incident of holding property for this purpose and therefore also covered by section 6. Given the fact that the relevant property clause is a "standard" variation of a "double" property guarantee, it is important to keep in mind that compensation is also provided for deprivation of property, which complicates matters somewhat. However, as in the Mauritian case of *Société United Docks and Others v Government of*

Mauritius; Marine Workers Union and Others v Mauritius Marine Authority and Others,[143] it is possible to argue that even "standard" "double" property guarantees leave room for regulatory deprivations that do not require compensation, and consequently the award of compensation in this case probably indicate the courts' opinion that the regulation in question actually amounted to an expropriation, just as much as the decision in *Société United Docks* indicated an opinion that the regulation in that case did not.

    Bank of New South Wales v The Commonwealth[144] concerned the Australian Banking Act 1947, which provided for the acquisition of shares in any private bank by the Commonwealth Bank by agreement or compulsion, the taking over of any business in Australia of any of the banks by the Commonwealth Bank by agreement or compulsion, the payment of compensation as determined by a Court of Claims and the prohibition of the carrying on of banking by the private banks upon notice given by the Treasurer. If put into full operation, the Act would have had the effect of creating a monopoly of banking in Australia in favour of the Commonwealth Bank of Australia. The plaintiffs challenged the validity of the Act on the grounds that it did not fall within the powers of parliament under section 51 of the Commonwealth Constitution 1900. The majority decision in this case followed the majority in *Minister of State for the Army v Dalziel*[145] in refusing to restrict the concept of an acquisition, for the purposes of section 51(xxxi), to the acquisition of full title, and in applying the requirement of just terms to compulsory acquisitions of "innominate and anomalous interests and ... the assumption and indefinite continuance of exclusive possession and control for the purposes of the Commonwealth of any subject of property".[146] The provisions of the Banking Act 1947 were held to be in conflict with the constitutional guarantee, because they amounted to a scheme for the compulsory acquisition of property, but failed to provide just terms[147] as required by section 51(xxxi). Important considerations in coming to this conclusion were that the scheme should not be allowed to effect a compulsory taking of the property by indirect means; that the empty husk which remains of the corporate shell of the private banks means nothing, and that the banks as such are in fact being acquired by the Act – "[t]he company and its shareholders are in a real sense, although not formally, stripped of the possession and control of the entire undertaking";[148] that the acquisition of property cannot change the nature of the property involved (shares and assets respectively), and the interest which the Commonwealth Bank would acquire would be anomalous, unknown to law and equity; and that the effect of the Act would be that the state would be in a position to act as judge in its own cause in determining the compensation.

Of particular importance in this respect are the recent Australian decisions referred to in the section on the cancellation of debts above. These cases made clear that not every deprivation of property amounts to an acquisition of property (depending on whether the state can be said to have acquired some benefit or advantage from it); and that not every acquisition of property will attract compensation (depending on whether the acquisition can be said to have been a proportionate, reasonable and incidental result of the exercise of a different head of power). These principles might well mean that many, if not most, regulatory interferences with the management of a private business can escape the compensation guarantee, even if there is substantial loss or deprivation of property at stake, either because the state does not acquire any benefit or advantage from the deprivation, or because the acquisition that can be identified was a proportionate and reasonable incidental result of the appropriate exercise of a different head of power, most notably the regulatory police power. If the main objective was to manage and administer conflicting private claims and interests and not to acquire property, and provided the results are reasonable and proportionate given the purpose served, it is possible that no compensation duty will accrue even if the state did acquire property in the process.

An extremely interesting perspective that seems to confirm this conclusion appears from the decision of the German Federal Constitutional Court in the *Contergan* case,[149] where it was decided that there are situations where the state has the power to interfere with the right to manage private property, without such interference amounting to an expropriation of the property. In terms of a settlement agreement between the victims and the producer of the medicine that caused the physical handicaps of the German Thalidomide victims, a private compensation fund was created, and each victim who was a party to the settlement agreement acquired a claim right against the fund. The federal government promulgated a law to create a public foundation to manage the compensation fund, supported by further state funds, for the benefit of all the Contergan victims. For all practical purposes this meant that the fund was nationalised, or at least placed under state management. The question posed by the complainants was whether the federal law was valid, and how it affected the rights of those victims who were opposed to the creation of the foundation. According to the complainants, the law infringed upon their property rights by taking away the rights they derived from the agreement with the company, and imposed a bureaucracy upon them which interfered with their right to manage their own private property interests in the fund as guaranteed by the Constitution. The effect of the Act was that the victims' private-law rights (deriving from the settlement agreement) in the compensation fund were replaced by public-law rights (deriving from legislation) in the foundation's funds. It was obvious that the original claims against the private fund would be reduced substantially by the fact that the new, public fund was open to claims from victims who were not parties to the settlement agreement. The most important change was that the rights in question were removed from the private sphere and subjected to the management of a specially created public-law body. The question whether the complainants' constitutionally guaranteed property rights were infringed has to be answered against this background.

The court accepted that the complainants' claims against the compensation fund in terms of the agreement were protected by the constitutional property guarantee: money debts can be regarded as property for the purposes of the property clause, especially when those debts and the claims deriving from them served the purpose to replace a loss of physical capabilities, and the property guarantee had to secure these debts and claims for the complainants in the same way as it does for all other protected property. The question was how the effect of the management law of 1971 should be explained. The court argued in the following way: the law transformed and changed the nature of these constitutionally guaranteed claims; the main question was whether the legislature was prevented by the Basic Law from doing so, and whether the law remained within the limits of what is allowed for such legislation; the substantive guarantee (*Bestandsgarantie*) in article 14.1 secures the right of a property holder to a specific, concrete property object, but does not make that property completely untouchable, nor does it exclude every possibility of affecting or changing it by law; on the contrary, article 14.2 allows and actually charges the legislature to restrict and give content to those rights, although this power has to be exercised within clear limits; this power to determine the content and limits of property rights gives the legislature the right to realise the social function of the property in question, depending on how strong or how weak the social function is; in the process a just balance between the autonomous sphere of freedom of the individual and the social interests of the community has to be found in view of the principle of proportionality; and even when a strong social interest justifies a regulatory limitation of the individual's autonomy, not every kind of limitation is justified, and the limitation has to be proportionate and has to respect the substance of the right. In view of these principles the creation of the public foundation has to be seen as a justified and legitimate regulatory provision, aimed at securing the social interest in the proper and just distribution and management of the compensation fund and the additional state funds. The law does not constitute an expropriation of the complainants' original claims against the compensation fund, but simply transforms these claims into public-law claims against the foundation funds. An important consideration in this regard was the fact that the compensation fund was not meant to satisfy only the complainants' claims against the company, but all possible claims deriving from the use of the relevant medicine. To ensure the just distribution of the fund under these circumstances, where new claimants might still come forward, it was unavoidable to manage the funds through a public foundation.[150]

The German Federal Constitutional Court assumed a similar position in the so-called *Mitbestimmung* case.[151] The question in this case was whether a law which provided for compulsory participation of employees in the management of large concerns was constitutional. The complainants, owners of a number of private and incorporated companies affected by the law, claimed that their property rights were infringed by the provisions in question. The Federal Constitutional Court decided that the law did not conflict with the property guarantee in article 14 of the German Basic Law. The court reiterated its position that, as far as the function of property in securing the personal freedom of the individual is at stake, property enjoys a particularly strong protection; but the stronger the social relation and function of property, the stronger and the wider are the regulatory powers of the legislature in determining the content and limits of that property – this principle is based on the fact that the use of property with a strong social function affects not only the property holder but also other people's lives and interests. The statutory provisions with regard to the participation of employees in the management decisions of large enterprises are regulatory determinations of the content and limits of the property rights of the owners and shareholders of the businesses involved, and not expropriations. In judging the legitimacy and justification of these regulatory provisions, the nature and social function of this kind of investment property has to be taken into account: it clearly has little direct bearing on the provision or security of the individual shareholder's personal freedom, and it equally clearly has a very significant social function in that the use and exploitation of this kind of property affects the lives of many other people, particularly the employees of the company. Therefore, in terms of the principles that govern the interpretation and application of the property clause,[152] the scope for legislative regulatory limitations of this kind of property is wide, although the substance of the property may not be destroyed. The specific provisions under review in this case were regarded, in view of the proportionality principle, as legitimate and justifiable restrictions of property. To arrive at this conclusion the court undertook a quite detailed investigation of the function and social effects of investment property.

These two German decisions suggest that not all state interferences with the right to manage private (commercial) property will amount to expropriations, not even when the interference is drastic and results in losses for those affected. In other words, it appears that it will be justified under certain circumstances for the state to interfere with or even take over the right to manage private (commercial) property when such a step is justified by the state's police power duty to protect an important aspect of the public interest.

A similar perspective appears from the decision of the US Supreme Court in *PruneYard Shopping Center v Robins*.[153] The private owner of a shopping centre appealed from a judgment of the California Supreme Court in which it was held that the California Constitution protects free speech and petitioning, reasonably exercised, in a privately owned shopping centre. The owner of the shopping centre claimed that the decision of the United States Supreme Court in *Lloyd v Tanner*[154] prevented the state from requiring a private shopping centre owner to allow access to people exercising their constitutional rights of free speech and petition when adequate alternative avenues of communication are available to them.[155] The question was whether the states are precluded from promulgating legislation (such as a state constitution) which requires a private shopping centre owner to allow access to people who want to exercise their right of free speech and petition in the shopping centre. Rehnquist J for the majority[156] made it clear from the outset that the reasoning of the court in *Lloyd v Tanner* did not limit the authority of the states to exercise their police power or their sovereign right to adopt their own constitutions in which individual liberties may be more expansive than in the federal Constitution. The states may exercise their police power in such a way that reasonable restrictions are imposed on private property, provided the restrictions do not amount to a taking of the property without just compensation or contravene any other federal constitutional provision. The effect of *Lloyd v Tanner*, according to Rehnquist J, was that when a private landowner opens a shopping mall to the public, the First Amendment does not create individual rights in expression beyond those already existing under applicable law. Rehnquist J confirmed that the right to exclude others from property (an important aspect of the owner's right to manage the property) is regarded as one of the essential sticks in the bundle making up property, and that the interpretation of the California Supreme Court indeed destroyed this right by allowing free expression rights to the public on the premises of a privately owned shopping centre. However, and this is the important point, he added that not every destruction of or injury to property by governmental action amounts to a taking in the constitutional sense. The question that had to be asked to determine whether there was a violation of the takings clause was whether the restriction on private property "forces some people to bear alone public burdens which, in all fairness and justice, should be borne by the public as a whole."[157] This entails considerations of factors such as the nature and economic impact of the regulation and its interference with reasonable investment-backed expectations. When the regulation goes too far, it will be recognised as a taking.[158] In the circumstances of the case, so Rehnquist J argued, there was nothing to indicate that the requirement to allow the petitioners to exercise their state-protected rights of free speech and petition in the shopping centre would amount to an unconstitutional infringement of the owner's property rights under the takings clause.[159] It was clear that the property owner did not have to suffer expressive activity under a blanket permission, and it was free to adopt and enforce regulations with regard to the time, place and manner in which these activities would be permissible so as to minimise interference with the regular activities of a shopping centre. From this perspective the actions of the petitioners could not be described as a physical invasion of the property. In fact, the point was that the property owner failed in this case[160] to demonstrate that the right to exclude others from the premises was so essential to the use or economic value of the property that the state-allowed limitation amounted to a taking of the property. Accordingly, the claim based on the takings clause failed. The claim based on due process was also rejected. Due process, it was pointed out,[161] demands only that the state action should not be unreasonable, arbitrary or capricious, and that the means selected to serve the public purpose should have a real and substantial relation to the objective served by it. There was no proof in the present case that the legislation complained of failed this test.

In view of the analysis above it seems that the right to manage (especially commercial) property is considered a sufficiently important aspect of property that a substantial interference with that right by the state may well establish a compulsory acquisition of the property involved. However, there are enough cases that indicate that not every interference with the right to manage property is a compulsory acquisition, and that not every acquisition should be subject to the compensation duty: the nature and public purpose of the interference (which may even assume the form of the state taking over the management of the property) can justify the inference that the state imposed this limitation on the right as a legitimate and reasonable exercise, in the public interest, of its police power. The proportionality test seems to be important in deciding whether it is justified not to compensate where property was actually acquired by the state.

Regulation By Way of Licences, Permits and Quotas

Regulation of commercial property by way of licences, permits and quotas gives rise to an especially important and interesting category of cases where it is often claimed that regulation has an expropriatory effect. These cases are distinguished from the ones discussed in earlier sections in that they do not involve the establishment of a state monopoly, and that they are not specifically concerned with the management of the relevant business. As a rule the most interesting cases originate in situations where a certain commercial branch or activity is subjected to (generally uncontroversial) regulation in the form of licences, permits or quotas, and the aggrieved party complains about the refusal, cancellation or amendment of a licence, permit or quota that is essential for the continued existence of her enterprise. In many cases the effect of the refusal or cancellation of a licence, permit or quota is that the business in question has to be closed down; in others an amendment of the licence, permit or quota or of the conditions under which it was issued or is held can render the business redundant or uncompetitive.

Tre Traktörer AB v Sweden (Tre Traktörer AB Case)[162] is a decision of the European Court of Human Rights,[163] and deals with liquor licensing in Sweden, a country with a long-standing policy aimed at the prevention of abuse of alcoholic beverages. This policy is embodied in the Act on the Sale of Beverages 1977, which regulates the serving of alcoholic beverages in restaurants and bars as well as the issuing of licences for these premises to sell alcohol. The applicant company's licence to serve alcoholic beverages in a restaurant was subject to regulatory conditions regarding the character of a restaurant and the serving of young people. When the sole shareholder of the applicant company was audited and the audit revealed discrepancies in the bookkeeping relating to the sale of alcohol, criminal proceedings were instituted against her. She was acquitted, and after an admonition the relevant authority nevertheless renewed her licence. The Social Council appealed against this decision on the basis of an inspection report stating that the restaurant was overcrowded, that most of its customers were 18 years old and that an all-night discotheque was operated in part of the premises. The National Board of Health and Welfare decided to revoke the licence. The applicant company claimed compensation from the government on the ground that the revocation violated her rights under the Convention. This claim was rejected and the applicant company complained to the European Commission, which allowed the matter to be heard by the European Court of Human Rights. The European Court had no problem in recognising the economic interests connected with the management of the restaurant (including the liquor licence) as "possessions" for the purposes of article 1 of the First Protocol to the European Convention on Human Rights, and accepted that withdrawal of the licence constituted an interference with the complainant's right to the peaceful enjoyment of its possessions in terms of the first rule. The court decided that, severe though this interference may have been, it did not deprive the complainant of its property, but constituted a measure of control of the use of the property. The third rule (dealing with the regulation of the use of property) rather than the second rule (dealing with expropriation) therefore applied to this case. Regulatory control of the use of property has to comply with two requirements in terms of the third rule: it has to be lawful and in the public interest; and it has to satisfy the proportionality principle. With regard to the lawfulness requirement, the court's power to review compliance with domestic law is limited, and there was nothing in the present case to suggest that the withdrawal of the licence was contrary to Swedish law. With regard to the public interest requirement, the court held that the interest served by the relevant law, namely control over the sale of liquor, was a legitimate action in the public interest. With regard to proportionality, the test is whether the measure of control strikes a fair balance between the general interest of the community and the protection of the individual's property rights; and there must be a reasonable relationship of proportionality between the means employed and the aim sought to be realised, bearing in mind that the states enjoy a wide margin of appreciation in this regard. The court held that the burden imposed in this case, though heavy, was not disproportionate under the circumstances, and that the state did not fail to strike a fair balance between the public interest and the individual property interest. There was, consequently, no violation of article 1 and the Swedish law was upheld.[164]

Patricia Hand and Others v The Right Honourable Lord Mayor, Aldermen and Burgesses of Dublin and Others[165] concerned a situation where renewal of a licence was denied because of criminal behaviour of the holder. Section 3 of the Irish Casual Trading Act 1980 requires a casual trading licence and a permit in order to engage in casual trading. The Act provides that a licence shall not be issued to anyone convicted of two or more offences under the Act. The plaintiffs had been convicted more than twice for offences under the Act, and when their applications for licences were denied, they claimed that the Act interfered with their right to earn a livelihood, which was said to be a property right in terms of the Irish Constitution. The court assumed, without deciding, that the right to earn a livelihood was a property right for purposes of the Constitution, but held that, even if the right to earn a livelihood was a property right, it could not be an unqualified right, and that it was subject to legitimate legal regulation. The regulations in this case were not considered an unjust attack on the plaintiffs' right to earn a livelihood.

In *Bahadur v Attorney General*[166] the Court of Appeals of Trinidad and Tobago reached a similar result, albeit along a somewhat unusual route. The appellant was the owner and driver of a truck which was involved in a fatal accident. The appellant was charged with manslaughter and dangerous driving. The Licensing Authority then suspended the appellant's driving permit in accordance with traffic laws, pending the determination of the charges against him. As the appellant's livelihood was affected by the suspension of his driving permit, his solicitors wrote to the authorities several times asking that it be returned. The appellant was acquitted of the charges of manslaughter and dangerous driving, but his driving permit was only returned eight months later. The appellant approached the High Court for a declaration that the notice suspending his permit was null and void and in conflict with sections 4 and 5 of the

Constitution. His application was dismissed and he appealed to the Court of Appeals. This decision provides an extensive discussion of the question whether a driving permit constitutes property for purposes of section 4(a) of the 1976 Constitution. The court subscribed to the generally accepted wide interpretation of this concept in constitutional cases, but nevertheless decided that a driving licence as such does not constitute property for this purpose. Of great significance in this regard is the additional qualification, which is particularly important in view of the fact that section 4 of the Constitution refers to the "enjoyment of property", that even though the licence does not constitute "property" for purposes of section 4(a), the improper withdrawal of a driving licence may constitute an unconstitutional infringement of the "enjoyment of property". The effect of the decision is, therefore, similar to that of the *Tre Traktörer AB* and *Patricia Hands* decisions discussed earlier.

A number of cases deal with the acquisition of a licence, permit or quota and its effect on the viability of the business enterprise in question. The first case, *Lawlor v Minister of Agriculture and Others*,[167] concerns the EEC Superlevy Regulations, which fixed an EEC limit for the production of milk and milk products and determined a national milk quota. The regulations provided that where land which was the subject of a quota was sold or leased as a whole or in part, the quota should be transferred and subdivided accordingly. The plaintiff sold one of his farms to the second and third defendants, who wanted to deliver their milk to a different co-operative, and a dispute arose as to the transfer of the plaintiff's milk quota. The first defendant, the responsible Irish minister, investigated and adjusted the various quotas allocated to the producers and co-operatives involved, and the plaintiff rejected these adjustments and the EEC regulations in terms of which they were made as an unfair attack on his property rights. The Irish court accepted that a milk quota is a valuable intangible asset, and that the quota regulations amount to a regulation or limitation of the use of farmland by individual producers, in an effort to reconcile such use with the exigencies of the common good. In what was described by the court as a teleological or schematic interpretation of the regulations, it was held that the purpose of the regulations was to ensure that quotas are allocated on the basis of milk production on given holdings throughout the basis year, so that any change in the ownership, subdivision or use of those holdings would be reflected in corresponding changes in the quota: the total quota for each holding in the basis year was to be allocated or subdivided between users of the total landholding in the same proportion as the use of the landholding itself. The court concluded that the regulations were not intended to abolish the right of private ownership or the general right to transfer, bequeath or inherit property, although they did limit the exercise of certain rights of ownership with a view to reconciling them with the exigencies of the common good. Furthermore, the court concluded that such a limitation of property rights did not require monetary compensation.

In another Irish case, *Hempenstall and Others v The Minister for the Environment*,[168] the question was whether an amendment of taxi regulations was valid. In terms of the Road Traffic (Public Service Vehicle) Regulations 1963 the minister created two classes of small public service vehicles, namely taxis and hackneys, the latter being somewhat more restricted in their operation in public places. In 1978 the number of taxi licences was restricted, and these licences were made transferable, thereby creating a market in them. In 1991, pending an investigation, the number of hackney licences was restricted temporarily, but in 1992 the moratorium was lifted. Subsequently, the applicants, a number of taxi operators, challenged the 1992 regulations, claiming that the unlimited issue of hackney licences constituted an unfair attack on their own taxi licences, these being valuable property rights. In this decision, it was assumed that taxi licences are indeed valuable property rights, and the only question was whether the regulations in question constituted an unjust attack on those rights. The court held that property rights originating in licences created by law are creatures of legislation, and that they are subject to changes in the relevant legislation and resulting diminution of those rights.

The most important trend in this category seems to be that licences, permits and quotas either are or form part of commercial property, and are protected as such by a constitutional property clause. However, the property rights inherent in or deriving from these control mechanisms are regarded as creatures of legislation, and are therefore open to change and amendment by or in terms of the same legislation. Such changes, amendments and controls (which may include the refusal, revocation or restriction of the licence or the conditions under which it is held) are not necessarily to be regarded as expropriations of the property interest in them simply because the property in question is destroyed or rendered less valuable or uncompetitive. The tendency seems to be that regulations of this nature have to be imposed by law and have to comply with some sort of proportionality requirement, which means that the regulatory regime must impose a reasonable and justifiable limitation that is designed and likely to protect the public interest and that establishes a just balance between the public interest and the private interests that are affected. This is in line with the general proportionality tests applied in various jurisdictions to establish whether a particular limitation of a fundamental right is constitutionally justifiable,[169] and also with the recent Australian case law discussed in the section above on the cancellation of state debts.

Regulation of Immaterial Property Rights

The "police power" regulation of immaterial property rights (copyrights, patents, trademarks, and confidential information) can of course also result in losses to commercial enterprises, since these rights often have great commercial value, and in certain instances they can be essential to the operation or competitive edge of a business. However, this paper is not concerned with the legal nature or with the constitutional protection of immaterial property rights as such. The position with the protection of existing immaterial property rights is not very problematic, and the principle is that an immaterial property right is regarded as property and protected accordingly in terms of the constitutional property clause if it is a vested right.[170]

A number of cases deal with the problems that arise when the regulation of immaterial property rights requires that information be made public by the holder of the right in such a manner that the right itself (or confidential information that is essential to it) is endangered. In *Smith-Kline & French Laboratories (Australia) Ltd and Others v Secretary, Department of Community Services and Health; Alphapharm Pty Ltd v Secretary, Department of Community Services and Health and Others*[171] the Australian Federal Court was confronted by such a case. The applicants in the first proceedings were the holders of a patent with regard to cimetidine, a compound used for the treatment of ulcers and related disorders. The patent was due to expire and the first applicants filed for an extension of the patent, providing information regarding the chemistry and quality control of the cimetidine product to the Department of Community Services and Health. In 1987 the first applicants instituted proceedings seeking injunctive relief on the grounds that the respondent department intended to use this confidential information for purposes other than those for which it was given. They were granted interlocutory relief. The applicant in the second proceedings was an Australian company who opposed the extension of the applicants' patent on cimetidine and applied for marketing approval for its own brand of cimetidine. The respondent department informed the second applicant that it could not evaluate their application due to the interlocutory relief granted to the first applicants. Second applicant instituted proceedings for a declaration that the respondent department was free to use the information supplied by first applicants in order to process its application and a *mandamus* that it should do so. First applicants contended that if the applicable regulation has this effect, it would be a law for the acquisition of property other than on just terms within the meaning of section 51(xxxi) of the Australian Commonwealth Constitution 1900. The Federal Court decided that the concept of "property" in section 51(xxxi) must be defined widely, and that it includes innominate and intangible interests, in addition to the usual estates or interests in land, chattels and choses in actions known to common law and equity.[172] It further held that the constitutional guarantee of just terms in section 51(xxxi) does not apply where the plaintiff supplies proprietary information to a state organ in order to obtain a permission or to have a prohibition lifted in terms of the regulations in question, because the regulations do not provide for a compulsory acquisition of the information in question.[173]

In a similar case, the German Federal Constitutional Court came to a comparable conclusion.[174] A federal amendment law aimed at the simplification and improvement of the existing patent law and registration procedure implied that the documents submitted for the registration of a patent would, at a certain stage, become publicly accessible. This could obviously affect the proprietary interests of potential patent holders detrimentally, and The Federal Patents Court submitted the matter to the Federal Constitutional Court for a decision concerning the validity of these provisions, in view of the potential implications for already submitted and future applications for the registration of patents. In its judgment, the court set out the position of the applicant for and eventual holder of a registered patent: according to settled law, the applicant can acquire a protected interest in the object of the patent even before its registration, even if this interest does not yet constitute an exclusive right; this protected interest which is awarded to the applicant even before registration of the patent enjoys the protection of the property guarantee in article 14; the regulatory provisions of the law are aimed at facilitating and administering the registration procedure, and these provisions serve the purposes of determining the content and limits of the relevant rights as meant in article 14.1.2; as such, these provisions have to conform with the normal duty to establish a just balance between the interests of the holder of the right and the public interest, in conformity with the general principle of proportionality; the provisions in question, seen against the background of their purpose and of the existing measures and principles (which protect the applicant against improper and unlawful use of the information which becomes publicly accessible in this process), are not unreasonable or in conflict with the constitutional guarantee.

An interesting aspect of the decision concerns the question of regulatory laws which change or amend an existing situation, thereby affecting existing rights. The court set out the general principles in this regard: in the case of necessary changes or amendments to existing law, the legislature is not bound to a simple choice between leaving existing rights unaffected or expropriating them against compensation – existing rights can be amended or affected by changes in conformity with the constitutional property guarantee; that means that existing rights may be subjected to new, possibly more onerous restrictions and burdens; however, in this process the legislature is still bound by the requirements and restrictions imposed by the Basic Law; the legality or justifiability of amendments or changes to existing rights are explained in terms of the general principle that they must be justified by the public interest, with due consideration for the fundamental principle of proportionality. In view of all the circumstances, the rationalisation law in question satisfied this requirement, especially considering the fact that the applicant was not left without a remedy, should her rights unlawfully have been infringed upon. This last aspect, regarding the effects of a change in the regulatory regime that may affect existing rights, was illustrated nicely in another German decision, the *Warenzeichen* case.[175] The case concerned a federal law aimed at rationalising and improving certain aspects of the wine industry. An aspect of the law was that wine labels could only display indications of the place of origin if the relevant place of origin was registered officially. However, estates or vineyards smaller than five hectares could not be registered. The complainant was the owner of a winery which has been marketing a quality wine from a small vineyard for many years, with a well-known label which indicated the place of origin of the wine in that specific vineyard. The new rules prevented her from continuing with the marketing of that wine, and her applications for an exception were denied. She alleged that her property rights had been infringed upon. In the course of its evaluation of the law, the Federal Constitutional Court set out the following principles regarding expropriation: the characteristic of expropriation in the terms of article 14.3 is that the state authority interferes with concrete subjective rights which are guaranteed as property in the terms of article 14.1; the question of an expropriation of the right to use indications of origin on a wine label can only arise in so far as that right qualifies as a property right in the terms of article 14.1, which it generally doesn't; however, in cases (like the present one) where the right to use that indication as part of a trademark (*Warenzeichen*) was actually registered, the holder of the trademark acquired an independent property right in the use of that trademark, and that property right enjoyed the protection of article 14.1. In that sense the trademark was an important aspect and instrument of the holder's business, and the constitutional court recognised the fact that property can also be protected by article 14.1 for its commercial value. The court held that the provision in question, in so far as it affected registered trademarks, was invalid because it conflicted with the constitutional property guarantee. The provisions were neither valid regulatory limitations of property (because they exceeded the limits of a legitimate determination of the content of the right in that they actually destroyed it completely) nor a legitimate expropriation (because they did not comply with the requirements for an expropriation in article 14.3). The validity of the provision in question could not be salvaged by means of a suitable compensation award either – according to the German Federal Constitutional Court, compensation is the result of a valid expropriation, and not a means of saving a disproportionate regulation.

The general tendency illustrated by these cases seems to be that property rights consisting in or deriving from immaterial property such as patents, copyrights, trademarks and confidential information are included in the protection of the constitutional property guarantee, subject to the normal provisos regarding the state's power to impose police power limitations, in the public interest, on the exercise of those rights. However, given the fact that these rights are normally recognised and protected under a statutory regime, their constitutional protection against police power regulation has to be judged in a context similar to the position with regard to licences, permits and quotas: being (largely) creatures of legislation, the rights in question are subject to changes and amendments in the applicable laws. Regulatory regimes that impose (or introduce new) police power limitations on the use and exercise of immaterial property rights may and often will cause losses (complete loss of the right or loss in value) for the property holder without thereby necessarily being invalid or attracting compensation claims. The rule seems to be that all property rights are subject to the potentially detrimental effect of police power regulation, but property created by or protected in terms of a statutory regime (including immaterial property) may be even more susceptible to these effects than other property rights.

Concluding Remarks and Evaluation

Of course there are many other cases that could have been considered here: the fairly extensive analysis above of 40 cases from 18 jurisdictions could have been extended a few times over. However, in my view the analysis suffices to illustrate a number of useful points about the police power regulation of intangible commercial property in terms of a constitutional property clause. I make no claims to methodological clarity or dogmatic certainty, but the following rather hesitant concluding remarks seem to justify the effort.

First, these case studies confirm the seemingly trite point that, for purposes of the constitutional property clause, the property concept is wide and flexible. This point is underlined by the very nature of the rights and interests that, in these cases, have been included under the protection of the property clause: a claim to a money payment based on a court judgment or on contract; a financial or commercial interest in a company or in the goodwill of a business or in a bank; the right to manage a business enterprise; rights or interests in a business licence, permit or quota; and immaterial property rights such as copyright, patent, trademark or confidential information. Generally speaking, the proposition that constitutional property is a wider concept than private-law property is fairly trite and unproblematic, especially for public law specialists or for lawyers with a common-law background. It may sound strange or more problematic to some property lawyers from a civil-law background. But, to me, that is not really the point of these cases at all: what is really interesting is that the case studies above suggest that we look at the admittedly wide property concept of constitutional law from a slightly different angle, and recognise that the inclusion or exclusion of a certain right or interest from the protection of a constitutional property clause is a matter of context.[176] In other words, the idea is not that the constitutional property concept is a wider one than the private-law concept, and that once we accept this basic point, the wider concept can be defined and circumscribed just as clearly and finally as the narrower one – the idea is that we should no longer focus on clearly described and defined concepts in our attempts to escape the hard and uncomfortable work of deciding cases on their merits.[177] What is and is not property for the purposes of the constitutional property guarantee is a judgement call, which means that we have to decide the matter, every time anew, with full recognition of the facts and the surrounding circumstances of each case. Of course there are guidelines and general trends that assist us in making the judgement, and in a sense this paper is an attempt to identify such guidelines. However, as the cases illustrate so clearly, one simply cannot rely on the guidelines to make the judgement. The guidelines suggest that cancellation of a state debt should normally be regarded as an acquisitive and expropriatory rather than a regulatory police power action, because the state acquires the benefit of not having to pay a debt. However, as the Namibian *Cultura 2000* case shows, there just may be cases where it is politically and morally justifiable for the state to repudiate a vested and acquired state debt – deciding when we are faced with such a case requires a careful evaluation of the facts and circumstances of each case, taking into account all kinds of difficult parameters such as the constitutional values enshrined in the Bill of Rights, the social, economic and political context in which the debt was created and in which it might be repudiated, the public interest in the case, the interests of those affected should the debt be repudiated, the possible social, political and economic effects and implications of either honouring or repudiating the debt, and so on and on and on. On the other hand it is equally important to realise that a case that seems to justify the repudiation of a state debt along the lines of *Cultura 2000* may be just slightly different from the Namibian case, requiring yet another judgement call on whether it might not be justified, in that particular case, rather to honour the debt. In many instances, the point of identifying guidelines and tendencies might not be to follow the guideline and simplify matters, but rather to avoid the mistake of following the guideline without realising that it is unsuitable. Perhaps we should only be identifying the tendencies in order to deviate from them.   Similar conclusions can be drawn with reference to the cases above dealing with business licences and with immaterial property.   In other words, the property issue in the constitutional context cannot simply be shrugged off with a dogmatic assumption that the concept is a wide one that includes a large number of intangible property interests: the question itself and the possible solutions, guidelines and tendencies that seem to offer or simplify the answers to it are contingent, contextual, continually changing. The dogmatic map that seeks to seduce us into believing that answers are not all that hard to find as long as one just follows the main routes of general principles and established precedent should be marked with the warning one finds on old maps of Africa: *Hic leones sunt.*[178]

As for the distinction between expropriation and deprivation and the various approaches to this conundrum, similarly uncomfortable conclusions are suggested by the case analysis above. The analysis of the Zimbabwean *Hewlett* and *Davies* cases illustrates the grave danger of an over-simplified inquiry based on the question whether the state acquired anything: in some instances, this question just does not make sense. This is not to say that it never makes sense, because the *Davies* case is a good example of a situation where it does: the effect of the relevant law in that case is easier to understand in terms of this question. It is in the context of other cases, like *Hewlett* or *Manitoba Fisheries* or *Selangor Pilot Association* that this question leads us into dangerous territory. Even when working with a more sophisticated conceptual and dogmatic framework than is displayed by the logic of *Hewlett*, the factual and contextual complexities of cases like *Selangor Pilot Association* and *Société United Docks* should serve as a warning that simplistic reasoning results in questionable decisions. Was the Canadian government merely rationalising the fishing industry, or was it actually establishing a state monopoly at the cost of the established private enterprises? Was the Mauritian government establishing a state monopoly at the cost of the private sugar handling concerns, or was it simply protecting and promoting the efficiency of a key industry in the national interest? These questions can only be answered with full recognition and consideration of the contextual factors mentioned earlier. The recent Australian decisions in which it was said that not every claim or right sounding in money was a vested right that qualified as property, that not every deprivation of such a right was an acquisition of property, and that not every acquisition of property attracted the duty to compensate are extremely important in this regard. They suggest a more complex and sophisticated set of principles in which the nature of the right or interest, the actual effect of a deprivation, the purpose of a state interference with property and the proportionality of purpose, means and effect have to be taken into account when deciding whether any given allegedly unconstitutional interference with property is valid, and whether it attracts the compensation duty.

A similar result is suggested with regard to another possible "bright line" rule designed to simplify the difficult question of distinguishing between expropriations and regulatory deprivations. Rubenfeld suggested,[179] with reference to the phraseology of the American Fifth Amendment, that the distinction should be made with reference to the question whether the property was actually "taken for public use", and not simply whether the property was taken. This indicates that property may in certain instances be taken without it being "taken for public use", so that a taking is either unconstitutional (if the public use aspect is regarded mainly as a requirement for a valid taking) or does not require compensation (in a different reading, where the public use aspect is read as a qualification of the compensation requirement) if it is not for public use. This reference to "public use" rather than the more general "public interest" is repeated in a few other property clauses,[180] indicating that Rubenfeld's reading of the Fifth Amendment has to be taken seriously if account is to be given of the textual differences between various property clauses. However, some problems deriving from a possibly dogmatic application of this suggestion[181] are immediately apparent: is the strict "public use" reading employed to subject expropriations to a stricter validity test, or is it used to limit the compensation requirement? The possible implications of the two approaches can be illustrated with reference to a situation where a constitution is supposed to protect existing property rights and to promote redistributory purposes like land reform. If a "public use" interpretation is employed to subject expropriations to a stricter requirement, it will mean that expropriation for the purpose of land redistribution is effectively blocked, because then it would be unconstitutional to expropriate from one private owner in order to give to another – use by another private owner would very possibly not qualify as "public use". There are indications that redistributory expropriation should be valid if it clearly serves a public purpose, such as a national land redistribution programme, but there are also legitimate fears that a more reactionary approach might prevail and block this kind of expropriation.[182] On the other hand, the "public use" requirement can be used to argue that only those expropriations that are actually for public use have to be compensated, while expropriations that do not result in public use of the property do not have to be compensated. The reasoning here may seem to be rather revolutionary, but in fact it is similar to what was argued in cases like *Hewlett*, *Manitoba Fisheries* and *Société United Docks*, and as long as the analysis is more sophisticated than in *Hewlett* it can be a useful tool:

the fact that the state "uses" the property (by saving on payment of debts, by trading on the goodwill of the closed down company) suggests there should be compensation. It can be argued that this approach should distinguish the situation in *Société United Docks* (where the state arguably did not use the goodwill of the redundant enterprises) from the position in *Manitoba Fisheries* (where the state indeed seemed to trade on the goodwill of the closed down businesses), which is useful.

However, in the final analysis it is again necessary to return to all the contextual determinants to reach a just and equitable decision: the values and purposes promoted by the Constitution (transformation of land holdings or the economy or society at large, national reconciliation, restitution of specific injustices, attraction of foreign investment, protection of the security of minorities, cultural upliftment, urbanisation, can all be relevant); the social, economic and political realities, the facts of the case, the nature of the property involved, the balance that has to be struck between the public interest and the individual interests of those affected, the kind of state power employed and the purpose for which it was used, the vulnerability of the individual or group affected, and so on. Rubenfeld's "public use" argument serves to open up new perspectives on the nature of expropriation, but it cannot (and was not meant to) be a hard and fast rule or a quick fix. State acquisition and public use of property are certainly relevant considerations when determining whether a police power regulation of property has crossed the line and actually effected an expropriation of the property, but it is not always a complete or a reliable or even a sensible test to employ. *Hic leones sunt.*

Even in the absence of the vexing question whether a police power regulation amounts to an expropriation it is still possible to question the validity of a regulation: normally, any police power regulation has to be imposed by law, it has to serve the public purpose protected by the state's police power and it has to be reasonable. In investigating this validity question the context of the case is once again important, as is illustrated by the proportionality tests usually employed in many jurisdictions.[183] The proportionality test is an excellent example, if used correctly, of the way in which a court should consider the context when deciding a regulation case. Proportionality means that a regulation is only constitutionally justifiable if it is demonstrably reasonable, taking into account all the relevant factors and the context. This once again involves consideration of and mutual weighing up of a huge variety of disparate factors, including the social, political and economic context, the facts of the case, the nature of the property, the harshness of the burden imposed and possible alternatives, and the possibility of establishing a fair balance between the public interest and the individual interests involved.   Any evasion of the difficulties involved in judging the proportionality issue runs the risk of arriving at an unfair, mechanical and irresponsible result.   Cases like the German *Contergan* and *Mitbestimmung* decisions illustrate the difficulty of and the necessity for this kind of judgement: it is very hard, but it has to be done.

This brings me to a last set of observations on the case analysis above. I think it is fair to say that the cases discussed illustrate the dangers involved in using precedent uncritically and indiscriminately.   Without making strong claims regarding the correctness or finality of the distinctions I introduced above, I think I can conclude that it is absolutely essential to analyse possible (and sometimes not so obvious) differences between precedents and the case in hand very carefully and critically before relying on existing decisions too heavily.   What looks like a sensible and reasonable decision in one case simply is not authority for another if the circumstances differ in one or two essential aspects, and this fact has to be taken account of in every situation where the case law method is employed.   Secondly, as far as case law in a comparative perspective is concerned, it is important to take account of the differences between the constitutional texts (and contexts) within which various precedents were created. In some cases the constitutional text and context makes little or no difference: despite the fact that the Australian Commonwealth Constitution does not actually include a property clause in the traditional sense, section 51(xxxi) is and has for a long time been interpreted as if it were such a property clause, and for the most part this textual quirk can simply be ignored when looking at Australian case law. Similarly, the property clause in article 1 of the First Protocol to the European Convention is simply read as if it referred to "property" although it actually refers to "peaceful enjoyment of possessions", and in this case the textual differences seem to make little or no difference. The same goes for the lack of a proper expropriation clause in the Irish Constitution, the absence of a general limitation clause in the German Basic Law, or the lack of a compensation requirement in either the European Convention or the Austrian Bill of Rights, and for the fact that the strictly correct translation for *Eigentum* in the German, Austrian and Swiss property clauses is "ownership" and not "property" – case law indicates that these textual differences are irrelevant. However, several case analyses above illustrate that this is not always the case: the finer textual differences between the "standard" variation of the "double" property guarantee in the Constitution of Mauritius and the unique variation of the "double" property clause in the Zimbabwean Constitution are essential to a proper understanding and evaluation of the *Société United Docks* and the *Hewlett* cases respectively.

This brings me to comparative methodology. There is such a wealth of case law on constitutional property, not to mention the large number of property clauses on which no case law is reported (or where the reported case law is inaccessible), that I cannot escape the conclusion that it would be folly to discuss or study this field without extensive use of comparative material. The problem is, there is no manual – there is not much of a developed methodology in this field, and the developed methodology that is available to us is either restricted by its focus on private-law (mostly in a civil-law context) or too generally aimed at the larger issues of comparative law or even human rights law. We need a properly sensitive methodology for the comparative study of constitutional property issues, with a strong focus on case law and a healthy sensitivity for context. Such a methodology has to leave us room for wide consultation of foreign law, with sufficient safeguards against unsuitable or insensitive comparisons. It should reflect the complexities of the shifting and opaque borderline between private law and public law, between the protection of private individual interests and the legitimate safeguarding and promotion of the public interest; and it should include careful consideration of the important role that the proportionality principle plays in human rights adjudication. It should provide us with suitable skills and strategies with which to negotiate the unknown and potentially dangerous terrain where both private individual property rights and the public interest struggle for recognition. *Hic leones sunt.*

Notes

*   Based on a paper read at the second conference, entitled "Contemporary Issues in Property Law", presented by the Centre for Property Law at The University of Reading from 25-27th March, 1998. The essay is based on sections from different chapters of the incomplete manuscript of AJ van der Walt *Constitutional Property Clauses: A Comparative Analysis* (forthcoming 1999, Juta and Co Cape Town - Wetton - Johannesburg). An electronic version of an earlier draft of the paper was published in the *Electronic Journal for Comparative Law* (http://www.law.kub.nl/ejcl/), and for this purpose helpful editorial suggestions were

made by the assistant editor Hildegard Penn. I am grateful to Denise Prévost, Karen Prinsloo and Marjan Gerbrands for research assistance, and I owe a huge debt of gratitude to Frank Michelman, Joe Singer, Laura Underkuffler-Freund, Clement Ng'ong'ola, Johan Erasmus, Peter Butt, Klaus Stern, Neville Botha, Josef Krüger, Kate O'Regan, Gretchen Carpenter and John Murphy for comments on and suggestions regarding different chapters of the manuscript of *Constitutional Property Clauses*. I am further indebted to Tom Allen for providing drafts of his own paper at the same conference, as well as other papers he wrote earlier and drafts of his book *The Right to Property in Commonwealth Constitutions* (forthcoming, Cambridge UP), and for discussing the issues with me. The final result is much improved thanks to his assistance and input. The Centre for Research Development (Human Sciences Research Council, Pretoria), the Research and Bursaries Committee (University of South Africa, Pretoria) and the Alexander von Humboldt-Stiftung (Bonn) supported different stages of the research process during 1990, 1992 and from 1995 to 1998. The views and opinions expressed in this paper should not be attributed to any of these institutions.

1   In his chapter here (based on a paper given at the above conference), Tom Allen discusses some of the issues revolving around the nature of the property interest: Allen "Limitations on Constitutional Property Rights", especially the section entitled "Limitations Based on the Nature of the Affected Interest" at 188 *ff.*

2   Such as the nature of land as a limited resource, considerations relating to planning and development theory and policy, conservation principles and practices, and so forth.

3   Is it a "police power" regulation or an "eminent domain" expropriation of the property; or does it fall into the middle category of "inverse condemnations"?

4   Even if it is accepted that the limitation constitutes a "police power" deprivation rather than an "eminent domain" expropriation, is it constitutionally justifiable in view of the harshness of its effects for the property owners involved?

5   1997 (11) BCLR 1489 (CC); 1998 (1) SA 300 (CC). For a discussion of the case see AJ van der Walt and H Botha "Getting to Grips with the New Constitutional Order: Critical Comments on *Harksen v Lane NO*" (1998) 13 SA Public Law 17-41.

6   The property clause appears in s 28 of the interim (1993) Constitution; s 25 of the final (1996) Constitution. Both versions feature a deprivation clause (s 28(2), s 25(1)) and an expropriation clause with provision for compensation (s 28(3), s 25(2) and 25(3)). S 28(1) also included a positive property guarantee, and s 25(5)-(9) contains land-reform provisions. S 28 referred to "rights in property", s 25 to "property". For a discussion of s 25 see AJ van der Walt *The Constitutional Property Clause: A Comparative Analysis of Section 25 of the South African Constitution of 1996* (1997) Juta and Co. In the so-called *First Certification Case* (reported as *In Re: Certification of the Constitution of the Republic of South Africa, 1996* 1996 (10) BCLR 1253 (CC); 1996 (4) SA 744 (CC)) the Constitutional Court was asked to certify the constitutional validity of the initial draft of the Final Constitution, and a few interesting remarks were made on the nature and purpose of a property clause in s 25 (at paras [70]-[75]1286D-1289C; 797D-800B). S 28 of the 1993 Constitution was referred to in *Transkei Public Servants' Association v Government of the Republic of South Africa and Others* 1995 (9) BCLR 1235 (Tk) (whether state contracts, pension and employment benefits were "property" for the purposes of s 28; answered in the

affirmative in principle); *Transvaal Agricultural Union v Minister of Land Affairs and Another* 1996 (12) BCLR 1573 (CC) (whether certain provisions in the Restitution of Land Rights Act 22 of 1994 were valid in view of s 28; see further T Roux "Turning a Deaf Ear: The Right to be Heard by the Constitutional Court" (1997) 13 SA Journal on Human Rights 216-227).

7 Constitution of the Republic of South Africa 200 of 1993, now replaced by the Constitution of the Republic of South Africa 1996. The 1996 Constitution was accepted by the Constitutional Assembly on 8th May, 1996 and, after the final draft was certified by the Constitutional Court, it came into operation on 4th February, 1997. In the so-called *First Certification Case* (reported as *In Re: Certification of the Constitution of the Republic of South Africa, 1996* 1996 (10) BCLR 1253 (CC); 1996 (4) SA 744 (CC)) the Constitutional Court was asked to certify the constitutional validity of the initial draft of the Final Constitution, which had to comply with certain constitutional principles referred to in the interim Constitution. For a discussion of the process see D van Wyk "'n Paar Opmerkings en Vrae oor die Nuwe Grondwet" (1997) 60 Tydskrif vir die Hedendaagse Romeins-Hollandse Reg 377-394; M Chaskalson and D Davis "Constitutionalism, the Rule of Law and the First Certification Judgment: *Ex Parte Chairperson of the Constitutional Assembly in re: Certification of the Constitution of the Republic of South Africa 1996* 1996 (4) SA 744 (CC)" (1997) 13 SA Journal on Human Rights 430-445.

8 1997 (11) BCLR 1489 (CC); 1998 (1) SA 300 (CC). References to this case below cite the relevant paragraph number in the decision. The discussion of this case below is based partly on sections of AJ van der Walt and H Botha "Getting to Grips With the New Constitutional Order: Critical Comments on *Harksen v Lane NO*" (1998) 13 SA Public Law 17-41.

9 The applicant also attacked ss 64 and 65, but for present purposes this aspect is ignored.

10 Now the High Court; see the 1996 Constitution s 166(c).

11 1992 (1) SA 9 (A) at 15I-J.

12 Now the Supreme Court of Appeal; see the 1996 Constitution s 166(b).

13 S 21 provides certain safeguards to protect the solvent spouse, amongst others that the solvent spouse can reclaim the property upon providing proof of ownership of the property in question, but this cannot occur without action (and often litigation) from the side of the solvent spouse, regardless of the nature of the property in question and the actual position of the insolvent spouse with regard to such property.

14 In her minority judgment, O'Regan J conducted an excellent comparative overview (at paras [105]- [110]) to indicate that a similar procedure to the vesting provision in s 21 is used only in the Netherlands. In the UK, Canada, Australia and New Zealand the corresponding law provides for a series of voidable or reviewable transactions to protect the interests of innocent creditors of the insolvent. A provision in German law that creates a presumption that movable property in the possession of the insolvent spouse (or in the possession of both spouses) at the time of insolvency belongs to the insolvent spouse is of far more limited scope, even though it resembles the South African provision in some respects. The fact that provision for voidable transactions offers a less burdensome and better alternative is underlined by the fact that this approach has already been recommended by the South African Law Commission for implementation in South African law. O'Regan J concurred in the majority judgment

on the property issue in *Harksen*, and used the comparative analysis only for purposes of the equality issue (to indicate that a less burdensome alternative is available, which makes it possible to argue that the differentiation between solvent spouses and others who had dealings with the insolvent amounts to unfair discrimination).

15   The majority (and the minority judgments did not raise any objections on this point) held that the attacks on ss 64 and 65 are unfounded, since it is clear that the kind of questions that are allowed in the procedure contemplated by these provisions cannot infringe on the solvent spouse's rights in any way: a question that would infringe the constitutional rights of the solvent spouse cannot be "lawfully put" in the terms of the Act (at paras [69]-[76]).

16   Now the Cape High Court; see n 10.

17   *Per* Goldstone J, with whom Chaskalson P, Langa DP, Ackerman J and Kriegler J concurred.

18   *Per* O'Regan J, with whom Madala J and Mokgoro J concurred, and *per* Sachs J in a separate minority judgment.

19   That s 21 of the Act is not inconsistent with s 28(3) of the interim Constitution.

20   That ss 64 and 65 are not inconsistent with s 8 of the interim Constitution.

21   That s 21 is not inconsistent with s 8 of the interim Constitution.

22   This subsection corresponds with s 25(2) of the 1996 Constitution, and deals with the power to expropriate and the requirements for a valid expropriation: it has to be effected in terms of law of general application, be for a public purpose or in the public interest, and be subject to just and equitable compensation as provided for.

23   As was pointed out earlier, the former Appellate Division of the Supreme Court stated *obiter* in *De Villiers NO v Delta Cables (Pty) Ltd* 1992 (1) SA 9 (A) that the effect of this provision was to transfer ownership (*dominium*) of the solvent spouse's property to the master or trustee. The term "transfer" in this statement has to be read with circumspection, since the vesting of property by s 21 (like expropriation in general) is obviously a case of original acquisition of property, which takes place without the consent or co-operation of the previous owner, thereby rendering the term "transfer" somewhat confusing.

24   S 25(1) and 25(2) of the final Constitution.

25   At para [32].

26   *Beckenstrater v Sand River Irrigation Board* 1964 (4) SA 510 (T) at 515A-C.

27   *Hewlett v Minister of Finance and Another* 1982 (1) SA 490 (ZSC) and *Davies and Others v Minister of Lands, Agriculture and Water Development* 1997 (1) SA 228 (ZSC).

28   The court's reference to an Indian case, *HD Vara v State of Maharashtra* 1984 AIR 866 (SC), is probably inappropriate in the circumstances, as this decision dealt with the distinction between expropriation or compulsory acquisition and requisition of property, the latter term being an old-fashioned reference to the temporary dispossession of tangible property for use by the state or the armed forces during a war or an emergency situation. Although Goldstone J at para [34] found it unnecessary to consider the question, it is important to note that this distinction is not identical to the distinction at hand, namely between expropriation and deprivation, since a deprivation of property can be and often is permanent and not merely temporary, and it can involve the property or certain rights in the property and not just the possession or use of the property. S 37 of the 1996 Constitution makes provision

for states of emergency, under which some of the rights in the Bill of Rights may be derogated from. Property (s 25) is not included in the table of non-derogable rights.

29   At paras [35]-[37].

30   *Beckenstrater v Sand River Irrigation Board* 1964 (4) SA 510 (T) at 515A-C.

31   *Hewlett v Minister of Finance and Another* 1982 (1) SA 490 (ZSC).

32   *Davies and Others v Minister of Lands, Agriculture and Water Development* 1997 (1) SA 228 (ZSC).

33   And especially the Zimbabwean cases. The *Beckenstrater* case was decided by the Supreme Court (now the High Court) and has no real constitutional authority or interest. The case concerned the expropriation of water servitudes under the Water Act 54 of 1956 s 94.

34   Especially *Australian Capital Television Pty Ltd and Others v The Commonwealth and Others; The State of New South Wales v The Commonwealth of Australia and Another* (1992) 177 CLR 107; *Australian Tape Manufacturers Association Ltd and Others v The Commonwealth of Australia* (1993) 177 CLR 480; *Health Insurance Commission v Peverill* (1994) 179 CLR 226; *Mutual Pools and Staff Pty Ltd v The Commonwealth of Australia* (1994) 179 CLR 155; *Re Director of Public Prosecutions; Ex Parte Lawler and Another* (1994) 179 CLR 270; *Georgiadis v Australian and Overseas Telecommunications Corporation* (1994) 179 CLR 297.

35   1997 (1) SA 209 (ZSC).

36   Although the court is not at all clear about this; statements concerning the question of acquisition confuse the issue considerably.

37   Some of the relevant cases are discussed later in this paper.

38   1982 (1) SA 490 (ZSC).

39   The property clause, which is a unique variation of a "double" property guarantee (see n 42 below), appears in the introductory s 11 and the special s 16 of the Constitution of Zimbabwe 1980. Generally, the property clause provides for compulsory acquisition against compensation and subject to certain requirements and procedures. It is accepted that the relevant provisions also allow for regulatory deprivations of property without compensation. The amendment, which is mostly concerned with land reform and the question of compensation for expropriation of land, does not affect the decision or the discussion here. For an overview see C Ng'ong'ola "The Post-colonial Era In Relation to Land Expropriation Laws in Botswana, Malawi, Zambia and Zimbabwe" (1992) 41 Int and Comp LQ 117-136.

40   Under the Act, a board was set up to determine whether or not compensation should be granted to victims of "terrorism" and to set the amount of such compensation.

41   In s 38.

42   The Zimbabwean Constitution 1980 is one of the (mostly post-colonial "Lancaster House") constitutions that contain a "double" or combined property clause, one part of which appears in the general, introductory s 11 and a second part in the special s 16 dealing with property only. For an analysis and a discussion of the problems deriving from this "double" format, and of the different variations of the format, see AJ van der Walt "'Double' Property Guarantees: a Structural and Comparative Analysis" forthcoming (1998) 14 SA Journal on Human Rights. The Zimbabwean variation is unique in that both sections refer to compulsory acquisition of property, which makes it more difficult to justify the traditional distinction between deprivations and expropriations, but avoids the problem of deciding whether or not compensation is

required for both.

43   At 497H.

44   At 497G, *per* Fieldsend CJ.

45   At 497H.

46   [1985] LRC (Const) 921 (CA) (St Christopher and Nevis).

47   [1970] EA 523 (UHC) (Uganda). See the discussion of the case below.

48   At 501G.

49   Charles Reich's "new property"; see C Reich "The New Property" (1964) 73 Yale LJ 733.

50   At 501A.

51   Further references to this principle appear in the other cases discussed below.

52   Based on the classic example of a property clause in the American Constitution, which refers to deprivations and takings of property. A very clear example of the distinction appears in s 13 of the Malaysian Constitution. Most constitutions (including both the 1993 and the 1996 South African constitutions) now either provide for this distinction explicitly, or the distinction is accepted even without a textual base in the property clause. A major source for the interpretation of this distinction is JL Sax "Takings and the Police Power" (1964) 74 Yale LJ 36-76, but the *Selangor* case (n 96 below) might be an example of the instances where Sax's distinction (on the basis of the question whether the state acted in its regulatory or its competitive capacity) does not work all that well.

53   For which compensation is not normally required. Deprivation of property is associated with the exercise of the state's "police power", which involves regulatory controls over the use and exploitation of property. These controls are imposed in the public interest, and normally affect all property owners (of the relevant category) equally.

54   For which compensation is normally required. Expropriation (also compulsory acquisition, taking, or condemnation of property) is usually associated with the state's power of "eminent domain", and involves state acquisition or use of the property for a public use or purpose. These actions usually benefit the public as a whole or serve a public purpose, but they affect one or a small group of property owners in a particularly detrimental manner.

55   *Per* Fieldsend CJ at 503A-E, 5-6D-507G, and *per* Baron JA 508B-509D.

56   At 501H-502H.

57   [1970] EA 523 (UHC). The property clause appeared in ss 8 and 13 of the original Constitution of the Republic of Uganda 1967 (a "double" property guarantee; see n 42 above); and now in s 26 of the Constitution of the Republic of Uganda 1995. The 1967 clause contained the usual deprivation and compulsory acquisition with compensation provisions. The 1995 clause contains a positive guarantee of the right to acquire and hold property, and more or less standard deprivation and expropriation against compensation clauses. The *Shah* case was decided in terms of the 1967 Constitution.

58   See n 42 and n 57 above.

59   At 531C, *per* Jones J and 533C-G, *per* Mead J.

60   At 534B. Wambuzi J dissented on this point; see 540E.

61   (1991) 104 ALR 449 (FC). It must be pointed out that s 51(xxxi) of the Australian Commonwealth Constitution 1900 is not a regular property clause in a regular Bill of

Rights. The section basically just establishes the federal government's power of expropriation, but has been interpreted as a standard constitutional property clause; see the decision *per* Burchett J at 454 ff.

62   At 456.49.

63   At 458.22 *ff*, particularly 459.43.

64   In *Nobrega v Attorney-General of Guyana* (1967) 10 WIR 187 (CAG), the appellant was employed by the government of British Guiana (now the Cooperative Republic of Guyana) as a teacher at a salary of $251 a month. After initially failing to comply with appointment formalities, she was informed that her appointment had been rescinded and that she would be paid as an unqualified assistant mistress pending the submission of the requested documents, and that her status as a teacher would be determined on receipt of the required documents and a new letter of appointment would be issued to her. She sent the documents the same day but received no further communication. When she received her salary, it had been reduced to $92 *per* month. She brought an action for a declaration that she was entitled to receive a salary of $251 and that the purported reduction in her salary was *ultra vires* and of no effect. Given the nature of this case, the major part of the judgment is concerned with unlawful dismissals. Ultimately this decision turns on the question whether or not the reduction was in breach of the contract between the applicant and the state: if it was, the deprivation of salary amounts to an unauthorised compulsory taking of property, if not, the reduction could not be unauthorised or unconstitutional.   The majority allowed the applicant's appeal, but just one of the two majority judgments (*per* Cummings JA, see 208D-I) referred to the property question. Cummings JA held that the reduction of salary was in breach of the applicant's contract with the state, and therefore illegal.   As such it amounted to an unauthorised compulsory taking of property in contravention of the constitutional property guarantee. In *Deokinandan Prasad v The State of Bihar and Others* AIR (58) 1971 SC 1409, the petitioner was a teacher who was found guilty of certain charges. The Disciplinary Authority passed an order demoting the petitioner to a lower position and directing that a censure entry be recorded against him. The Director of Public Instruction then passed an order terminating the employment of the petitioner due to absence from duty for more than five years. When the petitioner reached the age of 58, he applied for the payment of his pension. An order was passed stating that the petitioner's application for his pension was refused in terms of rule 46 of the Bihar Pension Rules, according to which no pension may be granted to a public servant whose service was terminated due to misconduct, insolvency or inefficiency. The petitioner challenged all the above orders, claiming that the order of 12th June, 1968 violated his rights under arts 19(1)(f) and 31 of the Indian Constitution. (The property clause was removed from the Indian Constitution in 1978; see ns 112 and 114 below.) In an earlier decision of a single judge in the Punjab High Court, *Bhagwant Singh v Union of India* (AIR (49) 1962 Punj 503; confirmed by the Letters Patent Bench in *Union of India v Bhagwant Singh* ILR (1965) 2 Punj 1, and again by a Full Bench of the Punjab and Harayana High Court in *KR Erry v The State of Punjab* ILR (1967) 1 Punj and Har 278 (FB)), it was decided that the right to receive a salary and a pension constitutes property and that any interference with it will be a breach of art 31(1), with the result that this right can only be taken away by the authority of law, and not by an administrative action. These decisions denied, therefore, that a pension was a "bounty" which was payable

and retractable at the pleasure of the government. The Supreme Court confirmed that the right to a sum of money was property in *State of Madhya Pradesh v Ranorijao Shinde* [1968] 3 SCR 489 = AIR (55) 1968 SC 1053. The cancellation of the petitioner's property was therefore declared unconstitutional in *Deokinandan Prasad*.

65   In *Attorney General v Alli and Others* [1989] LRC (Const) 474 (CAG), the Court of Appeal of Guyana had to decide on the validity of a statutory wage-freeze. In 1977 the Trades Union Congress entered into a collective agreement with the government of Guyana for minimum wages and an annual increment in respect of public servants. In *Guyana Sugar Corporation Ltd v Teemal* (1967) 10 WIR 187 (CAG) the court held that an employer who withheld payment of an agreed increase in salary and other benefits in 1979 on the ground that the collective agreement took effect, committed breach of contract as the collective agreement was unenforceable and of no effect unless expressly incorporated in an employee's contract of service. In April 1984 the Labour (Amendment) Act 1984 was enacted to amend s 142 of the Constitution. S 3 of the Amendment Act excluded wage regulation legislation, with retrospective effect dating back to before the coming into effect of the Constitution, from the operation of s 142, which requires a written law and compensation for compulsory acquisitions. S 7 of the Act provided that the wage agreement of 1977 was deemed to be legally enforceable and that wages were to be frozen at their 1978 level, notwithstanding any judgment, decree or court order, so that the decision in the *Teemal* case was effectively reversed. In 1984 the respondents challenged the constitutionality of this Act and the trial court struck down ss 7 and 28C of the Act. The question is whether a so-called "wage-freeze" imposed by law amounted to an unconstitutional acquisition of property. The court referred to the exclusions in s 142(2) and 142(3), and specifically the exclusion of provisions that regulate wages in terms of s 142(3)(iia). The "wage-freeze" was analysed with reference to two questions: (a) whether the law in question could be valid, although it purports to have retroactive effect going back to a time before the introduction of the Constitution itself; and (b) whether the "wage-freeze" is a law regulating wages as meant in the exclusion in s 142(3). With regard to the second question the court decided (*per* Massiah C, at 511a-b) that the provisions in question did not amount to wage regulations, because they did not have the beneficial objectives usually associated with wage regulations. Therefore the measures in question were outside the scope of the exclusion in s 142(3), which means that they amounted to unconstitutional acquisitions of property without compensation.

66   1997 (1) SA 209 (ZSC).

67   See n 42 above.

68   *Per* Gubbay CJ, Korsah JA and Ebrahim JA, at 216D, 217A-C.

69   At 219G, 221C-E.

70   *Per* McNally JA and Muchechetere JA at 226B.

71   At 224H-J, 225A-B.

72   See *Hewlett v Minister of Finance and Another* 1982 (1) SA 490 (ZSC); compare the discussion of the case above.

73   (1994) 179 CLR 226.

74   Compare the German decision in the *Eigenleistung* case: BVerfGE 69, 272 (1985), where it was decided that welfare rights will only be protected as property in terms of the German property clause if (among other requirements) the claim was based

substantially on own effort (such as contributions to a scheme).

75 Brennan J correctly pointed out that this cannot be the decisive factor, since some laws do create money claims that are in the nature of vested debts: see *Health Insurance Commission v Peverill* (1994) 179 CLR 226 at 241.

76 The nature of the legislation and of the rights created by it must determine whether this is the case.

77 With reference to *National Provincial Bank Ltd v Ainsworth* [1965] AC 1175 at 1247-1248 *per* Lord Wilberforce. The characteristic of assignability also mentioned in this *dictum* is said to be important (see Brennan J in *Australian Capital Television Pty Ltd and Others v The Commonwealth and Others; The State of New South Wales v The Commonwealth of Australia and Another* (1992) 177 CLR 107 at 166) but not vital.

78 In *Australian Capital Television Pty Ltd and Others v The Commonwealth and Others; The State of New South Wales v The Commonwealth of Australia and Another* (1992) 177 CLR 107 it was held that such a vested right was not affected when a law provided that broadcasters had to provide free time for political parties during an election period. The law was eventually overturned because it infringed the right to free political discussion, but no property right was identified.

79 (1994) 179 CLR 297. The same principle was again confirmed in the majority opinion of Brennan CJ, Toohey J, Gaudron J, McHugh J and Gummow J in the *Industrial Relations Act Case* (reported as *The State of Victoria v The Commonwealth of Australia; The State of South Australia v The Commonwealth of Australia; The State of Western Australia v The Commonwealth of Australia*) (1996) 187 CLR 416 at 559; but see the minority opinion of Dawson J at 573, where he adheres to the view he expressed (with Toohey J) in *Mutual Pools and Staff Pty Limited v The Commonwealth of Australia* (1994) 179 CLR 155, namely that the mere extinguishment of a money claim does not effect an acquisition of property by the state.

80 Dawson J, Toohey J and McHugh J.

81 With the result that a legislative reduction or extinguishment of claims or debts sounding in money can never qualify as an acquisition, since the acquirer can never "acquire" anything more than freedom from the duty to pay, which is neither what the plaintiff lost nor in itself a right of a proprietary nature.

82 Not necessarily the federal government, since it is sufficient that anybody acquires the property.

83 See particularly *Australian Tape Manufacturers Association Ltd and Others v The Commonwealth of Australia* (1994) 179 CLR 480 at 509 *per* Mason CJ, Brennan J, Deane J and Gaudron J, in an *obiter dictum* clearly inspired by the need to contradict the view taken by Dawson J, Toohey J and McHugh J in various other cases.

84 Hence, once it is clear that a loss of property is caused by a tax, the property clause is not applicable and there is no question of compensation: *Australian Tape Manufacturers Association Ltd and Others v The Commonwealth of Australia* (1994) 179 CLR 480.

85 *Re Director of Public Prosecutions: Ex Parte Lawler and Another* (1994) 179 CLR 270. This is also the heading under which the loss and "acquisition" of property in the South African *Harksen* case should have been considered.

86 (1994) 179 CLR 155.

87 See *Mutual Pools and Staff Pty Ltd v The Commonwealth of Australia* (1994) 179

CLR 155 for authority and further explanations.

88   *Ie* there is no other constitutional authorisation, or the state action did not pursue another purpose because its sole or main object was the acquisition of property, or the means chosen were not appropriate to the other purpose served, or the result was disproportionate to the purpose served.

89   However, the finding that nothing was acquired is still not a good reason for the decision; the court would have had to decide that property was lost and acquired, but under a different head (cancellation of debts of the former government?), and that it was reasonable and justifiable to do so without compensation given the situation. The fact that the debt was already confirmed by a court (judgment debt) makes this kind of finding unlikely in the circumstances. See in this regard T Roux "Constitutional Property Rights Review in Southern Africa: the Record of the Zimbabwe Supreme Court" (1996) 8 African Journal of Int & Comp Law 755.

90   1993 (2) SA 12 (NHC); 1994 (1) SA 407 (NSC). The property clause appears in art 16 of the Constitution of the Republic of Namibia Act 1990, and contains a positive guarantee of the right to acquire, own and dispose of property as well as a provision for expropriation with compensation. The general limitation provision in art 22 indicates that non-compensable deprivations are also possible.

91   At 25H.

92   *Per* Levy AJP at 26G.

93   *Government of the Republic of Namibia and Another v Cultura 2000 and Another* 1993 (2) SA 12 (NHC).

94   *Government of the Republic of Namibia and Another v Cultura 2000 and Another* 1994 (1) SA 407 (NSC).

95   At 420G, *per* Mahomed CJ.

96   (1977) 1 MLJ 133.

97   The property clause in s 13 of the Federal Constitution of Malaysia 1957 is perhaps one of the clearest examples of a "traditional" property guarantee based on the distinction between deprivations and expropriations: s 13(1) provides for deprivations and s 13(2) for expropriations with compensation.

98   (1975) 2 MLJ 66.

99   S 13(1).

100 S 13(2) Although this interpretation is based on the phraseology of s 13 of the Malaysian Constitution, it is interesting to note that it corresponds with Rubenfeld's argument regarding the phraseology of the US Fifth Amendment; see J Rubenfeld "Usings" (1993) 102 Yale LJ 1077.

101 (1978) 88 DLR 3d 462. See n 102 on the property clause.

102 The case was heard subsequent to the enactment of Canadian Bill of Rights 1960, which contains a property guarantee, but prior to the enactment of the Canadian Charter of Rights and Freedoms 1982, which contains no such guarantee. It was not decided with reference to the Bill of Rights, although it was concerned with federal legislation which caused what amounted to an expropriation of the plaintiff's property. The reason why the Bill of Rights was not mentioned probably is that s 1(a) of the Bill of Rights applies to natural persons only, and not to legal persons such as the plaintiff company. It should be added that the Bill of Rights, which is still in force, applies to federal legislation only and is just a normal statute, not an entrenched bill of rights like the Charter.

103 (1977) 1 MLJ 133. See the discussion of the case above.

104 Another reason why the decision is important is that, having found that the legislation effected an expropriation, the court relies on the decision of the UK's highest court in *Attorney General v De Keyser's Royal Hotel Ltd* [1920] AC 508 (HL) to find that there is a common law presumption in favour of compensation for expropriations of private property. It is possible for a legislature to provide for expropriation without compensation, but then the law in question has to be framed so as to exclude compensation explicitly. Since that was not done in this case the plaintiff is entitled to compensation on the basis set out in *De Keyser's* case.

105 (1985) LRC (Const) 801 (SC, PC). The property clause is a "standard" variation of a "double" property guarantee (see n 42 above), and appears in s 3 and s 8 of the Constitution of Mauritius 1968. S 8 contains the normal provisions regarding deprivation and expropriation against compensation.

106 For criticism along these lines see T Allen "Commonwealth Constitutions and the Right Not To Be Deprived of Property" (1993) 42 Int & Comp LQ 523-552 at 540-542.

107 A distinction set out by JL Sax "Takings and the Police Power" (1964) 74 Yale LJ 36-76.

108 (1993) 42 Int & Comp LQ 523 at 540-542.

109 See n 42 above. The article of Van der Walt referred to there analyses the different variations of the "double" property clause. The Mauritian *Société United Docks* decision is a major source of authority for the very proposition that the "standard" variation of the "double" property clause requires compensation for deprivations of property in terms of the introductory s 3 of the Mauritian Constitution. The decision of the Privy Council to the effect that the introductory clause does indeed create a separate and independent guarantee of compensation for deprivations of property has been cited quite widely, and is probably authoritative for all Commonwealth jurisdictions where the constitutional property clause assumes the form of the "standard" variation of the combined property guarantee. The discussion of Rault CJ in the initial hearing by the Supreme Court of Mauritius is more incisive and convincing than the discussion of Lord Templeman in the later decision of the Privy Council, but the Privy Council nevertheless confirmed the earlier decision in this respect.

110 [1995] 3 LRC 494 (PC) at 500-501. See the discussion of the case in Allen's chapter here: Allen "Limitations on Constitutional Property Rights" under the heading "Limitations Based on Proportionality" at 199 *ff*.

111 Specific reference is made to the decision in *Sporrong and Lönnroth v Sweden* [1982] 5 EHRR 35.

112 [1955] 1 SCR 707. See n 114 below on the property clause. The property clause in the Indian Constitution 1950 used to be a "double" property guarantee (see n 42 above) that appeared in arts 19 and 31 of the Constitution, but in 1978 the property clause was removed from the Constitution as a result of the preceding constitutional battle between the courts and the legislature. *Ulster Transport Authority v James Brown and Sons, Ltd* (1) [1953] NI 79 (CA) was also concerned with commercial road transport regulations. (The property clause appeared in s 5(1) of the Government of Ireland Act 1920 (art 16 of the Free State (Agreement) Act 1922 contained a similar provision), which was subsequently repealed by the Northern Ireland Act 1962 and

the Northern Ireland Constitution Act 1973. The provision in s 5 dealt mainly with religious freedom, but added that property shall not be taken without compensation and for works of public utility.) In answer to a criminal charge under the Transport Act (Northern Ireland) 1948 (concerning the transport, by a person other than the Ulster Transport Authority, of passengers or luggage or merchandise on a public highway for reward) the respondent claimed that the relevant section was a taking of property without compensation contrary to s 5(1) of the 1920 Constitution. The respondent was a firm of furniture removers who carried furniture from a mart to the premises of a dealer who bought the furniture at the mart. The court decided that the interest which the plaintiff had in the continuation of its business either was or included goodwill, which is a valuable aspect of its property that would be lost if the Transport Act (Northern Ireland) 1948 was valid; the term "taking of property" as used in s 5(1) was a general one which at least included the situation where the state prohibition results in part of the plaintiff's business being taken over by the state (although the question whether a simple destruction of the property would have constituted a "taking" was left undecided); and the point of the law was clearly to destroy the business in question, and the law could therefore not be saved by claiming that, while it did not make provision for compensation, it did not prevent compensation being paid to the plaintiff.

113   1954 (5) SCR 587, *per* Mukherjea J at 729-730.

114   Two later decisions of the Indian Supreme Court provide illustrations of an interesting change of direction. In 1978 the 30-year long struggle between the Indian courts and the legislature was terminated by the introduction of the Forty-Fourth Amendment. This amendment deleted arts 19(1)(f) and 31 from the fundamental rights in Part II of the Constitution, and replaced them by the insertion of art 300A in Part XII of the Constitution (see ns 112 above and 131 below). Art 300A provides that "no person shall be deprived of his property save by authority of law". Being inserted in Part XII of the Constitution art 300A establishes a constitutional (as opposed to a fundamental) right, which guarantees nothing more than the assurance that deprivations of property shall not be effected simply by administrative decree. In line with the interpretation of the rest of the Constitution this article does require a valid law, which means that it should be within the legislative power of the legislature enacting it, and that it should not violate fundamental rights or other constitutional restrictions. The change of direction implied by this constitutional amendment is also apparent from subsequent case law on the regulation of private enterprise. In *State of Tamil Nadu v L Abu Kavur Bai and Others* [1984] 1 SCR 725 the operators of private transport enterprises challenged the Tamilnadu Stage Carriages and Contract Carriages (Acquisition) Act 1973, which was aimed at the progressive nationalisation of the transport industry. The Act provided that on a date specified by the government, the permit issued to a transport operator would vest in the government, free from all encumbrances, and the operator's interest would be limited to the compensation provided for in the Act. The operators whose carriages were taken over challenged the constitutional validity of the Act. Their action in the High Court was successful and the State of Tamil Nadu appealed against this decision. The Supreme Court accepted that it was necessary, in "building an egalitarian society in order to achieve socio-economic emancipation [to accept] the policy of nationalisation of industries" (at 732D, compare 741E-G, 742F-H), and the amended property clause in ss 19 and 31 (which were still valid at the

time, but fundamentally changed by the Twenty-Fifth Amendment) were interpreted and applied accordingly. On the basis of these principles it was decided that the Tamilnadu Stage Carriages and Contract Carriages (Acquisition) Act 1973 was valid. *Coffee Board, Karnataka, Bangalore v Commissioner of Commercial Taxes* [1988] SUPP 1 SCR 348 was decided after the property clause was scrapped altogether. The Coffee Act 1942 was passed in order to regulate the coffee industry in India. The Act was administered by the Coffee Board. In terms of the Act, coffee growers were compelled to deliver their coffee to the Coffee Board, which then sold the coffee. Failure to deliver coffee to the Board was an offence under the Act and penalised by a fine and confiscation of the undelivered coffee. All marketing and other rights of the growers were extinguished by the Act, except for the right to receive payment under the Act. The Karnataka Sales Tax Act 1957 provided for the payment of sales tax on coffee. The Board instituted an action in the High Court claiming that the compulsory delivery of coffee to it under the Coffee Act 1942 was not a sale, but a compulsory acquisition of coffee and was therefore not subject to sales tax. The High Court dismissed the action and the Coffee Board appealed to the Supreme Court. The point raised in this case is the distinction between the exercise of the state's power of eminent domain (compulsory acquisition) and the police power (regulation). In this case, it was decided that the scheme of control and delivery imposed by the Coffee Act 1942 did not amount to compulsory acquisition. The Coffee Board was instituted to regulate the coffee industry, and not to acquire coffee from producers. In effect the transaction between the producers and the Coffee Board was interpreted as a contract of sale and purchase, which excludes the possibility of a compulsory acquisition.

115 15th November, 1950: *Hanreishu IV no 11 2257 (Criminal)*. Translated by JM Maki, published in JM Maki *Court and Constitution in Japan: Selected Supreme Court Decisions, 1948-1960* (1964) Univ of Washington Press, Seattle 273-281. The property clause in art 29 of the Constitution of Japan 1946 provides that the right to own or hold property is inviolable; that property rights shall be defined by law in conformity with public welfare (compare art 14.1 and 14.2 of the German Basic Law); and that private property may be taken for public use upon just compensation.

116 At 275-276.

117 At 276.

118 In *Attorney-General v Lawrence* [1985] LRC (Const) 921, the Court of Appeal of St Christopher and Nevis held that legislation that gave the minister the power to appoint the majority of directors of a bank amounted to an expropriation of the shareholders' right to appoint directors, which was an important aspect of the right to manage (and own) the bank. By contrast, the Privy Council held in *Government of Mauritius v Union Flacq Sugar Estates Co Ltd* [1992] 1 WLR 903 (PC) that legislation that barred companies from exercising voting rights did not effect an expropriation, because the company and its property were left unaffected by the legislation. See Allen "Limitations on Constitutional Property Rights" at 190-191.

119 AIR (38) 1951 SC 41. See n 114 above and n 131 below on the Indian property clause.

120 At 53 para [44].

121 At 54 para [49].

122 At 55 para [53].

123 At 59 para [65].

124   At 49 para [29], at 67 para [87].

125   At 61 para [77].

126   At 62 para [77].

127   At 62 para [77].

128   At 62 para [78].

129   AIR (41) 1954 SC 119.

130   At 137 para [52].

131   The original property clause in the Indian Constitution was a "double" property guarantee of the "standard" variation; see ns 42, 112, 114 above. The differences concerned the relation between the introductory art 19 and the special art 31: Sastri J wanted to regard art 19 as an institutional guarantee that had nothing to do with individual property rights and art 31 as a guarantee of individual property rights, while Das J thought that s 19 pertained to deprivations of property and art 31 to both deprivations and expropriations. An implication of Sastri J's position was that he was left in a rather curious position on the relation between art 31(1) and 31(2): whereas the former obviously related to deprivations and the latter to expropriations, Sastri J's position meant that he had to argue that both the deprivations in art 31(1) and the expropriations in art 31(2) required compensation, and that only the deprivations in art 19 did not require compensation. Das J defended the position that art 31(1) and art 19 both related to deprivations that did not require compensation, and art 31(2) to compulsory acquisitions that did require compensation. The Sastri position frustrated the legislative attempts of the reform-oriented government in that the conjunctive reading of art 31(1) and 31(2) eradicated the distinction between non-compensable deprivations of property and compensable acquisitions of property, thereby restricting the possibility of introducing non-compensable regulatory limitations of property and throwing the possibility to claim compensation for non-acquisitive regulatory limitations of property wide open. The legislature responded to these decisions with the introduction of the Constitution (Fourth Amendment) Act 1955, which streamlined and re-phrased art 31 in such a way that it became clear that the conjunctive reading of art 31(1) and 31(2) was mistaken, and that art 31(2) was concerned with compensable acquisitions of property against compensation, and art 31(1) with non-acquisitive, non-compensable regulatory limitations of property in terms of the police power.

132   1954 (5) SCR 587.

133   AIR (37) 1950 Pat 392.

134   At 400 para [6], and compare 399 para [6].

135   At 420 para [48].

136   At 427 para [71].

137   Such as preventing the collapse or closure of a key industry, or preventing unemployment.

138   AIR (57) 1970 SC 564. See ns 114, 131 above on the Indian property clause.

139   AIR (47) 1960 SC 1080.

140   AIR (52) 1965 SC 1017.

141   [1985] LRC (Const) 921 (CA). See the next note on the property clause.

142   The relevant ss 6 and 16 of the old Constitution are substantially similar to the property clause in ss 3 and 8 of the Constitution of Saint Christopher and Nevis 1983. This property clause is a "standard" variation of a "double" property guarantee, with

the normal provisions for compulsory acquisition against compensation. See n 42 above.

143 (1985) LRC (Const) 801 (SC, PC). The property clause is a "standard" variation of a "double" property guarantee (see n 42 above), and appears in s 3 and s 8 of the Constitution of Mauritius 1968. S 8 contains the normal provisions regarding deprivation and expropriation against compensation.

144 (1948) 76 CLR 1. See n 61 on the property clause in the Australian Commonwealth Constitution.

145 (1944) 68 CLR 261.

146 *Per* Dixon J at 349.

147 "Just terms" is the equivalent of compensation in the Australian property clause.

148 *Per* Dixon J at 349.

149 BVerfGE 42, 263 [1976]. The property clause appears in art 14 of the German Basic Law of 1949, and provides that property is guaranteed; that the content and limits of property is determined by law, and that property brings responsibilities with it which imply that its use should also serve the public interest; and that property may only be expropriated for a public purpose and with compensation.

150 Compare in this regard the decisions in BVerfGE 24, 367 *(Deichordnung* case) [1968]; BVerfGE 53, 257 [1980]; which also concern the transformation of private-law property into public-law regulated property.

151 BVerfGE 50, 290 [1979]. See n 149 above on the German property clause.

152 In reaching this conclusion the court set out the main principles which govern the interpretation and application of art 14: (a) the right to property is a fundamental right which is closely related to the right of personal freedom; (b) it secures for the holder a sphere of freedom in patrimonial matters, which makes it possible to take responsibility for the management of her own life; (c) as such the property which enjoys this constitutional protection is characterised by its value and use for the private individual; (d) however, the exact content and limits of the property so protected are determined by law, which must ensure that the use of property should also serve the public interest; (e) in determining the content and limits of property the legislature finds both its point of departure and its limits in the interest of the community; (f) and the substantive guarantee of property in art 14.1.1, the regulatory duty in terms of art 14.1.2 and the social responsibility and limitations of property in terms of art 14.2 form a fundamental unit, and have to be kept in balance.

153 447 US 74 (1980). The Fifth Amendment to the US Constitution guarantees that no person shall be deprived of property without due process of law, and that property shall not be taken for public use without compensation. The Fourteenth Amendment provides a due process guarantee that binds the states, as opposed to the federal government.

154 407 US 551 (1972).

155 In *Lloyd v Tanner* the court held that property does not lose its private character merely because the public is invited to use it for designated purposes, and that the essentially private character of a store did not change merely because it was large or clustered with other stores in a shopping centre. See JW Singer "No Right to Exclude: Public Accommodations and Private Property" (1996) 90 Northwestern Univ LR 1283-1497 for a full discussion of the exclusion issue in the area of public accommodations.

156   There were separate opinions by Blackmun J concurring in part; by Marshall J concurring; by White J concurring in part and in the judgment; and by Powel J (in which White J joined) concurring in part and in the judgment.

157   At 83 para [5], quoting from *Armstrong v United States* 364 US 40 (1960) at 49, 80.

158   With reference to *Pennsylvania Coal Co v Mahon* 260 US 393 (1922).

159   At 83 para [5].

160   At 84 para [6] Rehnquist J contrasted this aspect of the present case with the position in *Kaiser Aetna v United States* 444 US 164 (1979).

161   At 85 para [7], with reference to *Nebbia v New York* 291 US 502 (1934).

162   [1989] ECHR Ser A Vol 159. The property clause appears in art 1 of the First Protocol to the European Convention on Human Rights of 1950, and provides that every natural or legal person is entitled to the peaceful enjoyment of his possessions; that no one shall be deprived of his possessions except in the public interest and subject to the conditions provided for by law and by the general principles of international law; and that the preceding provisions shall not impair the right of a state to enforce such laws as it deems necessary to control the use of property in accordance with the general interest. The three parts of the provision are referred to as the first, second and third rules respectively; the second rule is interpreted as an expropriation clause (despite the somewhat confusing use of "deprived") and the third rule as a regulation clause. Note that the expropriation provision makes no mention of compensation, leaving the requirement up to the law of individual states. However, in recent case law of the ECHR there is a strong tendency towards requiring compensation in terms of the proportionality test; see *James v United Kingdom* [1986] 8 EHRR 123; *Lithgow and Another v United Kingdom* [1986] 8 EHRR 329.

163   The relevance of decisions of the European Court of Human Rights is, of course, controversial in view of the fact that the European Convention is an instrument of international law that binds only its signatories, but in my view it is justified to consider these cases because they are so many in number and cover so many interesting aspects of the property issue; they are relevant when considering the case law of member states of the EU; and they tend to follow (and sometimes also influence) the general trends established in many national jurisdictions.

164   In a recent decision, *S v Lawrence; S v Negal; S v Solberg* 1997 (4) 1176 (CC), the South African Constitutional Court upheld a liquor law that prohibits the sale of any liquor on Sundays. The attack against this law was not based on the property clause, but on the right to engage in economic activity (s 26) and the right to freedom of religion (s 14) of the 1993 South African Constitution. The court held that the prohibition was neither unreasonable nor an infringement of freedom of religion. Basically this decision echoes the European Court of Human Rights in stating that control over the sale of liquor is a legitimate exercise of the state's police power. A more interesting (additional) question would have been whether the control measures satisfied the proportionality requirement, given the purpose of control, the results it had for private business, and the possibility of using different, less onerous means for the same result.

165   [1991] 1 IR 409. A unique property clause appears in art 40.3.2 and art 43 of the Constitution of Ireland 1937. Art 40.3.2 requires the state to protect citizens' property rights from "unfair attack", and art 43 acknowledges a natural right to ownership of external goods; guarantees that no law shall abolish the right of private ownership or

the personal right to transfer, bequeath and inherit property; recognises that the exercise of property rights ought, in civil society, to be regulated by the principles of social justice; and allows the state to delimit the exercise of property rights by law, with a view to reconciling their exercise with the exigencies of the common good.

166 [1989] LRC (Const) 632 (CA). The property clause in s 4(a) of the Constitution of the Republic of Trinidad and Tobago 1976 looks like the first, introductory part of a "standard" variation of a "double" property guarantee (see n 42 above), but there is no second, special property section. Accordingly, the property clause simply protects the enjoyment of property and the right not to be deprived of it except by due process of law. Ss 5 and 6 provide for limitations of the fundamental rights.

167 [1988] ILRM 400 = [1990] 1 IR 356. See n 165 above on the Irish property clause.

168 [1994] 2 IR 20. See n 165 above on the Irish property clause.

169 In Canada this test is applied in terms of the general limitation provision in s 1 of the Charter of Rights and Freedoms 1982, the most widely cited authority being *R v Oakes* (1986) 26 DLR 4th 200. In South Africa the test is applied in terms of the general limitation clause in s 36 of the 1996 Constitution (s 33 of the 1993 Constitution), the best authority probably being *S v Makwanyane and Another* 1995 (3) SA 391 (CC) at 436B-439E *per* Chaskalson P. See AJ van der Walt "The Limits of Constitutional Property" (1997) 12 SA Public Law 275-330 for a discussion of different approaches to this provision. In Germany, the test was developed in the case law of the federal Constitutional Court without any textual foundation in the form of a general limitation provision; compare L Blaauw-Wolff and J Wolf "A Comparison Between German and South African Limitation Provisions" (1996) 113 SALJ 267-296 for authorities. The European Court of Human Rights also developed a similar test through case law, the earliest and most authoritative decision being *Sporrong and Lönnroth v Sweden* [1982] 5 EHRR 35; see W Peukert "Protection of Ownership Under Article 1 of the First Protocol to the European Convention on Human Rights" (1981) 2 Human Rights LJ 37-78. See also the last part of Allen's paper here: Allen "Limitations on Constitutional Property Rights" (ch 10).

170 German case law offers a useful series of decisions that concern all the major immaterial property rights. Compare BVerfGE 31, 229 [1971] (copyright and confidential information); BVerfGE 36, 281 [1974] (patents); BVerfGE 51, 193 [1979] (trademarks). In the South African so-called *First Certification Case* (reported as *In Re: Certification of the Constitution of the Republic of South Africa, 1996* 1996 (10) BCLR 1253 (CC); 1996 (4) SA 744 (CC)) the Constitutional Court was asked to consider the proposition that the property clause in s 25 was deficient in that it did not protect intellectual property rights explicitly and separately from property in general. The court rejected the argument and noted (at para [75]) that international and foreign law does not create the impression that it is necessary to protect these rights separately.

171 (1990) 95 ALR 87 (FC). See n 61 above on the Australian property clause.

172 In considering the question whether confidential information should be regarded as property for the purposes of s 51(xxxi), Gummow J pointed out that knowledge *per se* is not proprietary in character (at 135.11); that the protection of information against actual or threatened abuse is not based on a proprietary right in Australian law, but rather on a special obligation of conscience arising in the circumstances of the case (at 135.19); and defined property in rights and interests with reference to a *dictum* of

Lord Wilberforce in *National Provincial Bank Ltd v Ainsworth* [1965] AC 1175, which was followed in later Australian decisions: "before a right or interest can be admitted into the category of property, it must be definable, identifiable by third parties, have some degree of permanence or stability, and be capable in its nature of assumption by third parties" (at 135.43). Gummow J therefore accepted the claim that there was a proprietary right in the information in question, but only because he accepted (at 136.13) that, for purposes of the constitutional guarantee, "one should lean towards a wider rather than narrower concept of property, and look beyond legal forms to the substance of the matter" (at 136.17).

173　In arriving at the conclusion that the compulsory supply of proprietary information in order to obtain a permit or to escape a prohibition does not constitute a compulsory acquisition of the information for purposes of s 51(xxxi), Gummow J reiterated the Australian courts' view that s 51(xxxi) has assumed the status of a constitutional guarantee of just terms which has to be interpreted according to "the liberal construction appropriate to such a constitutional provision" (at 127.7). See n 61 above.

174　BVerfGE 36, 281 [1974]. See n 149 above on the German property clause.

175　BVerfGE 51, 193 [1979].

176　By "context" I mean social, economic and political context, and not just the interpretative context of the relevant constitutional text. I am indebted to Henk Botha for pointing out this misapprehension of what contextual interpretation means in some decisions of the South African Constitutional Court: see AJ van der Walt and H Botha "Getting to Grips With the New Constitutional Order: Critical Comments on *Harksen v Lane NO*" (1998) 13 SA Public Law 17–41.

177　It is a matter for debate whether (or how far) this point is reflected accurately by the opinion of the United States Supreme Court that constitutional property cases are essentially a matter of ad hoc decisions; compare *Penn Central Transportation Co v City of New York* 438 US 104 (1978) *per* Brennan J at 124 (2569) para [4,5]: "In engaging in these essentially ad hoc, factual inquiries, the Court's decisions have identified several factors that have particular significance."

178　I have to admit that this idea was prompted by reading the chapter "The end of the road" in Tim Cahill's very amusing and entertaining *Road Fever* (1991, ref here 1995 ed Fourth Estate, London). Cahill refers to the marking "Here there be dragons", but for aesthetic reasons, and coming from Africa, I prefer the more realistic and dangerous version usually associated with that continent, rather than with the supposed end of the (flat) world.

179　See J Rubenfeld "Usings" (1993) 102 Yale LJ 1077-1163.

180　Such as art 29, Constitution of Japan 1946; sec 13(2), Federal Constitution of Malaysia 1957; s 5(1), Government of Ireland Act 1920.

181　Which is not what Rubenfeld had in mind. I am trying to think through possible applications of his argument in foreign law.

182　This fear inspired the over-cautious efforts to ensure that expropriation for the purpose of land redistribution will be constitutionally valid in South Africa: see s 25(2)(a) (expropriation has to be for a public purpose *or* in the public interest, on the assumption that the latter is wide enough to allow for redistribution) and s 25(4)(a) (the public interest includes land reform) of the 1996 Constitution.

183　Some examples are referred to in n 169 above.

12 The Reform of South African Land Law in its Roman-Dutch Context - New Wine?

DL CAREY MILLER*

Introduction

The root and branch reform of South African land tenure dates from the De Klerk Government's White Paper put before Parliament in March 1991 but the fundamental basis of the reform process might be seen as the long-standing agenda of the ANC Government in waiting. This paper is concerned with the extent to which the reforms represent a departure from the relevant South African Roman-Dutch based common law. The first part seeks to identify the most significant features of that system; the second, and main part of the paper, aims to determine the priorities and outstanding features of the developing land law of the new South Africa. The final part attempts a succinct overall analysis of the nature and scope of the changes. The treatment will proceed under the following three headings: priorities of the pre-reform law; priorities of the new land law; analysis and overview of the changes. The reform of substantive South African land law and practice cannot be divorced from the considerations of justice and social and economic policy which are driving it but the primary focus of this paper will be on the changes in the law with particular emphasis upon those which reflect a departure from existing common law priorities or thinking.

Priorities of the Pre-Reform Law

Two features are very much apparent in the land law of South Africa prior to the reforms which commenced in the early 1990s. The first is the dominating character of the Roman-Dutch common law principles applicable to rights in land,[1] the second, the racially discriminatory controls over the actual allocation of rights which were principally developed in the twentieth century but had roots deep in the history of South Africa's colonial past. The development of the Roman-Dutch common law of property gave a virtually absolute right of ownership, very much superior to lesser rights, which was the foundation factor in a system of derivative acquisition in principle involving only transferor and transferee. The "apartheid" legislation, which grew significantly from the 1950s, operated as a "bolt-on" to the common law based system to curtail and control the allocation and transmission of rights in land in terms of a grand plan of racial ordering which was manifestly driven by ulterior motives. The priorities of the South African ruling class were reflected in these two principal features of land law; the uncomplicated, thoroughly ordered and secure system of the common law, working in conjunction with a rigidly enforced system of external controls to limit entry on a racial basis. Both aspects suited white social and political interests.

A central feature of pre-reform South African land law was the comprehensive and effective Deeds Registry system working on the basis of the Registration of Deeds Act, 47 of 1937 (the "Deeds Act"). The prevailing position was that ownership could only be acquired on a derivative basis by an act of registration and, from the mid-1900s, it increasingly came to be that racial control over land ownership was exercised through the Deeds Registries.[2] The system of the Deeds Act reflected the simple delivery requirement of the civilian common law - the act of registration being a manifestation of the intention of the owner/transferor to convey the property concerned to the transferee.[3] The emphasis of the Deeds Act upon the concept of an absolute right of ownership, open to allocation and division in only particular prescribed ways, reflected South African common law development. As Professor D P Visser has shown, the influence of nineteenth-century German "Pandectist" dogma - exemplified in Savigny's definition of ownership in terms of the "unrestricted and exclusive domain over an object"[4] - was very much apparent in decisions of the South African courts from the early twentieth century, the beginning of the period in which South African common law was developing a particular identity.[5] Savigny's definition was quoted by Wessels J in an early Transvaal case[6] and this approach to ownership, characteristically civilian[7] and very much distinct from the approach to property of English law,[8] came to be standard in South Africa.[9] But, of course, the absolute nature of the right of ownership did not mean that an owner's rights of use and enjoyment were not subject to restrictions.[10] It is significant that an original title based on possession was only admitted subject to definite limits and, even following modern legislative reform, only on the basis of a minimum thirty-year period of possession.[11] But the availability of a basis for the acquisition of rights through possession has to be seen in the context of the registered owner's clear entitlement to recover possession of property held by another without right to do so. As an Appellate Division judge noted in 1974, one of the incidents of the right of ownership was a right of exclusive possession which necessarily entailed a right to recover possession.[12] The relevance of this in the present context is that the primacy given to ownership over possession by the common law gave a basis for the development of the land-economy of South Africa in a manner which favoured the registered owner over holders of lesser rights. The significance of access to the Deeds Registry is illustrated by the concern of the then Transvaal Government - recorded in the compelling writing of black political spokesman Sol Plaatje[13] - at the decision of the Transvaal Supreme Court[14] that there was no legal reason why a black person should be barred from becoming the registered owner of land.

In the rural context - prominent in South African social and economic development - the general picture which developed was one of the dominating control of white registered landowners over the land rights of black labour tenants. The precarious vulnerability of tenant families to the legal power of landowners has been demonstrated in two notable modern works making the case for South African land reform.[15]

In the urban context the racial control over the occupation of land which dominated social development for the major part of the 1900s had two features which fitted conveniently with the system of land ownership and acquisition. The first was that black residential rights were generally only granted in the urban areas of "white" South Africa on a lesser basis than full registered ownership. The second was the point already mentioned that the Deeds Office system of comprehensive regulation of access to ownership gave a more or less fail-safe vehicle for ensuring compliance with the racially determined basis of access to land ownership.

Priorities of the New Land Law

Constitutional Entrenchment of Reform Priorities

The course of the ongoing process of reform of South African land law is chartered by the Constitution of 1996[16] (hereafter "the Constitution") which superseded the interim Constitution of 1993.[17]   The 1993 interim Constitution, however, retains a particular residual relevance in relation to the process of restitution of land rights as well, of course, as having potentially general application by reason of being the ultimate law in the limited time-frame of its duration. The precise controlling shape and form of the property provisions of the Constitution will emerge only on the basis of ruling interpretations by the Constitutional Court but the tenor of what the Constitution stands for in terms of property rights is patent.

Property is protected and its deprivation only permitted for "a public purpose or in the public interest" and always "subject to compensation".[18] This said, the manifest thrust of the property provisions in the Bill of Rights part of the Constitution is reformist. As the White Paper published in April 1997 notes "[t]he property clause itself now provides clear constitutional authority for land reform".[19] The "public interest" - which may justify expropriation - is defined to include "the nation's commitment to land reform, and to reforms to bring about equitable access to all South Africa's natural resources".[20] Moreover, the Constitution declares a number of specific mandates to the state which clarify the balance of priorities beyond any doubt. The state must "take reasonable legislative and other measures, within its available resources, to foster conditions which enable citizens to gain access to land on an equitable basis."[21]   Specific separate provision is also made for tenure reform legislation to deal with the insecure tenure of individuals or communities "as a result of past racially discriminatory laws or practices"[22] and for restitution or equitable redress, "to the extent provided by an Act of Parliament"[23] in respect of dispossessions after 19th June, 1913 which also occurred on the basis of racially discriminatory laws or practices.[24] The final substantive provision seeks to clarify the position regarding the tension between the basic protection of property and the Constitution's reform agenda in stating that no provision of the property section of the Bill of Rights "may impede the state from taking legislative and other measures to achieve land, water and related reform in order to redress the results of past racial discrimination".[25]

The subsection making this critical prioritisation of the reform agenda goes on to define the extent of the entrenchment in stating that any departure from this statement of priorities must be in accordance with the general approach of section 36 concerning the limitation of a right provided for in the Bill of Rights.[26] Insofar as the question of a limitation of the basic property right by something identifiable in terms of the reform agenda is concerned, it is significant that section 36 provides that "the importance of the purpose of the limitation" shall be taken account of as one of all the relevant factors.[27] The extent to which the property clause itself gives priority to the reform agenda must necessarily mean that measures properly identifiable as aiming "to redress the results of past racial discrimination" should be seen as highly important.

The Constitutional Court, in the context of the restitution legislation, has indicated its recognition of the constitutional land reform mandate.[28] It may be noted that the Constitution's Bill of Rights housing clause guarantee against eviction from or demolition of a home without an order of court[29] has been invoked in a High Court decision in which the court ruled that provisions of the Prevention of Illegal Squatting Act 52 of 1951 "which permit the demolition of structures without an order of court are clearly no longer of application".[30]

An extensive debate has taken place in South Africa concerning the constitutional protection of property and, in particular, the tension between existing property rights and the reform agenda; however, a considerable proportion of the relevant comment is concerned with the interim Constitution which reflected a weaker commitment to land reform than that eventually adopted. The Constitution - in its respective enjoining and inviting of an interpreting court to consider international ("must consider")[31] and foreign ("may consider")[32] law - has been accepted as the starting point by the writers of the first two major juristic contributions on the property clause.[33] On the critical issue of the tension between existing rights and reform measures Professor A J van der Walt provides an analysis with which the present writer would respectfully agree. With regard to the common law perception of property as a right in the realm of the absolute and inviolable the learned writer notes that the development of "a properly and overtly constitutional perception of property" via the property clause "will inevitably also affect the private-law perception of property, and will enable lawyers and the courts to move away from the traditional view that property is basically and fundamentally an unrestricted right, and that restrictions can be imposed only with the consent of the property owner or against compensation".[34] As to the active capacity of the reform elements of the property clause van der Walt comments as follows:

Leaving the positive rights created by section 25(6)-(9) aside for the moment, it can be argued that section 25 resurrected land rights that were undermined during the apartheid era, and that new legislation administers and controls rather than creates these rights in the new dispensation. The rights that were undermined now enjoy constitutional recognition, and land reform laws are needed only to give effect to and administer the process of reincarnation of these rights.[35]

The benefit of this interpretation is that it is more appropriate and preferable to justify a weakening in the position of existing rights on the basis of the specific recognition of the equal entitlement of those unfairly denied rights rather than on the simple basis of a radical change of socio-economic policy introduced by the new government. On this analysis the denial of black rights from an early stage in South Africa's colonial past produced a quantifiable debit against the accumulation of property interests, supported by powerful common law rights, enjoyed by the ruling minority - a debt which must now be called up.

The Roman-Dutch common law's bulwark protecting the *status quo* of legally accorded property rights does not reflect any sort of intrinsic legal value norm; rather, it does no more than reflect the policy priorities which influenced the development of the system in sixteenth and seventeenth century Europe. Its protection of what was unjustly put in place in South Africa was no more than an incidental consequence. While, in principle and practice, Roman-Dutch law holds out against any challenge to the property *status quo* other than by lawful process, there is no foundation for any idea that Roman-Dutch law, as a matter of proper principle, sets out to protect the *status quo* regardless. On the contrary, Grotius saw expropriation by higher authority as permissible provided it proceeded on the basis of sufficient cause.[36]

The position adopted by the 1993 interim Constitution - now confirmed subject to some clarification by the Constitution - requires the introduction and implementation of a range of positive measures towards the provision, restoration and protection of land rights determined on the basis of the policy of providing particular and general redress to citizens directly or indirectly affected by the racially discriminatory laws of the former regime. In one sense the necessary change required appears to be primarily about access to land and land rights as a matter of policy imperative in substitution for what all previous South African governments, prior to the De Klerk administration, saw as a necessary policy involving the limitation and control of land rights in respect of the majority of the population. Taking this generalisation further, one might conceive of a new land order as the removal of racially biased controls and the adoption of social and economic measures to remedy the legacy of discrimination without necessarily affecting the substantive land law. This analysis is accurate up to a point. Indeed, the long history of measures to restrict access to land on a racial basis was largely represented by law which did not need to make inroads into the ruling common law of property.[37] That radical change to the basic system of South African property is limited reflects partly the general policy decision to retain an essentially capitalist structure wedded to the concept of private ownership. But while the reform measures are more to do with the restoration and delivery of land rights than about departure from the existing system of land law they do reflect a number of important changes to the law of property, in both substance and emphasis.

Access to Legal Rights as a Primary Basis of Reform

A comprehensive *Land Policy* White Paper published in 1997 took forward the constitutional agenda in developing the mandated matters of redistribution, restitution and tenure reform as sub-programmes of the reform process.[38] But the boundaries between the three sub-programmes do not have any dogmatic basis, being no more than the three broad areas of reform identified in the Constitution. This means that there may be overlap in the sense of a particular statute, or even provision, serving more than one of the sub-programmes, but, of course, this is only significant from the point of view of exposition. Redistribution and restitution are both essentially concerned with the direct provision of legal rights in land; the former process being motivated by the relatively open-ended notion of the needs of disadvantaged people and the latter driven by the more particular matter of dispossession on the basis of a racial law passed after 19th June, 1913. Land tenure reform is a more complex concept with a broad scope generally directed towards the provision of a choice of meaningful legal rights over the entire range of situations presented by varying urban and rural circumstances and contexts. Forms of tenure reform developed early in the reform process include the device of upgrading a lesser right to ownership[39] and the facilitation of derivative acquisition by tenants.[40]

    An innovatory tool with an important role in the implementation of the new land law is the Communal Property Associations Act 28 of 1996 which makes it possible for a group or community to acquire land as a legal entity.   The Act will be commented on under the headings of "Redistribution" and "Tenure Reform Legislation".   Another aspect of tenure reform involves the development of the common law concept of ownership to allow the acquisition of a form of property right known as "initial ownership"; this will be mentioned again in the context of redistribution and considered in some detail in the section on tenure reform.

The fundamental common law concept of a "real right" in land - as reflected in an officially registered title deed recording an act of transfer of the right of ownership - superior to lesser "personal" or contractual rights not amounting to ownership, remains inherent in the thinking of the reform process.   A feature of the land tenure reform programme is the emphasis upon the provision of the real right of ownership; the 1997 White Paper declares this in unambiguous terms: "[a]ll land which is redistributed, restored or awarded to beneficiaries must be registered in one or other form of ownership".[41]   This, of course, suggests an expanded role of the deeds office system - something tacitly acknowledged in the 1997 White Paper, in which a rationalisation of the system is proposed but without derogation from the long acknowledged "importance of a unitary land registration system".[42]

The three reform sub-programmes will be considered in more detail under separate heads.

Redistribution

As a generalisation subject to certain particular qualifications one might say that this branch of the reform strategy is less about actual legal change and more about the facilitation of access to land than the other two sub-programmes - restitution and tenure reform.   The purpose of redistribution is set out in the 1997 White Paper as being to provide the landless - particularly the poor, labour tenants, farm workers, women and emergent farmers - "with access to land for residential and productive uses, in order to improve their income and quality of life".[43]   What the White Paper goes on to say confirms that from a general perspective redistribution is essentially an actively directed administrative process to facilitate the acquisition of land by those whose needs are seen as most pressing.

> Redistributive land reform will be largely based on willing-buyer willing-seller arrangements. Government will assist in the purchase of land, but will in general not be the buyer or owner. Rather it will make land

acquisition grants available[44] and will support and finance the required planning process.[45]

Indications are that this approach is having a measure of success but, if recent press reports are accurate, not on a scale which the government regards as sufficient. In the context of warnings that expropriations would be unavoidable if the landowner community did not co-operate Minister of Land Affairs Derek Hanekon was reported to have stated that in the three months up to February 1998, 31,128 hectares of land had been redistributed across the country in 39 projects involving a total of some 4,000 households.[46]

It may be noted that the Communal Property Associations Act is intended to have a role in the redistribution process with "[i]n many cases, communities ... expected to pool their resources to negotiate, buy and jointly hold land under a formal title deed".[47] At the same time this legislation is very much a matter of tenure reform and is considered as such below.

Another new statute, the multi-faceted Development Facilitation Act 67 of 1995 has a major role in the redistribution process in introducing "measures to speed up land development, especially the provision of serviced land for low income housing".[48] Partly taking further 1993 legislation providing for the designation of land for settlement,[49] the Development Facilitation Act also makes a major departure from the common law in introducing the concept, already mentioned, of "initial ownership".[50] The White Paper explains the rationale for this device as providing for "the initial registration of tenure in such a way that subsidy money will flow at any early stage in the process, having the potential to ease considerably the pressures on the delivery process".[51] The concept of "initial ownership" will be examined as an aspect of tenure reform legislation.

Restitution[52]

The political imperative of an equitable process to deal with the grossly unfair and large scale deprivations of property in pursuit of racist policies was recognised at an early stage in the formulation of the reform agenda. Modest restitution proposals introduced by the De Klerk Government[53] were overtaken by events in the rapidly changing scene of the early 1990s. The 1993 interim Constitution declared that the restitution of land rights should be provided for by an Act of Parliament[54] and comprehensive legislation followed in 1994.[55] The watchword for restitution is "state-direction" demonstrated by a demanding timetable which calls for deadlines of three, five and ten years from 1st May, 1995[56] to be respectively met for lodgement of claims, finalisation by Commission and Land Claims Court and implementation of orders.[57] The White Paper recognises that these deadlines may be too ambitious in the "difficult and very lengthy process" of restitution in which "it may be necessary to review time frames".[58]

As a vehicle designed to give access to the restitution of land rights lost through the application of racially biased laws scope is obviously a critical feature. In this regard the significant policy decision to limit claims under the Act to post-1913 dispossessions and so steer away from an "aboriginal title"[59] basis has been identified as a "pragmatic compromise"[60] - very probably one in which particular political considerations played a part.[61] The 1997 White Paper appears to speak from a socio-political standpoint concerning future stability in justifying the limitation in terms of the difficulty of unravelling historic claims and counter-claims and the danger of prolonging "destructive ethnic and racial politics"[62] But on another view a failure to deal with the roots of the unjust system will only store up potential conflict for the future.[63] An original title basis for a claim to land may not be a completely dead letter because at least one High Court claim is pending in which it is one of the alternative causes of action.[64]

A Land Claims Court (the Court) which has a central controlling role in the restitution process - indeed, in the land reform programme generally - represents a major legal innovation in the South Africa context. Significantly, the advent of a specialist court does not mean a system in which claims are simply pursued in an adversary setting. The work of the Court is closely allied to that of a Commission with national and regional offices. The Commission operates at grass-roots level in publicising the option of restitution, assisting with and receiving claims, investigating their merits, mediating and settling disputes and reporting to the Court on unsettled matters. The role of the Court is to approve and authenticate solutions arrived at by the Commission as well as actually to try cases in which the Commission's active solution seeking process fails to produce a settlement. The nature of the restitution process as a joint one involving the administrative role of the Commission and the authenticating and (where necessary) adjudicating function of the Court in a co-operative exercise is well illustrated in the first major decision of the Court, *In re*

Macleantown Residents Association.[65] As a means of resolving questions concerning particular rights in property the restitution process is radical by comparison to the standard South African system in which disputed property rights must be pursued by the parties before superior courts functioning in adversary format.

The restitution of land rights under the 1994 Act has a development-directed and group resolution character. Although the system provided for has its starting point in a right to restitution open to an individual claimant, certain structural features of the legislation promote a development-directed and group-focused character. The 1997 White Paper acknowledges this, essentially interventionist, approach as a feature of the restitution programme which "provides the opportunity to initiate a process of healing, re-integration and reconstructing the cities and towns which still bear the scars of racial zoning".[66] Certain features are identified in the White Paper as aspects of the "development-directed, group resolution" orientation of the Act. These are the prioritisation required in respect of claims affecting substantial numbers or involving particularly pressing cases;[67] an intervention mechanism allowing the Commission to consolidate claims within a particular area,[68] in competing claims provision for a directive that the parties resort to mediation;[69] a power in the Court to disallow the restoration of land on the basis of developmental or public interest grounds[70] and, finally, the possibility of successful claimants being included as beneficiaries in state-supported programmes.[71]

An aspect of the restitution process with obvious potential implications as a derogation from common law property rights is the Act's system under which the official publication of notice of a claim[72] has the effect, pending finalisation of the claim, of curtailing a landowner's normal rights of use and enjoyment.[73] These provisions were challenged in the first case to go to the new Constitutional Court on the land restitution process. In *Transvaal Agricultural Union* v *Minister of Land Affairs*[74] the Constitutional Court rejected the applicant commercial farmers union's claim to a right of direct access under the Court's rules and accordingly no definitive decision was required on the issue of constitutionality. However, the Court indicated that it did not see the relevant parts of the Act as infringing constitutional rights of property. Constitutional Court President Chaskalson observed as follows:

> The restitution of land rights is a complex process in which the rights of registered owners and other persons with an interest in the land must be

balanced against the constitutional injunctions to ensure that restitution be made where this is just and equitable. Parliament is given a discretion by the Constitution to decide how this process is to be carried out. Provisions in such legislation that are designed to protect claimants and maintain the *status quo* pending determination of a claim serve a legitimate purpose.[75]

At a recent University of Cape Town conference[76] two associated points emerged: dissatisfaction with the through-put rate of restitution claims and a call for the extension of deadlines. The available statistics indicate a significant number of urban claims met but a smaller rate in rural areas.[77] This difference is not surprising in the circumstances of urban development producing a number of claims which go forward together on the same basis, as against rural claims applying to larger parcels of land which are likely to be distinguishable.

Tenure Reform

Addressing the general legal bases under which land may be held has potentially greater implications for the reform of property law than the redistribution sub-programme - essentially concerned with facilitating the allocation of new rights within the existing property system, or with restitution - a timetabled process of restoring rights or otherwise dealing with a defined category of claimants affected by post-1913 racial laws or practices. The White Paper speaks to this in commenting on the complexity of the process of tenure reform in finding solutions which "may entail new systems of land holding, land rights and forms of ownership, and therefore have far-reaching implications".[78]

The Department of Land Affairs has published a set of "guiding principles" to inform the policy development process and these will be considered with the substantive developments which have already occurred. The "guiding principles" of tenure reform may be summarised as the aim to achieve a unitary non-racial system without "second-class" forms; to provide tenure options which allow choice according to circumstances but conform to the Constitution's commitment to basic human rights and equality; to develop a "rights-based" approach with new tenure systems and laws brought into line with existing forms and practice. The rights-based objective has distinct facets. It demands a departure from a "permit based" approach and it is intended to achieve security of tenure by the accommodation of *de facto* vested rights including "interests which have come to exist without formal legal recognition". The aim of introducing new systems "in line with the reality" requires fit with existing interests including "established occupation" and "long term historical ownership of land which exists in practice but which is not recognised in law"; of particular significance is the commitment to recognise *de facto* vested rights and the recognition that "[t]he most basic form of vested rights in land is established occupation".[79] This must necessarily point to reforms which will depart from the primacy of the right of ownership of a registered title holder of the existing law.

This is the least developed aspect of the reform programme with a Green Paper expected at the time of writing.[80] The most recent relevant material available to the present writer is a draft policy document with important preliminary proposals relating to land tenure reform.[81] Considered comment should necessarily await proposals in more final form but the gist of the Department's thinking may be noted at this stage. On the basis of the constitutional duty to remedy legally insecure tenure which has resulted from past racially discriminatory laws or practices by Act of Parliament[82] the paper recommends three interrelated measures, summarised as follows.

> The first is a law which defines and confirms underlying land rights and which describes the relationships between different land holders. The second is a registration system which enables people to register their rights. The third provides the holders of group-based rights with access to fair systems of day to day administration of their land rights.[83]

These proposals relate to rural circumstances in which the problem is not simply one of working towards the provision of secure tenure to separate units of residential property on a widespread basis. Rural tenure reform will have to be worked into a complex *status quo* reflecting various different forms of traditional African landholding which may, of course, be entirely stable and which communities may wish to maintain.

Tenure Reform Legislation

The first major development in positive tenure reform, the Upgrading of Land Tenure Rights Act 112 of 1991, was passed by the De Klerk Government and took effect soon after the termination of race-based land laws removed all statutory restrictions in respect of the acquisition or occupation of immovable property.[84] The Act provides for the upgrading of various forms of limited land tenure rights which were representative of the prevalent practice in apartheid South Africa of according lesser rights in land to blacks. Depending upon the right, upgrading under the Act is either automatic or on the basis of a process of registration initiated by the holder. In its initial form the emphasis was on the acquisition of individual ownership but amendments by the ANC Government have brought the Act into line with the policy of providing a range of protected tenure options. The 1997 White Paper notes that the amendments will continue to facilitate the upgrading of tenure rights in townships while ensuring that rural upgrading will neither damage tribal or communal landholding nor pre-empt tenure reform.[85]

The Communal Property Associations Act, already commented on,[86] is an important positive tenure reform measure making possible the holding of legal title to land by a simple "people based" entity. This legislation represents the first stage in a development which is intended to provide for meaningful landholding by a community or group entity. The Deeds Act provides only for the acquisition of title by one or more identified parties, whether natural persons or juristic entities. Thus while A may transfer land to B or to B, C and D in undivided shares, there was no provision for transfer to a group on a collective basis in which individual members are not identified. A trust basis is sometimes used to provide for a form of community ownership but in a trust arrangement the community members do not hold themselves but, rather, as beneficiaries to property held by a trustee. The Communal Property Associations Act allows a community group to form itself into a juristic person for the purposes of acquiring, holding and managing property on a basis agreed by the members in a written constitution - the primary purpose being the provision of a suitable basis for landholding by a community group. The essential rationale of the legislation is to give meaningful defined rights to individual members where the circumstances relating to the existing or projected holding of the land are not consistent with the provision of individual ownership. The Act provides for the establishing of a communal property association with a written constitution with the assistance of an officer of the Department of Land Affairs designated the "Registration Officer".[87] Following final approval by the Director-General of Land Affairs, the community association may be registered and, subject to the provisions of its constitution, it may acquire and dispose of or otherwise deal with immovable property.[88] In providing for the identification of a community group as a juristic person which may acquire and dispose of land by normal deeds office process, the Act has an important role in the land reform process. Its provisions apply where the Land Claims Court orders restitution of land on condition that a communal property association be formed or where a community is entitled to receive property from the state subject to such a condition.[89] It is also competent for the Minister of Land Affairs to approve the constitution of a community under the Act subject to being satisfied that "the community is disadvantaged and that it is in the public interest that such approval be given, having regard to the nature and current use of the land".[90]

With regard to the critical issue of the identification of the members of a group or community recognised for the purposes of the Act the body concerned must supply, in its application for registration as a communal property association, a list of names.[91] However, where it is not reasonably possible to provide the names of all intended members of the group the application must include principles for the identification of other persons entitled to be members.[92]

The concept of "initial ownership" introduced by the Development Facilitation Act 67 of 1995 has been mentioned. As this is also very much a matter of tenure reform it will be considered in some detail here. The nature of "initial ownership" can be assessed from the corpus of constituent rights which are identified in the legislation creating the device. In this regard the Act provides that the registration of transfer of initial ownership shall vest in the holder the right to occupation and use, the right to acquire (full) ownership, the right to encumber the initial ownership by means of mortgage or personal servitude and the right "to sell such initial ownership" but, significantly, "not the right otherwise to encumber or deal with the initial ownership".[93] Pending conversion to full ownership under the Act the position will be that the parcel of land held in initial ownership is part of a larger parcel held by another in full ownership. This situation necessarily requires a limitation upon the normal rights of the owner of the parent parcel until all the infant parcels have been converted into full ownership. The Act accordingly provides that land in respect of which initial ownership has been transferred shall not "in any way be alienated or further encumbered by the owner".[94] The nature of the concept of initial ownership is further revealed by the provision that a transfer of the right under the Deeds Registries Act 47 of 1937 is competent - and, by implication, only competent - in the circumstances of a deceased estate, insolvency or liquidation, sale in execution or "where some other event occurs requiring the transfer of such initial ownership".[95] As would be expected a transfer may "not confer upon the transferee any right which the previous holder of initial ownership did not have".[96] As no more than a right to acquire ownership, lacking any power of disposal of the property, initial ownership's only real claim to the status of ownership is in the according, in advance, of certain rights of ownership. This limited status is consistent with the power of a registrar of deeds to cancel a deed of transfer conveying initial ownership upon agreement to this by the owner of the parent land, the initial owner and any mortgagee or holder of a personal servitude;[97] cancellation, of course, not being competent in respect of ownership proper, being incompatible with the right of disposal of property which distinguishes ownership from lesser rights. The extent to which the concept of initial ownership departs from the common law dogma of a unitary concept of ownership as the absolute and final proprietary right is debatable. On one view it would appear to be no more than ownership in name and anticipation and, accordingly, not an erosion of the general concept of ownership. Although it is a meaningful right, applying conventional thinking one would probably conclude that it does not cross the threshold into property proper because it does not reach the point of conferring a right of disposal but only that of the right to acquire, a right which is open to cancellation. On the other hand it is clearly a real right available "against the whole world" rather than only against another party - in this case the owner of the parent entity of land. Without resort to circular reasoning, it may be noted that the fact that the right of initial ownership came into being as a registrable right is in itself significant to the extent that common law thinking tends to see as synonymous the criteria of a real right and registrability - an approach reflected in the Deeds Act.[98] But to apply conventional Romanist property dogma to a new property jurisprudence is more of an exercise of demonstrating change than one of rational analysis.[99]

Another relevant initiative of the new Government is a passive interim measure to provide for the continuation of certain interests in land, not otherwise protected;[100] the rationale being to protect the *status quo* for a wide category of holders of different forms of insecure tenure pending permanent reform measures.[101] The Interim Protection of Informal Land Rights Act 31 of 1996 reflects a major departure from the position of the Roman-Dutch common law under which a title-holder's strong right of vindication is a logical corollary of a supreme right of ownership.[102] The Act's title proclaims its radicalism from the perspective of the common law. The category of interests protected by "informal land rights", as a new term of art in South African property law, represents a wholesale creation of rights which amount to a major inroad into the traditional concept of ownership. The various "informal" interests protected are in the main specific forms of holding of land which vests in the state but the protection accorded by the general concept of "beneficial occupation" is a notable exception. This is defined in the Act to mean "the occupation of land by a person, as if he or she is the owner, without force, openly and without the permission of the registered owner".[103] This form of occupation is protected as an "informal right to land" provided the "beneficial occupation" has endured "for a continuous period of not less than five years prior to 31 December 1998".[104] Subject to the provisions of the Expropriation Act 63 of 1975 "no person may be deprived of any informal right to land without his or her consent".[105] That "beneficial occupation" does not include a precarious holding is made clear by the Act which excludes the situation of "temporary permission" granted on the basis that it may be withdrawn.[106] From the point of view of pre-existing property law, reflecting common law principles, the effect of the protection of "beneficial occupation" is to give standing to an interest of five years duration which would otherwise only have the potential to mature into a right on the basis of acquisitive prescription after thirty years.[107] That this Act is only intended as an interim measure appears in the provision that subject to the possibility of extension for a further maximum period of twelve months it will lapse on 31st December, 1997[108] - an extension which has been made.

On 4th February, 1997 a Bill was published which was enacted on 28th November, 1997 as the Extension of Security of Tenure Act 62 of 1997. The positive aspect of this legislation is to provide for security of tenure and possible acquisition by occupiers of rural land.[109] It may be noted that an element of retrospectivity is present in that an occupier's rights under the Act are established from the date of publication of the Bill on 4th February, 1997 and, indeed, from prior to publication provided continuous residence was maintained up to that date.[110] This device was, of course, intended to forestall possible adverse action by landowners pending the passing of legislation involving the restriction of their common law rights. The Act, not applying to any form of "township" land, is essentially applicable to all land outside urban areas.[111] The Act's three principal strands are represented in separate chapters. Chapter II ("Measures to facilitate long-term security of tenure for occupiers") provides for subsidised land development directed towards providing land, or rights in land, to "occupiers, former occupiers and other persons who need long-term security of tenure".[112] Criteria prescribed as relevant to the exercise of ministerial discretion include "a mutual accommodation of the interests of occupiers and owners" and "an urgent need for the development because occupiers have been evicted or are about to be evicted".[113] The Subdivision of Agricultural Land Act 70 of 1970 - widely perceived by the agricultural establishment as a crucial control in maintaining an efficient national farming industry but increasingly challenged as inhibiting reformist development[114] - is disempowered in respect of a development undertaken in terms of the Act.[115] In Chapter III ("Rights and duties of occupiers and owners") the Act establishes a correlative right/duty position between the defined categories[116] of "owner" and "occupier"; in Chapter IV ("Termination of right of residence and eviction") it establishes a legal framework on the basis of which differences can be resolved. Given the high prevalence of residential rights as part of an employment package, a provision of considerable practical significance is that an employee's right of residence which arises solely from an employment agreement, may be terminated if the occupier resigns or is dismissed in accordance with the provisions of the Labour Relations Act 66 of 1995, any dispute over termination to be dealt with under that Act.[117] In its general regulation of the basis under which consent to reside on land shall be terminated, an innovatory feature of the Act limits the owner's right of termination in respect of certain defined classes of long-standing occupiers vulnerable through age, ill health, injury or disability.[118]

The contractual right of a tenant, labour tenant, share-cropper or employee is not protected by the Interim Protection of Informal Land Rights Act 31 of 1996[119] but the Land Reform (Labour Tenants) Act 3 of 1996 had been passed earlier in 1996 to deal with labour tenancy - an area of long-standing discriminatory practice. The weak position of tenants *vis-à-vis* owners in terms of the common law as it had developed[120] meant that the former were vulnerable to agricultural economic policy,[121] in particular the shift to wage labour farming which had started in nineteenth-century South Africa.[122] The plight of non-owners who contributed to agricultural production as labour tenants or share-croppers has been identified by Albie Sachs in terms of the following stark equation: "Ownership, whiteness, and absolute control became synonymous, as did rightlessness, blackness, and subordination."[123] The reforming Act has two distinct purposes: to protect the circumstances of established labour tenancy and to accord to labour tenants the right to acquire the land occupied. A labour tenant is defined in terms of three conjunctive elements: a right to residence; a right to the use of farmland for cropping or grazing in return for labour; and an ancestral connection through parents or grandparents living on a farm of the landowner on the same basis;[124] but the definition excludes farm workers, predominantly remunerated for personal services rather than given a right to use land.[125]

Under the common law a labour tenant's position was a vulnerable one especially in the circumstances of a change of ownership of the farm;[126] the Act allows eviction only in certain circumstances and only on the basis of an order of the Land Claims Court.[127] In view of concern that evictions would occur pending the coming into force of the Act the Bill provided for retrospective protection backdated to the date it was gazetted - 2nd June, 1995. Thus while the commencement date of the Act was only 22nd March, 1996 the passage of the legislation accorded protection against any eviction which had taken place after 1st June, 1995.[128] The security of a labour tenant family against eviction is achieved by the Act's close and rigorous control of the owner's right of eviction. The tenor of the Act is illustrated by the fact that an order for removal pending a final determination may only be made if the Court is satisfied that "a real and imminent danger of substantial damage to the owner or lessee or his or her property"[129] exists, that no other effective remedy is available and that the balance of likely harm lies with the owner or lessee rather than the party against whom the removal order is sought.[130]

Chapter III of the Act provides for the acquisition of ownership of land and appropriate servitudes on the basis of the circumstances of labour tenancy. A labour tenant or his or her successor may apply for an award of land to the Director-General of Land Affairs but must do so within four years of the commencement of the Act. The legislation aims to promote a negotiated settlement, failing which one reached by arbitration, but the option of litigation before the Court is open to the parties.[131]

Analysis and Overview of the Changes

The major part of the very considerable body of new law passed since the active commencement of the reform process in the early part of the decade is concerned with giving effect to policy initiatives in implementation of the reconstruction and development programme in its application to land. The lengthy and complex Development Facilitation Act[132] is a prime example of new law in the critical area of reform and restructuring driven by long-standing social imperatives which, fortunately for South Africa, have finally become political priorities. The complete revision of land tenure policy means that a particular matter previously perceived as a policy priority may now be seen as an obstacle to the necessary direction of development. The Subdivision of Agricultural Land Act 70 of 1970 is an example of this.[133]

The reform programme is proceeding on the premise of the Constitution which, of course, is now the ruling feature to the extent that the common law no longer has its former pre-eminence. To this extent it is difficult to see the scope for an assertion of common law rights against a position supported by the reform agenda;[134] a conclusion which would appear to be supported by the first relevant *dictum* of the Constitutional Court.[135] This said, what is largely involved in the reform process has not, and apparently will not, affect the fundamental substance of the working system of the law of property although significant adjustment is taking place. On one view of the developments the radical aspect appears to lie primarily in features external to the law of property which are present to facilitate the implementation of the reform process; the form of adjudication applied to restitution being an instance of this.

But although the new order is primarily concerned with facilitating a reallocation of land rights without major departure from the pre-existing model it has brought significant changes and more are promised by the Department of Land Affairs. Ownership no longer rules in the close to absolute manner in which it previously did; its power and position has been and is in the process of being devolved and fragmented; it is now open to competition from possession to a degree which it was previously more or less invulnerable to. The overall position would appear to be that the general scope and significance of the changes wholly overshadows the fact that the new system is working within the basic principles of the common law.

Notes

*　This paper is a product of work done on research visits to South Africa in 1997 and 1998. The visits were made possible through financial assistance by the British Academy and the Carnegie Trust for the Universities of Scotland in 1997 and by the British Academy in 1998. I am grateful to Professor DP Visser, Dean of the Faculty

of Law, University of Cape Town, for making available a physical and intellectual base for both periods of work.

1 Professor CG van der Merwe's definitive modern work, *Sakereg* (2nd ed, 1989), shows the extent of the Roman-Dutch common law influence over the entire area of property.

2 See JT Schoombie, "Group Areas legislation - the political control of ownership and occupation of land" 1985 *Acta Juridica* 77.

3 Accordingly in *Preller & others v Jordaan* 1956(1) SA 483 (A) 496 the Appellate Division recognised that in principle ownership would not pass in the situation in which an owner did not intend to transfer his land but had been induced to sign a power of attorney to transfer on the basis that it was some other document.

4 DP Visser "The 'Absoluteness' of ownership: the South African common law in perspective" 1985 *Acta Juridica* 39, 46-7.

5 *Idem*, 47.

6 *Johannesburg City Council v Rand Townships Registrar* 1910 TPD 1314.

7 See Peter Birks "The Roman Law concept of dominium and the idea of absolute ownership" 1985 *Acta Juridica* 1.

8 See WW Buckland and Arnold D MacNair, *Roman Law and the Common Law* (2nd ed 1952, FH Lawson) 62-71; see also DL Carey Miller "Systems of property; worlds apart: a miscellany of works" 1985 *Acta Juridica* 369.

9 In *Gien v Gien* 1979 (2) SA 1113 (T) 1120 the court quoted a definition given in R Sohm's *Institutes* (3rd ed, 1907, 309) which describes ownership as "however susceptible of legal limitations ... nevertheless absolutely unlimited as far as its own contents are concerned".

10 See *Dadoo Ltd v Krugersdorp Municipal Council* 1920 AD 530; *Gien v Gien* 1979 (2) SA 1113 (T).

11 See s 1 of the Prescription Act 68 of 1969; for commentaries see CG van der Merwe (*supra*, n 1) 273-88 and DL Carey Miller, *The Acquisition and Protection of Ownership* (1986) 63-101.

12 *Chetty v Naidoo* 1974(3) SA 13 (A) 20. Many other judicial statements support this trite point; see generally van der Merwe (*supra*, n 1) 347-53 and Carey Miller (*supra*, n 11) 255-6. But it should be noted that the common law has had an important role in the protection of an occupying possessor in circumstances involving moves by the owner to recover physical possession; see, *eg, George Municipality v Vena and Another* 1989(2) SA 263(A).

13 See Brian Willam (ed), *Sol Plaatje: Selected Writings* (1996) 102-4.

14 *Tsewu v Registrar of Deeds* 1905 TS 130.

15 See, generally: Laurine Platzky and Cherryl Walker, *The Surplus People; Forced Removals in South Africa* (1985) and Christina Murray and Catherine O'Regan (eds), *No Place to Rest; Forced Removals in the Law in South Africa* (1990). South African periodical legal literature has been a vehicle for much valuable comment concerning land reform. This literature is far too extensive to cite in detail but the following contributions may be mentioned: Derek van der Merwe, "Land tenure in South Africa: a brief history and some reform proposals" (1989) 4 TSAR 663; Geoff Budlender and Johan Latsky, "Unravelling rights to land and to agricultural activity in rural race zones" (1990) 6 SAJHL 155; Nic Olivier, Willemien du Plessis and Juanita Pienaar "Legislation affecting land" 1990 SAPR/PL 266 and Olivier, "Grondreghervorming:

die erwe van ons vaad're..." Obiter 1991 1; TW Bennett and JW Roos "The 1991 Land Reform Acts and the future of African customary law" (1992) 109 SALJ 447; AJ van der Walt, "Land reform in South Africa since 1990 - an overview" (1995) 10 SAPR/PL 1 and "Tradition on trial: a critical analysis of the civil-law tradition in South African property law" (1995) 11 SAJHR 169; CG van der Merwe and JM Pienaar, "Land reform in South Africa" in Paul Jackson and David C Wilde (eds) *The Reform of Property Law* (1997) 334-380.

16   Constitution of the Republic of South Africa 108 of 1996.

17   Constitution of the Republic of South Africa 200 of 1993.

18   S 25(2).

19   White Paper on *South African Land Policy*, April 1997, 3.1.5.

20   S 25(4)(a).

21   S 25(5).

22   S 25(6). It may be noted that s 25(9) provides that "Parliament must enact the legislation referred to in subsection (6)".

23   The Restitution of Land Rights Act 22 of 1994.

24   S 25(7). The starting point is based on the commencement date of the Natives Land Act 27 of 1913; see White Paper, *supra* n 19, 4.14.2.

25   S 25(8).

26   S 36(1) provides that "[t]he rights in the Bill of Rights may be limited only in terms of law of general application to the extent that the limitation is reasonable and justifiable in an open and democratic society based on human dignity, equality and freedom, taking into account all relevant factors, including - (a) the nature of the right; (b) the importance of the purpose of the limitation; (c) the nature and extent of the limitation; (d) the relation between the limitation and its purpose, and (e) less restrictive means to achieve the purpose".

27   *Ibid.*

28   See below n 74.

29   S 26(3).

30   *Per* van Rensburg J in *Despatch Municipality* v *Sunridge Estate and Development Corp* 1997(4) SA 596 (SECLD).

31   S 39(1)(b).

32   S 39(1)(c).

33   A monograph by Professor AJ van der Walt, *The Constitutional Property Clause* (1997) and a chapter by Geoff Budlender (Director General of the Department of Land Affairs, but not expressing views to be attributed to the Department) "The Constitutional Protection of Property Rights" in Geoff Budlender, Johan Latsky and Theunis Roux, *The New Land Law* (1998) - both publications by Juta.

34   Van der Walt, *supra* n 33, 163.

35   *Ibid.*

36   *de Jure Belli ac Pacis*, 1625, 2.2.6.2; 2.7.1. See my summary, *supra* n 11, 107.

37   In my 1986 textbook the racial legislation is described as "a creature of its own, an external factor, a twentieth-century accrescence which, it would seem, can only be of a transient nature" and which "is of no relevance to the principles of the passing of ownership in land although it obviously has major implications from the point of view of practical conveyancing". See *supra* n 11, 192.

38   Minister of Land Affairs Derek Hanekom in a foreword to the White Paper notes the link between the three key elements of the land reform programme and the provisions of the Constitution; see *supra* n 19, foreword and at 4.1.
39   As in the Upgrading of Land Tenure Rights Act 112 of 1991.
40   As in the Land Reform (Labour Tenants) Act 3 of 1996.
41   See *supra* n 19, 4.19.
42   See *supra* n 19, 6.15.3.
43   See *supra* n 19, 4.3.
44   At the time of writing set at R15 000 per household; see *supra* n 19, 4.7.
45   See *supra* n 19, 4.3.
46   Report in *The Sunday Independent* (South African) of 15th February, 1998.
47   See *supra* n 19, 4.3.
48   See *supra* n 19, Box 4.1 (the White Paper's identification of the eight "Principal National Land Reform Laws").
49   The Provision of Certain Land for Settlement Act 126 of 1993.
50   See s 62. Note also the amendment to the Deeds Registries Act 47 of 1937 in s 3(1)(d) *bis*.
51   See *supra* n 19, 4.8.
52   Now see, generally, Dr Theunis Roux's valuable chapter "The Restitution of Land Rights Act" in *The New Land Law*, *supra* n 33, 3A-3 to 3C-93.
53   See the Abolition of Racially Based Land Measures Act 108 of 1991, s 87; a Commission on Land Allocation was introduced by the Abolition of Racially Based Land Measures Amendment Act 110 of 1993.
54   See *supra* n 17, s 121(1).
55   See *supra* n 23.
56   Fixed by GN 575 in Government Gazette 16370 of 21st April, 1995.
57   See *supra* n 19, 4.13.
58   *Ibid.*
59   See TW Bennett "Restitution of land and the doctrine of aboriginal title in South Africa" (1993) 9 SAJHR 443.
60   John Murphy "The restitution of land after apartheid: the constitutional and legislative framework" in MR Rwelamira and G Werle (eds) *Confronting Past Injustices* (1996) 113, 121.
61   See Daniel Visser and Theunis Roux in MR Rwelamira and G Werle, *supra* n 60, 94.
62   See *supra* n 19, 4.14.2.
63   See Durkje Gilfillan, "Restitution: Can Entitlement to Tenure Reform Break Through the Constitutional Barrier of the 1913 Cut Off Date?" in Michael Barry (ed) *Proceedings of the International Conference on Land Tenure in the Developing World*, Department of Geomatics, University of Cape Town, 1998, 186.
64   Information kindly provided by Cape Town Legal Resources Centre.
65   1996(4) SA 1272 (LCC).
66   See *supra* n 19, 4.14.6.
67   See *supra* n 23, s 6(2)(d).
68   S 12(4).
69   S 13.
70   S 34.
71   S 35(1)(d).

72   Under s 11.

73   *Eg*, disallowing the removal or destruction of any improvement without the written authority of the Chief Land Claims Commissioner.

74   1997 (2) SA 621 (CC).

75   At 633E.

76   See *supra* n 63.

77   The Internet Home Page of the Department of Land Affairs (http://www.wn.apc.org/dla) gives statistics as of 2nd June, 1997 which show a total of 15,874 claims in the nine provinces with the majority (5,936) in Kwazulu-Natal. See also the *Annual Report 1997* of the Commission on the Restitution of Land Rights, published by the Department.

78   See *supra* n 19, 4.15.

79   See *supra* n 19, 4.16.

80   *Idem*.

81   The third draft of a paper *Proposals for Securing Vulnerable Rights in Land* submitted by the Tenure Reform Directorate to the Land Reform Policy Committee of the Department of Land Affairs on 20th November, 1997.

82   S 25(6) read with s 25(9) of the Constitution.

83   Tenure Reform Directorate Paper, *supra* n 81, 5.1.

84   See *supra* n 53. See Peter Rutsch and Fred Jenkin, *The New Land Laws of South Africa* (1992 loose-leaf), 138-167 for details as to repeals, amendments and adjustments made by the State President in terms of ss 12 and 87 of the Act.

85   See *supra* n 19, box 4.10.

86   See *supra* n 47.

87   S 1.

88   S 8(5)(c).

89   S 2(1)(a) and (b).

90   S 2(2).

91   S 5(1)(d).

92   S 5(1)(d)(i).

93   S 62(4) of the Development Facilitation Act 67 of 1995.

94   S 62(5)(a). The subsection admits two necessary exceptions: complying with a condition of establishment and, of course, the registration of ownership under the normal land development process of the Act (s 38(1)).

95   S 62(6).

96   *Ibid*.

97   S 62(5)(b).

98   S 63(1) of the Deeds Registries Act 47 of 1937. See Kenneth GC Reid "Obligations and property: exploring the border" 1997 *Acta Juridica* 225, generally relevant to this issue and featuring particular comment on the Deeds Act section in question (at 240).

99   Another feature of the Development Facilitation Act 67 of 1995 shows its capacity for innovation, at least to the extent of labelling, not only unconfined by the conventional common law thinking but even by philosophical limits. The concept concerned is that of "non-statutory land development" which may be authorised under s 42 of the Act. In essence the law says here that land development which falls outside the system of the Act may none the less be recognised, provided that it meets certain basic

standards. This, of course, is a device to deal with the vast problem of the "informal settlement" of land.

100 Interim Protection of Informal Land Rights Act 31 of 1996.
101 See *supra* n 19, box 4.9.
102 See *supra* n 4.
103 S 1 defining "beneficial occupation".
104 S 1(c) defining "informal right to land".
105 S 2(1).
106 S 1(f).
107 See *supra* n 11.
108 See s 5(2).
109 See the "Memorandum on the Objects of the Extension of Security of Tenure Bill, 1997" published with the Bill.
110 S 3(2).
111 See details regarding application in s 2. The Memorandum (*supra* n 109) states: "the Bill will apply to land which is commonly understood as rural land - commercial farm land, rural land owned by tribes, and peri-urban land".
112 S 4(1)(b).
113 The full list of criteria appears in s 4(2).
114 See Johan van Zyl "The farm size-efficiency relationship" in J van Zyl, J Kirsten and HP Binswater, *Agricultural Land Reform in South Africa* (1996) 259. (See below n 133.)
115 S 4(7).
116 S 1.
117 S 8(2) and (3).
118 S 8.
119 See *supra* n 100, s (1)(e).
120 See Moray Hathorn and Dale Hutchison "Labour Tenants and the Law" in Murray and O'Regan (*supra* n 15) 194.
121 See Johann Kirsten and Johan van Zyl "The contemporary agricultural policy environment: undoing the legacy of the past" in Van Zyl, Kirsten and Binswanger (*supra* n 114) 199.
122 See, *eg*, W Beinart "Settler accumulation in East Griqualand" in William Beinart, Peter Delius and Stanley Trapido (eds) *Putting a Plough to the Ground* (1986) 275-8.
123 *Protecting Human Rights in a New South Africa* (1990) 125.
124 S 1.
125 *Idem.* Land Claims Court cases under the Act are *Mahlangu* v *De Jager* 1996(3) SA 235(LCC), *Zulu* v *Van Rensberg* 1996(4) SA 1236 (LCC), *Klopper v Mkhize* 1998 (1) SA 406(N) and *Tselentis Mining v Mdlalose* 1998 (1) SA 411(N).
126 See *De Jager* v *Sisana* 1930 AD 71 and *Crous* v *Crous* 1937 CPD 250; both cases are commented on by Hathorn and Hutchison (*supra* n 120) 209-10.
127 Ss 5 and 7.
128 Ss 3 and 12.
129 S 15.
130 *Idem.*
131 Ss 17-22.
132 See *supra* n 48.

133 See The White Paper, *supra* n 19, 3.14: "There is general agreement that the Subdivision of Agricultural Land Act must be phased out to free up the land market". (The Act is subject to repeal, on a date to be proclaimed, by the Subdivision of Agricultural Land Act Repeal Act 64 of 1998.)

134 As in *Diepsloot Residents' and Landowners' Association* v *Administrator, Trannsvaal* 1994 (3) SA 336 (A).

135 See *supra* n 75.

13 Extending Security of Tenure in South Africa: Labour Tenants and Farm Workers

JUANITA PIENAAR

Introduction

The racially based land control system in South Africa, as introduced by the Black Land Act 27 of 1913[1] and confirmed by the South African Development Trust Land Act 18 of 1936[2] until the abolition thereof in 1991, is by now well-known and well-documented. That these Acts laid down and perfected the principle of territorial segregation is undeniable. The effect these Acts had on the farming potential of, especially, black South Africans is, however, not always emphasised or fully understood. Letsoale[3] contends that any analysis of South African land reforms, both formal and informal, would always reveal an underlying agenda that links them with labour management and that the South African experience fits into the patterns of capitalist and labour exploitation.

In this paper I argue that the principles laid down in the ground-breaking legislation mentioned above effectively led to the uprooting of a well-established, independent farming community, resulting in *inter alia*, present-day farm workers and labour tenants. For the purposes of this paper I would like to draw a distinction between (a) black farming as such and the need for reform and development of the black farming sector in general and (b) labour tenants and farm workers providing labour and services for, mainly, the white farming sector. Although both these sectors are in the need of land reform, the former does not fall within the ambit of this paper. It is the object of this paper to give a background as to the reasons why labour tenants and farm workers' interests particularly need to be addressed, why pilot legislation (*eg* the Abolition of Racially Based Land Measures Act 108 of 1991) did not improve their plight and how these matters are presently dealt with.

The next section to the paper comprises an historical overview in order to place the present-day problems of tenure insecurity of labour tenants and farm workers in perspective. This will be followed by a critical discussion of the Land Reform (Labour Tenants) Act 3 of 1996; after which consideration is given to the Extension of Security of Tenure Act 62 of 1997. The specific rights provided for in these Acts and the classification thereof within the present legal framework will be dealt with in the penultimate section. Final remarks conclude the discussion.

Background

Measures issued by European influenced governments promoting colonialism had an immediate effect on land use patterns and tenure in South Africa.[4] Annexation of the colonies usually coincided with the institution of reserves for blacks that were too small to support independent African agriculture.[5] Under these circumstances share-cropping and labour tenancy were the two main forms of production accessible to black Africans.[6] Share-cropping entails the division of duties and factors of production on the one hand, and the produce on the other, between the cultivator and the non-cultivator, the latter usually being a white landowner.[7] The cultivator contributes the inputs (*eg* seed, labour and equipment) while the non-cultivator contributes the land. Under the labour tenancy system the labour tenant was awarded a place to live on the land, a plot to plough and grazing rights in exchange for labouring for the landowner.

Although obviously beneficial to landowners[8] complaints were raised concerning the making available of land (albeit indirectly) to blacks and not to poor whites which finally led to legislation in order to curb the evil of "squatting" and labour tenancy. The following laws were passed: Vagrancy and Squatting Act of 1879 (Cape); Ordinance 2 of 1855 (Natal);[9] Orange Free State Squatters Law (Document 90);[10] and Transvaal Squatters Law II of 1887.[11]

With large numbers "squatting" on land, early legislation promulgated to regulate the black presence on farmland was initially ineffective and unenforceable.[12] However, pressure from the mining sector and the desire to obviate food imports, led to new legislation during 1892. At this stage all tenants had to be registered and the number of tenants allowed on farms was restricted to five. This way tenancy was more structured and easier to control which also led to the more equal distribution of labour.

In 1894 the Glen Grey Act restricted farm ownership in the reserves to one parcel of no more than slightly above three hectares. It furthermore levied a labour tax on all men living in the reserves who did not own land and banned the sale, rental or subdivision of land by introducing a form of communal tenure that was vastly different from traditional tenure.[13]

Despite legislation, labour tenancy and share-cropping were still fairly common practice. This continued to affect the labour supply to the mining industry and disturbed the traditional master-servant relationship. It was therefore envisaged that the introduction of the Black Land Act would rid farm land from black ownership and share-cropping while at the same time prohibiting the purchase of land by blacks outside the so-called "scheduled areas".[14]

The introduction of the Black Land Act in 1913 and the later introduction of the South African Development Trust Land Act in 1936 are well-documented. These provisions confirmed the Glen Grey Act concerning communal tenure, the maximum holding sizes and restrictions on land transactions. It furthermore barred blacks from buying land outside the scheduled and released areas and prohibited them from share-cropping and cash rentals. The significant feature of the Act was the unequal distribution of land between black and white. The area for white occupation was ten times larger than that of the black majority.[15] Two key issues determined the amount of land: (a) the superior needs of whites as opposed to the more "primitive" needs of blacks and (b) the need to supply black labour for the white economy, that is the mines, industries and farms. This would result in the gradual transformation of the South African labour force from mainly labour tenants to wage-workers. The law was aptly nicknamed "a law for the mining houses".[16]

Other underlying reasons were to "curb black farming practices at a time when white farming was beginning to pick up ... to check black share-cropping ... and to prevent the purchase of land by syndicates of blacks who ... were beginning to move ahead fast".[17]

The Beaumont Commission proposed that further land be set aside for black occupation.[18] Although not all of the proposals were accepted, additional land was eventually provided for in the South African Development Trust and Land Act 18 of 1936.[19] Provision was made for "released areas" where blacks could also vest rights. This Act also instituted the South African Native Trust (later known as the South African Development Trust) that was responsible for the acquisition of land for blacks, the development of such land and the promotion of agriculture in the reserves. It furthermore had the general task of advancing the material, moral and social well-being of blacks.[20]

Concerning the farming activities of blacks, the above-mentioned legislation had the following effects: it forced African families, formerly independent farmers on share-cropped land, to accept wage-labouring and give up their equipment; it eventually ended African farming above the subsistence level; and it degraded the scheduled and released areas to dormitories for cheap African labour.

Having lost their right to acquire land outside the restricted scheduled and released areas, black farmers were gradually removed from farms.[21] It is rather ironic that, despite these measures, labour tenancy continued in white areas (in other words the rest of South Africa excluding the scheduled and released areas). During the 1930s, however, official policy proclaimed the withdrawal of support for labour tenancy.

Not only have black farmers lost their land and means to farm successfully, but they were also destined to become labourers by effective legislative engineering; for example: the Masters and Servants Laws 26 of 1926 restricted mobility by preventing Africans from changing occupation without their employer's written consent; and the Mines and Work Act 25 of 1926 excluded blacks from skilled jobs.

The provisions of the 1913 and 1936 Acts, as well as the exclusion of blacks from skilled jobs except agriculture, resulted in the class of farm workers being dominated by blacks.[22]

The labour tenant system was formally abolished in 1980.[23] Large numbers of former tenants were relocated to the national states and self-governing territories where they were allocated a dwelling plot. Allocated land was not only insufficient in extent but also inferior in quality. In some areas in South Africa, mainly in Mpumalanga and KwaZulu Natal, the system of labour tenancy continued.

During 1991 the former government embarked on a process of deracialising the land control system. Although the White Paper on Land Reform[24] was published and various Acts promulgated,[25] the following problems remained:

(i)   continued diversified land control forms in various parts of the country;[26]

(ii)   urban and rural planning continued on an ad hoc basis without specific formulated policies and strategies;

(iii)   insufficient protection of people without formal land titles;

(iv)   continued forced removals;

(v)   no provision for the restitution of land resulting from racially discriminatory measures;

(vi)   no provision for the redistribution of land;

(vii)   continued illegal occupation of land; and

(viii) unprotected rights of certain categories of land users, namely rural women, labour tenants and farm workers.

Although the land control system was deracialised, this did not have meaningful effect for persons actually living on the land and therefore did not automatically improve their livelihood. Rural living was characterised by tenure insecurity, social instability and conflict. In particular, the system of tied housing continued unabated.[27]

During 1994 the present government announced[28] an all-encompassing land reform programme consisting of three inter-connected, although separate, subprogrammes:

(i)   land redistribution;

(ii)   land tenure reform; and

(iii)   land restitution.

The plight of labour tenants was addressed under the redistribution programme by the formulation and commencement of the Land Reform (Labour Tenants) Act 3 of 1996.[29] The position of farm workers (and other persons living on land of which they are not the registered owners), was finally addressed in 1997 when the Extension of Security of Tenure Act 62 of 1997 was implemented in accordance with section 25(6) of the Constitution.[30]

Labour Tenants - The Land Reform (Labour Tenants) Act 3 of 1996

The aim of the Land Reform (Labour Tenants) Act 3 of 1996 is twofold: to provide for the protection of existing land rights on the one hand, and the acquisition of land or rights in land by labourers on the other.

Labour Tenancy in the Terms of the Act

For the purposes of the Act a labour tenant is defined as[31] a person:

(a)   who is residing or has a right to reside on a farm;

(b)   who has or has had a right to use cropping or grazing land on the specific farm or another farm of the owner and in consideration of such right provides or has provided labour to the owner or lessee; and

(c)   whose parent or grandparent resides or resided on a farm and had the use of cropping or grazing land on such farm or another farm of the owner and in consideration of such right provided or provides labour to the owner or lessee thereof,

including a person who has been a successor to a labour tenant, but excluding a farm worker.

In contrast to the above, a farm worker is defined as being a person who is employed on a farm in terms of a contract of employment which provides that, in return for labour, the worker shall be paid predominantly in cash or some other form of remuneration and not predominantly in the right to occupy and use land.[32]

The burden of proof is on the applicant to show that he is a labour tenant.[33] In *Mahlangu v De Jager*[34] Gildenhuys J stated that the applicant had to establish every requirement of the definition and that paragraph (c) of the definition was problematic. However, it was decided that paragraphs (a) and (b) had to be read conjunctively. In *Zulu and Others v Van Rensburg and Others*[35] reference was made to the *Mahlangu* case concerning the burden of proof; however, the impression was given that all three paragraphs had to be proven cumulatively:

> ...in order to qualify as a labour tenant, there must be compliance cumulatively with paras (a), (b) and (c) of the definition... The Act is intended to protect a very particular class of rural tenant and in isolating that class of tenant paras (b) and (c) must come into play... (1253H, 1254E)

Following these two decisions, it was generally very difficult to discharge the burden of proof. Recent developments in case law contribute to a more equitable approach regarding the onus on applicants. Galgut J found in *Klopper and Others v Mkhize and Others*[36] that the definition of "labour tenant"

> is in more than one respect obscurely worded, but it would in substantial measure stultify the object of the Act if para (c) of the definition were required to be read conjunctively with both paras (a) and (b). It may well have been intended that paras (a) and (b) should be read conjunctively,

but it seems that the further intention was that para (c) should either be read in its own or conjunctively with para (a) only. There is, in any event, no warrant for reading all three paragraphs conjunctively. (408H-J)

This approach, that the paragraphs not be read conjunctively, was followed and broadened in *Tselentis Mining (Pty) Ltd and Another v Mdlalose and Others*.[37] In fact, Meskin J found that paragraphs (a) to (c) are not to be read conjunctively, but that paragraphs (a) and (b) of the definition are to be read conjunctively and paragraphs (a) and (c) are to be read conjunctively but disjunctively from paragraphs (a) and (b).[38] He is of the opinion that most applicants would fall within the ambit of paragraphs (a) and (b), but that paragraph (c) in fact creates additional means by which a person who as at 2nd June, 1995 resided or had the right to reside on the farm but who did not have in his own right the rights to use cropping or grazing on such farm can nevertheless qualify as a labour tenant if his parent or grandparent had such rights. This would ultimately mean that the onus of proof is relieved by this new approach.

In 1997 the Act was amended by the Land Restitution and Reform Laws Amendment Act 63 of 1997. The amendment entails that if in any proceedings it is proved that a person falls within paragraphs (a), (b) and (c) of the above definition of "labour tenant", that person shall be presumed not to be a farm worker, unless the contrary is proved. For the purposes of establishing whether a person is a labour tenant, a court shall have regard to the combined effect and substance of all agreements entered into between the person who avers that he or she is a labour tenant and his or her parent or grandparent and the owner or lessee of the land concerned. This amendment, as well as the recent developments in case law, again relieved the heavy onus of proof on applicants.

The Right to Occupy Land

If a person met all the requirements above on 2nd June, 1995[39] that person has a vested right to occupy land with his or her family.[40] Such a right may only be terminated in accordance with the Act, namely the waiver of rights, the death of the labour tenant, eviction and the acquisition of ownership or vesting of other rights in land by the labour tenant.[41]

Deprivation of Right to Occupy

The labour tenant's right to occupy the specific parcel of land may be lost in two instances: eviction and relocation. In the latter instance the labour tenant merely loses the right to that specific parcel of land and can continue his rights on other land allocated to him after a relocation order.

Labour tenants may only be evicted under the terms of the Act. The Act provides for usual eviction[42] and urgent eviction proceedings.[43] Labour tenants may normally be evicted when it is fair and equitable and if

(i)   the labour tenant has committed a material breach of any obligation to provide labour and has failed to remedy such a breach after one calendar month's notice has been given; or

(ii)   the labour tenant or person occupying the land on account of his alliance with the labour tenant has committed some other act which amounts to a fundamental breach of the relationship between the labour tenant and the owner or the lessee which cannot be remedied.

An urgent removal of a labour tenant pending the outcome of a final order may be issued if the court is satisfied that:

(i)   there is real and imminent danger or substantial damage to the owner or lessee of the property;

(ii)   there is no other effective remedy available; and

(iii)   the likely harm if the order is not issued to the owner exceeds the likely harm to the person against whom the order is sought.

The owner is in principle the only person who may institute eviction proceedings.[44]

Labour tenants who have reached the age of 65 or who are unable to provide labour personally due to disability and have refrained from nominating a substitute shall not be evicted under section 7(2)(a). If the owner is prejudiced by this provision, he may apply for equitable relief. No specifics are contained regarding this form of relief other than that it has to be just and equitable in the circumstances.[45]

Any order of eviction shall be subject to the owner's paying the labour tenant compensation equal to the replacement of all structures and improvements made by the labour tenant or his predecessors together with the value of the crops of the labour tenant unless he is given reasonable opportunity to reap them.[46]

Reinstatement

Provision is made for the reinstatement of labour tenants after eviction and relocation proceedings. Regarding relocation proceedings, the labour tenant may apply for reinstatement to their former parcel if the owner has not used the land for agricultural or developmental purposes within one year after the relocation order has been carried out.[47]

Section 12 deals with reinstatement after eviction. Any person who would have had the right to occupy land if the Act was in force on 2nd June, 1995 and vacated the land or was evicted therefrom between that date and the commencement date of the Act (22nd March, 1996) may institute reinstatement proceedings. If the applicant was evicted before the commencement of the Act, additional factors will be taken into account, for example whether the eviction order would have been issued at all if this Act had been in operation at that time[48] and whether the person was effectively represented.

The Court is empowered to issue the following orders:[49]

(i)   that the applicant be regarded as a labour tenant for purposes of the Act;

(ii)   the reinstatement of the person;

(iii)   payment of compensation; and

(iv)   costs.

Acquisition of Ownership or Other Rights in Land By the Labour Tenant

Security of tenure is promoted by (a) confirming the right of labour tenants to occupy land and to ensure that such occupation may only be terminated in conformity with the terms of the Act, and (b) provisions enabling labour tenants to acquire ownership or other rights in land traditionally held by the landowner. Labour tenants meeting all the legislative requirements may apply for an award of land or land rights and for financial assistance.[50] In applications concerning land allocation, tenants can apply for the specific parcel of land being occupied by the tenant or for land that was occupied by the tenant or predecessors for a period of five years prior to the commencement of the Act and of which they were illegally deprived.[51] They can also apply for rights in land elsewhere on the farm or in the vicinity which have been proposed by the owner. Servitudes of water, way or any other servitudes reasonably necessary or reasonably consistent with the rights previously enjoyed by the labour tenant may also be awarded.[52]

Enforcement of these rights starts by lodging a claim with the Director-General of Land Affairs, after which notice is given to the landowner, who is entitled to dispute whether the claimant is a labour tenant. If the landowner does not dispute the claimant's status, he is deemed to have admitted that the claimant is a labour tenant and this admission will be sufficient proof of that fact in any proceedings in court. If the applicant's status is indeed questioned, either party is entitled to institute proceedings in court for an order determining the issue.

Once the question concerning labour tenancy is settled, the owner may submit to the Director-General alternative proposals for an equitable means of disposing of the claim other than by the acquisition of a right in the affected land. An arbitrator may be appointed to discuss any proposals.[53] However, any proposal may be rejected by the claimant as he may persist with the original claim. If the matter is not resolved, the claimant may institute court proceedings for an order or apply to court for appropriate relief. The court may then order the owner to transfer a right or rights in land to the claimant. In that event the court must determine the definition and nature of the right(s), the compensation to be paid by the claimant, the manner and period of payment, the time when the right(s) shall pass to the claimant and any other matter which requires regulation.

In the process of determining the nature of the order to be made by the court various factors will be taken into account:[54]

(i)   the desirability of assisting labour tenants to establish themselves on farms on a viable and sustainable basis;

(ii)   the achievement of the goals of the Act;

(iii)   the requirements of equity and justice;

(iv)   the willingness of the owner of affected land and the applicant to make a reasonable contribution; and

(v)   the report and any determination made by the arbitrator.

The owner is entitled to just and equitable compensation "as contemplated in the Constitution".[55] In the absence of an agreement the compensation will be determined by the court.

Discussion of the Act

The formulation, discussion and implementation of the Act were met with fierce opposition especially from agricultural unions and landowners. The following aspects were identified as major concerns:

(i)   that it was unthinkable that landowners had to undergo financial expense to defend their rights in court when a claim was instituted against their land: the potential huge legal costs were unacceptable;

(ii)   the state was in effect side-stepping its own responsibility in addressing landlessness and providing housing;

(iii)   the implementation of the Act would influence the land market negatively;

(iv)   the implementation of the Act would lead to the expropriation and fragmentation of valuable agricultural land;[56]

(v)   criticism was raised concerning the taking away of powers of the lower courts and transferring them to the Land Claims Court: it was argued that this court could only operate in the interim and that it would also lead to the inflation of legal costs;

(vi)   further, concerns at the lack of credibility the Land Claims Court has in the eyes of the farming community;

(vii)   that the minister should be drawn into agreements traditionally between the farmer and the worker only was found to be unacceptable.

The undemocratic way in which the Act was implemented was particularly criticised, making the implementation a very contentious issue. The farming community also commented on the fact that labour tenancy has been outlawed for decades, but that the Act now serves to perpetuate it as a legal practice. The Minister has himself in the past referred to labour tenancy as a form of slavery, which he now acknowledges and legalises. The comment was made that the Minister ought to be asked whether he was promoting a form of slavery. In the former dispensation prior to the implementation of the Act the practice of labour tenancy could well have been equated to a form of slavery. That in itself was one of the motivations behind the implementation of the Act, the other being the extension of security of tenure. In view of the new formalised form of labour tenancy and the whole framework within which labour tenancy presently functions, the same equation could hardly hold water. The Act does not perpetuate the original form of labour tenancy with its numerous shortcomings, but a revised form in which the tenant has security of tenure and could become a landowner himself. For the person who has not applied for the acquisition of rights in land, the basic elements of labour tenancy remain the same; that is exchanging labour and service for utilising the land. The difference is that such a person can only be evicted in accordance with the Act. He may not have applied for the acquisition of rights, but has definite security of tenure. The labour tenant who successfully applies for the acquisition of rights does not fit in the traditional mode of labour tenancy since one of the basic elements, namely exchange of labour for the use of land, has lapsed. A successful applicant is technically not a labour tenant any more; he is an independent landowner.[57] He can still provide labour and service for the farm owner, but not on the traditional basis of labour tenancy. The implementation of the Act consequently introduced a totally new dispensation with regard to the provision of labour and services, as the Memorandum to the Bill clearly stated:

> The aim of the Bill is neither to promote nor to entrench the system, but to ensure that in the process of its transformation the basic human rights of all parties are protected under a stable legal system.

It was furthermore problematic for some sectors of the community to comprehend why legislative measures such as these should be drafted when it is uncertain how many people may benefit from it. The reason why it was uncertain as to how many labour tenants existed was that the institution had been outlawed and one would not easily admit to contravening legislative measures. The estimated number of labour tenants is 40,000.[58] (The correct numbers might be higher). This number will in all probability increase when more applications are published in the Government Gazette and more people realise that they fall within the ambit of the Act. It is interesting to note, however, that in 1997 only 277 applications were published in the Government Gazette under section 17(1) of the Act, concerning mainly the provinces of Mpumalanga and KwaZulu Natal.[59] It is furthermore uncertain as to how much effort has gone into informing potential labour tenants of their rights.

It was also argued that the implementation of the Act would lead to massive land invasions. However, the clearly defined entitlement to government subsidy is modified by the period over which the tenants must have lived on and worked the land which pre-empts precipitated land invasions.

With regard to the formulation of the Act, the following remarks might be made concerning the onus of proof. Although the act has been amended and the onus is probably lighter than prior to the amendment, it can still be very difficult in practice for a labour tenant to prove that he benefits more from living and working the land than from earning mainly wages.[60] It is imperative that precautions be taken against arbitrary quantifications in establishing the value of a tenant's use and occupation rights. For the tenant these aspects could in fact be worth far more than mere economic value.

Regardless of the criticisms raised against the Act and the shortcomings thereof, the necessity of the formulation and implementation of the Act speaks for itself considering the historical background. It should not only redress some of the historical imbalances due to the racially based land control system, but should also enable black people with a knowledge of agriculture to own land for the first time for productive and residential purposes. This step should automatically strengthen the fabric of rural society.[61]

Farm Workers - Extension of Security of Tenure Act 62 of 1997

The Extension of Security of Tenure Bill 47 of 1997 was first issued for public information and comment on 4th February, 1997.[62] The Extension Act 62 of 1997 was eventually assented to on 19th November, 1997 and published on 28th November, 1997.[63] Similarly to the commencement of the labour tenancy legislation, the publication and commencement of this Act have drawn strong criticism from organised agricultural unions and several political parties. The preamble to the Act states that many South Africans presently do not have security of tenure of their homes and land and are consequently vulnerable to unfair eviction and that these evictions have led and will continue to lead to great hardship, conflict and social instability. It is therefore desirable that the law should promote the achievement of long term security of tenure for occupiers of land and that the rights of such occupiers should be extended. Due recognition to the rights, duties and legitimate interests of owners, however, will also feature. The law should further regulate the eviction of vulnerable occupiers in a fair manner while recognising the owners' right to apply to court for eviction orders.

Scope and Application of the Act

The Act, forming part of the land tenure reform programme, applies in rural areas, nation-wide.[64] The provisions of the Act are not applicable to land in a township established, approved, proclaimed or otherwise recognised in the terms of any law. The Act is, however, applicable to any land within a township (of any sort) that has been designated for agricultural purposes and any land within a township which has been established, approved, proclaimed or otherwise recognised after 4th February, 1997[65] - only if the relevant person was an occupier immediately prior to the establishment, approval, proclamation or recognition.[66] The Act therefore in essence applies to rural areas only and not urban areas and aims to protect all people living on such land.

"Occupier" Under the Act

The following is the meaning of "occupier":

> a person residing on land which belongs to another person, and who has or on 4th February, 1997 (or thereafter) had consent or another right in law to do so.[67]

> The Act specifically excludes the following categories of persons:

(i)   labour tenants,[68]

(ii)   a person using or intending to use the land mainly for industrial, mining, commercial or commercial farming purposes,

(iii)   a person who has an income exceeding R5000 per month.[69]

With regard to being an occupier, section 3(4) provides that for the purposes of civil proceedings under this Act, a person who has continuously and openly resided on land for a period of one year shall be presumed to have consent unless the contrary is proved.

Thus, if a person falls within the above-mentioned categories or has been residing openly for a year and the land in question is rural land, the Act is then applicable and the provisions may be utilised to extend these persons' security of tenure.

Long Term Security of Tenure

Chapter II[70] deals with the measures to facilitate long term security of tenure for occupiers. It targets projects which are aimed at providing long term security of tenure for funding, subject to the conditions the Minister may determine. Either on-site or off-site developments can take place with the assistance of the Minister of Land Affairs.[71] The latter occurs where the development provides the occupants with an independent tenure right on land owned by someone other than the owner of the land on which they resided immediately prior to the development. Priority will be given to applications which accommodate the interests of occupiers and landowners and which are cost-effective. If the development is not on the farm, satisfactory reasons must be provided why an on-farm development is not feasible.

Section 26(1) confirms the powers of the Minister of Land Affairs to exercise equivalent powers to those exercised under the Expropriation Act 63 of 1975 to enable developments in accordance with the Act. However, all expropriations for the purposes of this Act have to be preceded by a hearing[72] and compensation has to be paid with due regard to the Constitution[73] and sections 12(3)-(5) of the Expropriation Act.[74] The issuing of regulations and guidelines by the Minister is provided for in section 28 of the Act.

Although similar, the main difference between this subsidy and the general land acquisition grant lies in the implementing agent. Land acquisition grants may be used in private sector development, subsidies granted under this Act will only be paid to the local government who may contract private sector firms to undertake development.[75]

Rights and Duties of Occupiers and Owners

Chapter III sets out the rights and duties of occupiers and owners. General rights for owners, persons in charge of the property and occupiers are set out in section 5. These include the right to human dignity, freedom and security of person, privacy, freedom of religion, freedom of belief and expression of opinion, freedom of association and freedom of movement. An occupier further has the right to reside on the land and utilise it in a balanced way with the right of the owner or the person in charge.[76] A list of special rights and privileges are set out in section 6(2) (*eg* to receive postal or other communication, to enjoy family life, *etc*). It is clearly intended to limit the exercise of property rights of landowners. The introduction of the reasonable and justifiable limitation provides further means whereby the Land Claims Court can demarcate between competing rights of the worker and the landowner. This constitutes an intervention which could threaten traditional paternalism and foster a rights culture in rural areas.

An occupier is prohibited from intentionally and unlawfully causing harm to other persons or material damage to property.[77] The rights of owners are likewise set out in section 7 of the Act.

Termination of Rights and Evictions

Chapter IV deals with the termination of rights and evictions. As mentioned earlier, the main aim of the Act is to provide for security of tenure. Naturally this would imply that occupational rights may only be terminated under certain conditions and that evictions would only be possible under provisions of the Act. Provision is made for two categories of evictions: (a) for persons who were occupiers on 4th February, 1997[78] and (b) persons who became occupiers after that date.[79] In general the right of residency may be terminated on any legal ground.[80] These would include *inter alia*

(i)   if the occupier breached section 6(3) relating to the prohibitions placed on occupiers (*eg* the intentional causing of harm or damage);

(ii) when the occupier has breached a material and fair term of the agreement reached by the occupier and owner where the owner has fulfilled the agreement;[81]

(iii) where the occupier has committed such a fundamental breach of the relationship between him and the owner that it is not practically possible to remedy it;[82] or

(iv) where the occupier was an employee whose right of residence arose solely from that employment and has voluntarily resigned in circumstances that do not amount to a constructive dismissal in the terms of the Labour Relations Act 66 of 1995.[83]

Section 8 will also apply to occupiers who have been granted permission to stay on the land, but who do not work for the owner.

The right of residence of an occupier who has resided on the land for ten years and who has reached the age of 60 may normally not be terminated unless the occupier has committed a breach contemplated in section 10(1)(a)-(c). If there is no legal ground for eviction, an occupier may therefore not be evicted merely on the ground of old age. (This prohibition does not protect pensioners or the disabled who cause malicious damage or cause harm to others.) This limited real right of the occupier is sometimes extended beyond his lifetime, as section 8(5) provides that the right of residence of the occupier's spouse or dependant may only be terminated on 12 calendar months' written notice to leave the land, unless such a spouse or dependant has committed a breach contemplated in section 10(1) of the Act. The court also has a discretion to grant an eviction order on shorter notice if it is of the opinion that the owner of the land will be unfairly prejudiced.

Section 24 states that the rights of occupiers are binding on successors in title.

The Lodging of Eviction Orders

When an application for an eviction order is lodged, various factors have to be taken into account, *inter alia* the fairness of any agreement, provision in an agreement or provision of law on which the owner or person in charge relies, the conduct of the parties giving rise to the termination, the interests of the parties and the fairness of the procedure followed by the owner or person in charge.[84] Despite the legal termination of the right to occupy, the person seeking an eviction order must also satisfy the court that the eviction would be fair. A court that orders eviction shall determine a just and equitable date on which vacation shall take place and determine a date on which the eviction order may be carried out if the occupier has not vacated the land on the date contemplated earlier.[85] When determining these dates, the court has to consider all relevant factors - fairness and the balance of the interests of the parties being only two of these factors.[86]

An eviction order can coincide with orders regarding the payment of compensation for structures and buildings erected by the occupier, as well as compensation for improvements or crops planted by the occupier.[87] The payment of any outstanding wages or other related amounts may also form part of the eviction order.[88]

Urgent Eviction Proceedings

Apart from the usual eviction proceedings, provision is also made for urgent eviction proceedings.[89] Such an order may be granted in identical circumstances as those of the Labour Tenancy legislation.[90]

Dispute Resolution and Courts

Chapter V deals with dispute resolution and courts. Applications for evictions or for the restoration of residence and use of land, can either be made in the magistrate's court for the area concerned or in the Land Claims Court.[91] The Land Claims Court[92] has jurisdiction under the Act throughout the Republic and has all the ancillary powers necessary or reasonably incidental to the performance of its functions, including the power to decide on any constitutional matter in relation to the Act, to grant interlocutory orders, declaratory orders and interdicts, to review acts, omissions and decisions of any functionary acting or purporting to act under the Act and to review arbitration awards. If all parties to the proceedings agree, applications can also be made in the Provincial High Court.[93]

Mediation is provided for in section 21 of the Act. By this section any party may request the Director-General to appoint one or more persons to facilitate meetings of interested parties and to attempt to mediate and settle disputes. If the parties to a dispute under the Act refer the dispute to arbitration under the terms of the Arbitration Act 42 of 1965, they may appoint as arbitrator a person from the panel of arbitrators established by section 31(1) of the Land Reform (Labour Tenants) Act 3 of 1996.[94]

Reinstatement

Any person who has been evicted contrary to the provisions of this Act may apply for reinstatement under section 14(3) of the Act. A reinstatement order may be issued on such terms as the court deems just. Such an order may include provisions regarding the repair, reconstruction or replacement of any building or structure and the payment of compensation.

Discussion of the Act

Although the basic intent of the Act to provide tenure protection was sound, the lack of prior consultation with interested parties and general lack of transparency were found to be serious concerns by some sectors of the population. Other objections to the Act included:

(i)   the vast powers of dispossession of the Minister of Land Affairs,
(ii)   the availability and acceptability of alternative accommodation as a prerequisite for eviction procedures,[95]
(iii)   unfair onus of proof on landowners,
(iv)   virtual scrapping of the Prevention of Illegal Squatting Act 52 of 1951 without providing alternative measures,
(v)   the burden of unwanted occupiers on land,
(vi)   allegations that the state is shirking responsibility by dumping the provision of land and housing in the laps of farmers and local government,
(vii)   arguments that the Labour Relations Act 66 of 1995 gives adequate protection to employees regarding lawful termination of their employment contracts and that there is no necessity of protecting employees' rights any further,

(viii)   concerns that the implementation of the Act would reduce the market value of farm land, and

(ix)   that new owners would have to endure unwanted occupiers on their land.

The implementation of the Act necessarily entails a working partnership between landowners and local government to provide housing, financed by the Departments of Housing and Land Affairs.   Local Government does not, however, automatically have the expertise to facilitate these new developments. It is likely that there will be some delay in getting the necessary mechanisms up and running. Although the aim of the Act is sound, it could take some time before the benefits are reaped. It will also depend on the specific circumstances which development schemes will be more effective. In intensively cultivated areas such as the Western Cape province, agri-villages would probably be very sensible. In regions where farms are huge, agri-villages would probably not be as efficient and other solutions may have to be created, depending on the circumstances. Another factor that might become an obstacle is the lack of finance.   Although R200-R300 million have been allocated for land redistribution in 1997-1998, it could still turn out to be inadequate.[96]

It cannot be denied that the implementation of the Act goes a long way in limiting the exercise of property rights by creating basic rights for occupiers of rural land and preventing their unfair eviction. This step in itself has many positive consequences, most notably the creation of a rights culture in rural areas, previously non-existent.

Despite the positive effect of the Act in general various problems still remain: farm occupants are still not provided with real tenure security. While the Act makes it more difficult to evict occupants from farm housing, evictions are still possible in many instances. Given their locality on private property and the history of power relations that have operated between farmers and workers, farm dwellers may face particular restraints in accessing housing and development opportunities. The need for mechanisms to be set in place by the Department of Land Affairs that will ensure the facilitation of on-site developments where the property owner does not take the initiative, has to be specifically noted in the Act.

The separation of occupational rights from employment contracts needs to be further promoted.

It is also interesting to note that there is no built-in protection for dwellers in cases where the landowners apply for the re-zoning of land. This would entail re-zoning the land from agricultural to residential use.

Residential or urban areas are particularly excluded from the application of the Act. A re-zoning would have the effect that occupiers lose the protection of the Act. The Act ought to stipulate that the Department be notified of any re-zoning application and that the rights of occupiers would not be extinguished through such an application.

The most critical section of the Act is the one providing for measures to facilitate long term security of tenure. However, it does not receive the necessary attention. The Act does not clearly define what is meant by "on-site" and "off-site" development. It furthermore fails to identify the various actions required on behalf of the various levels of government to facilitate the different forms of development. It also refrains from identifying the services different levels of government are obliged to provide to facilitate access to tenure security and housing. The jurisdiction of local government over on-site developments needs to be clearly stated. It would also have been very useful if the Act created an enabling framework for an integrated approach to rural development. The commitment to link initiatives to the facilitation of sustainable rural livelihoods is imperative and needs to be stated. Measures to facilitate appropriate land use planning need to be included.

The Act does not identify the measures the various tiers of government need to take in order to ensure that farm dwellers are aware of their rights. The protective measures with regard to the prevention of unfair evictions assumes a knowledge of rights and an ability to enforce these rights.

The housing subsidy granted by the state is too little to ensure farm workers a real right in housing, unless farmers or financial institutions are prepared to make up the shortfall. It is highly unlikely that loans from financial institutions would be secured, in light of the low wages earned by farm workers. There will undoubtedly be much reliance on farmer co-operation and assistance in order to achieve real security of tenure for workers.

Evicted workers are likely to seek accommodation in municipal areas. There is already a huge backlog in the provision of housing, consequently farm workers are given a low priority on waiting lists.

Classification of Newly Developed Rights

Legal development has occurred *inter alia* with regard to the rights of labour tenants, farm workers and other occupiers of land of which they were not the registered owners. How are these new rights to be classified within the current property law system in South Africa?

There is no *numerus clausus* of limited real rights in South African law.[97] New *iura in re aliena* can be developed if need be. According to the tests usually applied to determine whether a right is real or personal, for example the subtraction from *dominium* test,[98] it is argued that the land reform programme led to the development of new limited real rights. The Extension of Security of Tenure Act 62 of 1997 guarantees long term security of tenure rights. Persons who vest this right, are occupiers on land of which they are not the registered owners. However, the occupier indeed vests a special right enforceable against the landowner as well as the successors in title. The content of the tenure right includes the right to use a specific parcel of land, reside on it and to have access to services. The special rights referred to above (*eg* right to family life, *etc*), are also included. This tenure right may only be terminated on a valid ground and only if termination is fair and reasonable in the particular circumstances. In some instances occupiers vest a permanent tenure right in that they cannot be evicted after ten years of service and when they have reached the age of 60. Following the death of the occupier, his spouse and dependants can remain on the land for another 12 months. If eviction occurs the eviction order can contain particulars regarding the payment of compensation for improvements and structures erected by the occupant. This right may also be expropriated in accordance with the provisions of the Expropriation Act 75 of 1963.

Similar developments have occurred with regard to labour tenants. When a labour tenant exchanges his labour and services for the right to utilise and cultivate the land, he in fact vests a limited real right enforceable against the landowner. When he is successful with an application to acquire ownership of the specific parcel of land, he is technically a labour tenant no longer, but an independent landowner himself.

Conclusion

As a result of racially and gender structured discriminatory legislation and practices, female and male farm workers and rural dwellers in South Africa experience extremely tenuous access to land and housing. As occupiers of private land their position is even more precarious. Due to their locality and marginalisation within rural society, they are excluded from urban and rural town housing markets and subsidy processes. These factors appear to have played a role in their falling between the cracks of the land reform programme in general.

It was therefore imperative that specific legislation addressing these problem areas be formulated and implemented. It is envisaged that these legislative measures should act as an enabling framework to ensure participation of all stakeholders in the provision of long term security of labour tenants and farm workers. New real rights are developed that are enforceable against landowners and third parties in general. It is even possible for labour tenants to vest ownership in land resulting in a new dispensation regarding traditional labour tenancy. Although the positive effects of the legislation introduced in 1996 and 1997 cannot be denied, various problems, especially regarding the practical implementation thereof, remain.

Notes

1   Originally the Natives Land Act 27 of 1913.
2   Originally the Bantu Trust and Land Act 18 of 1936.
3   Letsoale EM *Land Reform in South Africa* Skotaville Publishers (Johannesburg 1987) i.
4   See in general Letsoale *Land Reform in South Africa* 4; Bennett TW "African Land - A History of Dispossession" in *Southern Cross - Civil and Common Law in South Africa* Zimmermann R and Visser D (eds) Juta (Cape Town 1996) 65-94; Cross C and Haines R (eds) *Towards Freehold: Options for Land and Development in Black Rural Areas* Juta (Cape Town 1988). See also Ng'ong'ola C "Land Tenure Reform in Botswana: Post-colonial Developments and Future Prospects" 1996 SA Public Law 1-29.
5   For example, 0.76 million out of the 69 million hectares in Transvaal and 0.84 hectares of the 5 million in Natal. See also Letsoale *Land Reform in South Africa* 33.
6   Binswanger HP and Deiniger K "South African Land Policy: the Legacy of History and Current Options" in *Land, Property Rights and the New Constitution* Community Law Centre University of the Western Cape (1993) 104. This point can be further illustrated with reference to the position in Natal in the early 1800s: 55% of the native population lived as tenants - 35% on privately owned land and 20% on Crown land.
7   Also referred to as farming on the halves.
8   In some instances landowners were absent but their land was still being worked without them having to do any physical labour.
9   Provision was made for the removal of black squatters from public and private land. Furthermore, no more than three families were allowed on farm land.
10   This limited squatters to five families per farm.
11   Confirming the five-family rule.

12   As reflected by the 1904 statistics referring to Transvaal: of the 900,000 blacks in the Transvaal, 14% farmed their own land, 20% lived on Crown land and the majority - 50% - continued living as labour tenants on European-owned land (13% were in the reserves and 5% in wage employment).

13   It is interesting to note the effect that legislation had on the traditional communal tenure forms. Many colonial powers have interfered with the flexibility and adaptability of communal tenure systems and with the democratic institutions that prevailed in some of them. This was done by *inter alia* rigidly codifying the systems and by awarding hereditary rights to chiefs to manage land relations in the community and to allocate land to community members. See Davenport TRH *South Africa: A Modern History* Macmillan (Johannesburg 1987) 43-56. See also Letsoale *Land Reform in South Africa* 26-27 for a discussion concerning criticism that communal land ownership is inherently counter-productive.

14   Despite these provisions a general stipulation provided that share-crop agreements could remain in place for the time being. In the Cape province, Transvaal and Natal this arrangement prevailed for a limited time but in the Orange Free State share-croppers were evicted with the commencement of the Act.

15   The area for black occupation comprised 34,750 square miles, that is 7.3% of the total of land available. See Letsoale *Land Reform in South Africa* 35-36; Jaichand V *Restitution of Land Rights - A Workbook* Lex Patria (Johannesburg 1997) 10.

16   Davenport *Modern History* 176.

17   Davenport *Modern History* 334.

18   Beaumont (Native Lands) Commission (1916) - see Davenport *Modern History* 119, 178.

19   The Beaumont Commission proposed the acquisition of additional 27,000 square miles. The Act provided for an additional 24,000 square miles - Jaichand *Restitution of Land Rights* 11.

20   Letsoale *Land Reform in South Africa* 40.

21   Referred to as "black spots".

22   Recent figures show that it is still the case today: of the total of 1,051.2 million farm labourers in South Africa in 1992 14.9 were whites, 210.9 coloured and Asian and 825.4 blacks - Central Statistical Service: Agricultural Censuses and Surveys.

23   GN 2089 of September 1980.

24   WP-W-91.

25   The Abolition of Racially Based Land Measures Act 108 of 1991, the Upgrading of Tenure Right Act 112 of 1991 and the Less Formal Township Establishment Act 113 of 1991.

26   For example, different land control forms in the four national states (Transkei, Bophuthatswana, Venda and Ciskei), in the six self-governing territories (QwaQwa, Gazankulu, Lebowa, KwaNdebele, KwaZulu and KaNgwane) and in areas under the trusteeship of the South African Development Trust. With regard to aspects such as town planning and development, diversity of legislative measures increased in that the various provinces promulgated own measures.

27   See in general Hamman J "A Guide to the Extension of Security of Tenure Bill" Centre for Rural Legal Studies, Stellenbosch (1997).

28   Sections 121-123 of the Constitution of the Republic of South Africa 200 of 1993 made provision for the programme and the formulation of legislation. The legal basis

of the land reform programme is presently section 25(5)-(7) of the Constitution of the Republic of South Africa 108 of 1996.

29   The passage of the bill through parliament was met with fierce criticism mainly from agricultural unions - see discussion of the Act at p 316 *et seq*, *supra*.

30   "A person or community whose tenure is legally insecure as result of past racially discriminatory laws or practices is entitled, to the extent provided for by an Act of Parliament, either to tenure which is legally secure or to comparable redress."

31   Section 1(xi).

32   See *Mahlangu v De Jager* 1996 (3) SA 235 (LCC) - 242 E-F.

33   See also Pienaar JM "Land Reform, Labour Tenants and the Application of the Land Reform (Labour Tenants) Act 3 of 1996" 1997(3) TSAR 538-548 with reference to *Mahlangu v De Jager* 1996 (3) SA 235 (LCC).

34   1996 (3) SA 235 (LCC) at 241C-242A.

35   1996 (4) SA 1236 (LCC) at 1253E-1258B.

36   1998 (1) SA 406 NPD. The case was decided during February and March 1997.

37   1998 (1) SA 411 NPD. The case was decided during June and July 1997.

38   At 419G-J.

39   The date of first publication of the Bill. This date is important since it coincided with large scale evictions of labourers from farms.

40   Section 3(1).

41   Section 3(2)(a)-(d).

42   Section 7.

43   Section 15.

44   Section 6(1) - the lessee can act with the support of the landowner.

45   Section 9(3).

46   Section 10.

47   Section 8(5).

48   Section 12(3)(b).

49   Section 12(d)(a)-(d).

50   Advances and subsidies made available under section 26 of the Act.

51   Section 16(1)(a)-(b).

52   Section 16(1)(d).

53   The President of the Land Claims Court has, under section 20 of the Act, prescribed rules regulating the procedure to be followed in arbitrations conducted under the Act (GN 299 in Government Gazette 17804 of 21st February, 1997).

54   Section 22(5).

55   Relevant factors include the following - section 25(3): the current use of the property, the history of the acquisition and use of the property, the market value of the property, the extent of direct state investment and subsidy in the acquisition and beneficial capital improvement of the property and the purpose of the expropriation.

56   The provisions of the Subdivision of Agricultural Land Act 70 of 1970 (or other legislation relating to the subdivision of land) are not applicable in cases where the court or arbitrator orders that any land, right in land or servitudes be awarded to an applicant - section 40 of the Act.

57   Once ownership has been acquired or other rights in land vested in the labour tenant, his or her rights as a labour tenant lapse in accordance with section 3(2)(d) of the Act.

58   "Labour tenants: defusing conflict" Financial Mail; vol 139, 26th January, 1996, p 36.

59   Especially in the district of Vryheid.
60   Which would make the person a farm worker resulting in the non-applicability of the
      Land Reform (Labour Tenants) Act 3 of 1996.
61   "Labour tenants: defusing conflict" Financial Mail; vol 139, 26th January, 1996 p 35-
      36.
62   General Notice 285 in Government Gazette 17773 of 4th February, 1997.
63   In Government Gazette 18467 of 28th November, 1997.
64   Section 2.
65   The date of first publication.
66   Section 2(1).
67   Section 1.
68   Already provided for, see the discussion above.
69   Section 1(1)(x)(c).
70   Section 4.
71   Section 4(1).
72   Section 26(2).
73   See p 315, *supra*.
74   Section 26(3).
75   Hamman J *Guide to the Extension of Security of Tenure Bill* Centre for Rural Legal
      Studies (Stellenbosch 1997) p 10.
76   Section 6(1).
77   Section 6(3).
78   Section 10.
79   Section 11.
80   Section 8(1).
81   Section 10(1)(b).
82   Section 10(1)(c).
83   Section 10(1)(d).
84   Section 8(1).
85   Section 12(1).
86   Section 12(2).
87   Section 13(1)(a).
88   Section 13(1)(b).
89   Section 15.
90   In cases where there is real and imminent danger of substantial injury or damage to
      any person or property if eviction does not take place, if there is no other remedy
      available and if the likely hardship to the owner exceeds the likely hardship to the
      occupier if the order is not granted.
91   Section 17(1).
92   Section 20.
93   Section 17(2).
94   Section 22(1).
95   This would apply where the right to occupy was terminated due to no fault or choice
      of the occupier (*eg* a retrenchment exercise of the farmer). In these cases suitable
      alternative accommodation has to be provided by the landowner. Alternative
      accommodation entails accommodation that is safe and no less favourable than
      previous accommodation and suitable, having regard to the reasonable needs of

occupiers, their joint earning abilities and the need to live close enough to employment opportunities or other economic activities.

96   "Farm workers: whose responsibility?" Financial Mail vol 143, 7th February, 1997, p 36. The amount allocated includes putting farm workers into business for themselves by buying farms as well as building houses for the lawfully evicted.

97   Van der Merwe CG *Sakereg* Butterworths (Durban 1989) 63; Olivier NJJ, Pienaar GJ and Van der Walt AJ *Law of Property Students' Handbook* Juta (Cape Town 1992) 26; Van der Walt AJ *Law of Property Casebook for Students* Juta (Cape Town 1995) 1; 11.

98   Sonnekus JC and Neels JL *Sakereg Vonnisbundel* Butterworths (Durban 1994) 102-120; Van der Walt *Casebook* 1, 11.

14 Finland's New Electronic Title and Mortgage Register

MATTI ILMARI NIEMI

The 1995 Land Law Reform

Land law was completely reformed in Finland in 1995. An essential part of this new law is the *Land Code* (statute 540/1995) which came into effect on 1st January, 1997 and replaced the old land code of the Swedish General Code of 1734. The new Code regulates the conveyancing of real estate, the positions of the parties and their relationships to third parties, registration of acquisitions of ownership and agreement-based encumbrances of estates and the mortgage system. At the same time, some other important new statutes were enacted and many changes made in several other statutes. This was a reform of law and not a land reform, which would have affected the bases of land ownership.

Conveyancing of real estate has been strictly controlled and rigidly regulated for a long time in Finland. The new law relaxes the formalities to some extent but, on the other hand, contains a larger catalogue of prohibited provisions than earlier. Notable reforms are the modern regulation of conditional sale, the drawing of a parallel between a parcel of land and an entire piece of real estate, the strengthening of the positions of holders of limited property rights and the adoption of a new mortgage system based on the Swedish model.

The most important reform concerning the register is, in accordance with the models of Germany and other Nordic Countries, *the public trustworthiness (publica fides) of the Title and Mortgage Register* and its *electronic implementation*.

However, the principle of public trustworthiness is not taken as absolute but, rather, is combined with the principle of *good faith (bona fides)*. This signifies that a person who has trusted information in a register is protected, even if it becomes apparent that the recorded rights were not valid or that the power of the person making the transaction was defective. In contrast, if he actually had proper information or he had reason to be suspicious of data in the register, he is not protected. Besides the acquisition of ownership, the transferees of the limited property rights, which are important in practice, can enjoy this same protection. In cases of exception, where protection is not granted, material protection is provided through the *damage compensation liability of the state*.

The reforms signify a very broad and efficient real estate *information system* for both authorities and private individuals. Obtaining information for private individuals was inefficient and slow prior to the reform. Efficiency for the authorities has been improved, too. Both the provision of information and the supervision of real estate are so efficient that we can speak of a bureaucratic power base. An efficient data processing system allows for highly efficient monitoring by the authorities. "Big Brother is watching all the time and sees everything".

However, monitoring also helps to protect various rights of people and prevent the loss of those rights. From this point of view we can speak of *a social register law*. The official's active supervision of property rights and, for example, their rapid publication is the reverse side of the public trustworthiness.

Registers

The register system had already been reformed between 1985 and 1997, before the new Land Code. This first phase of register reform involved the transfer of information onto the electronic register, adopting decision making by register entries and other changes in the registration process. The second phase of the reform consisted of the changes in the registration methods made in the new Land Code.

Before the reform, maintenance of registers was decentralised amongst local authorities. In practice, every authority had its own register. Unit-based registers, which were maintained by courts, were unofficial. Registration occurred, in principle, in the same manner as other court decisions, by making an entry in the manual minute books. This resulted in, for example, mortgages having to be renewed every ten years on the threat of their expiration.

The new registers are *national, electronic* and *unit specific*. In addition to the operating database there is also a back-up. The decision making process occurs in data entry form, and every entry is immediately seen at all workstations. The job of judges and lawyers is, nowadays, to work at computer terminals and networks. For example, most of the information needed for the registration of the title is obtained directly off a computer network.

The division between the *unit* and *judicial* sides has still been preserved. As a matter of fact, there are two separate registers, although from the point of view of the judicial side they are combined. This means that holdings as such, as certain registered areas, and as concrete objects (*res corporales*) in legal processes are recorded in the *Real Estate Register* (cadastral) maintained by the survey administration. Conveyed areas (parcels) and each piece of real estate, when constituted in a survey process, are recorded in the register as *units*. Easements are recorded as well. This register is national and in electronic form, too. The Real Estate Register is a part of the judicial register, that is, the *Title and Mortgage Register*. Information on the units forms the basis for the legal process and for the judicial register, the basis of the *rights* of individuals (*iura*), ownerships, limited property rights and securities. The register also features in municipal planning and in other information related to estates. I will concentrate only on the judicial side.

The Finnish Title and Mortgage Register is national, that is, it is *centralised, public* and *maintained by authorities*. A modern electronic register can, however, be based on rather different principles. In 1991 Finland started to use the share and mutual bonds *value-share system* (statutes 826 and 827/1991) based on the example provided by the other Nordic Countries. This system is decentralised, non-public and privately maintained. Banks are important registrars. The system includes shares of all exchange-listed and other larger limited companies.

The value-share system is *paper free*. Shares, rights to those shares, and bonds appear on both computer monitors and statements (extracts), but no other forms of security papers or documentation are used. The system operates under principles similar to those used in modern bank accounts and electronic money. Shares and bonds are transferred electronically from one account to another. Security rights, distraints and bankruptcies are marked in the accounts as burdens of the shares or bonds. The tradition (in most cases the normal conveyance of possession) of security papers has been replaced by account entries. There are many problems associated with this regulation and the statutes have been changed frequently. In addition, plans are being made to centralise the system.

There is a general *obligation to know the information included in the Title and Mortgage Register* in Finland. This is an implication of the principle of public trustworthiness. As a general rule, no one can be in good faith regarding a right or other information which appears in the register. In practice, this applies to purchasers, other transferees and creditors. Obtaining register information is, as a matter of fact, quite easy. The authorities and many private companies, who continually make agreements concerning real estate (for example banks, insurance companies and real estate agents) have *direct access* to the register. Everyone with this access can follow events at their own workstations in real time and take unofficial paper extracts. However, only regionally authorised officials who make decisions can enter new information onto the register and alter old data. Official extracts can be provided by numerous officials irrespective of the location of the estates.

Conveyances of Real Estate

One distinctively Finnish feature of the system is what is known as *"corroboration of sales."* In Sweden they also planned to adopt this practice, but the idea was dropped. This system ties ownership conveyances directly to the registration. The conveyance of a piece of real estate or a part thereof has to be done in writing, the most important conditions must be written into the document, and the transaction has to be witnessed by a particular official known as a *Public Corroborator of Sales* (a special kind of Notary Public). Neglecting this regulation makes the conveyance void, and the acquisition cannot be registered.

The Corroborator informs several official agencies of the conveyance within a week. These, in turn, forward this information so that in practice all authorities concerned with issues relating to real estate receive details of the transfer very soon. In practice, notification is carried out on computer terminals directly into the registration system and to the designated recipients. The transfer will also be seen very soon in the Title and Mortgage Register. This is the so-called *"acquisition information"* registration, but this phase does not yet constitute the actual registration of title. Acquisition information has, however, a notable *legal effect* because after registration it is considered as having come to the attention of all. In fact, the acquisition information is the quickest way to publish a transfer.

It is also a duty of the Corroborator, to a certain and limited extent, to investigate the *validity of a sale*. At the point of sale he can ensure the observance of the rules of form, note possible lack of consent, confirm the identity of the parties or their representatives and check the correct date of the conveyance. This is intended to prevent invalid agreements. The investigation of the Corroborator supplements the broader investigation of the title registration. During the latter, however, one can use only register information and written documents. Correspondingly, the stronger legal effects are connected with the title registration. For example, the faith of a purchaser in the registered title of the vendor is protected, and the registration granted to the purchaser immediately corrects errors of form in his deed.

Registration of Titles

The Quickening and Expansion of Registration

One of the major faults of the earlier system was the slow and imperfect registration of titles. The registration period as such was reasonably short but numerous exceptions, which deferred the commencement of the period, could result in decades of delay. There were two principles: the obligation to register applied only when the title of the transferee was final and complete, and the right to register began at the same time as the obligation. Moreover, because the acquisition information was unknown very often the register did not display the correct ownership of real estate. On the other hand, the principle of public trustworthiness was not in existence.

In Sweden, in some cases, they have tried to solve this problem by allowing registration noticeably earlier than the obligation begins. In Finland both the obligation and the right to register are still considered as one but from Sweden we have adopted the so-called *resting procedure* (a special kind of postponement procedure or a qualified title). This procedure is used when the deed or other documents provide evidence that prevents the final title and registration (absolute title) from being granted and the hindrance is mentioned in the Land Code as a reason for resting. These reasons are the most common limitations of the transferee's title but are generally temporary in nature. The transferee has to apply for registration within the normal period, six months after making the deed of conveyance, even though the final and affirmative decision cannot yet be made. The application is postponed; that is, an interim decision is issued.

The general aim is a quick and comprehensive announcement of changes in legal relations concerning real estate. One method is to enter the application into the register on the same day as the application is made, even when this would result in a resting procedure or the applicant would be ordered to *supplement* his application. The latter has some similarities to the British possessory title.

A notable change is the *obligation to register* a conveyed *right of use* to an estate. It is registered as a burden of ownership. This usually refers to a *lease* and the obligation is parallel to the traditional obligation to register the title of ownership. This obligation is, however, limited to rights in which the holder is allowed to build and where the right and the holder's buildings may be used as loan security. Holders of the other practically important rights of use have an entitlement to register their rights. All registrable types of rights are mentioned in the Land Code (*numerus clausus*). The concept of settlement is unknown in Finland, but there are some statutes which grant similar rights or burdens of estates.

Conditional Sale

Conditional contracts for the sale of real estate are regulated in Finland as they are in Sweden. They refer to a form of agreement in which one of the parties has reserved the right to *rescind the contract*, or as often in the wording of an agreement, *the vendor retains ownership*, for example, until the purchaser has paid the entire price. These types of conditions are considered equivalents with respect to their regulation.

The essential principles are as follows: conditionality has a fixed period of validity, at the most five years; the term is understood to be a *security for price receivable* (a real or property security), when the vendor has provided the purchaser with credit in the form of a payment period; during the intermediate state, that is, as long as the conditionality lasts, the *purchaser is considered the owner* of the estate, although, according to the wording, the vendor has retained ownership. As a matter of fact and despite the suspension of transfer of ownership by the wording, the vendor retains only the right to rescind the agreement and regain ownership. During the intermediate state, the purchaser is seen to have *conditional ownership*, which is limited by the right of the vendor to rescind the contract on the agreed basis. The owner's possession is viewed as transferred immediately to the purchaser although there is a term of remaining limited possession for the vendor for a fixed period. If the parties want to establish a stronger position for the vendor and, at the same time, to commit themselves to a binding sale in the future, a preliminary agreement (*pactum de contrahendo*) has to be made.

The above-mentioned maximum period is substantive and mandatory in that its expiration nullifies the right of the vendor to rescind the agreement even if the agreed period is longer or if no time limit is set at all. This means an *"automatic procedure"* in which the purchaser's conditional ownership develops into an absolute one, the vendor's right to rescind is lost and the purchaser's name is entered in the register as the normal owner at the close of the period.

The purchaser in a conditional sale has to apply for title registration within the normal fixed period after making the contract, but the application has to be made to rest for the conditional period. When the intermediate period has ended, after five years or less, the computer program decides that the issue must once more be raised for final decision, and the purchaser is granted final title registration to the estate directly by the registration authorities (*ex officio*). Conditionality, or the intermediate state, can terminate by returning the ownership to the vendor only if the parties have made a voluntary agreement to rescind in the same form as the original sale or through a court decision. Hence, the rescinding of the sale and the return of ownership is also made public with the aid of the register.

During the intermediate state the purchaser has the *right to convey the estate* to another, but the right of the original vendor to rescind the contract and, for example, to claim the remaining debt for the sale price, binds and has effect on the new purchaser, too. The new purchaser will easily notice his predecessor's limited ownership (a special kind of qualified title) in the register. However, the purchaser cannot convey limited rights which burden the estate without the approval of the vendor.

The real estate is considered the property of the purchaser (limited ownership) during the intermediate state. The vendor's property is the right to rescind the sale and return the ownership on the agreed terms. These rights are considered the properties of the parties if they go into *bankruptcy*.

During the intermediate state the estate can be distrained by the execution authorities only for the debts of the purchaser. However, it is possible to distrain the estate for the vendor's debts if the creditor has a security right and the estate is mortgaged. Formally, the object of the distraint and the resulting compulsory auction is the real estate, even though the purchaser-debtor as the distrainee has only conditional ownership of that estate. The vendor's position is secure, however, and there are several alternatives open to him: he can keep the conditionality in effect, thus binding the compulsory auction buyer, too; he can, usually on the ground of prejudiced delay and irrespective of the distraint, claim rescission of the sale and regain ownership and possession; or he can claim payment for the entire price receivable at the compulsory auction. When the conditionality is bound to the payment of the sale price, the vendor is able to file his claim at the compulsory auction and he has a certain *priority, vis-á-vis* other debtors. As a security debtor, he has a particular *privileged* position. His priority is inferior to that of the mortgagee but better than other that of normal debtors. Only the receivables on the sale price with its securities or another right to rescind the sale can be distrained from the vendor.

The Sale of a Parcel of Land

The fact that publication of conveyances is more efficient than earlier is also seen in the obligation to register the received ownership to a parcel of land (*pars quanta*) within the normal fixed period. According to the old law the registration of the title of a parcel of land used to take place only after the parcel had been transformed into a registered estate or some other form of surveying proceeding had occurred.

The purchaser of a parcel of land now has just as strong a position as the purchases of a registered piece of real estate. Earlier, the parcel was, according to German doctrine, considered a constituent part of a legal thing (in this case a registered piece of real estate), and the right of the purchaser was focused as a right on that material part. The right of the purchaser was seen as weak, and being based on an agreement only, and as an ability to separate a certain material part from a thing (a right *in personam*). Ultimately, this kind of right was included in the law of obligations, not in the property law as normal form of ownership (a right *in rem*).

Nowadays, registration is directly related to the initiative of the authorities, where the person receiving a parcel is guided in the surveying proceeding and the title registration is granted for the newly constituted and registered real estate. First, acceptable conveyance requires the affirmation and notification of a competent Public Corroborator of Sales. Second, the obligation to register a title can be monitored through computer information. These phases are also applied to other forms of ownership conveyance. Third, the authorities initiate *ex officio* the procedure for the surveying proceeding without application when the receiver has been granted a registered title and the parcel is to become a new piece of real estate. However, the owner of the parcel may demand, with a statement of reason, that the proceeding be cancelled. Fourth, once the surveying proceeding is completed the registered title of the parcel is changed directly and *ex officio* into registered title to the real estate into which the parcel is transformed.

In other respects the conveyed parcel runs parallel to the registered real estate; it can be a registered base for mortgages and, in this way, be used as a security.

Real Estates as Security

This part of the new system in Finland has been adopted from Sweden. Conceptually, the creditor's security right to real estate resembles the right of lien over a movable thing, that is, a pledge.

Earlier, the Finnish system was based on the mortgaging of a promissory note. As a general rule, the one applying for a mortgage was the creditor who presented the note with the owner's acknowledgement of the debt and mortgage. This note was secured by a mortgage on the real estate, that is, it was registered. However, the registered note was normally only a proof of security and it could be reused later. In practice, the actual promissory note was not usually registered. The debtor had to sign another promissory note which showed the true sum of credit. Together these two notes indicated the credit and its security. Hence, the system was known as the dual promissory note procedure.

The new system recognises only one actual promissory note. The proper debt obligation remains a matter between the creditor and debtor only, and it may be verbal. Only the owner of the real estate or a conveyed parcel can apply for *a mortgage*. On the basis of his application he is granted a mortgage to a fixed sum and a document as a certificate is provided as proof of this. This document can be called a "*security deed*" (in Swedish *pantbrev*). A security deed is not a promissory note. It proves the existence of a mortgage and its sum and provides a fixed sum reserve as a part of the security value of a real estate (as a certificate). However, most important is that the *deed is a document for the possible use of the estate as a credit security*, to be delivered to creditors.

The essential idea of the securing of real estates and parcels is that an *owner*, after having received the security deed and by virtue of the value of his real estate, *conveys the security deed* as security *to the creditor* who, by the *tradition* of the deed, receives the position of a security creditor.

This operation presupposes also the existence of a security agreement and a granted credit. Instead of conveying the possession of the deed *traditio longa manu* and *brevi manu* may be used, but *constitutum possessorium* may not. Hence, in the hands of a creditor the document of the mortgage is a deed although it is not written by the owner. The parties can also use the so-called agreement of *general security*.

There is actually double publication in the forms of register and the tradition of security deed. The security deed can be reused later to obtain new credit. The creditor, when transferring his claim, can also transfer the security of that claim to another creditor (in practice the security deed and the promissory note together). By proving his receivables, usually in the form of a promissory note, and presenting the security deed the creditor legitimises his position as a mortgage creditor, *eg* at a compulsory auction.

In Finland, unlike in Sweden, possession of a security deed by the owner himself is not seen as providing security or constituting a dividend at a compulsory auction. Besides, the difference between the mortgage sum and the receivable amount is not an advantage to the owner, but it is for the benefit of the creditors with a poorer priority rating

A mortgage is granted to the owner by a court, but a mortgage and a security deed as such are only formalities and necessary phases in establishing the proper security. The actual substantive security is established between the owner and the creditor on the ground of a security agreement. The person giving the security indicates his power to the creditor by possession of the security deed and a register extract. In practice, most creditors can check his title at their workstations. The owner is often also the debtor but the security can be established, as in the case of a loan guarantee, as a security for *another person's debt*.

The same process is also applied to a *leasing right* and the tenant's buildings when they are used together as a loan security.

In practice, the procedure is often that the owner of real estate or a parcel of land *empowers a creditor*, usually a bank, to apply for a mortgage and the security deed is naturally given directly to the creditor. The application of an owner can also ensure that the *security deed is addressed* for delivery directly to a certain creditor. In this case the security of the creditor is considered as having arisen at the same time as registration, if a credit has already been granted. Empowerment can be cancelled and so the latter process is more secure for the creditor.

Following the Swedish model can be seen as an attempt to ensure *real protection of faith* for the secured creditor on the ground of public trustworthiness of the Title and Mortgage Register. This is apparent in the creditor being able to trust old register extracts for six months: it is possible that the security remains in effect for the entire estate even though the giver of a security may have sold that real estate, or a certain area thereof, to another before conveying the security deed. This can be criticised because similar possibilities are not granted to real estate purchasers, although banks and other credit institutions have direct access to the register, while private individuals usually do not.

There are several statutory credits in Finland which are connected to the so-called *legislated securities*. This right of a creditor is based directly on the law, without any agreements, by specific regulation when a defined claim (usually to the benefit of the state) comes into existence. On the other hand, the existence of an efficient security requires registration according to the principle of public trustworthiness. Hence, the legislated security refers only to the fact that the owner's consent is not needed, not to the immediate constitution of the security. This comes close to a proper *compulsory mortgage* to the benefit of an individual.

The Future

From the *de lege ferenda* point of view one interesting question is the possible transition to the *paper free real estate mortgage system* in Finland. This would be similar to the share and mutual bond value-share system. The registered title of an owner would be the starting point, and the creditor's right of security could be marked in the register as a burden. A written agreement of security would entitle the creditor to apply for registration, or the entry could be made on the application of the owner. Registration could, in practice, be handled by the creditor before providing credit. Security deeds would no longer be drawn up and would not be used when creating security. The creditor's security and identity would both be seen as a record entry and in extracts.

This type of system is already in use in Sweden (in Swedish *datapantbrev*). There is a separate computer-based register in which the new owner's applications for mortgages and creditors are entered. This register was established in 1994. Both the sum of the mortgage and the name of the secured creditor must be registered. Existing mortgages may also be entered onto this register, in which case the security deeds have to be given to the registration authorities. This new system in Sweden is used in parallel with the old one and only certain credit institutions are accepted as secured creditors, as these have sufficient technical ability to work directly with the computer-based system.

In Finland, the establishment of a new separate register does not seem reasonable. Rather, the aim should be to enter the creditors' security attached directly to the ownership information in the electronic Title and Mortgage Register. Separate mortgage entries would be pointless.

In Sweden, after the transfer of a secured claim and on the ground of the registered transferor's application, the transferee can be recorded as a new secured creditor. The transfer could just as well be entered into the register on the application of the transferee and the presented agreement of transfer. The system in this form would provide new practical possibilities for a secondary market of loans and their securitisation through stocks and bonds in Finland, too.